# ... a Walk on the Downhill Side of the Log

# The Life of Maurice K. Goddard

**Ernest Morrison**

*Forward*s **by George M. Leader**
**and**
**William C. Forrey**

The Pennsylvania Forestry Association
Mechanicsburg, 2000

The Pennsylvania Forestry Association

As the nation's oldest state organization devoted to forest conservation,
The Pennsylvania forestry Association's mission is to encourage the proper
management of every acre of the Commonwealth's forests.
Our members are individuals, landowners, loggers, forest industries, resource
professionals and businesses concerned about the stewardship of
Pennsylvania's forest resources.

With grateful acknowledgment to the United States Department of Agriculture, United States Forest Service, and the Pennsylvania Department of Conservation and Natural Resources, Bureau of Forestry for their support in the production of this book.

Printed in the United States of America
Published and distributed by
The Pennsylvania Forestry Association
56 East Main Street
Mechanicsburg, PA 17055

# CONTENTS

# FORWARD

By December 1954, I had pretty well completed the selection of my cabinet in anticipation of taking office in January 1955. I had a good balance of professionals and persons with a political background. In fact my cabinet was referred to by some as Pennsylvania's first cabinet made up of professionals.

There was one post, however, that was still open in December. It was for the Department of Forests and Waters. I was under heavy pressure to fill this post with a "party person," but resisted it.

Years before concern for the environment became a widespread public issue, I promised the voters to develop Pennsylvania's natural resources, to purify its streams, to increase its opportunities for outdoor recreation, to keep a sense of the forest and the field in our lives. And I intended to keep that promise.

Genevieve Blatt, who was a friend as well as a running mate, had been elected the Secretary of Internal Affairs. Genevieve suggested we talk to the head of the School of Forestry at Penn State. Her brother Joe had always raved about the dean of the school, Maurice K. Goddard.

We met with Maurice a few days later when he was coming through Harrisburg on his way to the Penn State Mont Alto campus. He not only had impressive credentials for the position, but Genevieve and I immediately liked his honest, direct style as well as his philosophy on reforestration and recreation. When I called Dr. Milton Eisenhower, president of the university the following day, it was especially reassuring to have him tell me, "Well you sure know how to pick them."

Maurice had all the motivation and zeal of a Gifford Pinchot. In fact, I always thought of him as a modern-day Gifford Pinchot. He immediately began seeking ways to professionalize the Department of Forests and Waters. He pushed hard for civil service for skilled positions, but we weren't able to get it through legislative means, so we did it by Executive Board action. Maurice was then able to begin recruiting graduates from Penn State and other forestry schools. His department soon gained a reputation for its professionalism.

Parks were always high on Maurice's agenda. He told me that state parks were the best possible source of recreation for people of limited means. He said to me, "Anyone with a tank full of gas can take a whole family to a state park for the day at no more cost than they would have staying at home. They have to eat no matter where they are!" And he also felt strongly about lakes. He said a park without water isn't a park. According to Maurice, "We need water for fishing, swimming and boating." And, as usual, he was right.

When Maurice took over the department, there were very few seedlings in the state nurseries. He got the nurseries started up again so that we could go forward with our program to replant the areas that had been denuded by the strip mining industry.

The high regard in which Pennsylvania's forests and state parks are held today owes a great deal to the efforts of Maurice Goddard. His leadership on behalf of protecting those in existence when he took office, and with improving and extending the state's holdings of these valuable resources stands as a monument to his dedication and sacrifice. The results of his 24-year stewardship over them is something each of us can be deeply grateful for.

It was a mark of his professionalism that the four governors who followed me into office, reappointed Maurice to oversee the state's forest and park resources. The successive legislatures with which he worked also held him in high regard. When he told them he would do something, they knew he would follow through on his promise.

Ernest Morrison's biography of Maurice Goddard is a welcomed addition to the existing literature about important Pennsylvanians. Maurice's life is certainly one of those we should not only long remember, but also celebrate. Hopefully this biography will help keep his deeds and memory alive so that future generations of the Commonwealth's citizens will know of, and be able to appreciate more fully the many achievements he brought about on their behalf.

George M. Leader

# FORWARD

During a period of 19 years, from 1960 to 1979, I served in various capacities in the Department of Forests and Waters and in the Department of Environmental Resources.

During those years, I was privileged to work under the leadership of Maurice K. Goddard, a man of enormous intellect and of unblemished integrity. He had an incredible memory along with the ability to analyze problems and move quickly toward their solution. Once he set a policy or determined a course of action, he never wavered. His honesty in dealing with citizens, elected officials, the news media and fellow employees was always foremost in the decisions he made and the actions he took.

He always approached his responsibilities as Secretary of Forests and Waters and later with the Department of Environmental Resources with a sense of urgency. No matter how big or how small a problem, he would move to solve it. There was never a case of easing off if the problem belonged to the minority party. It did not matter whose problem it was. If a situation needed attention, it received the necessary attention.

Through his leadership, he set an example that attracted well-qualified people to work for the Commonwealth. During his 24 years as a Cabinet Secretary, employees of State Parks and Forestry worked long hours (many of which were without pay) in order to complete work to their satisfaction and to present first-class facilities to the park and forest users.

He worked tirelessly to achieve the goals which he set for the Commonwealth. The Project 70 and Project 500 bond issues were dear to his heart. He campaigned virtually around the clock to convince legislators and the citizens that they would be a positive factor in the lives of all Pennsylvanians. The value of these programs is obvious today.

His love for the outdoors and for Pennsylvania's natural resources did not stop with his own department. He supported causes and projects for all of the Commonwealth's natural resource agencies. He was a great friend of the sportsmen, recreationists, park users and open space advocates. His personal integrity, honesty and forthrightness were obvious traits that impressed all who knew him.

During my years with Dr. Goddard, his never ending sense of excitement for his work permeated throughout the staff. Speaking personally, his love for his profession gave me the same desire to work at my highest level of performance. I consider it my good fortune and enormous pleasure to have had the opportunity to spend 19 years with a great man.

Ernest Morrison is to be commended for his leadership and literary acumen in writing this marvelous biography of one of Pennsylvania's finest leaders. Maurice K. Goddard's legacy can be viewed and enjoyed by millions of Americans every year as they utilize and pass through Pennsylvania's state parks and state forests. It is fitting and appropriate that his life and his accomplishments are chronicled in this biography.

William C. Forrey

# PREFACE

Maurice K. Goddard was a remarkable man living in a remarkable time.  As a boy, he knew the privations of the Great Depression.  As a man, he experienced the horrors of the second Great War of his century; then came home to a nation consumed with a desire for growth, an explosive growth that threatened to change the very face of the land.

This is the story of the man, and of the part he played in that time, and of his attempt to provide some respite, some stay in the nation's unbridled pursuit of economic expansion.

A biography, of course, is more a portrait of its subject than a history.  To a biographer, Why? is as important as What?  But unlike a painter, whose brush may give no more than hints at the subject's emotions, character, worth, a biographer must probe for clues beneath the external image, probing the mind and soul of his subject.  This portrait of Maurice Goddard became then a question of who he was, why he did the things he did, why he said the things he said.  The search for answers to these questions was far from easy; it is my sense that, being an empiricist, he probably never posed them to himself.

The record of Maurice Goddard's life presents a biographer with a difficult assignment.  The written, official Goddard material is at variance with the oral record.  The speeches, the articles, the reports of the Secretary of the Department of Forests and Waters and later the Department of Environmental Resources sound, with only a few exceptions, dry and officious and appear to provide few glimpses of the man making them.  On the other hand the Goddard oral tradition — the stories told about him — is lavish in the extreme.

Ideas and stories, when transferred to print, often lose much of their vitality — except in the hands of the skilled — but when repeated orally, they often become suspect for their reliance on the faulty memory or for a tendency to self-serving extravagance — the "I shook his hand" syndrome.

Everyone who knew Maurice Goddard seems to have his or her favorite tall tale to tell. People are drawn to strong individuals and want to be identified with them. In the case of the stories about Maurice K., it is frequently impossible to corroborate them, to connect them with some official action or record, to trace them to their origin, or — assuming any of the account is true — to confirm which is the more likely variant. Like Paul Bunyan and his great Blue Ox, many of these stories are probably apocryphal. Which then is the true Maurice Goddard: the larger-than-life, respected-by-everyone dragon slayer, or the dry, driven bureaucrat?

Those tales that I have elected to use in the text were chosen to illustrate some essential point about, or character trait of, Maurice Goddard that I was able to confirm, or at least reasonably adduce by other means. The tale itself may or may not be true, but that is unimportant. I have not, however, used such stories simply to produce an agreeable narrative. Where the story is critical to the point or the character trait being considered, but is doubtful, I have given the contradictory evidence so the reader may decide.

A word, too, about the final chapter. Modern biographers generally eschew closing their work with an assessment or an "evaluation" of their subject's contributions. The tendency today is to let the reader decide about the worth of the accomplishments, the individual's character strengths or weaknesses, his or her possible motivations, and the importance of the life. This I think is unfair. The biographer leads the reader in one direction or the other through the choice of material and its organization. (In the hands of one writer, for example, President Dwight Eisenhower is an irresolute hypocrite for not coming to Secretary of State George Marshall's defense when he was attacked as a Communist sympathizer. In the hands of another, Eisenhower is a shrewd politican, co-opting the election away from Adlai Stevenson.) Having taken positions in this artful manner, the biographer should have the integrity to be forthright and state a personal opinion in summary.

This is difficult, however, with Maurice Goddard. He was a private person on a public stage. He seldom, if ever, shared his feelings with those he worked with, certainly not with the members of his family. What he thought on the critical matters he dealt with, or especially of the individuals with whom he had dealings, was seldom openly expressed, even to his closest associates. When coupled with the manner of his death, it seems the reader can reasonably expect some assessment on the part of his biographer. It may not be in the current mode, but I have not been one to follow fads.

The events in a biography are usually offered to the reader — with good reason — in chronological order. On the other hand, it has always seemed to me to be important to tell stories with a sense of completion. Stringing a dozen threads from the front to the back of a biography, finally resolving them all on the final pages — thus adhering slavishly to the calendar in recounting a life — yields a false picture. We live our lives in bits and pieces, frequently moving from one thing to another, returning to some of them later, never again visiting others. But a life is actually a single, composite existence, a journey of the mind and soul, and it is this that the biographer must try to uncover.

Because of the nature of the Goddard material, the early chapters of my narrative do follow in the order of their occurrence. In Chapters Eight, Fourteen and Fifteen, however, I step back in time to pick up a different thread, one that began earlier. Rather than, for example, introduce Maurice K.'s initial involvement in efforts such as the development of Pittsburgh's Point State Park or with the problems of the Delaware River Basin at the time they began — both of which commenced at the start of his state career — I have covered them in separate chapters devoted to those topics. I have placed them, however, in the time when his critical or more significant involvement in them occurred.

A prefatory word, too, about Maurice Goddard and dams. During his lifetime, dams became a lodestar for his version of conservation, both his successes and his failures. Although building dams for water-based recreation makes sense to many individuals, what does one make of his persistence, his apparent blind insistence on continuing to build high dams for flood control and low-flow augmentation, in the face of great public resistance?

It cost $152 million for example, to build Kinzua Dam in Warren County, Pennsylvania yet we continue to have floods along the Allegheny. This raises the question, Was it flood control or folly? Although I started with a general and uneducated bias against dams, eventually I came to appreciate Maurice Goddard's desire to build them, a mistaken, irrational interest according to many individuals. I hope I have been able to convey this part of the Goddard story (of his desire to balance the need of future generations for water, with a sacrifice of some portion of the environment) so that the reader who may not agree, will realize that, like the settler who, without thought for ecological damage, cleared away the forest for land on which to grow crops to feed his family, it was a decision made in good faith, and with reasonable expectation that it was the right one for the future.

I believe, moreover, that his faith in dams was not just a sign, a measure of his persistence, but of his integrity. Individuals who refuse to *blow with the wind* seldom win popularity polls, but are often judged to have had foresight. Maurice Goddard believed that providing and controlling water for an ever-growing population was the key to the future, as it had been of the past, and thus he fought for them on principle as an essential ingredient of an intelligent, overall conservation program.

The existence of dams is really not a question of "salmon versus watts," as one recent magazine writer put it, when a dam on Maine's Kennebec River was removed. From the dawn of civilization, man has depended on the availability of useful water. Civilizations have risen and fallen over it. And from the time of Hammurabi, gathering water in support of a great civilization has meant the construction of dams and water works.

A closing note or two for the reader. Aside from a few cases (where clarity seemed to call for their inclusion) I have omitted the name "Pennsylvania" following place names, such as those of the counties, cities, mountains, and streams of the Commonwealth. Any places in states other than Pennsylvania are so indicated throughout the text.

Except where noted the definitions serving as chapter heads were taken from the Second Edition of *Webster's New International Dictionary of the English Language*. It was published by G & C Merriam Company, at Springfield, Massachusetts in 1934, Maurice K. Goddard's senior year as an undergraduate at the University of Maine. A forestry student in 1934 would have looked in Webster's in vain, however, for definitions of words such as *bio-diversity, flood plane, smoke eater, or wetland* — all ones that would come into currency during Maurice Goddard's lifetime.

Finally a word about the title, . . . *a Walk on the Downhill Side of the Log*. Woodsmen and foresters always walk on the up-hill side of a fallen log. In this way, if the log starts to roll they can jump away from it rather than down-hill and into its path. Maurice K. Goddard was not what we would call a risk taker. He left little to chance by laboring long and hard building a consensus to support each of the major initiatives he undertook. But the steps he took were large, bold ones, ones to which, except for his perservance and energy, would have attached high probabilities of failure. The title, therefore, seems appropriate.


Many individuals assisted me in the research for this book. I would be remiss if I neglected to recognize them. First, without the patient persistence of Norman Lacasse, this work would not have been written. It was he who introduced me to the subject, led me to the reference material at Penn State, and invited me to the Maurice K. Goddard Symposium in 1996. He pursued me in the expectation, I suspect, that I would bring Maurice K. Goddard and his work alive for a wide audience. I hope I have justified his faith.

Libraries have been a life-long love. They hold and protect our collective memory as does no other organization. And librarians and archivists — as did Maurice K. Goddard — labor as conservationists. Like him, they not only want to conserve, they also want to share that memory with others. In my experience they have been more than helpful, they have been gracious in the extreme. Among those who should be singled out for taking such a role during the research on this book were: Betsy Paradis of the University of Maine; Dr. Linda Rambler of the Department of Conservation and Natural Resources; Carolyn Pfeifer, Librarian for the Joint Legislative Committee; Judith Strong, Librarian for the Delaware River Basin Commission; and numerous other unnamed assistants in the Pennsylvania State Library, the Pennsylvania State Archives, the Western Pennsylvania History Center, and in the consortium of college libraries throughout Central Pennsylvania.

I conducted more than fifty interviews in the course of writing this book. Several of these were memorable for the unreserved assistance the interviewee provided. Numbered among these were Goddard intimates: former Pennsylvania Governor George M. Leader, William C. Forrey, Pennsylvania Parks Bureau head under Maurice K.; John Rex, his Land Acquisitions manager; Joseph E. Ibberson, who was in charge of Forestry Advisory Services; and Darrell Albright, Pretty Prairie, Kansas, historian. I should mention, too, Steve Williams and David Higgins, who shared with me the information and interview tapes they gathered as producers of a Goddard-retrospective video for Penn State. Finally, a note of thanks to Alfred A. White, Robert H. Rumpf, Eleanor Maass, Caren Glotfelty, and my brother, Robert B. Morrison, who read the entire manuscript and made valuable suggestions for improving it.

# CHAPTER I

# PRETTY PRAIRIE

**prairie** n. [F, an extensive meadow, fr. OF, praerie fr.
(assumed) VL prataria, fr. L *pratum*] A meadow or
tract of grassland: specif; an extensive tract of level or
rolling land in the Mississippi Valley, characterized in
general by a deep fertile soil, and except where
cultivated, by a covering of tall coarse grass without
trees.

Maurice Goddard was born on September 13, 1912 in Lowell,
Massachusetts, to Norman O. and Susan Kimball Goddard.
Lowell, "The City of Spindles," was the home of the nation's textile
industry at the time of Maurice's birth. According to Charles
Cowley's *Illustrated History of Lowell*, ten major textile
corporations were operating in Lowell by the end of the Civil War.[1]
There were more than forty mill buildings, most of brick
construction, the largest of which was six stories tall. (Many are
still standing as part of a National Park Service site.) More than
seventeen thousand men and women were employed on the mill's
twenty-five thousand looms. They produced 6.5 million yards of
cotton cloth a week.

The revolution in the textile industry occurred early in the
nineteenth century as a result of the invention of the spinning
machine, and the development in 1814 of the first successful water-
powered loom. Although the industrial revolution was largely
water driven until the end of the nineteenth century, in another
sense it was also wood powered. As if to mark this twofold nature,
one of the largest, well-known, frame-construction dams was
located at Lowell. [2]

1

As were those in many other industries, these early textile factories were filled almost exclusively with wooden machinery. The massive forests that extended from the slopes of the Allegheny Mountains east to the ocean and west to the plains were used extensively in manufacturing as well as for erecting buildings, making furniture, providing fuel, and in constructing ships. When he traveled up the Susquehanna River in 1743, the botanist John Bartram noted, for example, that even farm fences between Lancaster and Harrisburg were of the post and rail variety. Moreover the nearly mile-long bridges across the Susquehanna at Harrisburg and at Wrightsville, between Lancaster and York, were built of timbers.

Water-power is mentioned in history books in connection with the industrial revolution, but as Increase Lapham, a respected ninetenth-century scientist wrote, "Few persons . . . realize . . . the amount we owe to the native forests of our country for the capital and wealth our people are now enjoying, yet without the fuel, the buildings, the fences, furniture and a thousand utensils, and machines of every kind, . . . we should be reduced to a condition of destitution." As Lapham evaluated America's astounding prosperity, "Anyone who studies closely and carefully the elements that have contributed to the greatness will find cheap lumber and cheap fuel [wood] the greatest of all factors." [3]

While this use of the nation's prime resource led to its tremendous growth, it was as much a cause for concern as for celebration. Approximately five billion cords of wood, for example, were consumed for fuel in the first half of the nineteenth century in homes, industry, steamboats and by the railroads. This is estimated to have required cutting the trees on two hundred thousand square miles of woodlands. In a report Lapham wrote at the request of the Wisconsin legislature, he surveyed the "experience of other countries, ancient and modern, whose forests have been improvidently destroyed . . . [and] . . . the effects of clearing land of forest trees, upon springs, streams and rainfall . . . how [forests] temper winds, protect the earth . . . enrich the soil and modify the climate." [4] His synopsis title, "Report on the Disastrous Effects of the Destruction of Forest Trees Now Going on So Rapidly in the State of Wisconsin," makes his appraisal clear.

Even when iron machinery replaced wooden equipment in the New England textile industry, the bullet-shaped shuttle was still made of wood. Although initially boxwood had been used, by the middle of the nineteenth century, shuttles were made of dogwood and persimmon. Eventually the wood of the flowering dogwood, *Cornus florida*, became the wood of choice. Arnold Arboretum archivist Shelia Connor reports in her *New England Natives* that as late as 1926, 90 percent of the harvest of the nation's flowering dogwood went into these shuttles. Although by then the wood was taken primarily from southern trees, most shuttles were manufactured in Massachusetts and Rhode Island for domestic as well as foreign use. [5]

When Maurice Kimball Goddard was born, the nation's streams and its forests and their products were still a major source of the nation's wealth. And Lowell was still an important industrial center when his mother took young Maurice to church on Sunday mornings.

□ □ □ □

At the time of Maurice's birth, his father, Norman Goddard, was a Swedenborgian Church ministerial student. (He graduated from the New-Church Theological School in Cambridge, Massachusetts, in June 1913, and was ordained as a Swedenborgian minister the following year.) Emanuel Swedenborg (1688-1772) was a Swedish scholar and Biblical theologian, but he also made important contributions to science and philosophy. Among his inventions were a dry dock of new design as well as a system for moving large boats overland. And his discoveries in metallurgy advanced the science and technology involved, while in biology he was the first to accurately understand the importance of the cerebral cortex. [6]

3

Swedenborg never sought to organize a sect, but believed in a "new Christianity" that would in time spread over the earth. In his *Heaven and Hell*, he "rejected traditional doctrines of the Trinity, original sin, a chief devil, and eternal punishment as an expression of divine vengeance," but taught that "eternal life was an inner condition beginning with earthly life, and that gradual redemption occurs through personal regulation of spiritual states." The primary view of his writings by the Swedenborgian or New Church is "as inspired commentaries on the Bible." The Swedenborgians were never a very large group, but "stirred some interest" in England and America in the nineteenth century. [7]

Emerson was fascinated by Swedenborg. Beside his essay, *Swedenborg, or the Mystic*, there are more than eighty references to him in Emerson's writings, with forty of these being in the *Journal*. Other writers linked Swedenborg to the "spirit of America," by which they meant the scientific, technical spirit, because Swedenborg was primarily a scientist and an engineer. The unique contribution of the New Church, however, has been to eschew the literalism of other sects and instead find meaning in the Scriptures, in the "sense of metaphysical truth awaiting investigation." [8] In her study of Swedenborgianism in America, Marguerite Beck Block claims that Robert Frost once expressed something of this essential Swedenborgian attitude in an interview:

> What's my philosophy? That's hard to say. I was brought up a Swedenborgian. I am not a Swedenborgian now. But there's a good deal of it that's left with me. I am a mystic. I believe in symbols. [9]

While Norman Goddard was Swedenborgian, Susan Goddard could trace her family back directly to Puritan stock. Susan Harriet Kimball was born November 1, 1875 in Lowell to William Henry Kimball and Laura Ann Whitehead of Chateaugay, New York. She was the first of their seven children. Susan's father, who was a "man of enterprise and integrity," served two enlistments in Company G of the 6th Regiment of Massachusetts Volunteers between 1862 and 1864. [10]

There is nothing to indicate that their differing religious backgrounds were an issue in Susan and Norman's marriage. By the nineteenth century, the amalgamation of religious stock had become commonplace in America. The early efforts at separatist communities, such as those of the Moravians, had been opened to all following the American Revolution. The Europeans came to America for religious and political freedom; most of them were determined not to let old enmities become new ones. There were those who objected individually to mixed religious marriages, but society in general and state governments viewed it neutrally, and perhaps taking their cue from Darwin, some writers even described it as being the source for the development of a new "American" race.

□ □ □ □

When Maurice was three years old, his father became the minister of a church in Pretty Prairie, in south central Kansas. This was probably a "call" from the church congregation, as Swedenborgian ministers are not assigned by church authority. (Opportunities to serve churches in the east probably went to well-established ministers, not recently ordained ones such as Norman Goddard.) The town of Pretty Prairie, which lay along the Santa Fe Railroad, is forty miles west of Wichita and fifteen miles south of Hutchinson, the Reno County seat. The Goddards undoubtedly traveled west by train, which probably was an exciting adventure for Maurice.

The part of Kansas to which they moved is drained by the two branches of the southeast flowing Ninnescah River. Although devoid of trees [11] and generally flat, by an Easterner's standards, some gentle hills rise to the west of the town. The soil is primarily sandy, but excellent for growing wheat. The town of Pretty Prairie was small with a population that seldom exceeded more than six hundred souls, all of whom were served by a one-block-long business district.

The area was first settled by Mary Collingwood, a widow who came west from Indiana in two prairie schooners with her nine children in 1872. Stopping first in Hutchinson, she moved out onto the prairie when land became available in the Wichita area. Among the early settlers who followed Mary Collingwood into the area, Mennonites from the Black Sea area of Russia predominated. In 1874 they bought a hundred and fifty thousand acres from the Santa Fe Railroad. It was the Mennonites from the Ukraine who brought with them the Turkey Red winter wheat that proved so adaptable to the Kansas climate and started an agricultural revolution on the plains. [12] People of English, German, and Swedish descent also settled in eastern Kansas during this period.

By the early 1880's a few residents of Pretty Prairie, mainly Mennonites, chartered themselves as Swedenborgians. Initially they met in a rural schoolhouse, but in 1906 they built a church on three-quarters of an acre of land in the town. The following year they erected a residence for their minister. [13]

The Pretty Prairie Swedenborgian Church was a small but attractive one-story frame structure with a steeple. The floors and pews were of finished wood, but the walls were of white plaster. The ceiling of the sanctuary was overlaid with metal that had a design pressed into it. Three steps led to the chancel. They symbolized Swedenborg's three "levels of maturity," or the "life experience": the *natural*, the *spiritual*, and the *celestial*. [14] The structure, which housed an organ, stood over a full basement, which was used for Sunday School, Ladies' Aid meetings, social functions and church congregational meetings. Although, when the Goddards were there, the total number of families in the congregation was no more than ten or twelve, families were large so the membership numbered between seventy and eighty. [15]

The town fathers initially wanted to name the community Collingwood, after the town's first settler, but Mary Collingwood vetoed the idea and suggested it be named for what she felt was the best description of the area, a pretty prairie. To Susan Kimball Goddard, however, the vast stretches of flat land (considered as part of the great "American desert," when Congress opened the territory for settlement) [16] were anything but pretty, so she planted trees all around the house.

The planting of a few trees for summer shade and as shelter from winter blasts was a common practice among homesteaders living in isolated houses standing on the open prairie. (Travelers across the continent by land even today can see many of these pickets still faithfully standing guard over long-abandoned turn-of-the-century farm houses.) For Susan Goddard, however, the trees were more than shelter and shade. They were psychic shields from the hated vista of the unadorned prairie landscape. Like photographs of distant loved ones, they were warm, comfortable reminders of her Massachusetts home with its many deciduous species. Whatever his mother's tree plantings were - Maurice was too young to recall specifically - they were remembrances of the ashes, cottonwoods, maples, cherries, flowering dogwoods, towering oaks, and black walnuts she had known in New England. [17]

From the very earliest, Maurice was impressed with how essential these reminders of eastern forests were to his mother's well being, the spiritual sustenance she drew from their presence. Years later he recalled that every time a big summer thunderstorm swept across the prairie to threaten the Goddard property, she would "whip out" with the three-year-old Maurice close behind to "check on the trees." Only when their well-being was assured, would she finally turn her attention to the house. [18]

Although flat and lacking forest coverage, Kansas was an excellent state for the growing of many fruits, berries and vegetables. According to Liberty Hyde Bailey, the early twentieth-century authority on American horticulture, by 1900 orchards and gardens were scattered all over the eastern portion of the state. And the location of the state was such that commercial growers could ship their produce north to Nebraska, Colorado, and Iowa when those states were still gripped by cold, and then later to Texas "when the heat of summer had paralyzed Texan products." [19] The

7

Goddards probably enjoyed Kansas tomatoes, cherries, blackberries, raspberries, melons, plums and especially strawberries. The sandy soil, which to Susan Goddard's chagrin sometimes blew under the door of the parsonage, seemed to be ideal for producing them as well as the state's more famous wheat. [20]

Reading between the lines of the scant material that remains, we get the impression that Susan Goddard was more of an influence on Maurice than his father. Notwithstanding the small size of his congregation, Norman Goddard was a busy minister. Not only were his sermons scholarly, well-reasoned, and carefully crafted — showing long hours of study and preparation — he also appears to have been gone from home frequently. During his first years at Pretty Prairie, for example, he worked on a second degree at the Hamilton College of Law in Chicago, from which he received a Bachelor of Law Degree in March 1918.

□ □ □ □

The name Maurice is usually thought to be of Norman or French origin; it is actually a derivative of the Latin, *Mauricius*. Instances of its use were known during the Byzantine era. A Maurice (Mauricius Flavius Tiberius) was Roman emperor from 582 until 602. This early Maurice was a competent organizer and administrator renowned for his "austere realism." And austerity and realism are both traits the adult Maurice Goddard brought to the management of Pennsylvania's natural resources. As one summary of his life stated: "[In] the economic and environmental needs of the commonwealth, . . . Dr. Goddard's position consistently has been that of a pragmatist." [21]

Goddard, on the other hand, *is* Norman in origin. It is derived from *Godhard*, which is composed of the elements *god* (or *good*) plus *hard* implying hardy, brave, or strong. It was a popular name in the Middle Ages as a result of the fame of St. Goddard, an eleventh-century bishop, who founded a hospice on the pass between Switzerland and Italy that bears his name. Almost universally those who knew or worked with Maurice Goddard would agree, his surname of *good* and *hardy* or *brave* was as appropriate to the man as a name can be. [22]

□ □ □ □

The Swedenborgians in Pretty Prairie owned 80 acres of land about five miles outside the town. It had been bequeathed to them by a veteran who settled in the area following service in the Civil War. Swedenborgians are primarily congregationally oriented, so the ties between individual churches are more familial than hierarchical. Being an autonomous group, the Swedenborgians at Pretty Prairie — as reflected in the minutes of their congregational meetings — debated over how to manage this land: who would work the soil, what and when they would plant, and what they would do with the money from the sale of the crops.[23]

Harvest time, of course, was the major community event of the year, an especially exciting one for an energetic young boy. For weeks, the town was flooded with workers who came to help bring in the wheat. One of the events Maurice especially enjoyed watching was the unloading of the huge threshing machines at the railroad depot. Each day, the streets were filled with the "pageantry of the harvest," as Ben Hibbs, editor of the *Saturday Evening Post*, called it. Hibbs, who grew up in Pretty Prairie at about the same time as Maurice, described the harvest as consisting of

> the sweating men, the horse-drawn headers and the great steam threshing rigs clanking down Main Street on their way out to the endless stacks of yellow grain. [24]

Then as the fields were stripped and the grain separated from the stalk, the wagons would line the town's one main street, waiting to transfer their loads of wheat into the Collingwood or Security Elevator Company's grain elevators that stood by the railroad in long, majestic rows. And then later as the wheat was sold by the elevator operators, the cars of the Santa Fe would take on their fill of grain from the giant silos and carry it to Hutchinson for eventual reshipment elsewhere. [25]

The ever-active Maurice also enjoyed other boyhood diversions. He shot marbles, went skating and to parties, took rides in a friend's donkey cart, and attended picnics on the church grounds and hot dog roasts along the Ninnescah River. The Ninnescah is broad, but shallow. It is dotted with sand bars that are easy to wade to. And when he was a little older, he probably joined other boys in following the tracks of the Santa Fe south from the town to the ponds that dot the prairie or, perhaps, took bike rides along the dusty roads that passed the "banks of lazy little creeks," where he could "catch sun perch or bullheads and swim in the buff." [26] On a hot summer afternoon the creeks and ponds would have been a welcome relief from the Kansas sun. To a friendly, outgoing boy such as Maurice, who was given to jollity and pranks, it would have been all sun, splashing and shouts as he and his friends frolicked in the water.

The girls of the community considered Maurice to be an "ornery" boy. By this they meant not so much that he had an irritable disposition, as a playful one. Susan Goddard, an accomplished musician, gave piano lessons to a number of the town's young women, who in those days wore long, full dresses that were gathered at the waist by a sash tied in the back. One of Maurice's tricks consisted of dashing into the room and behind the bench during a lesson, quickly pulling open the girl's sash, and then racing from the house with Susan Goddard's shrill *"Marr—ress—"* following him out the door. [27]

Maurice's practical jokes and generally playful nature were apparently more than Susan Goddard was able to handle, at least, calmly. Where in other families, older children might have helped keep the younger disciplined, with Maurice's boundless energy and his mother's apparently vexatious disposition, she was unable to curb or learn to accept his boyhood appetites for action, noise, and boyish peccadillos. When it came time to enroll him in the Pretty Prairie Elementary School's first grade, she reportedly appeared on the first day with him and told the teacher: *I can't do anything with him, see if you can!* [28]

□ □ □ □

There were also books, magazines and copies of the *Pretty Prairie Times* in the Goddard home, which Maurice read as he grew older. (The publisher of the *Pretty Prairie Times* was Claude Claybaugh, who lived across the street from the church.) And, although young boys would not have been welcome in the town's two banks or its heavy-implement store, he probably hung around the general and hardware stores listening to the yarns of old sodbusters. There were men of foreign extraction, veterans of the Civil War, even some old Indian fighters. These, in Hibbs' words, were the

> leathery pioneers who had lived through drought and blizzard and the devastation of the grasshopper years, and who had taken this raw plains country by the scruff of its neck and turned it into a gracious, smiling land. [29]

According to a diary the twelve-year-old Maurice began keeping in January 1925 — it was apparently a Christmas gift — he had many friends among not only the children but also the adults in the community. On New Year's Day that year he was busy shoveling snow for the neighbors as well as playing in it with his friends Dean Bay, Vernon Krehbiel, and Glenn Voran. They went sledding and ice skating, built snow forts, had snowball fights, and took long walks out into the fields looking for wildlife. On one such hunt several days later, Krehbiel, who had a gun, shot four rabbits, one of which he gave to Maurice for his cat. And in an entry a week later Maurice recorded that his "best girl," Hilah Field, "rote me a note." [30]

Maurice also liked to make the evening rounds with the milkman, who paid him ten cents to help with his deliveries. Maurice doesn't say so but the milk was probably delivered from a horse-drawn van. Once in making their rounds the milkman "about scared" him "to death" by starting across the tracks when a southbound Santa Fe train was approaching. When Maurice returned from helping to deliver the milk, Susan would read to him, or he might work with his erector set. He also had chores: he carried out the ashes, cut wood, walked to the post office to pick up the mail, and carried chairs and tables back to Mrs. Claybaugh's following a meeting of the "Social Hour Club," a collection of the town's women who met together regularly to sew, talk, and eat. [31] And, as he reported in his diary on at least one occasion the mischievous only Goddard son "hung up" his clothes.

Maurice studied not only in the evening, but also worked on his lessons before he left for school in the morning. [32] Although he frequently wrote in his diary of preparing lessons for his seventh-grade classes, his test scores didn't appear to reflect natural gifts as a scholar. He did well in mathematics, but his grades in history, classics, and reading were no more than average.

The Pretty Prairie grade school was the pride of the town. The two-story brick building had been put up only a few years before the Goddards' arrival. It had a central-heating system in the basement, and a large assembly room on the second floor, which doubled as a lunch room for the children from the surrounding farm lands. While the town didn't grow much in size over the years, as outlying one-room school houses were closed, more and more students began coming into Pretty Prairie for their education. Moreover, farm families at that time not only were numerous but also very large, so the school was well populated. [33] By the time he was in the seventh grade, Maurice regularly practiced shooting hoops and went to watch Pretty Prairie High School basketball games, dutifully recording the team's wins and losses in his diary.

❑ ❑ ❑ ❑

In the spring of 1925, when Maurice was twelve, the Goddards moved from Pretty Prairie to Toronto, Canada where Norman had accepted another Swedenborgian congregation's offer to be its minister. [34] Beginning in mid-May Maurice began to help pack furnishings, clothes, and chairs; helped his father "fix" and then crate the "piano box"; and assisted Norman in taking items to the train station for shipment. They sold some articles including an oil stove and Maurice's old coaster — he didn't mention whether it was a sled or wagon — and on May 25 left Pretty Prairie on the morning train to Hutchinson accompanied by the Claybaughs. While the Goddards waited to change trains in Lawrence, Kansas, Maurice and his father went to a picture show. Rather than the train ride during their three-day trip, the tall buildings and all the people Maurice saw as they rode around Chicago seemed to impress him more.

Maurice apparently didn't suffer too much over the change from Kansas to Canada or from a small town to a sizeable city. He left behind a lot of good friends but was soon writing in his diary of playing ball with boys named Rich, Purvis, and Douglas, and although he seemed to spend more time with adults — he tells of frequent shopping trips to College Street with his mother and of playing games like "Authors" with his father — he continued to ride his bike around town, especially to the parks. At Toronto's High Park, a vast expanse of downtown greenery, there were bicycle paths, picnic areas, and a multitude of interesting niches where Maurice was delighted by the wide variety of animals he saw. And at Sunnyside on Lake Ontario, there was a marvelous beach from which he could go swimming, no longer, of course, in the buff. That same year, too, he joined the Y.M.C.A. [35]

Maurice undoubtedly spent time in church, probably sitting with his mother in the front pew on Sunday mornings while his father preached on topics such as *The Blessedness of Silence on the Soul,* *Belief and Success,* and *Eternal Goodness.* Then, following supper, came the evening church worship in which Norman replaced his sermon with a "lecture." The content and order of these services were typical of Protestant sects: prayers, hymns, Psalm and responsive readings, and a daily lesson all opened with a voluntary and closed with an offertory and benediction, played by Susan Goddard, who served as the church organist.

The effect of all this religious worship on Maurice is unclear. He seldom went to church in later life — there were those who claimed it was a reaction to his upbringing — and he was certainly not given to quoting Bible verses in his talks or articles, but as Ben Hibbs said of the Kansas heavens and prairie, the experience must have "flamed with [enough] majesty that some dim comprehension of the Infinite entered even into the heart of a young lad." [36] Still from the very earliest, Maurice's bent seems to have been practical, not philosophic or artistic. His seventh-grade journal writings, for example, are brief and direct, and except for one short entry while he was still in Pretty Prairie — "I took a little walk in a wheat field and saw one rabbit" - show little introspective interest or reflective nature.

Ninety years later, Norman Goddard — viewed as a strict, New England minister type, and thus probably a stern parent often is suspected as having been the source of Maurice's authoritarian manner as an adult, and his unexpected outbursts of anger. This, however, may simply be based on a stereotype of the nineteenth-century preacher. Those who knew him during Maurice's formative years, describe Norman as soft spoken and always pleasant to children on the streets of Pretty Prairie.

Although Norman was never seen publicly without his formal minister's garb, it was Susan Goddard who, according to first-person accounts, was tall, stern looking, and severe of manner. Hilah Field recalls, for example, that she left the Goddard's living room in tears following many a piano lesson with Mrs. Goddard. And Florence Steward, at whose wedding in 1919 Norman officiated, and who sang in the Pretty Prairie New-Church choir, which Susan Goddard led, remembers her as always looking like an "old-maid," tall and slender, dressed in unfashionable, no-frills dresses, and with an unchanging "stern look" on her face. [37] Even Ethel Goddard, who only knew Susan when she was much older, remembered her as still being "very well organized, perhaps overly so." [38] Such an unyielding manner might well account, moreover, for Susan's inability to "manage" her rambunctious son.

But his mother's influence seems to have predominated. Neither of Maurice's sons is named Norman; his first is Kimball, and his second, Mark, bears Kimball as a middle name.

❑ ❑ ❑ ❑

The Goddards' stay in Toronto lasted only five years and then Norman accepted a pastorate in Portland, Maine. Their new church home was a little larger in size — the bulletins Norman printed each Sunday now numbered in the hundreds — although the building was hardly impressive as churches go. A large A-frame structure, its roof was interrupted only by a chimney at the spot a steeple might have risen. With the larger congregation, the social activities probably increased in frequency and size. Susan Goddard would have been even busier with the Ladies' Aid than she had been in Pretty Prairie. The women of the Ladies' Aid in Portland always seemed to be setting up tables of "fancy-work" or aprons, having basket lunches, cooked dinners, or fish chowder suppers.

It was in Maine that Maurice's desire to work in forestry first asserted itself. He became impressed with the stands in which each acre of the forest contained thousands of young spruces and firs, often decorated with a heavy accumulation of snow. His instructor at the University of Maine, Dr. Robert I. Ashman, recalled years later how Maurice told him he considered it a "privilege" to "plunge into them." [39] And it was at this time, too, that his long legs also began to figure in track competitions at Portland's Deering High School.

In addition to his normal pastoral duties in Portland, Norman and Susan Goddard became involved in running the New-Church Assembly at Fryeburg, Maine, each summer. This summer church camp was situated near the New Hampshire state line outside of the town of Fryeburg. A brochure for the camp described Fryeburg as a

15

"lovely little village on the edge of the White Mountains." The Assembly grounds comprised thirteen acres of wooded land along the Saco River, reportedly one of the "finest rivers in the state for canoeing." There were beautiful views of the mountains from the grounds and idyllic walks throughout the surrounding lands. Young people could enjoy swimming, canoeing, hiking, tennis, and mountain climbing. [40]

Norman, along with several other church leaders, taught classes in religion and Susan managed the camp: bought the food, hired the help, ran the kitchen, oversaw the dining room, baked the bread, and paid the bills. When years later Ethel Goddard suggested to Susan that, rather than spend so much time each Monday baking bread (which she was still doing), she should go to the store for it, Susan told her, "I wouldn't know how to buy a loaf of bread." [41] The tuition for a three-week session at the camp was a modest one dollar (with another dollar for a "cot in a tent," and daily board of $1.50). Maurice K. helped pay his way by serving as camp grounds keeper. He mowed the grass, trimmed the brush, pruned the trees, cut the firewood, helped erect the tents the students lived in, and performed the other handyman chores required around the camp site. [42]

The purpose of the Assembly, of course, was study and instruction in religion as "revealed in the Lord's Word and as explained in the writing of Emanuel Swendenborg." In addition to lectures on the Bible, there were also ones on New-Church music and singing, even one on Astronomy. Norman Goddard's lectures — he was listed in the camp announcements as a "Doctor of Divinity" — were described as "scholarly considerations of unusual topics too rarely presented in the light of the New Church." Among these were *Art in Relation to Life* and *The Books or Literature of the Ancient Church.* [43]

In the spring of 1931, Maurice graduated from Deering High School and finished making arrangements to enter the University of Maine that fall to study forestry. His interest in forestry had been increasing rapidly since his arrival in Portland. Maurice's uncle, who was the supervisor of the Coconino National Forest in Arizona, frequently  sent him nature books as did his aunt, the librarian at Boston University. So following his graduation, entering the University of Maine seemed the natural thing for him to do. And to help pay for his education, he signed up for membership in ROTC (Reserve Officer Training Corps).

Thirty years later, in the face of student protests against the military, many colleges across the nation would drop ROTC from their curriculum. In the depression of the thirties and forties, however, ROTC was an important means of financial support for students who might otherwise never have been able to go to college; it was also a form of governmental backing for the educational institutions themselves, many of which were in uncertain financial positions. Moreover, the corps provided a ready reserve of trained officers for the U.S. Army, an army that would soon need them in great numbers.

# CHAPTER II

## FROM MAINE TO PENNSYLVANIA

**sil-vi-cul-ture** or **syl-vi-cul-ture** n. [F, fr. L
*silva*, forest + E *culture* fr. L *cultura*] a phase
of forestry that deals with the art of producing
and caring for forest trees — compare
Arborculture.

The University of Maine is located in the New England Uplands
eight miles northeast of Bangor at Orono. The Uplands is a plateau-
like area that extends from the Canadian border to Connecticut. In
Maine the region, which ranges from thirty to seventy miles wide,
lies between the Maine coastal lowlands and the White Mountains.
In the eastern portion, the plateau is distinguished by its deep,
fertile soil where one of the nation's largest potato crops is grown.
The western portion is heavily forested — mainly with softwoods
— and is sparsely settled.

The town of Orono is located very near the geographic center
of the state; half way between Kittery, the most southerly town in
Maine, and Fort Kent, the most northerly. When Maurice was a
university student in the early 1930s, Orono was a pleasant town of
fewer than thirty-five hundred individuals.[1] One guide book
describes it as "part college town, part typical Maine village." The
six-hundred-acre school campus is situated about a mile from the
center of Orono along the Stillwater River, a branch of the
Penobscot, the longest river in the state. [2] The school's 1935-36
catalog described the Stillwater as a stream of "great beauty."

When the town was first settled by Europeans, it was called
Stillwater, but in the 1770s the community was renamed after the
Penobscot Indian chief Joseph Orono. By 1840 the area had
become prosperous from the lumbering industry. Sawmills lined the

18

banks of the town's Marsh Island, which lies between the Stillwater and the Penobscot Rivers. Huge log drives, that came down the Penobscot from the forests of northern Maine, ended at Orono making the town's economy boom as well as the local timber merchants wealthy. Many of the magnificent Greek Revival, Queen Anne, and Federal homes built with lumber dollars are still standing as part of Orono's Historic District.

During the years Maurice K. was at the university, the Maine Central Railroad's mainline, over which regular passenger service was available, still ran through the community. There was a hard-paved road between Bangor and Orono, but the most often used local transportation was that of the Bangor Hydro-Electric Company's trolley-line to Bangor. Cars ran each half-hour for those students who wished to avail themselves of the city's entertainment, social, and religious amenities. Few, if any, of the eighteen hundred men and women studying at the school when Maurice K. graduated had an automobile. Orono did have one theater, the Strand, and the Maine Masque, a campus group, periodically staged "professional" productions with "complete" sets. In an effort, moreover, to overcome a sense of the area's cultural isolation, the university regularly brought in outside speakers.

Buildings on the campus, which was extensive, were widely placed; and although Maine is 84 percent forested, the level ground on which they stood was also sparsely populated with trees. Many of the school structures were old and those that had been built since the beginning of the twentieth century often "showed a rather Spartan asetheticism." [3] If Maurice K. was fortunate he was housed in Hannibal Hamlin Hall, which was built in 1911. The other men's dormitory was Oak Hall, which dated from 1871.

First World War I and then the depression produced hardships on the school's sources of income, including the state's mil tax on property, and often placed construction of new facilities out of reach. When they were considered, new dormitories and instructional facilities included only those of the most restrained design or features. It was not, for example, until a number of years after Maurice K. graduated that the old concrete bleachers, whose paltry dozen rows of seats lined half of one side of the athletic field, were replaced with more modern, more substantial facilities. Budget austerity, like the flat campus with its few scattered trees, always seemed to characterize the school. By the standards of the day, however, the school was not unattractive; it simply reflected the Spartan efficiency that was current.

The University of Maine was established as one of the nation's land-grant colleges under the provisions of the Morrill Act, which President Lincoln signed in 1862, in the midst of the Civil War. The purpose of this legislation was to encourage the states to establish higher-educational institutions to stimulate and then propel a technical revolution in the nation through the application of scientific knowledge that would make industries, especially agriculture, more efficient, more productive. The substance of the act was the giving of federal land to those states that agreed to establish such schools. The land to be purchased under the Morrill Act was intended not only for the erection of the schools, but as bankable assets for raising funds to put up buildings and buy furniture and equipment. This philosophy of training the young along technical lines was, of course, dramatically at variance with the centuries-old European idea of a higher education based on a classical emphasis.

Long, then, before its more obvious mid-twentieth-century stance — with a plethora of agencies and a GI Bill of Rights — the federal government was influencing the direction the nation took in areas such as agriculture and education.

The University of Maine opened in September 1868. By 1871 four curricula had been set up. These grew eventually into a College of Agriculture, a College of Technology, the College of Arts and Sciences, and the Maine Agricultural Experiment Station. By 1931, forestry — a late arrival sometime around the turn of the century — was one of the sixteen curricula in the College of Agriculture. The four faculty members in the discipline taught a wide range of courses including: logging and wood technologies, nursery practice, seeding and planting, forest mensuration (the measurement of logs, trees, and stands of timber), forest management, regional silviculture (the study of commercially important timber species, the application of thinnings, and methods of natural reproduction), even courses such as "game food and cover planting," and "forest recreation" — often thought of as more recent innovations in forestry. [4]

The course of instruction was arranged to make students eligible for positions in the United States Forest Service, or to prepare them for private firms needing foresters, or for a career educating future generations of foresters. The first two years of study dealt with fundamentals or pre-technical subjects (English composition, trigonometry, botany, zoology, surveying, and economics), the last two with specialized work in the technical aspects of the field. Time was spent in lectures, recitations and laboratory work, but the largest single amount of the men's involvement was devoted to field work in which they were exposed to practical problems and experiences. [5] This was accomplished in large forest areas already under permanent management (one of the college's areas was located near Princeton, Maine, eighty miles to the east), and by visits to large private manufacturing plants that used forest products.

□ □ □ □

Maurice was soon drawn into school activities in which he became an active participant. There was the traditional fall "Festival of the Night Shirts," a rivalry between the incoming Freshman and the Sophomores that was held on the "Night-of-the-yellow-moon." It apparently involved ripping off each others shirts as a reporter for the school newspaper, *The Prism*, wrote, "Clothing was flying; naked bodies were everywhere," while men and women crowded around egging the participants on — the words "naked bodies" undoubtedly carrying a different connotation than they would today. Three years later Maurice K. was designated, as a member of the Senior Skulls, to supervise the fight, but in his freshman year he undoubtedly took part in it as he was known as a "cut-up." The senior's supervision of this fall rivalry, of course, tended to be mainly *managed-encouragement*. In his first year, Maurice K. also captained the Freshman class to a win over the upper classmen in the Sophomore-Freshman track meet. His track and Senior Skulls involvements were among his "fondest memories" of his years at Maine.

By his second year "Gramp" Goddard, as he was known, was one of the stalwarts of the university's track team, his specialty being both the high and low hurdles. According to *The Prism*, he "performed capably in his speciality" helping the Maine "Pale Blue," as they were called, win or at least stay in many a meet. In the spring of 1934, for example, he led the university to a stunning 79 to 56 victory over state-rival Bates College in Lewiston. "Lanky" Maurice K. scored 15 points as he led the "Pale Blue" to any early lead which was never threatened. He earned his letter that year and by his senior year was captain of the varsity track team. During his final year at Maine, he "performed capably all season," according to *The Prism*, although an injury kept him out of several meets.

□ □ □ □

There was a Pale Blue football team. Maurice tried out, broke a tooth during a scrimmage, and withdrew when Susan Goddard told her son, "No more football!" [6] Track, however, was equally as or even more prominent a school sport. Maurice K. was good enough as a track man that, on one occasion, he traveled to New York City to compete in the prestigious Millrose games held each year in Madison Square Garden. [7] If, as is probable, he went in 1935, his senior year, he saw two of the country's all-time track greats. The *New York Times* was filled for days with stories about national stars such as Jesse Owens, of Ohio State, and to the

22

"blazing foot rivalry" between Bill Bonthron of Princeton and Kansan Glenn Cunningham. Although no press attention was paid to unseeded athletes such as Maurice K., he always felt honored just to have participated. To be in the same national meet with Cunningham, who had overcome crippling adversity as a boy to become holder of the mile record, was an exhilarating, awe-inspiring experience. [8] Moreover, he got to see Cunningham, the holder of the world's indoor record for the mile, win the event before a frenzied crowd of sixteen thousand fans packed in the Garden, and at only 2.6 seconds off the Kansan's record mark of 4:08.4.

Maurice K.'s was also busy as a member of the Maine chapter of Phi Kappa Sigma. His involvement in its activities and his popularity led, in his final year at the university, to the fraternity presidency. Phi Kappa Sigma was an old fraternity, having been founded at the University of Pennsylvania in 1850; the chapter at Maine in 1898. While the fraternity was not a scholastic one, it did have a reputation for educational achievement. The University of Pennsylvania chapter, for example, held a "high position socially" in Philadelphia. According to *Baird's Manual of American College Fraternities*, the chapter had established a prize in English literature, the first ever established by a social fraternity. [9]

As talk of the troubles in Europe grew in frequency, and discussions of whether America should be involved became more heated, "Strikes Against War" were held on campuses across America, including Maine's. At the same time, Maurice K. also drilled regularly with the campus ROTC unit. At graduation, he was commissioned a 2nd Lieutenant in the Infantry Reserve.

As important as Maurice K's sport and frolic were to his development, he also undoubtedly felt the influence of the newly appointed Maine president, Arthur A. Hauck. Young, personable and informal in many campus situations — it was described as an "everyday style" — Hauck urged his charges to "take a constructive part" in civic life, to maintain "high standards in everything" they undertook, to "cooperate closely" with others, and to "emphasize those elements that make for good citizenship and abundant living." [10]     Although Maurice K. and Arthur Hauck were of different temperaments and personalities, a more accurate, more precise blueprint for Maurice's life could not have been devised.

Maurice K. was an outstanding scholar, in addition to his "star" status as an athlete and president of Phi Kappa Sigma. [11] He was the only forestry student in the class of 1935 who graduated with academic honors, having earned a "highest distinction." Moreover, the school faculty recommended him for a Rhodes scholarship based on his "consistently high scholarship" and "outstanding [involvement] in extra-curricular activities." [12]     The nation was divided into eight districts — New England was one — each of which could send four scholars to Oxford. Although a University of Maine graduate had been selected in a previous year, recipients of the scholarship typically came from schools such as Harvard, Brown, Bowdoin, Yale, and the Massachusetts Institute of Technology.

Maurice K. was not selected. He would not go to Oxford on a Rhodes scholarship, but did leave Maine well educated, well prepared for the future. He would get to London eventually, but not until ten years later, after much of the city had been destroyed by German bombs.

Maurice K. would probably have been unhappy at Oxford. He was the product of the land-grant educational approach; his was a pragmatic education — of the soil rather than the classics. And this conformed nicely with his natural bent, which was factual and scientific, not scholarly or artistic. The *Western Canon* was not central to his experience or interest. Beyond an introductory course in English, his education at the University of Maine did not include any literature, foreign language, art, or other *civilizing* courses.

As an adult, his written expression was usually businesslike — dry like well-baked macaroni and cheese — lacking the illumination one receives from the brilliant flash of a well-placed, well-turned analogy, metaphor, or simile. There are few flights of fancy and

24

little of the emotional in his writings and speeches. Unlike Robert Moses, Maurice K.'s was a pragmatic, not a poetic world. He would never have written of the Pennsylvania park system as did Moses, who, in envisioning a Long Island playground-park at the Montauk peninsula, described it as "an extraordinary mass of clay, gravel and rock with high bluffs on the south shore and, back of the bluffs, kettleholes and rolling hills clothed with bayberry, shrubs and gnarled and twisted trees." [13]

❑ ❑ ❑ ❑

Maurice K. wanted to work for the U.S. Forest Service, so following graduation from the University of Maine, he took the civil service exam. Decisions on selecting new hires in the Federal Government are often slow due to elaborate civil service rules and procedures. The summer of 1935 passed without word, so he accepted a position as an instructor of "general forestry subjects" at Pennsylvania State College. A week later the Forest Service made him an offer of a job in Michigan. Reluctantly he turned it down.

Penn State, like the University of Maine, was a land-grant institution. There were, moreover, other ties between the two schools. Their forestry curriculums were similar, although training in mensuration was considered a weak spot at Penn State, and the head of Maine's experiment station at Orono, Whitman Jordan, had come from Penn State. Earlier Jordan had established an agricultural experiment station at State College, although at that time the principal work done was restricted to the "analysis of fertilizer samples in support of state regulatory laws." [14]

Although John A. Ferguson, who had headed the Forestry School at Penn State since 1913, hired Maurice K., Victor A. Beede replaced Ferguson in Maurice's second year. Beede, like Ferguson, had graduated from Yale University, but he also had stayed to complete his M.A. there in 1912. He then studied forestry in Europe and eventually returned to become Assistant

Forester for Massachusetts and later for New Hampshire. He came to Penn State in 1931 following several years of private employment. Beede also taught Economics as well as Policy and Administration.

Initially, Maurice K. was assigned to the school's Mont Alto campus near Waynesboro in the south central part of Pennsylvania. He instructed first-year students in the basic principles of forestry dealing with the establishment, care, protection, reproduction and harvesting of stands of timber, as well as the influence of forests upon water supply, climate, soil and public health. He probably also taught an occasional course in dendrology (tree identification) which included extensive field observations of the budding, blossoming, leafing, and fruiting of specimens in the mountains behind Mont Alto.

Maurice K. undoubtedly started helping with the summer camp in his years at Mont Alto. Like elementary school youngsters looking forward to recess, forestry students always seemed to be itching to "get out in the woods." Professor John A. Ferguson, a Yale forestry graduate who came to Penn State in 1908 and headed the Department of Forestry from 1913 to 1937, attempted unsuccessfully for several years before he retired to have the camp held in the Allegheny National Forest in Pennsylvania's northwest corner, so it remained at Mont Alto through 1939. [15]

In the Mont Alto State Forest, first-year Penn State students received practical instruction in connection with a forest that had been managed on a sustained yield basis for more than thirty years, and had gained reputation as a woodland laboratory. There they could find examples of practically every forest activity carried on anywhere in Pennsylvania's state forests. And at summer camp the students were able to observe and participate in the "practice of technical forestry" and the "allied phases of conservation," as instructor Maurice Goddard wrote in an article for *Sylvan*, the forestry school's year book. [16]

In 1940, Maurice K. and a colleague, William H. Pfeiffer, met with representatives of the U.S. Forest Service and worked out the agreement that finally gave Penn State use of a camp in the Allegheny National Forest. "Blue Jay" as it was called had been built in 1935 under the depression-era Federal Emergency Relief Program as a camp for out-of-work transients. It had a capacity of 260 men, and was known to the locals as a "hobo" camp. The camp cook was an unemployed hotel chef, his assistant a former undertaker. According to Maurice K., two doctors, a lawyer, professional "hobos," carpenters, cabinet makers, and mechanics had slept side by side and worked together in the forest. [17]

At Blue Jay, Penn State forestry students were able to observe and participate in forestry and conservation practices being applied by the U.S. Forest Service to a national forest. Although the area had been heavily cut over in the early nineteenth century, by 1930 it had become a "laboratory of soil, plants, and trees," one that, according to Maurice K., made possible "an intensive cross-sectional study of forestry in Pennsylvania." There were also a number of commercial firms in the region which the students could visit, among them logging operations, furniture and paper companies, veneer and panel producing facilities, and a chemical plant.

The camp facility was similar in construction and arrangement to that of a Civilian Conservation Corps camp. The camp site consisted of frame, barracks-like structures: a headquarters building, which housed the camp store, library, office, and faculty quarters; a classroom building; four billets; a wash house; a mess hall and kitchen; along with various other maintenance and out buildings. A typical camp day started at 7 AM when the bell, a section of steel rail, was "rung" to call the men to breakfast. Following the morning meal beds were made and billets swept. Classes commenced at eight and ran until five. For evening recreation, the students engaged in various forms of athletics including softball, boxing, hiking, swimming, and fishing. [18]

The student's work in camp covered two main fields, forestry and surveying, with four weeks being devoted to each. The forestry instruction, which Maurice K. probably led, covered, in addition to the industry trips, two weeks of mensuration and one of silviculture. The silviculture course included not only class work, but a day trip to observe and study fire protection activities in a national forest, one on wild life studies, an examination of the Kane Experimental Forest, and a study of the Heart's Content virgin forest. The surveying instruction included general transit survey, topographic work, sketch-board work, exercises on cut and fill, railroad curves, and similar work related to surveying.

During the 1937-38 school year, Maurice K. took a leave of absence from Penn State to get a master's degree in forest management from the University of California at Berkeley. Although the forestry school at the University of California seems like an unusual choice for an eastern forester, his appointment as a teaching assistant at the school most certainly had something to do with his decision. He always showed concern over monetary affairs, which was brought on by the straitened circumstances in which he grew up. He probably first saw the announcement of assistantship appointments on a bulletin board in the Penn State Agriculture Department. In the thirties the University of California regularly offered annual stipends to unmarried scholars to come west and teach in exchange for a graduate degree.

The change from central Pennsylvania to Berkeley, both cultural and professional, must have been substantial for Maurice K. The university campus, with its exotic trees and masses of brilliant, flowering shrubs, contrasted against the August California landscape — its hills "bleached and sere" — would have been a far cry from the green, wildlife-filled hills of the eastern hardwood forests of Maine and Pennsylvania. And the yellow-buff facade of buildings like the International House with its large Spanish arches, and an interior that combined the mission style with the Moorish revival would have been in striking contrast to eastern architecture, which did not yet know even the "ranch house." [19]

Although much of the curriculum, especially for undergraduates, was little different from that at Penn State, including such courses as dendrology, forest measurements, and forest utilization, there was a strong emphasis on forest management and regulation at the graduate level. Although the forestry curriculum had a basic European flavor, by the mid-thirties, following the suggestion of Bernhard E. Fernow, the distinguished Cornell instructor, it had developed more of an American slant. Men such as D. T. Mason, Donald Bruce and Woodbridge Metcalf, who had all had experience with the U.S. Forest Service, had been appointed to the faculty. [20]

There was also a tradition of dissent at Berkeley, even at that early date. There were protests against living conditions and discrimination in the local boarding houses, and even student riots (the breaking of store windows and destruction to streetcars), although in 1937 and 1938 these were related to Big Game rallies, rather than political dissent. [21]    And this idea of dissent extended to, or perhaps stemmed from the university faculty.  John Kenneth Galbraith, who was a graduate student in Agricultural Economics at about the same time Maurice K. was there, stated:

> At Berkeley I suddenly encountered professors who knew their subject and paradoxically, invited debate on what they knew. They also had time to talk at length with graduate students." [22]

In addition to his formal studies and teaching duties, Maurice K. certainly would have roamed through the streets of San Francisco, visited the redwoods, and probably gone up to the Sierras and to tour Yosemite. He may also have spent time at the Davis campus, in the Sacramento Valley, which in the thirties was the center of agricultural research and instruction associated with orchards, insects, and soil. And he probably spent some time instructing — and learning — about the woods aspect of California forestry at the university's forestry camp at Quincy in Plumas County.

□  □  □  □

On his return to Penn State, Maurice K. was reassigned from Mont Alto to the main college campus at State College as an Assistant Professor of Forestry. He began teaching silviculture.

Already seriously depleted in the nineteenth century, the forests of the United States were under additional pressure to provide more and better products and benefits for the nation's increasing population. This pressure accelerated the development of procedures for managing the forests to serve these needs. This in turn meant that the nation's forestry schools had to provide instruction, not only in the important forest types of the country, but also the choices considered appropriate for their management.

The study of these methods is called "silviculture." Among the silvicultural systems available to the forester were: *selection*, which involved the removal of mature trees singly or in groups at varying intervals; *shelterwood*, in which the mature stand is removed in a series of cuts, with regeneration of the new stand occurring under cover of a partial forest canopy or "shelterwood"; the *seed-tree* system, with the harvesting of nearly all the timber in an area with a few of the better trees left standing to permit reseeding naturally (a system that applies mainly to conifers); and *clearcutting*, the cutting of all trees in an area to create a new, even-aged stand. [23]

Maurice K. was considered an outstanding teacher by his students. His lessons were well prepared, and he brought an enthusiasm to his classes that was infectious. His forestry students came to expect a stimulating lecture, high in energy as well as interest. With a voice that resonated beyond Maurice K.'s years, they were assured of a performance as much as a lesson. During his early years as an instructor, he was also assigned responsibility for the men's dormitory. He quickly earned a reputation as a strict disciplinarian. For this, the students began calling him "gramps" in recognition of his antediluvian admonitions. (It is unclear whether or not there was any connection between this and his University of Maine nickname of "gramp.")

During his years as an instructor at Penn State, he prepared several papers on forest subjects. These were marked by a careful and rigorous application of statistical methods. For example, in the "Effect of Animal Coaction and Seedbed Condition on Regeneration of Pitch Pine in the Barrens of Central Pennsylvania," which he co-authored with William C. Bramble, [24] he prepared tests to determine the prospects of germination and survival of seedlings under "protected" (with cages) and "unprotected" environments by three plant communities (Aspen, Scrub Oak and Grasses) for five different seedspot types — seeds sown on undisturbed soil, on uncovered mineral soil, on cultivated soil, and on that covered with litter, or sod, or soil.

The results of this two-year study showed that destructive animal co-action prevented establishment of pitch pine from seeds in the aspen and scrub oak communities. And while successful germination in grasses occurred, there was a low survival rate because of animal co-action. The two researchers did find that the cages reduced the light intensity by 35 percent, but as pitch pine survives in nature under 50 percent, good growth was obtained. They concluded that the greatest (side) benefit from the cages was the reduction of water loss. [25] The statistical exactitude that marked this study was a characteristic of Maurice K.'s work throughout his life.

□ □ □ □

By the spring of 1940, "Gramps" Goddard was eagerly anticipating the commencement of a quite different adventure, marriage. Maurice K. would find, however, that it required attributes rather foreign to his personality and to his upbringing as an only child. Unlike teaching, with its authority figure model and convention of largely one-way communication;  or research, with its requirement for "statistical exactitude," marriage is primarily experience-based, and encompasses a significant amount of human inexactitude.

Moreover, he would discover that to be successful, a marriage requires a great measure of restraint, in addition to a willingness to compromise — both attributes that were not among his stronger ones. It was not just as a teacher, but also as a person, that Maurice K. always let those around him know exactly what he thought. While this quality would stand him in good stead in the future as a soldier and as a Pennsylvania state cabinet officer, it placed him at peril as a husband and father.

This, however, was all beyond Maurice K.'s consideration in the euphoria of the moment.

# CHAPTER III

# I'M GETTING MARRIED THIS SUMMER

> **hardwood** n. [*hard* + *wood*] Any heavy, close-grained and resistant wood; in forestry the wood of any broad-leaved deciduous tree as distinquished from that of a coniferous tree; any tree having hardwood.

The spring 1940 issue of the Penn State *Sylvan*, quoted Maurice K. as telling his students on several ocassions, apparently with enthusiasm: "I intend to get married this summer." In a setting of teacher to pupil the pronouncement seemed to possess an air of boastful arrogance. Like the expression *having sex* rather then *making love*, it tends to trivialize the event at the same time it exalts it.

Rather than get married at the beginning of the summer, however, Maurice K. waited until just before fall classes started at Penn State. On September 7, he and Ethel Mae Catchpole were married in her family's church, New York's St. Agnes Episcopal Church. The Catchpoles' minister, Herbert Brown, performed the ceremony. It was a large wedding. Ethel's best friend Betty Heinz was her maid of honor, and Dorothy Catchpole, her sister, served as one of her four bridesmaids.

The newspaper coverage that Saturday consisted, however, of page after page of war news from Europe: "German Planes Raid London All Day;" "British Bomb Berlin," "Riots in Rumania as King Carol Flees." And, in the midst of a presidential campaign, the news on the home front also was war-driven: "Wilkie Condemns Destroyer Trade," "House Bars Change in Age Limits of Draft Measure," "Defense Bill Adopted Providing Enlarged Army, Planes, Warships," "Roosevelt Presses for Speedy Final Action on Bill." [1]

On a slightly lighter note, however, the New York World's Fair was in full swing in Long Island's Flushing Meadow. Ethel had worked one summer as a hostess in the Ford building directing visitors to exhibits. There was much to see and do at the fair, although the pavilions of several of the smaller European nations, including Poland and Czechoslovakia, which no longer existed as nations, were "Closed due to the emergency." Maurice and Ethel had spent time at the fair earlier, so the newlyweds took a honeymoon among the Thousand Islands in New York State. [2] Then they moved to State College, Pennsylvania.

□ □ □ □

Maurice K. met Ethel Mae Catchpole of New York during one of his trips to the city (probably for an athletic event at Madison Square Garden), but their relationship actually ripened at the Fryeburg, Maine, church camp that Norman and Susan Goddard ran each summer for the New-Church. Ethel had come to the White Mountains camp in the summer of 1934 at the suggestion of her friend, Betty Heinz. [3] Betty, who had described Maurice K. as an "interesting character," wanted to help Ethel get to know him better. It was between Ethel's sophomore and junior years as a history major at Hunter College in New York City. And, although she was a strong-willed young woman, she was reluctant to go to Maine alone, so she induced her sister Dorothy to come along. They had a good time. Both of the young women found tall, lanky Maurice K. to be a real "cut-up." He was fond of playing practical jokes, and always seemed to find ways to entertain them. [4]

One feature at the end of each summer encampment at Fryeburg was an August Christmas play in which, to everyone's amusement, Maurice took the part of Santa Claus. Maurice and Ethel also had the opportunity to take long walks along tree-lined paths through the pine woods. Ethel was drawn to him because he was different from most of the boys she had dated. He was a "take-charge kind of guy," she told one reporter years later. "I liked trying to figure out where he was going and how he was going to get there." [5]

Attendance at woodland camps was a summer-time activity that was considered appropriate for mixed groups of young people in the early decades of the century. The camps were supervised, often religiously oriented, and considered to be both physically and morally uplifting. Large amounts of fresh air and doses of mildly administered instruction in a wide range of subjects were regarded as healthy for both the body and the mind. As author Henry Wellington Wack wrote in Redbook after surveying 243 camps in six New England states, where the movement was first established: "The camping ideal is nothing less than the building of bigger, braver, better boys and girls as the progenitors of a better race." [6]

While, in the days before air conditioning, the very wealthy summered at elegant resorts such as Newport and the middle classes at "The Cape," those who couldn't afford summer vacations went to camps. There were camps in the mountains and along the streams throughout the northeastern United States. They were often run by churches, but other groups, including social clubs and corporations, sponsored some. These were, of course, the days before the average American could afford to own a house in town as well as a camp site in the woods, and with only a few individuals owning automobiles, most people relied on public transportation. Some of the camps and resort areas were even a side-business for the trolley and rail lines that served them.

□ □ □ □

As a minister, Norman Goddard had been poorly paid, and Maurice K. wanted to avoid any family-type commitment until he was able to afford it. It was not, therefore, until six years after they first met, when the forestry instructor was well established at Penn State, that the couple finally decided to marry. He never seemed to forget the straitened circumstances of his youth, for instance, the beans and Boston brown bread that seemed to be a mainstay of family menus during his boyhood. According to some who knew him well, these distressing conditions apparently contributed to his life-long desire to excel. While she waited for Maurice, Ethel worked at a variety of jobs, primarily as a Macy's salesgirl, but she also tried her hand as an elementary school teacher for a short period.

Although Maurice K. and Ethel returned to Penn State following their marriage in September, 1940, the couple only had a little more than a year to get settled. Shortly after the war came to the United States in December 1941, he was called to active military duty. In June 1942, he was ordered to report to Camp Croft, South Carolina, where he received his basic orientation in army life with the 35th Infantry Training Battalion.. Camp Croft was a small infantry installation, lying about ten miles southeast of Spartanburg in the northwest corner of the state near the North Carolina border. In the years preceding the war only about ten thousand men were assigned there. As an infantry replacement center, the base complement's job was administrative; they were responsible for assigning infantrymen to units throughout the southeastern United States. 7

While her husband was away, Ethel returned to New York and a Hunter College administrative job in the Registrar's Office. The new couple's separation was to be the first of many, although Ethel did come down to Spartanburg for a week in September where they had a "second anniversary" celebration. And in December Maurice K. had his first leave which they spent together in New York City.

At Camp Croft, Lieutenant Goddard began to keep the "books" for his platoon: the morning reports, duty rosters, reassignment lists, and records of courts martial that were prepared daily by each company commander for submission to regimental headquarters. His administrative skill and interest soon became apparent and after a few months Lieutenant Goddard was moved to the base Adjutant General's office. Then in December, 1942 he was appointed as the Battalion Adjutant, an appointment that left him "very pleased." In March of the following year he was promoted to Captain and attached to Battalion Headquarters for duty as a Classification Officer.

Following a stay in the hospital for a case of the measles, Maurice K. was ordered to the Adjutant General School at Fort Washington, Maryland, across the Potomac River from Mt. Vernon. [8] Although he did get to spend a brief weekend in the Hotel Statler in Washington, it was a "tough grind." At the Adjutant General School, students learned Army administration: manpower control, personnel management, preparation of orders, circulars and directives, records keeping, and postal operations. (The Adjutant General runs the Army Post Office.) The development of training materials and courses to be administered by other elements of the Army was also an important part of an Adjutant General's responsibilities. Officers in the Adjutant General's Corps are the army's office managers.

□ □ □ □

Records keeping in the U.S. Army is one of the most systematized spheres of human endeavor. Army manuals of the time dealing with "Office Training," for example, went into great detail covering each report: shape, size, color of paper, number of copies, order in which the copies are to be arranged (and fastened) for signature and then rearranged for filing purposes, down even to the order in which marginal "remarks" are to be annotated. And each report is covered by an offical Army Regulation. Moreover, only authorized abbreviations — for which there is a regulation — are to be used. Memorization of all this detail was probably a significant part of the course. [9]

In October 1943, Maurice K. graduated from the Adjutant General School and was assigned to Camp Edwards, Massachusetts, on the neck of Cape Cod, about seven miles from Buzzards Bay. Camp Edwards, which had a capacity for about thirty-five thousand men, was primarily a processing center for men going overseas to the European Theater. The permanent-duty staff, of which Captain Goddard was a part, had to make arrangements to handle arriving troop trains, to billet troops during their stay, and then to prepare them for shipment to overseas assignments.

Although some "complete" units arrived for trans-shipment, many men had to be classified and assigned individually on the basis of their MOS (Military Occupational Specialty) and the need for their job specialty in specific overseas theaters of operation. There is an MOS for virtually every civilian job. In 1942, for example, a baker's occupational code number was 017, a band leader's 020, a barber's 022 a biologist's 389, and a bookbinder's 416. A man typically has a primary and a secondary MOS; it is the basic classification tool used in assigning individuals to positions in the army. [10]

While at Camp Edwards Maurice K.'s reassignment from the Army's infantry branch to the Adjutant General's Corps finally took place. But at the base one of the new Adjutant General officer's administrative duties, which he disliked immensely, included working with German prisoners of war. He had an aversion to things "foreign," especially languages. He did get some relief from his responsibilities, however, in the form of alternate-weekend passes, which he usually spent in New York with Ethel. Finally in April 1944, he received orders to England. After spending a few days in Portland with his mother and father, he headed to New York and a hurried goodbye with Ethel at the 42nd Street B.M.T. subway station. [11]

❑ ❑ ❑ ❑

"Ike," as General Eisenhower was universally known, had arrived in London in January 1944 to set up SHAEF (Supreme Headquarters, Allied Expeditionary Force) for the invasion of the continent. SHAEF was an outgrowth of COSSAC, the "vast planning apparatus, consisting of more than 3,000 American and British officers and technical experts" which had been set up a year earlier to start the planning for the invasion of the Continent. [12] Maurice K. arrived in England on the eve of the Normandy invasion in June and was assigned to the Headquarters, Adjutant General's office at SHAEF.

Personnel duties at SHAEF fell across two divisions: G-1, which was run by Maj. Gen. Raymond W. Barker, who had held a similar position at COSSAC, [13] and the Adjutant General's Division, run by Brig. Gen. Thomas J. Davis. Barker was responsible for plans and activities concerning the procurement and utilization of personnel for military purposes, and, according to Lt. Gen. Walter Bedell Smith, Eisenhower's Chief of Staff, Ike considered him an "excellent planner" and "one of my most valuable assistants." [14] The Adjutant General, on the other hand, was responsible for handling incoming and outgoing mail, preparing orders and directives, and managing SHAEF files as related to individuals. Captain Goddard worked for Davis, although he did not report directly even to him. Maurice K. headed one of the seven sections (Emergency Returns) of the Military Personnel Branch under the Adjutant General's Division. [15]

Brig. Gen. Thomas Jefferson Davis was a florid, genial man. He was known affectionately among the SHAEF headquaters staff as "T. J." Davis, who had been with Ike since their prewar days on McArthur's staff in the Philippines, was the SHAEF Adjutant General, although from March to September 1944 he served as the command's public relations director. [16] He did this job extremely well, but Ike moved him back to the Adjutant General's Division following a stay in the hospital for an operation, and the fear that Davis might become completely exhausted if he continued in his grueling job as the SHAEF public relations director.

Both G-1 and the Adjutant General's Divisions were relatively small sections concerned with planning, personnel and other related matters connected with American and British forces and thus were staffed with both British and American officers and men. [17] Although all of the Division heads, including Barker and Davis, reported to Ike, in practice Maj. Gen. Walter Bedell Smith, Eisenhower's chief of staff, was their principal on-going contact.

One of Ike's key requirements for each member of the SHAEF headquarters staff was that he be part of the team. American and English officers predominated at SHAEF, but there also were others on the staff, including Canadian, Free French, and Polish members. [18] Any officer who, in spite of being highly capable, could not work well with others, especially with those of different nationalities, was quickly moved elsewhere. When General Omar Bradley first reported to SHAEF from Sicily, he was told: "No one will object if you wish to call someone a bastard. But you'd better watch out if you call him a 'British bastard.'" [19]

Ike also insisted that his staff exude confidence. After a plan was formulated, everyone was expected to express his faith in it. Maurice K., who from his earliest days at Maine had been a team player, was well suited for SHAEF. (Years later, when he conscientiously carried out a Pennsylvania governor's orders with which he did not agree, he was spoken of as a "good soldier.") But more important, as the head of the "Emergency Returns Section" of the Personnel Division, Maurice K. also learned lessons for the future in leadership and command. [20]

If Barker was an excellent planner, and Davis a good Adjutant, General Smith was the epitome of the tough executive. According to General Bradley, Smith was "an intense, tempestuous and harassed man." [21] He not only served as the door to, and took flak for Ike, he made many noncombat-related decisions for his chief, was given authority to sign Ike's name to letters and messages, and functioned as the SHAEF "boss," ruthlessly firing those officers who didn't work out. This left Eisenhower free to conduct the war. On a number of occasions, Ike had to soothe tempers when Bedell (pronounced Beetle) Smith had upset some other high-ranking official. Ike would clear the air by telling the offended officer that Smith "fights for what he wants but means no disrespect." It was a personal trait that would have drawn the approving attention of Captain Goddard.

Rex Melton, a Goddard colleague at Penn State after the war, recalls that Goddard mentioned General Smith several times and Melton concluded, therefore, that Maurice K. had reported directly to Smith. While the two officers would have had contact at SHAEF briefings and in meetings, and Maurice K. would have been impressed and probably influenced by Smith's brusque manner and tough management style, it is unlikely the general would have had time for detailed personnel matters. Given the army's adherence to chain of command, and that, as Ike's right hand man, Smith was extremely busy managing the entire SHAEF headquarters staff, he undoubtedly left such matters to Davis and his Adjutant General's staff that included Captain Maurice Goddard. [22]

❑ ❑ ❑ ❑

Captain Goddard's primary job in the Military Personnel Branch of the Adjutant General's Division was to handle correspondence received from the families of men throughout the European Theater, especially those requesting "Emergency Returns" of soldiers to the states. This required that Maurice K. know where the individual men of American Army forces in the European theater were. In the days before computers, this was recorded on cards. [23]

Each unit in the army, including one in the field, prepares a daily "Morning Report." It is the army's basic personnel management tool. It consists of four sections: the station and record of events, strength, rations, and remarks. [24]    A company commander's obligation to complete and submit the daily "Morning Report" is the primary reason for mustering the men of his unit for roll call the first thing in the morning. While the First Sergeant's bellowing out of the name of each man, who responds, "Here!" seems more like the stuff of a grade-B movie, a company's "Morning Report" indicates the status of each man in the unit. Those who aren't available for duty must be accounted for in the remarks section as on sick call or in the hospital, on leave, missing, wounded, killed in action, or transferred to another unit.

These reports are collected at battalion and regimental headquarters and then forwarded up the line to the army level. Although at the company level, each man is accounted for daily, by the time these reports have arrived at higher headquarters, they probably include only the information on men whose situation had changed from the previous day. In this way the SHAEF Morning Reports Section staff had to annotate the cards solely for those men whose status had changed.

SHAEF headquarters also used this information for a number of other purposes. From time to time, a mission would require some special skill. The ability to locate the man quickly who possessed it was vital. Then there were the letters from the states requesting information on soldiers who were lax in writing home. These naturally required an up-to-the-minute record of the soldier's whereabouts and condition before headquarters personnel could safely respond: "Your son is fine. He recently was in the hospital for two weeks with tonsillitis, but is now back with his unit." Then the man's company commander would receive a message to have the soldier write home.

After the war, Maurice K. told Joe Ibberson, one of the freshmen forestry students he taught in his first year at Mont Alto, that he had kept track of him throughout the war. This was no small feat. Ibberson, who as a Convoy Commander took ship loads of men back and forth across the Atlantic, made nearly sixty trips across the ocean, with trips to North Africa and the United Kingdom as well as between European theater stations. [25]

The most difficult of Maurice K.'s personnel tasks involved the preparation of large numbers of letters of a sensitive nature responding to "heartbroken mother" letters, as Ike called them.

Family members would ask for word on men missing in action (the Eighth Air Force alone was unable to account for 41,552 men who were shot down over Germany), [26] as to where a soldier's remains had been interred, or whether or not a soldier or airman might be able to come home for an "emergency." The replies had to be solicitous but frequently noncommittal, or in many cases even a rejection of the requested favor. They required, therefore, the utmost care in the preparation of responses.

Rather than draft or dictate these letters anew each time for successive review and revision, Maurice K. developed a set of one hundred stock paragraphs that covered every probable need. Then it was only necessary for him to scribble the three or four numbers between one and a hundred that were appropriate in putting together a reply to the incoming letter. No drafting, no dictating, no revision; just select the paragraphs, have the letter typed and get Ike, General Smith, or General Davis to sign it. [27] And, of course, when a return or reassignment of a man was recommended, appropriate orders had to be prepared, clearances through friendly countries obtained, and full transportation arrangements made.

When Maurice K. eventually became Executive Officer of the Military Personnel Branch, letters to stateside correspondents became only one of his responsibilities. The entire branch also reviewed and recommended action on all medals and awards, which meant that detailed records had to be kept of the theater and battle or engagement participation of both men and units. Moreover, the branch was responsible for keeping the "201" record jackets on officers and selected enlisted personnel including their assignments or reassignments, the reclassification of their Occupational Specialties, any disciplinary actions that were recommended, and requests for promotions, or for an appointment to Officers Candidate School or one of the military academies.

□ □ □ □

In the successive moves that the SHAEF headquarters units made between the date of the Normandy invasion in June 1944 and the final collapse of Germany fifteen months later, the men of the Adjutant General's Branch remained well behind Eisenhower's advanced headquarters. Two months after the invasion, in June 1944, for example, the advance headquarters (mainly intelligence and communications functions) was moved from England to the grounds of a school near Jullouville, Normandy, but Maurice K. remained with the bulk of the SHAEF staff at Bushy Park near London. Bushy Park was a large Eighth Air Force cantonment located in the London suburb of Kingston. The facility was Spartan, consisting of Nissen huts and tents. SHAEF administration offices were set up along a narrow corridor on a bare concrete floor in a damp, unheated building. [28]

Although by the time Maurice K. arrived the waves of Goering's bombers were no more, German V-1 rockets — "Doodlers" they were called by the staff — came over regularly. In the months before the invasion the Germans sent more than ten thousand of them at London and other targets in southeast England. The distinctive "buzz" these pilotless aircraft made before dropping on a target was particularly unnerving. Some days the men had to interrupt their work as often as eighteen or twenty times to go to the air raid shelter. [29] According to Captain Harry A. Butcher, Eisenhower's naval aide and SHAEF diarist, the men were "semi-dazed from loss of sleep and had the jitters" whenever they heard a door bang or the sound of motorcycles or aircraft. [30]

In September 1944, the main echelons of Supreme Headquarters, approximately 1500 officers and men, including Maurice K., were moved by air to Versailles. Versailles was chosen because Ike wanted the men away from the temptations of Paris. At Versailles, SHAEF offices were maintained in the Trianon Palace Hotel, a large, sumptuous building in the grand hotel style. Maurice K. occupied an office on the first floor. While the enlisted men were housed in a temporary camp arrangement, the officers were billeted in homes along the Seine between St. Cloud and St.

Germain-en-Laye. [31]   Although that December was an extremely difficult time for the American forces in the field, Maurice K. did get to Paris and bought earrings and a pin to send to Ethel along with a bottle of perfume for his mother.

A number of Goddard stories have come out of his time at SHAEF.  They included the: "How he 'lost' Ike's dog one weekend — when he was the duty officer — and sent the entire headquarters complement out scouring the French countryside looking for it before the general returned." And another tale of his brusquely ordering an unidentified junior officer — who was just casually nosing around — out of the Emergency Returns Section, only to be told that it was Ike's son, John.   Maurice K.'s reaction to being told this was a brusque and gruff, "Well, he had no business here!"

In February of 1945, Maurice K. was promoted to Major. General Davis pinned on his "leaves" in the presence of the whole staff.   Then in May the Pennsylvania forester was awarded a Bronze Star as well as a Legion of Merit for "exceptionally meritorious conduct" in the performance of his administrative work at SHAEF. His Legion of Merit citation not only mentioned the reforms and procedures which he devised, but also his "humane desire to alleviate the distress" of those he helped as head of the Emergency Returns Section.  Of the hundreds of awards he would receive in his lifetime, these two would remain among his more prized.

❑ ❑ ❑ ❑

In June 1945 following the Nazi defeat, Maurice K., by then a Lieutenant Colonel, moved to Frankfurt-Am-Main to work in the military occupation government.   The SHAEF staff, renamed as USFET (U.S. Forces, European Theater), operated out of the I. G. Farbenindustrie Building.  It was an immense, institutional-looking office  structure, several city blocks long, that was sited in the middle of a large open area on the outskirts of Frankfurt.   In a curious anomaly, Frankfurt was devastated by Allied bombings, but the Farben building was spared even a near miss. The story made the rounds that it had been deliberately saved so it could be used as the headquarters for the occupation army. [32]

Actually the Farben facility comprised seven identical rectangular office buildings standing like dominoes side by side, with each joined at the hip to its neighbor by a similar cross structure to form one enormous architectural composition. It seemed to exemplfy the unrestrained architectural megalomania of Hitler — "we will create stone documents" — and his chief architect, Albert Speer, who were planning for a monumental as well as a long-lasting Third Reich. [33]

According to Capt. Harry Butcher, there was a large pond in back of the Farben building. In it was a large bronze statue of a female nude. It became a popular place for both officers and enlisted men to pose for photographs. [34] Although given the right occasion, Maurice K. could be impish enough to have had his picture taken with the nude, he probably would not have sent a print home to Ethel.

One writer claims that the I. G. Farben building was deliberately selected by the Allies "to smash the worldwide chemical cartel system," that the company had established. [35] I. G. Farben had been an early supporter of Hitler as well as Germany's reindustrialization, and although relucant to manufacture them, the company had sold the patent for Zyklon-B crystals used in crematoriums to two firms that were more than willing to do so for the Nazis. Moreover, I. G. Farben directors had taken advantage of the cheap slave labor available and erected a new synthetic coal-oil and rubber plant near Auschwitz. [36] Following the war a number of the company's officals were convicted of war crimes, including "plunder of property" and "imposing slave labour and inhumane treatment on civilians and prisoners of war." The disposition toward complete liquidation of the company eased, however, as the Cold War heated up, and in 1952 the Western powers divided the company into three independent corporate entities: Hoechst, Bayer and BASF. [37]

❑ ❑ ❑ ❑

It was the assignment of the Allied military administrators to destroy the machinery of the Nazi government, and then re-create a new civilian government from the ground up. More than thirty thousand military and civilian personnel were employed in the American part of this effort. Although public schools, for example, were not closed, text books had to be purged of Nazi propaganda. Moreover, because Germany was divided into four zones of occupation (American, Russian, British, French) it was necessary to establish many completely new administrative services within each zone to replace ones that originally had been under the direct control of the central government. [38]

The American military became responsible, therefore, not only for denazification and democratization of the people, but also for such administrative functions as banking, basic governmental operations, transportation, and population control, including addressing unemployment and shortages of labor in various industries. One of their first jobs involved conducting a comprehensive census of the population of the U.S. Occupation Zone of Germany. It included demographic studies to determine such matters as population by age, sex, size of community, and marital status, as well as questions such as the effect produced by migration patterns brought on by the war and by the presence of female labor on the zone's work force.

Because of his experience as a military personnel locator, Maurice K. probably worked on organizing personnel issues for German nationals similar to those he did for GIs. Following the war, refugees flooded all areas and their relocation, the reunion of families, and the matching of these floating resources with jobs all became critical concerns. These were especially acute for individuals who previously had lived or worked in what had become the Russian sector. Lt. Colonel Goddard was assigned German clerical help and interpreters to assist in this work. (According to Ethel Goddard, he always considered foreign languages to be "anathema" and refused to study them.) [39]

Although the war ended in August 1945, Maurice K. remained in the army for another year to assist in the recovery of Germany and the emergency return to the states of GIs on occupation duty. He was discharged in September 1946 just in time to return to Penn State for the fall semester. [40]

□ □ □ □

Those who knew him years later often claimed that Maurice K.'s management style was sharpened, if not developed, by his army experience, especially his exposure to officers such as Bedell Smith. While there appears to be some truth in this, the gruff, take-charge military mold also seemed to be a perfect fit for his personality. Even as a child he showed evidence of an independent nature which may have been encouraged or at least reinforced by his lack of siblings as well as his mother's reported inability to control him.

Maurice K. carried his European experience and his aversion to things foreign, especially German, back into his personal as well as his professional life. When, years later, his teen-age son Kimball was about to buy his first automobile, he had his eye on a German import, which he told his father was well engineered and built. After several attempts to dissuade Kimball from a purchase which, to the boy, made very good sense, Maurice K. finally blurted out his objection: "Those people tried to kill me." [41]

48

# CHAPTER IV

# MONT ALTO FORESTRY SCHOOL

**mat-tock** n. [AS *mattuc*; akin to L
*mateola* mallet]   A kind of pick-ax,
having the iron ends broad instead of
pointed;  used for digging and grubbing.

When Maurice K. returned from Europe and the army to take
up university life again, he didn't begin where he had left off three
years earlier; he was promoted to Associate Professor of Forestry
and assigned to the Mont Alto Forestry School.   It was not,
however, as an instructor.  In the fall of 1946 he was appointed the
school's Resident Director.

The village of Mont Alto nestles at the foot of a cleft in the
Blue Ridge Mountains east of Chambersburg, Pennsylvania.   The
village consisted then of no more than a few houses and no stores.
For Ethel living there after growing up in New York City was like
"moving to the end of the world." [1]   The Blue Ridge Mountains,
which are also known as the Catoctin Mountains, rise steeply from
the limestone valley floor. The largest of the individual mountains
are named South Mountain and Montalto Mountain.   The rock
which is exposed along the ridges range in geologic age from the
Precambrian to the Ordovician period, while the core is made up of
granite and gneissic rock from the Precambrian period.   The
individual ridges of the mountains are separated by narrow valleys.
While the slopes of the mountain average around 10 percent, those
of the V-shaped valleys along the flanks sometimes run as high as
30 percent.

Near the top of Montalto Mountain, the West Branch of the Antietam Creek starts its meandering trip down the Cumberland Valley. Not too many miles distant its waters empty into the Potomac River after passing under the historic bridge named for Ambrose Burnside, the Civil War general who in 1862 had so much difficulty wresting it from an inferior force of Confederate defenders.

As the Antietam descends Montalto Mountain — out of what is now the Michaux State Forest — it passes beneath promontories such as Oak Knob, Eagle Rock, and Pine Knob, and is joined by waters from spots such as Pearl, Travelers, and Tarburner Springs. At the turn of the century, one forester noted that there were 144 species of native trees and shrubs in the area, among them chestnut, rock oak, hickory, red oak, white ash, black oak, and wild cherry; while hemlock, white pine, black gum, yellow poplar, and red maple lived happily along the streams and swamps. Almost pure stands of Jack pine and white pine could be found in many places. [2] At the point where the stream trickles out of the mountains it passes the Mont Alto Forestry School. Concentrations of houses in the valley through which it heads south possess picturesque names such as Tartown, Knepper, Fox Hill, Jugtown, Conboy Switch, and Slabtown.

For tens of thousands of years the great eastern hardwood forest spilled down the slopes of the Blue Ridge Mountains, covered the valley like a luxuriously piled emerald carpet, then climbed the next range of the Appalachians to disappear over the crest. With the coming, however, in the mid-eighteenth century of the Scotch-Irish, who were followed in the nineteenth century by the even more industrious German farmers, the valley soon was stripped of its tree mantle to get at the rich forest floor. Only the unfarmable mountains continued as haven to the forest.

❑  ❑  ❑  ❑

The forestry school at Mont Alto was the product in 1903 of the joint endeavors of two giants of early Pennsylvania forestry, Joseph Trimble Rothrock and Mira Lloyd Dock, a member of the Pennsylvania Forestry Commission. [3] In 1895, the legislature had given Dr. Rothrock charge of the state's "forest preserves." The idea was new — Pennsylvania's first preserves were largely small parcels of abandoned land that had been ravaged by strip mining and the logging industry. In the fall of 1898, Rothrock acquired his first land for a state forest preserve and he needed men to manage it. There were, however, few trained foresters available. Biltmore, in North Carolina, the first such training site in the country, only turned out one or two men a year and Yale's forestry school did not graduate its first student until 1902.

Beyond botany, which was available in American institutions, individuals such as Mira Dock and Gifford Pinchot learned their forestry practice mainly by self study in what remained of the nation's forests, but for formal study had gone to Europe, especially France and Germany. Several of the early textbooks used at Mont Alto, for example, were in German, there being no English texts on those subjects. Of necessity German was one of the courses in the school's curriculum.

After his appointment by the legislature, Dr. Rothrock [4] attempted to interest the Pennsylvania State College and the University of Pennsylvania in starting forestry schools, to no avail. According to Rothrock, his suggestion was rejected because their courses were designed to "train young men in the Arts that would provide them with a living hood and they could see no future in the profession of Forestry." [5] In truth, American land-grant colleges, of which Penn State was one, interpreted their charter as that of training scientists who would use their knowledge to serve others rather than that of training individuals to labor directly on the land. Moreover, the Hatch Act of March 2, 1887, which authorized federally funded experimental stations in each state and offered assistance for scientific research, gave further emphasis to the schools' position. [6] While this interpretation was drawn for their agricultural program — the land-grant schools' curriculum mainstay — the training of men to work in the forest preserves in the early twentieth century was as much practical work as it was scientific.

But, having been rebuffed, Rothrock began his own school for foresters at Mont Alto with Dock's help and encouragement. He chose the specific site in part because the former owner of the land, the Mont Alto Iron Company, had cut well-graded roads throughout the area to transport logs and charcoal. These would furnish easy access to all areas of the forest for men on horseback and also facilitate the removal of timber to be harvested later from any improved areas. Moreover, the village of Mont Alto would be a good source of gardeners, handymen, cooks, and cleaning women.

In addition to reforestation of the denuded land, Rothrock's charge from the legislature included fire protection, as that was an equal threat to the state's scarce timber resources. Tuition at the Mont Alto Forestry School was free for the first several years, but each man had to bring a horse; Rothrock's fire protection "apparatus" consisted of a man with a shovel and a horse with two barrels of water slung over its back. The students paid for their education (which was financed by the state) by fighting fires as well as working in the preserves.

□ □ □ □

By the time Maurice arrived in 1946 to take over as Resident Head of the school and serve as Associate Professor of Forestry, English texts had replaced those in German, Rothrock's "fire" horses had been replaced by trucks, and Penn State had decided that forestry was after all a part of its mission as an agricultural school. In 1907 less than a decade after Rothrock had established the Mont Alto Forestry School, Penn State had set up its own forestry program with four junior and eight sophomore students. The renowned Bernhard E. Fernow had been selected as the first head of the department.

The presence of two forestry schools in the state, both enjoying the support of the legislature was bound eventually to cause difficulty. Although there was jealousy between graduates, especially over appointments to state jobs, it was not until 1922 that the dispute broke into the open. Following his election that year as Pennsylvania Governor, Gifford Pinchot, who had been the nation's first federal forester, began a protracted struggle with the Penn State administration over the existence of two forestry schools in the Commonwealth, a situation he felt was a duplication of effort.

Pinchot "insisted" that Penn State give up its "program" in deference to the full-fledged school at Mont Alto and threatened to cut the college's appropriation. The Board and President of the Penn State refused to give in to the Governor's demands, but attempted to appease him by down playing the importance of their forestry training. For the next several years, it was listed in the Penn State catalog as "farm forestry." The program still included, however, fairly complete course offerings in lumbering, silviculture management, forest law, dendrology, forest economics, seeding and planting, milling and marketing, wood technology, and forest administration. [7]

Then when John Fisher (who was on Penn State's Board of Trustees) followed Pinchot as Governor, he had his Secretary of Forests and Waters, Charles Dorworth, advise him of the possibility of consolidating Mont Alto with Penn State. Hoping to be relieved of the financial burden of Mont Alto's budget, Dorworth recommend their merger. In 1929 the Pennsylvania General Assembly directed that the schools' forestry curriculums be consolidated After that date, Penn State College's freshman forestry students all went to Mont Alto, then completed their remaining three years at State College. It was not until eight years later, however, that all of Mont Alto's property finally was deeded to the college. [8]

□ □ □ □

The forestry school at Mont Alto had been closed between January 1943 and September 1946 for lack of students due to the war. Being all male, and rugged virile types, potential students in forestry had been in the military. When the campus was reactivated that fall, the entering class of 134 was made up, with the exception of two, of men who had seen service in the European and Pacific theaters. Many were married, some with children. They were a serious-minded group of undergraduates.

One of the new Resident Head's first tasks was to find quarters for these married students. Eileen ("Cookie") Middleton, who taught Home Economics at Penn State, was one of those who came under the spell of Maurice K.'s "charm and persuasiveness." Her husband, John B., had applied to the forestry school, so Goddard, who had conceived the idea of renting a summer resort and hotel in nearby Caledonia State Park as quarters for the fifteen couples, but who needed a manager, approached the Middleltons. He reasoned that, as a dietician, Eileen could handle the food and other housekeeping responsibilities while John could "take care of the rest." [9]

That September the five-months-pregnant Eileen took up residence in the Piney Mountain Inn with John and fifteen couples and miscellaneous small children. According to *The Seedling*, the weekly school newsletter, the "rhythm of the ping pong ball and the talk and laughter at the [Inn's] evening refreshment hour" disappeared when the students took up residence. It was as quiet as if the building were deserted. The men studied in the morning, before dinner and then following the evening meal until long after everyone else was in bed.

Maurice K. frequently interrupted his classes in tree identification and dendrology to stop by and check up on his "big experiment." He and Ethel also began to "chaperone" weekend dances and other social events. [10] The Resident Head was especially solicitous of his veteran students. In part this may have been because virtually all of the Penn State and Mont Alto student foresters between 1935 (the year he arrived from Maine) and 1944 had gone off to war, with forty-seven of them, all men he probably knew, paying the supreme sacrifice. [11]    John B. Middleton, for example, had been the commander of an infantry company in the battle across France and Germany. His unit was involved in some difficult fighting and Middleton led it into one of the concentration camps, a sight he never forgot. [12]

Maurice K. seemed to know intuitively how to handle these returning veterans.    One of his Penn State students, Robert H. Rumpf, recalls that midway through the summer of 1948, Professor Beede sent Maurice K. up to Blue Jay from Mont Alto to "restore harmony," when the camp director "was unable to handle a bunch of ex-GIs." [13]

Knowing what they had been through, Maurice K.'s former streak of determined disciplinarianism was now tempered somewhat. One story he delighted in telling in later years concerned a whippoorwill that took to crying his tiresome, rolling call each evening in a tree outside the veterans' inn.  After several nights of this singing, two ex-Marine demolition experts strapped some dynamite to the limb they suspected the bird perched on.  When the whippoorwill started that next evening, they set off the dynamite. They blew out some dorm windows and scattered mattress feathers all over the area, but the whippoorwill was back the following night to take up his mournful, monotonous song once again. [14]

Maurice K. and Ethel were also frequent hosts to his charges at dinner gatherings in the Goddard home. Several instructors would join them and after the meal the group would exchange stories and banter.    Although Maurice K. was no longer the "cut-up" he had been when Ethel first knew him, he enjoyed telling and listening to a wide-range of tales. Some of these were at Ethel's expense, according to one student at the school, who thought they and the way Maurice K. sometimes treated her were in poor taste. [15]

At one such dinner, during a winter snow storm, however, the normally quiet, retiring Ethel Goddard, who always took the ridicule without comment, did become quite agitated.  Ethel was a "nervous wreck" throughout the entire evening, as Eileen

Middleton was "so obviously" on the verge of giving birth to the Middletons' first son, John, who came the following day.

The residents of Piney Mountain Inn bought their staples — flour, sugar, eggs, milk, and coffee — in Fayettesville or Chambersburg, but most of their meat was dragged out of the mountains. John Middleton led the men on frequent forays into the woods. They bagged rabbits, deer, pheasant, an occasional turkey, and innumerable squirrels, which the men brought back by the sackfuls after almost every hunt. Eileen baked them, boiled them, turned them into casseroles, prepared them every conceivable way, but soon grew tired of fixing and eating the great quantities of squirrel the men shot.

□ □ □ □

According to Rex Melton, one of his colleagues at Mont Alto, Maurice was a stimulating lecturer. Moreover, he insisted on taking his students to their field classes or work sites regardless of the weather. On rainy days, reluctant students were apt to be told: "Your skin doesn't leak — lets go!" [16] The resident director also played first base on a "tough" faculty softball team that competed with the students in intramural sports programs. And he spent many evenings driving the campus basketball team to their games with other colleges. At these events the loudest voice in the arena was usually Maurice's as he rooted for the boys from Mont Alto.

One change after Maurice took over the forestry school was to increase the number of class and laboratory hours. The old system of spending a full day each week on practical woods and forestry work was changed to a half-day of forest practice. The mornings of "Forest Practice Day" were devoted to class practicums in the use of instruments, chaining, pacing, elementary mensuration and use of the compass. The student's afternoons were spent in practical woods work. They learned how to use the axe, crosscut saw, chain saws, small crawler tractors, and other tools of the profession. They also spent time in the Mont Alto State Nursery mulching the beds in the fall, lifting trees in the spring, and planting seedlings on abandoned fields and submarginal lands. The student foresters returned to the campus with sore muscles and blistered hands; those who were careless occasionally suffered cuts, leading to greater respect for the tools of forestry. [17]

The forestry profession was — and to a great extent still is — a field dominated by males. In the days of the supremacy of the axe, crosscut saw, and hand crank to start a truck engine, great physical strength was one of the attributes demanded of those who worked in the forests. Adding to this such duties as fire fighting and logging, and one is easily led to the idea of the forester as Paul Bunyan. The possibility that a latter-day botanist in the mold of Mira Dock might take her place next to men who were capable of performing heavy fieldwork, and make a significant contribution, was not even examined in 1946.

As early as the eighteenth century, however, botany had been considered an appropriate field of study for young women. It was even seen by some as "peculiarly adapted to females" because they "liked flowers," "were nurturing" by nature, and would benefit from "healthful but not strenuous outdoor exercise." But while Linnaeus's system for classification was considered satisfactory for female contemplation — it had been the basis for the popularization of plant study by amateurs — there was concern that, as his work made much about the sexual characteristics of plants and their methods of reproduction, it might offend some sensibilities. Therefore, "desexualized" texts were developed for female readers.[18]

It was not until several decades after World War II, with the coming of the technicians — to whom were given the heavy outside work while the "forester" moved from the field to the office — that women were given (sometimes grudgingly) such jobs. [19] In 1946, however, there was still a heavy emphasis at Mont Alto on practical, technical work. The intent of this was to give students an "appreciation of the elementary aspects of forestry." At the same time their academic work included botany, chemistry, dendrology, mathematics, and English composition. And although trucks were used rather than horses, the students were still organized into fire crews. [20]

□ □ □ □

During this period Maurice K. also performed some practical forestry work of his own. As a consultant, he and Rex Melton worked on various projects for the Corps of Engineers, for the Letterkenny Army Depot in Chambersburg, and the Glatfelter Paper Company. They marked trees and conducted inventories of wooded tracts. [21] Then, following a summer of personal research with the Great Northern Paper Company in 1948, Maurice arranged for twenty of his Mont Alto students to spend several months the next year in blister rust control with the U.S. Bureau of Entomology and Plant Quarantine. The jobs were in the national forests of California, Idaho, and Oregon. The students went with mixed feelings of eagerness and anxiety.

Although some of the men drove west many hitch-hiked. Most of them had extensive experience during the war in the art of bumming a ride, but *The Seedling* ran a page of advice before they left. It explained how to find the proper spots along the highway, what to do if stranded in the "middle of no-where at night," when to and when not to engage the driver in conversation, and to "close the car door gently" unless the driver directed that it be slammed shut.

When they arrived in the west, they discovered that the work was demanding. Certain species of ribes (a genus that includes the currant and gooseberry shrubs) are alternate hosts to the white pine blister rust, so the Bureau of Entomology and Plant Quarantine's method of control was through eradication of the ribes. It was this work that the Mont Alto men did. In three-man crews they removed the ribes root and all with a hoedag or mattock. When the plants were too large or the ground was too rocky for removal, they used chemicals sprayed from hand pumps.

58

They were deep in the forest. The areas were often overgrown with chaparral of chinquapin, ceanothus, and maxanito which quickly became the "object of much verbal abuse" over the nearly insurmountable task of penetrating through it. The camp food, however, was exceptionally good. And encounters with black bears and timber rattlesnakes were "thrilling" experiences for the Easterners. They were also called on at times for fire suppression work. Although it was even harder, dirtier work than ribes removal, many of them were eager to get on a fire for the extra money they earned through overtime. [22]

❑ ❑ ❑ ❑

In the spring of 1950, Resident Head Goddard worked out an agreement with the nearby borough of Waynesboro for the school to manage the lands on the town's watershed. This effective management of the forest returned revenues to the borough and improved the property, while at the same time the students received income which was used for dances, field day prizes, the printing of *The Sylvan*, the school yearbook, and other miscellaneous activities.

Perhaps the biggest job the students undertook in this cooperative arrangement was the preparation of the site for a new Waynesboro impounding dam the next year. The town, which drew its water from the Little Antietam Creek, was facing a critical water shortage. The new dam, which rose 75 feet above the stream bed, is 805 feet long and 20 wide at the crest. It created a lake of 150 million gallons of water. The Waynesboro *Record Herald* of September 29, 1951, showed Maurice striding along the trunk of a felled tree while directing the clearing operations. His work-gloved hands indicated he was an active participant in the effort. Most of the wood the Mont Alto "boys" removed from the reservoir site went for pulp and railroad ties.

When he brought the Pennsylvania Forestry Association back to look over the tract in 1955, Maurice K. proudly showed his colleagues the results of a timber-management and watershed-protection system begun when he was director of the school. He felt it had served as an excellent demonstration of a community's dependence on good forestry for its water. [23]

□ □ □ □

Several "innovations" were introduced at Mont Alto during the Goddard years, among them the acquisition of a chipper and a tree-planting machine and the construction of a sawmill. Portable chippers, like the tree-planting machine were new equipment at the time. The tree-planting machine consisted of a triangular frame pulled by a tractor, which was fitted with a special two-piece plow to open a trench, while "floating packing wheels" on the end of the frame were used to close it. [24] The operator sat across the frame and dropped the seedlings between his legs and into the trench, which was closed by the wheels at the back of the frame.

When Robert Rumpf was transferred to Caledonia in March of 1950 as the the new "Service Forester" (whose job is to furnish advice to and work with private woodlot owners), Dick Dalton, the Assistant District Forester for Caledonia, took him to Mont Alto. It was Easter break and the students were all gone, so Dalton took Rumpf to see the Waynesboro Watershed. When they got there they found Maurice K. operating the tree planter. He was wearing his G.I. trousers and combat boots, busily dropping seedlings between his long, wide-spread legs. [25]

The sawmill was situated near the college woodlots for instruction and research purposes. Instructor Orvel A. Schmidt designed it. The saw was powered by a 128 h.p. Chrysler engine which had a speed of 3800 r.p.m. It was capable of handling trees of twenty feet in length and forty-five inches in diameter. Unlike most mills, the college's was "left-handed." This departure was to "keep the lumber flowing in one direction from the saw to the planer and eventually to the dry kiln and preserving plant." [26]

According to Rex Melton, Maurice K. exhibited great "leadership and communications" skill as the resident director at

Mont Alto. Both the students and the faculty "trusted and respected" him. Moreover, he was "readily available for consultation" and really "listened to those who came to him with problems or suggestions." [27]

When Professor Beede decided to retire in June 1952, Milton S. Eisenhower, who had become President of Penn State two years earlier, announced that Maurice K. would be the new head of the Penn State Forestry Department at the State College campus. [28] According to William Bramble, the assistant head of the department, he had the unanimous support of the college faculty in the appointment.

Milton Eisenhower had excellent credentials as an educator and with the federal government, especially in agriculture. As the New York *Sun* wrote of Eisenhower: "He can tell you anything about agriculture from 'a' to 'e' because he knows his subject from the ground up." [29] He came to Penn State from Kansas State College, which he had transformed from a small school into a major institution. During his tenure there he had assisted President Truman in a variety of positions. Milton was not only a highly successful administrator at Kansas State but also beloved by the students and the faculty. When Dwight visited the campus in 1945 a woman told him cheerfully, "Ike, you may be a great big general, but in this town [Manhattan] you're just Milton's big brother." [30]

□ □ □ □

Maurice K. soon had the forestry faculty "analyzing and modifying" the school curricula to keep pace with the demands of the profession, and in 1953 started "short courses" in lumber grading and inspection. He also had the students re-inventory the university's farm woodlands in preparation for a second revision of the school's "management plan," constructed a two-mile access road in the Shaver Creek block of the Stone Valley Experimental Forest, conducted a large-scale test to determine the effect of chemical brush control on game food and cover on the right-of-way of the Pennsylvania Electric Company — an experiment considered at that time to be one of the "outstanding projects in chemical brush control in the country." [31]

As at Mont Alto, the students' course work at University Park was also heavy in practicums and field work. Between their sophomore and junior years, those who enrolled in Forestry 30, the course in Wood Utilization, took a six-week tour of various industries. These trips, taken in the back of a station wagon or truck, consisted of jouncing visits over rough roads to paper mills, tanning plants, furniture manufacturers, wood preservation plants, and a glue factory where they were "assailed by pungent, nerve racking stenches." [32] The two-week orientation preceding the trip, included instruction in kiln-drying, seasoning, and wood-manufacturing procedures.

The Penn State Forestry Department also worked closely with the Pennsylvania Department of Forests and Waters gathering data and doing some of the basic processing for Pennsylvania's first forest plan that came out in 1955. The school prepared some general volume tables as well as tree volume tables in both board and cubic feet for the entire state. Joe Ibberson, of the Division of Research in Forests and Waters — the state's point man in the effort — used to come up to Penn State for meetings on the project. He said it was not unusual when he arrived from Harrisburg to find Milton Eisenhower in the Ferguson Building talking to Maurice K. about some aspect of forestry. According to Ibberson:

> He and Dr. Eisenhower were very close. I would go to him [Maurice K.] for basic ideas on the forest plans, such as sampling techniques and especially for recruitments to the Department of Forests and Waters. I went up to State College a couple times a year to tell the students about some of the practical applications they would run into. [33]

At times there were disagreements over the school's research and work the that the Department of Forests and Waters had undertaken. According to Ibberson, the University (in November 1953 the college became the Pennsylvania State University), especially several members of the department and Milton Eisenhower, felt that the *practical* work of the state in reviewing the growth types that did well in restoring rights-of-way and strip mine overburden (the soil lying on top of the seams of coal) encroached on the university's *research* responsibilities under its land-grant status. Although Ibberson met with Dr. Eisenhower, Maurice K., and especially William Bramble on the issue, they never reached an agreement. After Maurice K. went to Harrisburg as Secretary of Forests and Waters, he appeased the University by simply changing the name of Ibberson's Division from "Research" to "Forestry Advisory Services." [34]

In the few years he spent as department head at Penn State, Maurice K. provided dynamic leadership for the Forestry Department. By 1954, he was able finally to convince the campus administrators to award the department status as a full school of the university, a change that had been under discussion for more than eight years. [35] Within the new School of Forestry, two departments were set up, one for each of the two major curriculums being offered. William Bramble became head of Forest Management; Newel A. Norton was named to the Department of Wood Utilization.

Writing for *Pennsylvania Forests* in the summer of 1953, Maurice K. proudly pointed out that Penn State had the second largest enrollment of forestry students in the country. He also announced his hope to develop a forestry center that would include a dry kiln, wood preservation plant, sawmill, greenhouse, and related facilities.

During these years, Maurice K. also became especially active in the Pennsylvania Forestry Association. Between 1950 and 1952 he served on the Association's board of directors, then on March 28, 1953, he succeeded Philip Glatfelter as president. Through the years, the two men worked closely on a number of forestry and water concerns. Maurice K. previously had induced the P. H.

Glatfelter Company to award a $1,000 fellowship for graduate study in the forestry school, and it was probably Glatfelter who pushed Goddard forward in the Forestry Association. Through the years Maurice K. continued to work closely with the Glatfelter firm and members of the family. One of their major joint efforts was the establishment of Codorus State Park, which benefited both the state of Pennsylvania and Glatfelter's firm.

Following his election as president of the Pennsylvania Forestry Association at the Split Rock Lodge, Maurice K. spoke on the great need for "unselfish cooperation of all groups" and for the "coordination of multiple uses" in Pennsylvania forestry. [36] Both cooperation and multiple use would later become watchwords for Goddard-style conservation across the state.

One of the special actions Maurice K. took during his three-year presidency of the Pennsylvania Forestry Association was to establish an ad hoc committee to look at "water resource development in the interest of business, industry, agriculture and forestry, recreation, and wildlife." Floods, water shortages, dry wells and streams, and low lake levels in recreational areas had become a concern; there was always "too little, or too much." The committee developed a "Resources Development Program for the Commonwealth of Pennsylvania," which later became the basis for Pennsylvania House Bill 1585 to set up a Pennsylvania Conservation Advisory Council. [37]

□  □  □  □

In 1955, incoming Governor George M. Leader appointed Maurice K. to his cabinet as Secretary of the Department of Forests and Waters. Pennsylvania State University granted him a leave of absence to accept the appointment and the trustees set up a committee consisting of William Bramble, Newell Norton, and Wilbur Ward to run the School of Forestry's activities in his absence. The faculty "deeply regretted" his departure; he had been more than just their director, and they considered him a "good friend they knew they would miss." [38]   Goddard told the students:

> Although reluctant to take leave from the University at this time, I felt the opportunity offered to strengthen forestry and water management in Pennsylvania should not go unchallenged. [39]

While he may simply have been trying to ensure he was not seen solely as a forester, his statement seems to mark a new direction. From this point on Maurice Goddard began to turn from the forest to "water." Within a few years this shift would take him to the time when water would receive more emphasis, be of more concern to him than forests, the day was not too distant when he would declare: *Water is Pennsylvania's future.* [40]

# CHAPTER V

# MR. SECRETARY

tree (tre) n. [ME *tree, tre, treo* fr. AS *treow, treo*, tree akin to Gk *drys* wood, *dory* spear] a woody perennial plant having a single main stem (trunk) commonly exceeding 10 feet in height and usually devoid of branches below, while bearing a head of branches and foliage or a crown of leaves at the summit.

George M. Leader put together a mix of professionals and politicians in his cabinet. It was a deliberate attempt to reform the executive branch in Pennsylvania by reducing the large number of party favorites that had always been picked to fill important state offices — usually in return for a substantial contribution to the party coffers. (A contribution of $25,000 was often expected for an appointment as a department head.) The Governor-elect did discuss appointments with U.S. Representative William J. Green, Jr. of Philadelphia and Mayor David Lawrence of Pittsburgh, perhaps the two most powerful leaders in the Pennsylvania Democratic party, but chose only a couple of the men they recommended.

Leader, who had served as the Supply Officer of the aircraft carrier U.S.S. *Randolph* in the South Pacific during the war, was, however, no political neophyte. He had been Secretary of the York Country Democratic Committee and later served as the party's chairman in several vigorous campaigns. When his father vacated his state senatorial seat in 1950, George was elected to replace him.

By late December 1954, Leader had filled most of his cabinet positions. One exception was a head for Forests and Waters. The

Governor-elect was determined to find someone who, at least, knew something about the subject. He was convinced that the state's conservation and recreation programs needed professional management. He came from York County, an area where, in the words of his biographers Richard Cooper and Ryland Crary, "Husbandry dictates conservation; a farmer destroys his soil only from ignorance — not intent." It was still a few years before ecology would become a major public issue, but the new governor was determined that his administration would

> develop for our wise use the natural resources of our state, purify its streams, increase its opportunities for outdoor recreation, keep a sense of the forest and the field in our lives. [1]

The new governor had a deep interest in the environment, but really didn't know anyone in the field, or even how to go about finding a person with a good technical background. The party bosses were pushing hard for him to give the position to John Torquato, a seven-term Democratic chairman of Cambria County, but Leader wanted another non-politician for this job, so he kept "elbowing everyone away" that the power-brokers recommended. He knew that most party appointees were more interested in their businesses back home than in the demands of a cabinet job, for which they usually had little technical background. They would come to Harrisburg on "Tuesday and leave on Thursday." [2]

Just prior to his January inauguration date, he asked a friend, Genevieve Blatt, who had been elected Secretary of Internal Affairs when Leader had won the governorship, for the names of professionals who might be good in the position. Blatt's brother, Joe, had attended the School of Forestry at Penn State and always "raved about the dean of the school"; she recommended to Leader that they talk to Goddard. [3]

A few days later, when Maurice K. was on his way from University Park to Mont Alto, the three met for lunch in Harrisburg. They ate in a nondescript restaurant on Cameron Street not far from where the Governor-elect had his transition office. It was convenient and efficient, and desk-clean efficiency was a Leader hallmark. Leader immediately liked Goddard's "honest, direct style," and his ideas on reforestation and recreation. It was clear at their first meeting that the two men saw eye to eye on all of the important issues affecting the state's environment. Maurice had barely completed the trip to Mont Alto, when the Governor-elect phoned and offered him the position. [4]

Maurice K. accepted conditioned on the agreement of Dr. Milton Eisenhower, the school president. In addition to Dr. Eisenhower's superb educational credentials, he had spent twenty years in federal service filling important positions at the U.S. Department of Agriculture and at the United Nations. If Eisenhower didn't actually counsel Maurice K. to accept the offer, he at least would have been supportive of Maurice K.'s decision to accept it. According to Leader, when he called, Eisenhower asked, "Who is it this time?" anticipating he was going to want someone in addition to Dr. William Henning, who had accepted the post as Leader's Secretary of Agriculture. On learning it was Goddard, Eisenhower replied, "Well you sure know how to pick them." Having just met Maurice K. the day before, Leader appreciated the reassurance. [5]

George Leader had studied at the University of Pennsylvania, following his return from the South Pacific, and he is reported to have said, "At Penn, I learned what a really professional government should look like." This idea of "professionalization" in Leader's administration — a revolutionary one for Pennsylvania in 1955 — was nowhere more obvious than in his choice of cabinet officers. Maurice Goddard was one of the beneficiaries of this new management tilt; and as Cooper and Crary stated, Goddard was an "undisputed professional."

The new Governor received a large number of messages and letters congratulating him on the wisdom of choosing Maurice Goddard to lead Forests and Waters. Conservationists throughout Pennsylvania seemed to sense that Leader wanted, as he said in his inaugural message, to "set new standards for the state's services; to improvise; to modernize; to excel"; and knew that Goddard was the man to shake the lethargy out of the department and was ready to follow the governor's willingness to "take risks" and "adopt bold measures" whenever they "promised to advance the interests of the state."

As one writer told the governor, "Your appointment plainly shows your determination to give first consideration to the calibre of man needed to bring expert guidance to this important work. It shows an encouraging departure from previous practices in this respect." [6]

Leader also received a letter from Joseph S. Illick, Dean Emeritus at the College of Forestry at the State University of New York at Syracuse. Illick was one of the early forestry authorities in Pennsylvania — a patriarch among state foresters. After study at Biltmore and in Germany, he had been an instructor at Mont Alto from 1905 to 1919. He then served as chief of the Bureau of Silviculture in Pennsylvania's original Department of Forestry, and then became the architect of an expanded research program. In 1931 he left Pennsylvania for New York. Even more important, he was the author of what was probably the first major American work on tree identification, *Pennsylvania Trees*. It was the definitive work in the field for many years, with more than forty-five thousand copies in print. Illick wrote George Leader:

> The good news has just reached me of the appointment of Maurice K. Goddard as Secretary of the Department of Forests and Waters. . . I want to compliment you most sincerely in placing . . . the Department in the hands of one who has demonstrated outstanding competence, dependable judgment, progressive leadership in matters relating to forestry not only in Pennsylvania, but throughout our nation. [7]

Less than two weeks after he moved into his new office, Secretary Goddard swung into action. Wielding what would soon be recognized as his strong administrative axe, he reversed a last-minute decision of the outgoing Secretary, Samuel Lewis. Lewis had "reinstated" a contract of a C. A. White (that had been suspended soon after it was issued nine years earlier) permitting him to cut four and a half million board feet of timber in Perry County.  In his telegram to White voiding Lewis's reinstatement, Maurice K. said:

> I consider the reaffirmation of a contract that had been dead for nearly nine years, then was reinstated at 1945 prices, extremely irregular.  If [you] have any rights they should be determined by proper legal action, not by a questionable legal maneuver in the dying days of an outgoing Administration. [8]

Another Lewis action that complicated his early years was the former Secretary's decision to plow under more than a million seedlings the department had earmarked for use in restoring strip mines and other scarred areas of the state. [9]  Secretary Goddard and the Governor had agreed at their first meeting that mine restoration was a major concern.

Strip mining had severely disfigured portions of Pennsylvania. The open mines were such an appalling sight from the air, Leader eventually asked his pilot to avoid flying over them on routine trips around the state.   The Bituminous Coal Open Pit Mining Conservation Act of 1945 and the Anthracite Strip Mining Law of 1947 required mine owners to "backfill near highways, homes and streams," to "level and round peaks of spoil banks," and to reslope and "plant exposed surfaces with trees, grasses or shrubs" when they finished removing the minerals, but many of them stalled. Among the deceptions they practiced was the setting of an old rusted bulldozer on the site so, if inspected, they could claim they were working on the problem.   Some even skipped the state, abandoning their properties, to avoid complying with the law. Although the owners were supposed to pay the costs, many of the mine sites actually were restored with state money. [10]  This, of course, included the cost to replace the lost seedlings.

Secretary Goddard was able to report a striking turn-around, however, two years later.  In 1957, the department's four nurseries shipped more than fifteen million seedlings, two thirds of which were provided to the Department of Mines for planting operations on pre-act spoil areas. Moreover, he was able to announce a goal of twenty million seedlings for mine restoration in 1958. [11] The techniques involved in collecting and treating large numbers of seeds, the preparation of soils, the proper sowing of the seeds, and the protection of the seedling from insects and disease made this a complicated job. He later attributed the program's success to having placed a professional forester in charge of each of the state's nurseries.

❑ ❑ ❑ ❑

A few months after he took charge, a thoroughly prepared Maurice Goddard appeared before the House Appropriations Committee in support of his department's budget of fourteen and a quarter million dollars for the years of 1955 and 1956. [12] He told them that Forests and Waters' income of nine and a half million dollars a year from timber and other sales was actually more than the sum of the department's budget lines for salaries and general expenses. Thus when compared to its basic costs, the department actually "showed a profit." Among his new ventures, however, was a request of one million dollars to acquire property for an Independence Mall State Park, and a like amount to continue the development work at Point State Park in Pittsburgh.

The new secretary described his department's responsibilities for the legislators. They were

> to develop and maintain recreation areas; engage in research studies of practical forestry problems; make studies and records of stream flows; regulate the placing of encroachments and design; construct and maintain dams in, along, across or projecting into all streams and bodies of water having a drainage area of one-half square mile or more; and allocate water to public water supply agencies. [13]

According to his testimony, visitors in the "State Forest Parks" had increased from five million to nine million between 1952 and 1954. Maurice K. closed his comments to the committee by describing himself as a "temporary administrator" of the department and told them, "I am obligated to the conservation of resources so that future generations, . . . may continue to received the benefits of nature's gift to mankind." [14]

He didn't mention it to them but his first look at the state of the parks had left him "pretty discouraged." The campgrounds in many of them looked "like shanty towns." There was almost no oversight and little management at many of the facilities. People even brought old refrigerators from home, placed them under tarps hung between trees or off of trailers, and then "stayed all summer." Moreover, there was no money in the capital budget and an inadequate general fund budget line to tackle the problem. [15]

❑ ❑ ❑ ❑

Goddard's personal imperative after taking over at Forests and Waters, however, was not parks or even forests. And it was not one the legislature was interested in grappling with. Maurice K. and the governor wanted to extend the civil service system throughout the department. They saw this as a necessary means to achieving their conservation goals. They wanted not only competent, well-trained foresters but also other fully proficient workers in Forests and Waters. And they quickly set to work to change the situation when the only man Maurice was able to hire from the fifty-five graduates of the 1955 class of the School of Forestry at Penn State, resigned because the position lacked civil service status. According to Cooper and Crary, the rest of the class went to neighboring states for more attractive and secure employment offers.

After an unsuccessful months-long struggle to get a bill through the legislature, Leader took the simple, but extraordinary action of issuing an executive order professionalizing several of the state's departments. The Governor's order, effective October 1, 1956, directed the Department Secretaries "to place . . . technical and professional job categories under the jurisdiction of the Pennsylvania Civil Service." As he told the press:

> It is imperative to the success of our programs . . . that we recruit skilled technical and professional personnel . . . and that we recruit them on the basis of merit, competence, and experience. The quality of our work depends upon the caliber of our people. [16]

The governor's directive explained that the "lack of job security is a principal deterrent to the recruitment of persons properly qualified," therefore, after ordering that all the professional jobs be placed "under the present Commission contract arrangements," it directed that "no incumbent and no persons appointed thereto be given security [permanent] status without having passed a qualifying examination." Once having passed the Civil Service examination, moreover, the employees were protected from dismissal for any reasons (especially political) other than cause.

While Maurice K. did not undertake wholesale firings in Forests and Waters, there were, of course, selective dismissals. In September 1955, he peremptorily abolished the Division of Nurseries, terminated T. G. Norris the head, and placed responsibility for the nurseries under Joe Ibberson, the Chief of the Division of Research, despite Ibberson's objections. Although Ibberson was concerned about the increased work load, it was the combining of a production unit with a research group that was his greatest worry over the move. [17]

From this point on all professional level postions — for example, Foresters I to V — were sent to Civil Service for development of job descriptions, standards and qualifying criteria, including competitive examinations. [18] Those who could pass the examinations were retained. All new job applicants, of course, were screened through Civil Service before they were even considered for hiring by department personnel. Equally as important, promotions within the department were now also based on "merit."

The Pennsylvania political establishment didn't give up, however, simply because the Governor issued an order. According to Goddard, "Fifty-five county chairmen came and visited me. I wasn't that naive that I didn't know I was being set up. None of

73

them wanted me to put any of the department's positions under civil service." His final political visitor was a Bedford County chairman who asked him to get rid of the local district forester, a Republican. Maurice K. told him: "OK, if you can prove to me the guy there now isn't competent, I'll get rid of him, but the person I replace him with won't necessarily be from Bedford County. I'll go out and get the best person for the job." As Goddard told the story the man "jumped about three feet off the floor." And he was no longer bothered by visits of the county chairmen. [19]

His professionalization efforts soon began to show results. Sales of timber started climbing at the rate of almost a half-million dollars annually. And to head up what *American Forests* was to call two years later "one of the best all-around resources staffs in the history of the state or nation," Maurice K. brought back Ralph Wible as Pennsylvania State Forester. [20] Then — after abolishing the several deputy secretary positions Samuel Lewis had established — he installed Wible as the director of the Bureau of Forestry.

Wible, who had graduated from Mont Alto in 1927, served as district forester in several Pennsylvania State Forests. During the Earle administration he had been dismissed in the "organizational upheaval" unleashed by the 1938 change in political parties in the governor's office. After his return he became responsible for improving fire control in the Wyoming State Forest. Moreover, he was the "prime mover" in the development of new state lands acquired from the Ricketts estate, which later became Ricketts Glen State Park. [21]

◻ ◻ ◻ ◻

Secretary Goddard quickly learned to work, not only within the executive branch, but also with legislators on either side of the House and Senate aisles. [22] At times he was blunt and direct — he never minced words, so was seldom misunderstood — but as a worker he was as hard as the heart of oak, and the members of the legislature soon realized his directness was an expression of his honesty and sincerity. As a result, they came to trust and respect him. Moreover, the state's legislators soon recognized that his vision for a better Pennsylvania environmentally embraced not just one or two counties, or only the metropolitan areas, or just the rural ones — the farmer, the hunter, the fisherman — but virtually all of the state's constituencies. His horizons were broad; they covered everything from the Delaware River to the Ohio, from the Great Lakes to the Mason Dixon Line.

Copying an idea from California, where following World War II, the state used the revenues derived from Pacific Ocean oil wells inside the state's three-mile limit to rebuild the California state park system, [23] Maurice K. proposed applying the royalties from gas and oil on state land directly to Pennsylvania's state parks.

Then like a shrewd third-term lawmaker, he put together a bill that placed the income received from royalties on the sale of the oil and gas reserves (except those under lands managed for fish and game) into a special, restricted fund to be used solely by his department. He proposed appropriating the proceeds — which at that time went into the state's general fund — "for conservation, recreation, dams, or flood control." Working both sides of the legislative aisle, he got the bill sponsored by four Republican senators, chief among them George B. Stevenson of Clinton County. [24] With bipartisan support, it became law as Act 256. Governor Leader, signed the Oil and Gas Lease Fund Act December 15, 1955. (There was no oil on state lands, but Maurice included it in the bill, apparently in case some was later found.)

Then following the advice of William F. Schulz, a University of Pittsburgh professor, who had done a pre-inaugural study of Forests and Waters policies, as well as an exhaustive study of the laws and administration of conservation and resource use in Pennsylvania two years earlier, [25] Maurice K. established a new Division of Minerals in the department to handle the leasing of the gas and oil reserves.

In addition to the leasing of the gas and oil wells, a plan was devised to use exhausted wells for storing gas. The emptied underground cavities were perfect places to store gas to ensure that the state (and east coast) would have adequate supplies during the winter months. In this way, there was no need to construct expensive, elaborate above-ground storage facilities.

The Oil and Gas Lease Fund Act granted the Secretary of Forests and Waters extensive powers. It was left up to him "to determine the need for and the location of any project authorized by the act"; moreover, he was given the authority "to acquire in the name of the Commonwealth by purchase, condemnation or otherwise such lands as may be needed."

According to Richard Thorpe, the Director of the Bureau of Forestry from 1977 to 1988, this act was the "most significant conservation-oriented legislation ever approved in Pennsylvania" since the one in 1895 that established the initial state Forest Reservations and put Dr. Rothrock in charge of their management. Nearly twenty million dollars poured into Goddard's "oil and gas fund" over the next fifteen years    Except for the acquisition of about seventy-nine thousand acres of interior holdings for state forest land, [26] the money was spent on parks,  almost all of it in building new ones.

□  □  □  □

In August of Goddard and Leader's first year in office, two hurricanes, Connie and then Diane hit the northeast. The blows staggered the state; destruction in eastern Pennsylvania from the resulting flash floods was extensive. A hundred people were killed. Thousands of children were stranded at camps in the Pocono area. The *New York Times* stated that "chaos and benumbed shock" overlay East Stroudsburg. There were thirty bodies in one funeral home, while helicopter pilots reported seeing nine bodies floating in the "wildly overflowing Delaware River" over which four bridges had been destroyed. [27]    The greatest single tragedy was at a summer colony of fourteen modest bungalows near Analomink, three miles northwest of East Stroudsburg. There the "normally placid" Brodhead Creek rose nearly thirty feet in fifteen minutes. The *Times* reported that eighteen dead were recovered by the next day, while nineteen persons were still missing.

The damage to roads, bridges, and streams was so massive that the legislature acceded to the administration's request for a temporary additional tax on gasoline and cigarettes to pay for repair of highways and the clearing of streams. (It was a difficult decision for Leader who had run for governor on a pledge of no new taxes.) During the height of the flooding, Route 309 between Allentown and Philadelphia was impassable, while sections of Routes 6, 611, 307, 502 and 11 in Luzerne and Lackawanna Counties were reported under as much as four feet of water. About thirty highway bridges were destroyed. Along with the State Police, Civil Defense, the Highway Department, and Health, Welfare, and Public Assistance, the Department of Forests and Waters became one of the agencies responsible for the cleanup. According to Cooper and Crary, many of Goddard's employees worked for the next three years clearing the streams and forests. There were mountains of debris, for example, along the banks of the Delaware. [28]

In testimony before the U.S. Senate Select Committee on Water Resources in Philadelphia several years later, Maurice K. estimated the cost of the floods "in the neighborhood" of $164 million. Approximately a hundred million of this was due, however, to losses of real, personal and industrial, not state property. He estimated the damages to highways, roads and bridges at about $35 million. [29]

President Eisenhower promised the governors of the northeast states $120 million in relief funds, but Pennsylvania only received about $3 million of this money. The bulk of the state's restoration effort was paid for by the gasoline and cigarette tax. Approximately $37 million were raised from this assessment. [30]

❑ ❑ ❑ ❑

The effect of Connie and Diane went well beyond the cleanup. In both Leader and Goddard the hurricanes produced a dramatic change. Flood control became a priority for the rest of Leader's four-year term. For Maurice K., however, the emphasis on water as a *primary* resource for the Commonwealth became a life-long concern.

In November 1955 the Governor launched a campaign to protect the state from the "ravages of floods." He gave the State Planning Board the assignment of studying flood control across the state and of recommending any projects it deemed desirable. During the next three years, nearly four hundred flood control projects were undertaken throughout Pennsylvania, and by the end of Leader's term as governor, the Department of Forests and Waters had a comprehensive flood control program in place. The Division of Flood Control undertook two basic kinds of projects — stream clearance and flood control construction. [31]

Floods disrupt stream equilibriums, leaving deposits and debris in stream channels. These deposits reduce channel-carrying capacities thus increasing the likelihood of future flooding. Stream clearance consisted of two types of operations — clearance and channel rectification. The second of these efforts was designed, as far as possible, to return waterway conditions to those existing prior to the flooding. These projects sometimes included improvement of channel alignment and the construction of overflow channels or dikes.

The department's first concern after a flood was, of course, to undertake stream clearance work for temporary or partial relief. At a later date, in areas suffering extensive damage, engineering studies were conducted to determine the type, extent, and justification for permanent flood protection work.

When feasibility studies indicated a need for such work, topographic surveys were made and contour maps prepared. These formed the basis for hydraulic and hydrologic studies. Several plans of protection were usually proposed. They invariably included various combinations of solutions — earth or paved channels, earth dikes or concrete floodwalls, or the construction of silting or debris basins. After Goddard's approval, all such plans were submitted for their final review and okay at the local level. All projects were built by contractors under the Department's supervision, [32] not with Bureau personnel. Moreover, their maintenance fell to the local communities benefiting from the Forests and Waters' work.

In a *Pennsylvania Forests'* review of the Department's accomplishments three years later, Maurice K. wrote that "nearly $14,000,000 worth of [flood control] projects are under contract, design, or construction this year." The two more expensive of these were a $1.8 million project at Scranton and a $2.7 million one at Stroudsburg, the largest one undertaken since the area was devastated by Hurricane Diane. The department also completed thirty-seven smaller stream-clearance and channel-rectification projects. [33]

All of these measures, of course, are engineering in nature. From a hydrologist's point of view non-structural actions such as flood-plain and storm-water management, along with the availablity of flood insurance are equally important. Although it is not clear when the change in attitude occurred, eventually (as we shall see in Chapter XIII) Maurice K. became a strong supporter of these alternatives to engineering works.

From this point forward the development of flood control projects took on greater urgency for Maurice K.. Twenty-five years later — when he stood alone against abandoning the plans to build the Tocks Island dam on the Delaware — Maurice was still thinking of two water concerns — *supply* and *control*. Diane was a lesson he never forgot.

□ □ □ □

In May 1957 Maurice K. and Governor Leader traveled to University Park for the Penn State-Mont Alto Forestry Alumni

79

Association's anniversary celebration marking a half-century of professional forestry instruction at Penn State. Among the more than 500 guests were Henry Clepper, executive secretary of the Society of American Foresters, and a distinguished author of articles and books on forestry; Professor John A. Ferguson, who headed the Forestry School on the main campus from 1913 to 1938 and George Wirt, the first director of the Mont Alto Forestry School and, according to *Pennsylvania Forests*, the state's "pioneer professional forester." [35] By this time the earlier rivalries and animosities between the two schools had dissipated. Although Governor Leader gave the highlight address of the two-day program, his remarks clearly echoed Maurice K.'s sentiments:

> The conservation of our forests is — first, foremost, and always — measurable only in terms of people and their well-being. We grow trees so that mankind can grow. And this realization is at the root of all our conservation laws. [36]

Although Leader's "well-being" of mankind from the forest was usually ascribed to the benefits derived from its timber harvest, the growing use of the forest for recreation became its more visible public contribution in the years following World War II. When Maurice K. took over Forests and Waters in 1955, for example, there were forty-five State Parks, five State Historical Parks, and four Commissioned Parks in the Pennsylvania system, along with seven Natural Areas, and two State Forest Monuments. By the time of their May trip to Penn State (midway through Governor Leader's four-year term), the steady inflow of dedicated funds from the gas and oil leases made it possible for Maurice K. to announce a bold new plan to establish a state park within twenty-five miles of every resident of the Commonwealth.

Earlier parks had been located mainly in more remote, sparsely settled areas where the state had acquired forest reservation land in the years since 1895. It was almost all land that was stripped by logging and surface mining, burnt over, or encumbered with tax debt, thus inexpensive for the state to buy. Much of this land was located in the north central and western portions of the state away from the more populous areas. When the forest finally began to return, it was in these areas that the first state parks had been placed.

Based on a mid-1950s survey that showed only 9 percent of the population of Philadelphia used the state parks, while 85 percent of the residents of Warren used them, Goddard drew twenty-five-mile-wide circles on a Pennsylvania map around each of the existing parks — the distance he believed it was reasonable to expect residents to drive to a day-use park. Seeing the lack of parks near the centers of population, he decided with the Governor's blessing to build a ring of parks around Philadelphia and Pittsburgh. He told the legislature:

> Parks are for people. . . . Every individual is important, whether he lives in a city or a small town. The goal of this program is a state park within twenty-five miles of every resident of the Commonwealth. [37]

The criteria and standards Maurice K. set for locating each new park were based on water, topography, subsurface conditions, availability of the land, and its scenic and historical interest.

Water was of prime importance. To the Secretary a "state park without a place to swim is like apple pie without cheese," [38] so he made certain that the center of attraction in the most heavily used state parks was a body of water. And he insisted that it be good water, free from contamination, located in a forested or agricultural watershed where conservation practices were already being employed. There had to be plenty of it, too, otherwise a crystal clear lake in spring might become an unhealthy stagnant pool in late summer. And its temperature had to be warm enough to permit comfortable bathing. In most cases the desire for a lake entailed the building of a dam. This meant the sub-surface soil and rock structure had to support such construction.

❑ ❑ ❑ ❑

After the Oil and Gas Leases Fund Act was approved, the department studied 175 potential sites and by April 1957, thirteen were under development, each in a separate county. Among the more ambitious of these were Prince Gallitzin State Park in Cambria County near Altoona and Gifford Pinchot State Park in Governor Leader's home county of York.

Prince Gallitzin covers 6,600 acres and includes a large tree-lined lake of 1,640 acres that has a shore line of 26 miles. In addition to boating and swimming, the lake is renowned for warm-water fishing, including muskie. In the winter the marina portion of the lake is home to iceskaters, while ice fishermen go after walleye and panfish. The park, which has become the focal point for the entire region, was named for Dimetrius Augustine Gallitzin, the prince-priest who established a mission at Loretto in the Alleghenies in 1795, and for whom a Pennsylvania forest district is also named. In addition to the usual park activities, significant protection against floods was provided to Coalport, Irvona, and other communities in the Susquehanna Basin. The project was planned jointly with the Game Commission, which agreed to an exchange of one thousand acres of land for "consent to flood additional acreage" to increase opportunities for duck hunting.

Prince Gallitzin State Park introduced two new concepts in Pennsylvania state park design. A double bathing area with two complete beach facilities was located on opposite sides of the lake. It solved problems common to older parks. The opening of two areas on days of heavy use distributed the traffic load more evenly on the local highway network; at the same time it permitted a less conspicuous and thus more aesthetic design for parking facilities. The "splitting" also permitted the "resting" of one of the areas during periods of minimum operation, giving them time to recover from the wear of heavy use. [39]

The ever-conservation-minded Goddard also insisted that the park contain an area dedicated to Conservation-Education. He felt that many of the problems besetting natural resource managers "can more easily be solved with the help of an enlightened public." The theme of the Conservation-Education area was "to demonstrate . . . the obvious effects of good and bad natural resource management practices." [40]

An important aspect of education, that Maurice K. quickly began taking advantage of as Secretary, was getting the department's story and activities to the public with the help of the local press. When he traveled with C. H. McConnell, his chief for flood control, to Prince Gallitzin in December 1960 to conduct the ceremonies marking the closing of the gates to the new dam, he made certain that reporters from area newspapers were in attendance. Managing Editor of the Johnstown *Tribune-Democrat*, James Whiteford, obliged by giving the event a quarter-page picture and three columns under the heading, "BY GODDARD." Whiteford's lengthy article described the features of the finished park and lake. He quoted Maurice K. as telling the audience (while standing in the biting cold and bitter winds at the end of the sixty-foot control tower at the breast of the dam to touch the button that activated the machinery to close the gate), "This is pretty simple, but it took two and a half years to do this." [41]

There was, however, one discordant note sounded over a park. At a public meeting in Ebensburg, northeast of Johnstown, to discuss the plans for the site with local residents, several people suggested that the benefits would be greater if the park program were abandoned and the area opened to mining. Maurice K. carefully explained to the group that their prime consideration should be that the park would be an "everlasting economic asset to the community," while the "influence of a coal mine would only be a temporary benefit, at best." He mentioned the economic distress that was common in many of the state's older mining communities because of their reliance on a single industry and a product that would eventually be exhausted or become unmarketable. [42]

❏ ❏ ❏ ❏

Gifford Pinchot State Park is about one-third the size of Gallitzin, but does contain a 340-acre lake that was formed by damming Beaver Creek near where it flows into Conewago Creek. The site, located near Lewisberry, in a unique upland valley in York County, was one the National Park Service had studied in detail years before and recommended to the state for development. (Maurice had found the Park Service's plans in a pile of papers in the back of a cabinet after moving into his office.) Governor Leader suggested naming the park after Gifford Pinchot, not only because he admired Pinchot, but because the park location was near the first road paved under Governor Pinchot's 1925 program to "get the farmers out of the mud." [43]

In addition to boating, fishing, hiking, and swimming, the park contains bridle trails and nature areas that are excellent for bird watchers. With numerous oak-hickory groves, heavy stands of cedar, and nearby overgrown fields, dozens of species can be sighted, including eagles, owls, and osprey. And the marshy shoreline provides good opportunities to sight loons, egrets, heron, grebe, ducks, rails and others.

Pinchot State Park was the first "metropolitan" park built under Goddard's plan to place parks near heavily populated areas. In order to meet his state-park standard of a wilderness or natural type of environment, it was necessary at Pinchot State Park, to "bottle up" the peripheral area. Surrounding farm land was planted with trees so that people on the lake wouldn't hear the noise of nearby highways, or realize there was a "big housing development a few feet away." [44]

Because Pinchot State Park is surrounded by farm fields, yet offers excellent wetlands along the lake's shoreline, it has become a rest stop for many migrating forest birds. Warblers, vireos and thrushes stop to rest and feed before flying on to their spring breeding grounds or winter homes. At the same time, the wetlands are a "beacon that lures waterfowl by the thousands." Mergansers, Canada geese, mallards, loons, teal and many other species of ducks come for the swimming, diving, and dabbling for vegetation and small fish. [45]

In later years, Pinchot State Park became an occasional Goddard-family recreation spot. Maurice K. would load a canoe on the top of the car, Ethel and the boys, Kimball and Mark, would pile in, and they would drive from Camp Hill for an afternoon on the lake. [46] To Kim Goddard, however, these events were less than the warm, happy family occasions they might have been. He and his father would boat on the lake, looking for frogs along the shore, or turtles sunning themselves on a log, with barely a word to each other. Maurice K. was there but, like the placid waters, quiet and inscrutable; the father distant and seemingly unavailable to his son. [47]

□ □ □ □

The estimated cost for the thirteen new state parks was $6,806,235. Two and a half million dollars of this was for Gallitzin and a little more than one million for Pinchot. The least expensive, Bendigo State Park in Elk Country cost only $45,500. [48] In the two years between June 1956 and May 1958, 324 separate properties were appraised, 108 land purchase contracts negotiated, and 14 properties condemned. [49]

During the same biennial, some twenty-eight thousand acres of State Forest Lands were leased for oil and gas exploration. Their average rental was $5.41 per acre per year. And one of the leases for gas storage was for what was the largest such field in Pennsylvania and possibly the world. Its anticipated capacity was 135 billion cubic feet of gas. It involved approximately 39,500 acres of state forest lands and the anticipated annual income was $82,000 per year for at least forty years. In addition the Department of Forests and Waters let twenty-four service contracts to provide associated pipe lines and compressor station facilities. [50]

□ □ □ □

Maurice K. traveled with John C. Rex, his land acquisitions chief, all over the state looking at prospective sites for parks or potential forest additions. According to Rex, Goddard had a "deep belief that land was fundamental — it was the engine that drove him." Jimmy Rankin, an ex-paratrooper Military Policeman, was assigned by the state to drive them. He was built like a bull, and was completely devoted to Maurice K.. Even though he was his driver, not a bodyguard, he fearlessly stepped between his boss and a man who threatened Goddard at one meeting. [51]

To the men in Forests and Waters, Maurice K. was usually known as "M.K." After he received an honorary Doctor of Science degree from Waynesburg College in western Pennsylvania in 1959, occasionally it was "Doc." [52] They, on the other hand, were invariably addressed the way an army platoon leader summons his men, by their last names. It was always: "Rex," "Rankin," or "Forrey." And his Bedell-Smith approach to handling his subordinates went beyond how they were hailed. Once when two division chiefs could not agree on which of them would get the better qualified of two recruits who had passed the entrance exam for a surveyor position, and insisted on laying out the issue before him for a decision, Maurice K. listened for a few minutes, then roared: "Out!" The assembly of men knew exactly what to do. They bolted from their seats and scurried for the door of his office, like a covey of birds flushed from a field by a shot. [53]

Ralph Widner, a young *New York Times* political reporter, who came to the Department of Forests and Waters in 1957 to handle public information operations, interpreted such explosions as filling Goddard's need for a "sounding board," someone to "blow up with," to "vent his anger and frustration on." Widner, in his "advise and trouble shooting position," was often nearby and took many of these outbursts, but saw this as a positive; it led him to insights into Maurice K.'s thoughts that "otherwise would never have ended up on paper and out to audiences around the state."

Widner also found Maurice K. to be a superb teacher. The day he arrived in Harrisburg, Debs Meyers, Governor Leader's Press Secretary, sent him to see Goddard. When he arrived at the Secretary's office, Maurice K. — without an introduction or even a "hello" — took Widner for a ride to Gifford Pinchot State Park, then under construction. During the thirty minute ride out, Maurice K. talked about all the things he was trying to do. At the park he gave Widner a lecture in log identification, another on identifying a tree by examining a twig, one on hydraulics at the dam site, and when they looked at the plans for the park, a lecture on the design of day-use facilities. By the end of the trip, both decided that they had "hit it off." According to Widner, this was apparently because he had said "scarcely a word." He conjectured that Goddard saw him as a "fun" student who would help him "get his ideas on paper and into channels where they could get acted on." [54]

In later years as Maurice K. flew over Pennsylvania, he often amazed fellow travelers with his ability to recall the details of the department's land transactions. Bouncing from one side of the plane to the other, like a child showing off his new Christmas toys, he would point out parcel after parcel that had been acquired for parks or state forest lands. He could identify the acreage involved, the names of the owners, and recount any unusual circumstances or difficulties that had been encountered during the negotiations. This may have been a trait inherited from his mother. One history of the Kimball family in America states: "They often possess the same pronounced and peculiar qualities of mind. Many of the stock have been noted for their powerful and retentive memories." [55]

Indicative of the importance that Secretary Goddard attached to the parks program, in 1962 he elevated the management of the state parks, which had been a division within the Bureau of Forestry, to bureau level. Four regional park offices were established: at Sizerville State Park in Potter County, Moraine in Butler, Shawnee in Bedford, and Nockamixon in Bucks. The state parks and picnic areas were transferred from the Bureau of Forestry to the new

Bureau of State Parks. While the Bureau of Forestry continued to administer all facilities in the State Forests, the Bureau of State Parks became responsible for all developed recreation areas . [56]

A number of writers have credited Maurice Goddard with having professionalized the Department of Forests and Waters as though it had been his idea. Governor Leader's Executive Order, removing 3,500 positions from partisan politics was consistent with the stand he had taken before becoming governor. It was directed at professional positions in a half-dozen Pennsylvania agencies, and covered positions from accountants and architects to bridge design engineers; from building and loan examiners and chemists to nurses, and from psychiatric physicians to veterinary pathologists. The idea, too, of a park within twenty-five miles of each Pennsylvanian was not original with the Secretary, but came from someone in the Bureau of Parks, probably Joseph Blatt. So how much of the credit should Maurice K. receive?

When questioned about Goddard's role in originating the Executive Order, Governor Leader sidestepped the question. He made it clear that to him the source of an idea was unimportant. In his cabinet meetings he promoted the active exchange and fine-tuning of thoughts and suggestions regardless of who had first suggested them. As Leader puts it, "To become useful, ideas must be tested in the marketplace." He asks, "Who should be credited with an idea, the individual who first thinks of it, or the person who reshapes it into one that makes it useful?" [57]

On this basis, of course, Maurice Goddard should get full credit, if not for originating the park idea and for professionalizing the department, then for seeing their merit and aggressively carrying them forward to brilliant fulfillment. Both were unusual actions for state government; together they were as rare as a Pennsylvania spring without a wildfire.

Studio portrait of Maurice Kimball Goddard as a boy during the period the Goddards were living in Pretty Prairie, Kansas. (from the private collection of the Goddard family.)

Two views of the opposite sides of the one-block long Main Street, Pretty Prairie, Kansas at the time Maurice Goddard was growing up there. The tip of the steeple of the New Church, where Norman Goddard was the minister, can be seen at the extreme right beyond the trees in the photo to the left. (courtesy of Darrell Albright)

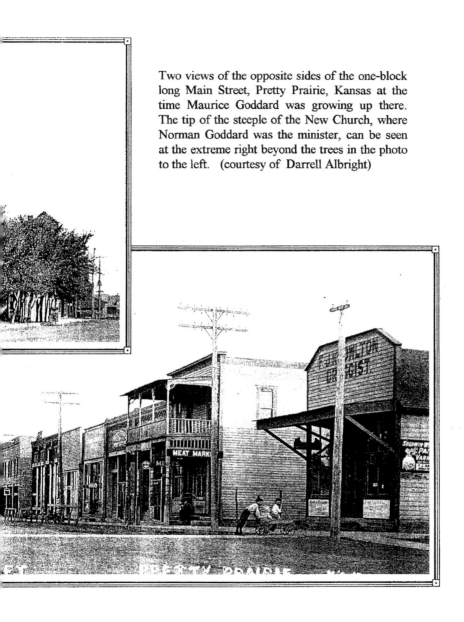

Left: Norman O. Goddard, Maurice's father. Norman was the minister at the Swedenborgian church in Pretty Prairie - at which time this photo was probably taken - and then later in Toronto, Canada and Portland, Maine. (from the private collection of the Goddard family.)

A studio portrait of Susan Kimball Goddard, Maurice Goddard's mother. The photograph was probably taken when the family was living in Pretty Prairie, Kansas. (from the private collection of the Goddard family.)

Right: Maurice Goddard dressed for an outdoor hike during a Maine winter in the early 1930s. (from the private collection of the Goddard family.)

Below: The University of Maine track team in the mid-1930s. Team Captain Maurice K. Goddard is in the center of the front row. (from the private collection of the Goddard family.)

Portrait of Ethel Mae Catchpole probably taken during the days of her courtship with Maurice Goddard. (from the private collection of the Goddard family.)

A happy moment with Ethel about the time she and Maurice were married in 1940. (from the private collection of the Goddard family.)

Secretary Maurice K. Goddard intently going over a Department
of Forests and Waters report.  (photo courtesy of the Department
of Conservation and Natural Resource, Bureau of State Parks.)

From left to right:  Otis B. Morse, IV, Secretary to the Governor,  Maurice Goddard, and
Governor George M. Leader closing the gate to commence filling the lake at Gifford
Pinchot State Park, December 1959.  (photo courtesy of the Department of Conservation
and Natural Resource, Bureau of State Parks.)

Signing of the Delaware River Basin Compact at the White House, November 2, 1961. Seated at the President's desk, from left to right: Governor Robert Meyner of New Jersey, Governor Elbert Carvel of Delaware, Governor David Lawrence of Pennsylvania, and President Kennedy. Maurice Goddard is standing immediately behind the President. Philadelphia Mayor Richardson Dilworth is standing behind Governor Lawrence. (photo courtesy of the Delaware River Basin Commission.)

Alternate Commissioner Maurice Goddard seated between Governor Nelson Rockefeller of New York (on Goddard's left) and Governor William A. Scranton of Pennsylvania. The basin commissioners along with several of their alternates were gathered at the 4th annual Delaware River Basin Commission meeting at Trenton, New Jersey, May 6, 1966. (photo courtesy of the Delaware River Basin Commission.)

# CHAPTER VI

# AIR BOMBING WILDFIRES

Someone once asked me how I could work for
both Democratic and Republican governors, and I
said, "Well a forest fire's not a Democratic fire or
a Republican fire. It's just a fire."

Maurice K. Goddard

In the final months of George Leader's term — Pennsylvania
chief executives could not succeed themselves in 1958 — Maurice
K. traveled to Pittsburgh to give his "Water Is Pennsylvania's
Future" speech. He told the Pennsylvania Electric Association that
"Water and progress go hand-in-hand"; that there was adequate
water in the state, but the state was "faced with the problem of
being able to make maximum use of it for industrial expansion."
Moreover, when the other users in the state, homeowners, farmers,
recreationists, and especially the electric power utilities, were added
to the equation, not only did the demand increase but conflicts
arose over use-priorities because the water was not always "at the
time and place it was needed."

He cited the situation in eastern Pennsylvania, where the area in
the vicinity of Lansdale, North Wales, and Souderton had "reached
the limit of its present sources of water supply." Then the Secretary
quoted some figures from a recent Department of Forests and
Waters study to support his contention: a projected population
increase from four to six million by the year 2010, and during the
same period an anticipated withdrawal rate increase from 569
million gallons a day to 1 billion, 55 million gallons. These figures

included water furnished only by water supply agencies; some large industrial users were taking water directly from the streams in unrecorded amounts.

After describing the problem, Maurice K. recited the steps his department was taking to address it:

> We are actively cooperating with the U.S. Army, Corps of Engineers, on their comprehensive studies of the water resources of the Potomac and Delaware River Basins. . . Unlike Corps of Engineers [flood control] studies of the past, these new studies are designed to embrace other water uses, such as, water supply, recreation, [and] power production. . . .
>
> Through our membership on the Interstate Commission on the Potomac River Basin, and the Delaware River Basin Study Coordinating Committee, we are able . . . to protect the interests of the Commonwealth.
>
> We are strongly in favor of multi-purpose projects where feasible, and in comprehensive planning for the future.
>
> We advocate the inclusion of power production in the proposed Delaware River dams. We believe that failure to provide for power production would overlook a major source of revenue necessary to off-set construction costs. [1]

He closed his speech by telling the association's members, "Thinking ahead and planning are not enough, . . . You cannot expect to win a race with a lame horse. Good tools are the prerequisite of a job well done." He was referring to the lack of adequate laws permitting the state "to allocate water." He stated that those dealing with obstructions and encroachments, flood control, and pollution were "good." Those covering allocations and equitable distribution of water, however, were "weak or non-existent." There was only one law, passed in 1939, and that brought less than 10 percent of the Commonwealth's surface water under the jurisdiction of the Water and Power Resources Board. Moreover, the act did not contain any penalty provision for violations of the statute. And there were no laws governing ground water supplies. The Department of Forests and Waters had begun work on a new act, but it was simply an outline in September 1958. [2]

Three months after Maurice K.'s trip to Pittsburgh, the mayor of that city, David L. Lawrence, succeeded George Leader as Pennsylvania's governor. Although he was frequently thought of as one, Lawrence never liked to be called "boss" — he once threatened to ban a reporter from future press conferences for applying the term to him. His management of the Pennsylvania Democratic party, however, turned it into a well-oiled modern version of the old political machine, one in which everyone knew who the boss *was*. The big difference, according Michael P. Weber, a Lawrence biographer, between his machine and those of the nineteenth-century was the new Governor's insistence that "political interests" were always "separate from governmental responsibility." [3]

He wanted the party faithful elected to office — and worked hard to put them there — but once in, they were expected to put the public interest first. The message to his subordinates was always:

> We are working for the same employer — the people. . . We'll work or get off the job. [4]

Accordingly, Lawrence welcomed experts into his administration. "It was brains," Genevieve Blatt said "He was "always on the lookout for someone he thought had the brains to be a good government official." [5] With this serious, no-nonsense business approach to running the state, the new governor retained many of the professionals that George Leader had appointed as department heads, including Maurice K.

Lawrence's main priorities, however, lay elsewhere than in the Department of Forests and Waters. George Leader had run four years earlier on a pledge not to raise taxes and consequently left the incoming administration with a large deficit. Balancing the budget became Lawrence's highest priority. He was a liberal when it came to social issues — medical care for the needy over age sixty-five, aid to public libraries, child care for poor children, support for public housing and urban renewal — but was proud of being a fiscal conservative. [6]

To get the budget back on track meant raising taxes and running the government on an austerity basis during the early part of Lawrence's four years in Harrisburg. The Governor had to work closely with the legislature to raise taxes, so there was little time for, or interaction between the department heads and the executive office unless a department got into difficulties. Lawrence was so set on addressing the budget deficit that when social legislation and fiscal responsibility came into conflict, the latter usually won. He was even known to fight hard to get bills passed, and then veto them if the legislature left them unfunded.

◻ ◻ ◻ ◻

When the new Governor first addressed the cabinet heads following his January 1959 inaugural — in a two-hour meeting that he opened to the press — Lawrence let them know who was boss. According to Weber, he gave them much the same warning he gave his top aides when he assumed the mayoralty of Pittsburgh; it was no idle threat. He told his cabinet and the assembled press corps:

> I will insist upon efficiency and honesty. We must perform the services offered by the State government better than ever before. . . . If at any time you find yourself in such serious disagreement with these [the governor's] goals and procedures that you cannot give this administration your unstinted loyalty, then you should no longer be a part of the administration. . . . [7]

Maurice Goddard had come to government from academia, Lawrence from politics, but both had essentially the same ideas on running a public agency. Years later someone asked Maurice K. how he worked with governors and members of both parties. He told his questioner: "Well a forest fire's not a Democratic fire or a Republican fire. It's just a fire." [8] The Secretary saw his job, however, not so much as putting out fires, but as establishing measures to prevent them — of planning for the future. Moreover, as he once said, he devoted "most of his energies not to day-to-day operational problems but to that delicate process known as reconciling the pressures of many interests." [9] It was an activist, not a reactivist view of his position; one that is not usually held by a bureaucrat.

Many believe that the mark of a good manager is the ability to make decisions — especially the "tough" ones. It is more important, however, for the chief executive to plan, to develop policies, to establish a coherent framework so that subordinates can execute without recourse to the boss for all but major decisions. While the original ideas were not always Maurice K.'s, the adoption of such policies as employing modern firefighting equipment, professionalizing the Department of Forests and Waters, emphasizing his cooperation-model and multiple-use philosophies, and, a few years, later building a park within twenty-five miles of each resident and extending the state park system into the heart of urban areas such as Philadelphia and Pittsburgh, is what distinguishes his management from that of others.

Maurice K. not only had the credentials — the brains that David Lawrence looked for in a colleague — but the Department of Forests and Waters had made some solid accomplishments during his first four-year tenure, ones that would make any governor look good. And unlike most of the potential political appointees Lawrence could have tapped, the secretary was tireless in the position. Maurice K.'s job was his only agenda. To continue him at the helm simply made good sense for the new Governor.

Both men were hard working in the extreme; unrelenting, like the spring flood waters of an undammed river. Each of Lawrence's days was divided into two parts: twelve to fifteen hours for politics and government, and three hours for family and leisure. Maurice K.'s, which started at 6:30 A.M., often ran to midnight, especially when he was traveling throughout the state. And he seldom took a vacation.

Once, after years as Secretary of Forests and Waters without time off, several of his staff members convinced him to take a week's leave. When they arrived for work on the second morning of his "vacation," they were surprised to see him back behind his desk. When they asked why he had returned so soon, he told them: "It was over, so I came back." According to William Middendorf, one of his deputies, he had gone to Codorus State Park, picked up trash and put it in the basket, watched the sailboats on the lake, and then, after a few hours, returned home. [10]

□ □ □ □

On July 8, 1959, Maurice K. was awarded the Army's Patriotic Civilian Service Award in recognition for having fostered "close cooperation" between Pennsylvania and the federal government on flood control projects. Governor Lawrence participated in the ceremonies. After declaring that "Pennsylvania has today in the Department of Forests and Waters one of the Nation's outstanding natural resource agencies," the Governor credited Maurice K. for having "infused the program with enthusiasm and direction." Lawrence went on to tell the gathering:

> Secretary Goddard's talent for gaining cooperation between State agencies, between the State and Federal Governments, and between his own Department and private citizens . . . has earned a wide distinction for Pennsylvania in the conservation field.
>
> Pennsylvania's State Flood Control Program today is rivalled only by California's, thanks to . . . Secretary Goddard's diligence. [11]

Having been mayor of Pittsburgh during the period of its renaissance, Lawrence was well aware of Goddard's ability to work with local groups. One of the urban park development that Maurice K. had supported wholeheartedly since taking office was Pittsburgh's Point State Park. "I can testify personally," Lawrence said, "to the excellent spirit of co-operation which exists between the people of Pittsburgh and Secretary Goddard.

Then three months later *American Forests* devoted an entire issue to "Pennsylvania's Resource Renaissance" under Goddard's leadership. The issue included articles on "Rebuilding Penn's Woods," "Water for the Future," and "Pennsylvania, the Has Everything State." In the lead editorial, Maurice K. was described as "a man capable of exploding with a self-starting, tireless sense of 'mission,' a student of practical government, an administrator with an almost uncanny knack for achieving co-operation, and a militant conservationist who believes it is high time conservation assumes its rightful place in national and state affairs." [12]

*American Forests* never explained what Maurice K. meant by conservation's taking "its rightful place in national affairs," but as the historian Samuel P. Hays has pointed out, the original conservation movement was predicated on the principle of "efficiency." Accomplishing the most good with the least amount of effort was the early conservationist's goal in managing resource spending for future generations. And Maurice K.'s approach to conservation seems to bear out this as the point the magazine was making.

According to the article's author, the "most remarkable thing" about Goddard's forestry program was its efficiency. Not only did the returns from oil and gas leases garner praise, but so did the curve representing timber sales, which kept going up. (Between 1955 and 1964 sales grew from five million to sixty million board feet.) Maurice K. attributed this to having placed twenty of his newly hired foresters in positions to coordinate the sales program with the required cut of the forest management plans, much of which previously was wasted.

The writer also cited the "tremendous efficiency" of his road building and maintenance programs. (Access roads into the forest, of course, are essential for removal of trees and key to any successful fire prevention program.) Under Maurice K., use of second-hand Army surplus equipment, "kept in the pink by the foresters," held down costs so that road construction and upkeep expenditures ran only $40 a mile, as compared to more than $200 for nearby Pennsylvania counties. The low costs for roads contributed substantially to the high margin the department realized on timber sales. One forester couldn't resist, however, placing a particularly disreputable-looking truck at a spot where some visiting state forest commissioners were bound to see it. Coming upon it, they gave the truck the once-over. Then one of the commissioners, Philip H. Glatfelter III, turned to the forester and observed, "Well, as Goddard would say, the tires are good." [13]

The magazine claimed, that the Secretary was not only politically astute and "knew a thing or two about tactics and maneuver," but also he had a "profound conviction . . . that politicians are useful people who protect our liberties and get things done." And it credited his success as a conservationist to one thing, "cooperation." [14] It was a thought that in a few years would take on even greater, national significance for the Secretary of Forests and Waters.

The Goddard cooperation-model was designed to work not only between the different levels of government — state, Federal and local — but also with private industry. Working closely with Philip Glatfelter III, the fourth-generation family president of P. H. Glatfelter Company of Spring Grove near Hanover, Maurice K. put together plans for a new state park, Codorus. Their joint effort, between 1965 and 1966, was designed to provide another star in the state's constellation of parks as well as a reliable source of water for Glatfelter's paper production. The company erected a $5.5 million earth dam on Codorus Creek while the Department of Forests and Waters acquired the adjoining lands. The resulting park is about 3,300 acres; its lake is 1,275 acres. Open fields began reverting to woodlands of hardwoods and pines, and marshlands filled with wildlife. Within a few years, as many as 250 species of birds were recorded as visitors to the park.

❑ ❑ ❑ ❑

Not all of Secretary Goddard's cooperative ventures were successful, however. Soon after his appointment to head Forests and Waters, the Leader Administration developed plans with the Curtiss-Wright Corporation for a venture it hoped would boost the depressed economy of the state's northern tier counties. Goddard's task was to find a sizable piece of available but remote land for the company's exclusive use. This effort was well outside any department mandate for management or conservation of forest land, but Maurice K. — always the good soldier — saw the value of the project to the state, fell in step and worked hard to advance it. He found a suitable tract of State Forest and Game Commission land in Clearfield County. The state sold eighty-six hundred acres and leased another forty-three thousand acres to Curtiss-Wright, on which the company planned to build a research and test facility for the development of rocket engines and a nuclear airplane. [15]

Except for several dozen leased camp sites and hundreds of rattlesnakes the area was isolated, ideal. The state canceled the existing camp leases, fenced in the entire area, and Curtiss-Wright erected several buildings, including one to house a reactor. It took a crew of eight men working under Forests and Waters land survey-engineer John C. Rex seven months to complete the survey and erect the fence. [16] The job of evicting the lease-holders fell to Maurice K.. Never one to shirk even a difficult task, he personally faced the angry campers. At several of the meetings he held trying to explain the administration's position, individuals came carrying rifles. Years later he told fellow cabinet officer Clifford Jones, it was the most difficult job he had ever had. [17]

Eventually Curtiss-Wright had nearly a thousand scientists, technicians and other workers at the site. But soon after the reactor was in place and operating, Defense Department cutbacks in the aerospace industry caused the company to abandon its plans for the location. In 1963 the leased lands were returned to the state, and four years later the commonwealth bought back the lands it had sold. Along with the Curtiss-Wright buildings, minus the reactor, which was dismantled, the plant site has been used by a firm that irradiates plastic-impregnated wood flooring with radioactive cobalt from the reactor pool. It has also been used as a dump for nuclear waste and for a variety of state ventures including a heavy equipment training center and a Department of Corrections boot camp, Quehanna. [18]

Relieved to have the property back, Maurice K. tore down Rex's thirty-two-mile-long fence — perhaps the longest continuous fence in the state — and, hoping to prevent the area's ever again being used for commercial purposes, turned the land (other than the plant site) into a "wild area." Tracts designated as *wild* are open to the public only for the "pursuit of peace and solitude." No development of any character is permitted; motorized conveyances are prohibited as well as are camp leases, mineral development, and utility rights-of-way. Hiking and overnight camping must be of the "primitive" type. Rules are stringent; if you carry water into a "wild area," you must carry back what you don't use. [19]

The Quehanna Wild Area, which is characterized by short streams and creeks, is one of Pennsylvania's last expanses of primitive back-country. Writing ten years later for *Pennsyvlania Forests*, Joseph A. Dague, Jr. described the area as including one of the "most magnificent stands of white birch" to be found anywhere in the state as well as "far-flung vistas overlooking the tributaries of the Sinnamahoning Creek." [20]

❑ ❑ ❑ ❑

In October 1959, Maurice K. testified at a hearing of the Select Committee on Water Resources of the U.S. Senate. He came to the hearings to recommend the establishment of a "wise national policy for the integrated development of the country's water resources" in the East, one that would parallel the policy that had long been in place in the West. He called for the Senate to enact a "comprehensive, far-seeing water policy," one that "no longer predicated construction upon a single disaster, or a single water requirement." [21]

As was typical of the Secretary of Forests and Waters, the emphasis was on planning and a shared Federal and state development. He described plans in which the states would take a "heavy and responsible part" but told the committee these efforts "must be integrated closely with Federal plans." He then proposed Pennsylvania's flood control program as the model for the future. [22]

Floods were, according to Maurice K., Pennsylvania's "pre-eminent problem," the result of the state's plentiful rainfall and miles of streams combined with long, narrow mountain valleys. Moreover, he told the Committee of a University of Chicago study that cited the state as the one having the most-acute flood problem with more people and more communities affected by floods than any other state in the nation.

He then called attention to the accomplishments that had been made in the last five years in Pennsylvania both by the state and the U.S. Army Corps of Engineers. During that period, Pennsylvania had completed nearly $17 million worth of flood control projects and had another $14 million worth of control works on the drawing board, under contract, or under construction. He made the point, too, that many of the these works were "predicated upon the benefits from the Corps' work" at other locations within the same watershed. Overall planning, integration, and cooperation were always the hallmarks of a Goddard project.

Maurice K. also made certain that the members were aware of his belief in "multiple-use" dams and flood control projects. He explained that the twelve-reservoir plan proposed by the Department of Forests and Waters for the Brandywine Creek Basin would help satisfy an increasing need for sources of safe water. And as a means to provide for periods of drought, he proposed that Congress authorize the Corps of Engineers to "take account of low flow benefits in computing the feasibility of a reservoir" such as those proposed for the Delaware River. Moreover, he told the Committee that recreation should no longer be considered an "intangible by-product" of water resource development efforts. With more people having more money and more leisure, recreation was no longer a nicety, an expedient; it was an "important justification for clean streams and multiple-purpose reservoirs." [23]

□ □ □ □

One joint Pennsylvania and Corps of Engineers flood control project, however, became a *cause celebre*. Its proposal caused a controversy that reached, and then ran for several years on the pages of the *New York Times*. Although there were Goddard plans to incorporate the 2,053-foot-long Kinzua railroad bridge, the highest railroad viaduct in the world, and 316 surrounding acres for the development of a park near the Allegheny National Forest in northwestern Pennsylvania, he also jumped into the fray over a Corps of Engineers scheme of the same name, Kinzua, about thirty miles to the west of the new state park location.

It was the Corps' intention to build a high dam on the Allegheny River above Warren, Pennsylvania near the mouth of Kinzua Creek as part of a low-flow and flood control scheme designed to protect the Allegheny and Ohio River basins. The Kinzua dam project had the backing of the U.S. Forest Service and the Army Corps of Engineers as well as Maurice Goddard, but met with opposition from the eleven hundred Senecas, who owned much of the land needed for the lake, and the Quakers who had befriended and backed them for nearly two hundred years. The land, however, was not simply *owned* land; it was *treaty* land that had been given to the Senecas in 1791. Therefore, the use of eminent domain to take the Senecas' land became a legal question. The case went all the way to the U.S. Supreme Court, where the Senecas were "found subject to the same public power of eminent domain as other Americans." [24]

Kinzua, which in Algonquian means a place "they gobble," has been rendered in English by the more prosaic "Turkey Creek." As was frequently the case, it was not the dam that was the problem, it was the resulting lake. It would stretch thirty-five miles upstream across the border into New York, "drown 10,000 acres" in the "heartland of the Seneca reservation" and "divide the land where 'the whippoorwill cries, the fox whimpers' "down the middle." [25] *New York Times* columnist Brooks Atkinson, who was the greatest print-foe of the project, called the plan the "annihilation of a moral obligation," one that he traced back to a personal promise by George Washington, who had signed the treaty for the United States. [26]

Chief Cornplanter, who was a Seneca war chief, had fought against the settlers in the Revolution. Following the war, however, he advocated a policy of reconciliation with the United States among the Iroquois nations. For this raproachment, the Senecas' "reservation" had been granted to Cornplanter and his family. Chief Cornplanter, who was the son of a Dutch trader and a Seneca woman of chiefly lineage, turned his grant into a "model community." He "established schools, brought in Quaker teachers, built good houses, developed agriculture, and bred large herds of cattle." [27]

The Cornplanter grant, which was not really an Indian Reservation, stretched forty-four miles from the mouth of Kinzua Creek into New York. At most places, it was a mile or less wide, as it wound along the flat, fertile shoulders of the Allegheny River. The Indians lived in "bright bungalows, white farmhouses and unpainted shacks" along both sides of the river and among the "pineclad foothills" that rose above it. According to the *New York Times*, the Cornplanter Senecas lived "amid vegetable gardens, cow pastures and henyards" that were little different from "any rural scene in western New York." [28]

When they lost their appeals in the case, representatives for the Senecas then recommended several alternative flood control techniques, including diversion of overflow flow waters northward to Lake Erie. At the direction of Congress, these alternatives were examined by a private engineering firm, which, according to Maurice K., concluded that the "estimated costs would add one-fourth to one-third more, require twice as much land, and dislocate nearly twice as many people as the reservoir" proposed by the Corps. [29]

In a letter to the *New York Times*, Tennessee Valley Authority expert, Arthur Morgan, called for a reexamination of these alternatives. Maurice K., rejected Morgan's request for another review, describing it as just another delaying tactic. In closing his own long, rebuttal statement to the *Times*, Maurice K. wrote rather disingenuously:

> I share . . . concern for the rights of the Senecas. All of us do. They are entitled to every right, every protection guaranteed to other Americans. . .
>
> It is unfortunate that any citizen, no matter what his origin, must give up his beloved home to make way for an urgently needed public project whether it be an airport, a highway or a reservoir. But I am certain that in the final analysis the Senecas will see the necessity for this project which most economically meets the needs of their fellow Americans downstream.
>
> I am firmly convinced that the Senecas will be among the leading beneficiaries of the project. For it will inevitably attract new people, new interests, new business into an area which, at the moment, is economically depressed. [30]

Maurice K. also had to answer a large number of letters sent to him and to then Governor William Scranton over their support for the dam. In his responses, he dismissed the "treaty" claim on the basis that the "Seneca Nation ceased to exist," and the treaty was "invalidated" when the Senecas voluntarily became citizens of the United States and thus subject to its laws along with all other Americans. He justified the dam because its "water is urgently needed for water supply, industry, and navigation, particularly during low-flow periods." [31] To one correspondent he described his "criteria for judging the worthiness of any public works" as being "whether the project, as proposed and designed, is the best possible project to do the job required from an engineering and economic standpoint." "In short," he concluded, "the project must afford the greatest benefit and protection to the largest number of people at the lowest cost." [32]

And in a long letter to another writer, he explained the specific "need" for the Kinzua Dam and its place in the water control scheme for the Ohio River Valley:

> The Allegheny River Reservoir is a single unit of an integrated and coordinated flood control system for the protection of the Allegheny River Basin and the Ohio Valley. . . . Omitting it from the system would be akin to owning a watch without a minute hand — the watch will continue to run, but it will not do the job it was designed to do! [33]

Despite appeals made to him, President Kennedy refused to step into the dispute. According to the President, the Supreme Court had settled the eminent domain issue and the dam "was needed for flood protection." In December 1965, after five years of work and several silent vigils at the site by the Quakers, the 169-foot-high dam was finished. The structure cost $117 million, the Pennsylvania Railroad received $20 million to relocate its tracks, and $15 million was appropriated to resettle the Senecas. [34] They were moved upstream onto a reservation, twenty miles across the New York border near Salamanca. The state of Pennsylvania also spent several million dollars rebuilding roads and a new bridge across the mouth of the Kinzua Creek, which with considerable irony was named "Cornplanter."

❑ ❑ ❑ ❑

While the importance of flood control and water-based recreational facilities grew in Maurice K.'s mind during his first years in state government, he did not abandon the forest side of his job. He took special interest, for example, in forest-fire fighting. While there had been changes in equipment, the essential character of fighting forest fires — a man with a hand tool on the fire line — had not changed very much by 1960 from the time early in the century when Dr. Rothrock put together the first Pennsylvania forest firefighting teams consisting of a mule, a man, a shovel, and two barrels of water. [35]

Large forest fires, raging out of control are awesome natural phenomena. Each year they destroy large amounts of timber and other valuable forest products. There are three kinds of forest fires: surface, crown, and ground. The most common of these is the surface fire. In it the leaves, debris and other residue on the forest floor are consumed. Almost all forest fires start as surface fires. Crown fires, which primarily occur in dense stands of evergreens, and are rare in Pennsylvania, leap from treetop to treetop. Ground fires are those in which the organic material beneath the surface debris burns, usually very slowly. They are sometimes called "duff" fires because they burn into the peat or "duff" several feet below the surface. [36]

There are three overall concerns in dealing with wildfires (the modern name for a forest fire): prevention, detection, suppression. From early in the century, the primary means of detection was the fire tower. "Lookouts" were posted in the towers during the peak forest fire seasons — spring and fall. These were lonely jobs but included rigorous duties. Hauling drinking and cooking water a mile or two up the mountain and then to the top of the tower was difficult in the extreme, and the twice-weekly washing of all the windows to maintain proper visibility was a highly detested chore. Water was used over and over, first for washing and brushing the teeth, then for shaving, and finally for cleaning the windows and scrubbing the floor. [37]

□ □ □ □

Each of Pennsylvania's twenty forest districts was supervised by a District Forester who also functioned as the District Fire Warden. Prior to the development and use of aerial firefighting techniques, the District Warden oversaw approximately twenty wardens, each warden heading up a team of about twenty firefighters. Today the numbers are about half this: ten wardens for each district, each managing teams of ten fighters. These teams, which train regularly to keep in readiness, work closely with city fire departments. They seldom fight wildfires, for example, near metropolitan areas, and with the encroachment of homes into the forest, have had to change some of their tactics in combatting fires.

On the ground there are two methods of fighting wildfires, going directly at the fire's head, or falling back some distance and constructing a control or fire line in an indirect attack. Direct attacks are only used on small fires that can be contained quickly; the indirect approach is the more common method used in Pennsylvania.

In an indirect attack the warden usually acts as the locator for the line. The rest of the team is divided into line cutters, rakers, torchmen, guards, and a mop-up crew as required. Typically there is one torchman and from two to four cutters, rakers and guards. The cutters are the axmen or brush hookers who open up the line to a width of three to four feet. The rakers clear away all debris in a fifteen to twenty inch-wide strip down to bare mineral soil. The torchman burns out the "fuel" between the line and the advancing fire, while the guards control the fire line to prevent breakovers. The fighters rotate among these assignments from time to time as some jobs are more arduous than others. [38] The line must be located by the warden so that the most good is accomplished with the least expenditure of time and energy. This means making best use of natural barriers, such as lakes, streams, and rock outcropping, and avoiding dense forest growth. Even more important, the line must be located so that the advancing fire cannot flank it, thus placing the crew in danger.

◻ ◻ ◻ ◻

The use of aircraft to assist in detecting wildfires began in 1932. Douglas Brown, a pilot who was a state forest fire warden, circled the Plumer Fire Tower between Clarion and Oil City pointing in the direction of some smoke until the tower man finally spotted it. During the remainder of that year Brown spotted twenty more fires from his Taylor Cub. He eventually developed the technique of gliding by the tower, with his engine idling, then yelling out the location of the fire. [39] By the 1940s reconnaissance aircraft were regularly used in detection roles.

It was not until after Maurice K.'s arrival, however, that the Division of Forest Protection, in Forests and Waters, first experimented with using aircraft in fire suppression work. In 1960 two Bell helicopters and a Stearman crop-dusting biplane were acquired for the spring wildfire season that year. The Stearman operated for two weeks from the Black Moshannon airport, covering eastern Clearfield and western Centre Counties; then it went to Hazleton to provide coverage of parts of Schuylkill, Carbon and Luzerne Counties. One helicopter was stationed at Black Moshannon while the second worked out of Hazleton for several weeks and then was moved to Big Pocono tower in Monroe County.

These two areas of operation were chosen, according to Maurice K., based on the department's having "broken our past experience down to show the two spots of heaviest fire occurrence in the state during the height of occurrence." [40] While there were a number of practice runs, the first drop on a going fire was made by the Stearman near Whiteside in Clearfield County in April.

Fifty-four missions were flown that spring in 115 drops. Fifteen thousand gallons of water were delivered. The largest single mission was a drop of thirty-five hundred gallons. An even more impressive action took place six miles from Black Moshannon. A fire was raging up a steep slope with the help of strong gusty winds. It was discovered as it broke over the top of the hill. Three men were sent on the ground and the air tanker was dispatched. After three drops by the tanker and appropriate mop-up action by the ground crew, no further help was needed. The fire was contained at a burn of 2.5 acres and everyone was back at the base in less than an hour. The worth of aircraft in fire protection work had been established convincingly. [41]

When, however, the Auditor General reviewed the statement of expenses in Maurice K.'s "use agreements" for the helicopters, he suggested they employ the Civil Defense helicopter rather than rent new equipment. Maurice K. explained that the Civil Defense helicopter was a "rather large affair" and more expensive to operate than the ones he was using. Moreover, as it was kept on standby for serious emergencies in the State, its pilot was only "on call." He then described how his fire crews employed the helicopter:

> To be useful it means that we must have this machine on standby like a fire company, pilot ready, water loaded ready to go, each day throughout the season.
>
> In addition we use the helicopter for reconnaissance of going fires, for supervision, communication, inspections, survey of fires and delivering men, water, tools and supplies right to the edge of the fire either by landing in a nearby field or dropping with a rope to the men below.
>
> This full time use of the helicopter in our hands at some field station assignment is what largely rules out the use of the Civil Defense helicopter.
>
> We hope this next Spring we are able to give the helicopter another run, under still better conditions and preparations. We hope if similar use agreements [those submitted by Forests and Waters] come to your attention you will give them your wholehearted support and approval. [42]

The following April and May the air attack was expanded. Five Stearman water bombers were placed strategically across the state. By 1962 the fixed-wing aircraft and helicopters had bombed 326 fires, delivering 94,570 gallons of water in 656 air drops. [43] It soon became apparent that the real value of the aircraft was in "first attack" work. Dumping large amounts of retardant on early burns contained them for ground crew mop up. Once a fire became large or widely spread the use of tankers was much less effective. [44]

While the number of fires statewide during each of the next twenty years did not change substantially, the acreage burned did decrease over time from an annual average of between thirty and forty thousand acres to between five and ten thousand. More dramatic, perhaps, was the reduction in the average size of the burn. During the 1950s, the average burn was about 26.6 acres. By the 1970s the average had fallen to 5.6 acres. [45] The value of the massive first-strike air bombing capability was clearly borne out.

It was a technical solution to a serious, long-standing problem, one that had plagued the state for more than seventy-five years. It was a solution, moreover, that pleased the Secretary. Most wildfires now could be controlled quickly, effectively, and efficiently.

There were occasions, however, when the conditions in the forests became such that Maurice K. had to recommend that the Governor issue a proclamation closing the forests and banning burning in their vicinity. There was one such occasion in the fall of 1963. He was reluctant to take such steps because they not only halted hunting and fishing activities, but also the personal and commercial activities of thousands of individuals and businesses. In a response to Representative James Kepler Davis, he cited lumbering, construction activities, farming, and disposal operations as being among those adversely affected when outdoor fires are banned. [46]

To Davis, who had suggested a system of "regional closings" so that recreational activities could continue in selected forests, Maurice K. wrote that "the elimination of every possible hazard that can result in a forest fire" was his primary concern and that he was reluctant to decide selectively by forests until they were able "to gear them [their detection techniques] to fixed measures of forest fire danger, based on fire weather measurements." But he reassured Davis that it had been twelve years since the last proclamation, and that only five had been issued in the forty years since the legislature passed the law permitting the governor to do so. [47]

❑ ❑ ❑ ❑

During his years as Secretary of Forests and Waters, Maurice K. always took a special interest in fire suppression and especially those who fought wildfires. Like General Eisenhower, who against the advice of his aides made visits to the troops at the front a part of his normal routine, Maurice K. frequently traveled around the state to inspect facilities and talk to the men and women who did the hard, dirty work of firefighting, and with whom he seemed to have a special bond. According to Stephen Cummings, the Executive Director of the Lancaster Forest Fire Crew, Maurice K. was the regular speaker for years at the annual meeting of the Lancaster group of those who battled forest fires. [48]

And, while the firefighters were not "professionals" in the strict sense of the word, Maurice K. knew the job of fighting fires was hard work that required dedication as well as training and skill. When the Chairman of the Democratic State Committee inquired on behalf of a constituent who had not received the promotion his local committeeman urged, he wrote back that while the man "was adequate as a smoke chaser," he "lacked the ability and initiative to become a Forest Inspector." Moreover, the man had refused to work on Saturdays and Sundays, which "are usually the most serious periods for forest fires." Maurice K. told the Chairman: "It has always been an order that our employees are definitely available and prepared for any emergency either day or night." [49]

At Maurice K.'s insistence, too, Pennsylvania was one of the earliest of the eastern states that put together a "specialized" group to help in out-of-state fire suppression. Since about 1973, Pennsylvania has been one of the few Eastern states that regularly contributes to suppression assignments throughout the Western part of the nation. When one such group of fighters was being flown back to Harrisburg directly from a fire site — still wearing their bulky gear as well as their sweat, and the grime and smoke from the fight — Maurice K., who by then was retired, happened to board the plane in Pittsburgh. He spent the entire flight finding out where they had been, the problems they had had with the blaze, and in giving them encouragement by telling them how important their work was.

When Stephen Cummings met them at the airport, one fighter asked him if he knew who the businessman was coming down the ramp wearing a suit and carrying a briefcase. When he told her it was Maurice K. Goddard, she told Cummings incredulously that he had given her a hug in appreciation for the job she was doing. [50]

Although Maurice K. gave priority to employee issues, sometimes the payments to contractors for the use of equipment, such as bulldozers were late. In responding in 1964, for example, to one Fire Warden, who apparently was being pressed by a contractor and also had concerns over the lack of funds to purchase certain items, he wrote:

> We have purchased large quantities of basic equipment over the past five years, such as new fire trucks, portable pumps, hose and similar items. The need to divert funds for fire bill payments have made it necessary to forgo purchase of much needed work tools such as rakes and spray tanks. We are working hard to secure sufficient funds in our budget to secure purchase of these items during the coming year. [51]

□ □ □ □

Maurice Goddard, not only worked hand in hand with other state agencies, private corporations and federal organizations, such as the U.S. Army Corps of Engineers and the Department of the Interior, he developed and maintained close ties with citizens' groups across the state. He considered input from organizations such as the Western Pennsylvania Conservancy important, and also valued their support for his land programs. In return, he became a promoter of their efforts. He told them that this "spirit of co-operation was a trademark of conservation in Pennsylvania," and that there was "no more outstanding example than the relationship between the Conservancy and the Department of Forests and Waters."

He frequently traveled west to the Conservancy's meetings and events, and wrote a number of articles for *Water Land and Life*, the organization's publication. This newsletter-magazine regularly featured pictures and news stories of him "hailing" the beauty of McConnell's Mill, describing the "unfolding" of plans for Butler Park, and praising both Conservancy and Forests and Waters projects — in plan, in progress, and when completed. [52]

In a long October 1959 article "Conservation for Self-Preservation," the Secretary of Forests and Waters explained to the readers of *Water Land and Life* his ideas on conservation:

> Too often people are inclined to think of us as impractical fellows whose high-minded interest in greenery sometimes gets in the way of "progress." Generally, we are considered too preoccupied with the landscape to worry about such realistic matters as earning profits. . . .
>
> The main concern of the conservationist is, and always has been, the conservation of humanity. Men, not trees, are still our chief concern and chief resource.
>
> It is precisely because the conservationist is primarily interested in the long-term survival of man that he studies man's dependence upon the rest of nature. "Water, Land, and Life" is his province and his principal field of endeavor. . . . Modern conservation, in my opinion, can best be described as the applied science of reconciling man's material demands upon nature with his biological dependence upon a balanced resource environment. [53]

He told the members of the Conservancy that there were "few new frontiers" from which to get additional raw materials, that we must stop farming "valuable land to sterility" and then moving on to greener pastures, that forests and natural areas were "essential for the retention of soil, for flood control," and that we cannot continue to give such resources away indefinitely to the "encroachments of urban civilization" without "upsetting the balance necessary to our economic vitality."

Maurice K. also defined "multiple use" for his audience, that what is "wise conservation practice on one piece of land is not necessarily so on another." He used Cook Forest as an example. In preserving the 170 acres of virgin forest, the Department of Forests and Waters was "concerned neither with creating marketable timber, nor with active public recreation." To him,

Cook Forest was a "natural museum — an area we want to preserve as long as we can as a reminder of the forest primeval." [54]

After describing a number of other programs offered by the Department of Forests and Waters that provided advice both to agriculture and industry, he told them: "Conservation is not solely the job of a small coterie of high-minded individuals. . . . It is a task for all of us working together in the economic as well as the esthetic interests of the community." Maurice K. then touched on an idea that in a few years he would bring boldly before the public:

> I have favored for a number of years authority for government to buy land today for development as parks sometime in the future. If such a policy is not soon adopted, we stand in danger of seeing all our desirable park sites swallowed up. [55]

It was the spark of an idea that two years later burst into flame, a flame that would illuminate Pennsylvania from the Delaware to the Ohio.

# CHAPTER VII

# THE PARKS COME OUT
# OF THE FOREST

*Poly-math* n [Gk *polymathes* knowing
much, fr. poly + *manthanein* to learn] A
person very and diversely learned.

In a major statement to the Society of American Foresters at the
Sheraton Park Hotel, Washington, D.C., in November 1960,
Maurice K. outlined — it was probably his finest speech — his
views on the relationship of state parks to the nation's future
recreation needs. In describing the new role he saw for parks, he
told the gathering:

> Our interests are no longer solely in great natural museums. They
> have shifted from mere preservation to development and management
> of our resources to meet skyrocketing interest in recreation as well as
> mushrooming appetites for water, timber, soil and minerals. [1]

Because of this, he claimed that "Recreation has taken on a
potent economic dimension;" therefore, the "state parks we build
today, and those of the past, are two different breeds." The older
parks took advantage of publicly owned forest land and unusual
scenic attractions and thus resembled the national parks. Most of
these parks, however, were "tucked away in state forests and forest
preserves," in the remote areas of the state and were often
"incidental to the main purpose of timber production." Today, he
told them, "The parks have come out of the forests and are moving
along slowly toward the metropolitan periphery." [2]

The only way in which it would be possible to "maintain the
livability of our metropolitan areas," Maurice K. averred, was to tie

the "need for water, flood control and the demand for recreation with the same facilities."   In Pennsylvania he described plans for four new parks built around U.S. Army Corps of Engineers' flood control projects, and four others being constructed in conjunction with joint U.S. Soil Conservation Service and Pennsylvania Department of Forests and Waters reservoirs.

To address any hesitancy that his audience might feel over the thought of separating the forests and parks, Maurice K. explained that a "forest-like environment is still desirable in our state parks," even though that might be difficult to achieve in many of the new metropolitan areas being considered.   Moreover, under this new view of forests and parks, he claimed "today's forester" is no longer so much a forester, as he is a "land-management specialist." Moreover, he claimed, the forester now has another job, that of "selling this program to the public for its own good." [3] He told the gathering:

> We must succeed if we are to get off this asphalt treadmill of billion dollar roads leading nowhere except to other congested places. . . . And to do so requires a sense of mission and dedication which, unfortunately, too few of us possess at the moment. [4]

❑ ❑ ❑ ❑

In November 1961, the Pennsylvania State Planning Board, of which the Secretary of Forests and Waters was a member, unveiled a bold initiative for the state's parks.   Described as a "Growth through Recreation Areas' Development" plan, the board's proposal was designed to fight urban sprawl through a network of parks, open-space sites and other recreation facilities.  Their project proposal — named "Project 70" — called for the creation of three federal recreation areas:  at Tocks Island on the Delaware River, near Kinzua Creek on the Allegheny River in Warren County, and on the Raystown Branch of the Juniata River in Huntingdon County — plus the expenditure of $70 million by the state which would be used to ring Pennsylvania's fourteen metropolitan areas with "belts of parks, open space sites, and fish and wildlife areas." [5]

Earlier that year, in March, Secretary Goddard had presented the plan at a meeting of the board. He reviewed New York's open-space program and then presented a proposal for Pennsylvania that resembled New Jersey's "Green Acres" program. In June 1961 the Planning Board approved the concept, and the following January Governor Lawrence, then starting his final year in office, sent a special message to the General Assembly outlining some of the program specifics. [6]

The Governor told the legislators that the plan had profound implications for the future of the Commonwealth, that it was "shaped in the traditions of William Penn, who prized the beauty of his province highly"; that it will mean a "richer life for all citizens," and that, it "aims for a healthier, more pleasant, more prosperous Pennsylvania." Lawrence told them that the "plans were not Utopian . . . . they are hard, realizable proposals, . . . bedrock economics, an investment in the future of our state." He closed his special message by declaring:

> This great, good land of Pennsylvania is ours — ours to till and mine, to build upon and use. But it is God-given. We are here in stewardship. It is as stewards that I ask you to consider this plan, for man as laborer thinks of his bread but for today. A steward thinks of his children tomorrow.
>
> That must be our guide and our goal. Project 70 will give us the implements to follow that guide and achieve the goal. [7]

The idea immediately "won widespread approval among conservationists, recreation groups and metropolitan area officials." And there was broad support among newspapers all across Pennsylvania. According to a report in the *New York Times*, a Philadelphia *Evening Bulletin* editorial hailed the plan, claiming it was deserving of the "wholehearted support of every Pennsylvanian" and that the Lawrence administration "should be complimented for its foresight in presenting this program." [8] This attitude was echoed throughout the state.

The name, Project 70 was derived from the year 1970 — the anticipated completion date of the new Interstate Highway system — not the $70 million they hoped to raise for new parks and other conservation efforts. Maurice K., Ralph Widner, former public relations director for Forests and Waters and now assistant executive director of the State Planning Board, and John P. Robin, Board Chairman, were the prime architects of the project. Robin, like Maurice K., was known for his encyclopedic learning; Widner called him a "brilliant polymath." [9]

As members of the State Planning Board, the three men were concerned about the pressures the federal highway system would exert on land, especially near the state's metropolitan areas. Coupling this with the expected increase in workers' time away from work, they reasoned that sites satisfying the people's future recreational requirements would mesh nicely to meet both needs.

The federal government would pick up the cost for the three national areas (Tocks Island, Kinsua Creek, and Raystown), but access to state money for such purposes was more difficult. The Pennsylvania Constitution limits — for purposes other than to suppress insurrection or rehabilitate areas affected by disasters — the amount of debt the state may incur to "one and three-quarters times the average of the annual tax revenues deposited in the previous five fiscal years." Any indebtedness above this amount must be submitted to the voters for approval. It was important, however, that the process of land acquisition begin as soon as possible before "urban sprawl made the sites unsuitable" or land costs "skyrocketed." [10]

Since any state expenditures for acquisition of land under "Project 70" had to be submitted to the voters, Maurice K. prepared a letter to newspapers around the state. In it he stated that the Lawrence administration "intends to put a bond issue proposal before the legislature next year with the goal of getting it on a referendum in 1963." [11] The two-year delay in getting the question on the ballot was necessitated because proposals to amend the constitution had to pass in two successive legislatures.

The Lawrence administration went ahead with its long-range plans for an enlarged park system, although there was an election coming up in November 1962. Months earlier Maurice K. had been mentioned among Democrats as a possible gubernatorial candidate. U.S. Senator Joseph S. Clark had announced his intention to run for another term, Genevieve Blatt was assumed to be interested in reelection as Secretary of Internal Affairs for a third term, and Richardson Dillworth, Mayor of Philadelphia, was the Democratic front runner for governor. Reports, however, indicated that Dillworth might have a tough time "campaigning in the hustings," in which case Goddard's chances "might develop." The Harrisburg *Patriot* said: "Politically, Goddard is one of the least controversial figures now in a cabinet post." The paper described him as "one of the rare policy makers who has not drawn the ire of Republican or Democratic lawmakers." [12]

Dillworth was nominated as the Democratic candidate, but Republican Congressman William E. Scranton was elected Governor by a landslide. On Christmas Eve 1962, the Governor-elect announced that he would keep Maurice K. as Secretary of Forests and Waters. When he made the public announcement, Scranton said:

> This is, of course, a tribute to the high regard in which we hold Dr. Goddard's ability and dedication as a conservationist. It is my hope the new administration will make a mark in the field of conservation and in the development of our natural resources. [13]

Maurice K., whom Governor Lawrence had called "The best public employee in America," pledged to run his department "on the same professional and technical basis as in the past." According to the news reports, Stewart Udall had offered him a position in the Department of the Interior, but Maurice K. wanted to remain in Harrisburg and complete the program he had started under Governor Leader. The Secretary of Forests and Waters, who was still "on leave of absence" from Penn State, told reporters he was "grateful and pleased" by Scranton's decision. [14] Newspapers around the state also were strong supporters of his reappointment.

□ □ □ □

Governor Scranton's action was even more remarkable, however, following as it did some contentious campaign disagreements over the management of the environment under the previous two Democratic administrations. In debates and speeches, candidate Scranton alleged that Pennsylvania had "reduced its conservation efforts during the past eight years." He also criticized a decision to drain the lake at Prince Gallitzin. And in a September 15, 1962 speech he called the Democrats, "politicians who strangle our future," and then specifically charged that the administration in Harrisburg has "failed to cleanse our rivers and streams, . . . and to conserve our natural resources."

Maurice K. could have left, as would most cabinet officers, any response to this campaign rhetoric to the Democratic candidate or the out-going Governor. He chose, however, to counterattack in the most political of fashions — as if he were running for office against Scranton. He fired off Department of Forests and Waters press releases alleging that Congressman Scranton "was at best ignorant of the facts or at worst guilty of reckless charges." One stated:

> Mr. Scranton's allegation that Pennsylvania has actually reduced its conservation effort serves as an indication of his appalling lack of knowledge about the many significant and dramatic developments which have occurred in this field during the past eight years.
>
> I am naturally distressed and disappointed when a candidate for Governor repeatedly makes such irresponsible charges as the Republican candidate has made about this vital function of our State Government. [15]

He had to set the record straight, that his department's budget had "doubled" in eight years, that "we lead the nation in stream pollution abatement," and that Pennsylvania ranked third in overall conservation effort, not forty-seventh as Scranton had claimed.

118

And in an earlier release from the Department of Forests and Waters, Maurice K. had stated:

> Any candidate for Governor owes it to himself and to the people whose support he seeks to know what he is talking about, and on this count, Mr. Scranton has exhibited an abysmal lack of information. [16]

In making his appointments Governor Scranton not only disregarded these remarks and retained Maurice K., but also warmly embraced Project 70. It seemed to have something for everyone: park land, flood control, fishing waters, hunting lands, and especially, economic development for all sections of the state. The promise of an improved economy may have made it especially attractive to Scranton. He had been elected by a margin of a half-million votes. He regarded lifting the state from its economic doldrums as a major initiative, but his support of conservation issues was also substantial. He referred frequently to Governor Gifford Pinchot's record and "tried to emulate his efforts in forest and game protection." [17] In addition to economic recovery, conservation and educational reform, one of the new governor's concerns was to extend civil service, considering the Pennsylvania system as "the worst in the nation." To ease his task, the voters had given him a majorities in both houses of the legislature.

In August, eight months after he took office — on a day on which he vetoed eleven measures — Governor Scranton signed into law his plan of broadened civil service coverage for state employees. It extended job protection to eighteen thousand additional patronage workers as well as to the twelve thousand that had been covered previously by executive order. The bill did not apply to supervisory and unskilled state employees, but it placed sixty-one percent of Pennsylvania's eighty-two thousand workers under civil service. At the same time, the Governor signed a legislative pension bill that permitted members of the House and Senate to retire on full pay after twenty years, and gave them retirement benefits of two-and-a-half times the rate for regular state employees. [18]

If Maurice K. had any idea what was involved in getting a bond issue approved, it did not lessen his enthusiasm for the plan. Between July 1, 1963, and November 5, 1963, he led a statewide campaign to promote approval of the bond issue. Accompanied by John Rex, his land-acquisitions chief, and Bill Forrey, chief of plans for state parks (in 1973 he became head of the Bureau of State Parks), Maurice K. traveled all over the state talking up the scheme at public meetings — there were, perhaps, as many as a hundred of these events prior to the referendum. He talked at Lions and Rotary Clubs, to sportsmen's organizations, to Chambers of Commerce and League of Women Voters chapters, and to Realtors and to township planning commissions, to any one or group anywhere in the state who would listen.

Maurice K. approached these meetings with the zeal of an evangelist seeking converts. He told the attendees of his concern about the "opportunities for recreational and conservation development" that would be "irretrievably lost" if Pennsylvania did not undertake the effort, and optimistically cited land-acquisition programs for similar purposes in California, New York and Wisconsin for similar purposes. In Butler County — after telling his audience that they could be the "best county" in Pennsylvania to live and work in, if they showed interest in the Moraine State Park project — he insisted, "These outdoor attractions are as important to growth as highways and schools." [19]

He was so enthusiastic in his presentations that he received letter after letter praising "his stimulating speech" and "his dedication to this work," and describing "the splendid reaction" to his "excellent talk," and hailing his appearance before one group as its "outstanding program of the year." The League of Women Voters of Lower Merion Township wrote: "It is rare, indeed, that we have the opportunity to listen to as solid a body of material as you presented." And from James A. Ream, Managing Director of the Lebanon County Chamber of Commerce came the following:

> In one evening's talk, you have done more to sell the Project 70 concept to our Lebanon County community then all that has gone before. One of our most prominent and local farm operators came to me after the meeting and indicated that, while he disagreed on a few minor points, you answered major questions that have been bothering farm people for two years. [20]

Maurice K. talked to both large and small groups. At the Pennsylvania State Association of Boroughs annual meeting in July 1964 — possibly the largest he met with — there were sixteen hundred delegates. And he usually talked with nothing more than a few skimpy notes. When he went before the Westmoreland County Planning Commission, in April of the same year, he had scribbled only a few notes on a single sheet of paper: the name of the organization and those of the half-dozen prominent guests (which included three members of the General Assembly), and then he gave his entire speech from the following thirteen words: *Ladies and Gentlemen: Project 70, Time, Energy, Money, Support, Destroy Values, etc., etc.*

After the referendum was approved (by a narrow majority of 113,109 votes out of the 2.2 million cast), it became Section 15 to Article VIII of the state constitution and authorized the "issuance of bonds to the amount of seventy million dollars" to be used for the "acquisition of land for State parks, reservoirs and other conservation and recreation and historical preservation purposes." [21]

While Project 70 was, and still is, thought of as a "land for parks" act, the legislation also covered the acquisition of land for such things as "reservoirs" and "historical preservation" and as Maurice K. explained in a letter to George Jenkins, Director of the Institute of Research at Lehigh University, the bill defined "conservation purposes" very broadly as

> any use of land for water supply, flood control, water quality control development, soil erosion control, reforestation, wildlife reserves, or any other uses that will maintain, improve or develop the natural environment of soil, water, air, minerals, or wildlife of this Commonwealth. [22]

Use of Project 70 monies also permitted participation with political subdivisions, for the same purposes — but mainly community parks — subject to any limitations the General Assembly would prescribe. The final step in the long process was the approval by the legislature of an enabling bill. On February 11, 1964, Governor Scranton called a special session of the legislature to enact the necessary legislation setting forth the guidelines for implementing Project 70, thus empowering the executive branch to proceed.

At this same legislative session, he also requested a revision of the Commonwealth's eminent domain laws. The two laws were finally in place by June, more than three years after Goddard had first brought forward the plan. The main provisions of the enabling act required not only public hearings before park development began, but also for the approval of each project by the State Planning Board and the governor. The new Eminent Domain Code clarified as well as simplified condemnation proceedings and increased the kinds of damages to which a property owner would be entitled. [23]

❑ ❑ ❑ ❑

Maurice K. wanted to ensure that in a "friendly" condemnation the owner would received the same benefits as did one who resisted. Generally he was sympathetic to those who lost their land. The story is told how he let two elderly sisters continue to live (under a life tenancy) in their cabin after the state acquired the land for Moraine State Park. According to Leonard Green of the Pennsylvania Federation of Sportsmens Clubs, "This led more to help sell the idea [of the park] . . . to the local folks in Butler than anything else." [24] As it turned out, one of the sisters died within the year and the other moved into a retirement home.

And Maurice K. attempted to allay the fears of those who became upset over the possibility their properties might be among those condemned. To one such woman in Wind Gap he wrote:

> I have read your letter with interest and I can certainly appreciate your deep attachment for your property and your present apprehension.
>
> I urge you not to be unduly concerned about the prospects of being dislocated. If a project is approved for this area, your property may not be involved in any way. If it is determined that all or a portion of your property is required to serve the public interests, every possible consideration will be given for your welfare. [25]

Where there was a clear public objective in acquiring land, Maurice K. moved resolutely. "No power of government, except taxation," he wrote in the U.S. Department of Agriculture's 1963 *Year Book*, "is more apt to inspire dispute than the power of eminent domain, the right of government to act on behalf of the people in acquiring land for public use," but he used the power without hesitation whenever he thought it appropriate. Acknowledging that zoning, easements, and purchase of development rights were methods that have their "place in the box of tools available to public bodies," he still was convinced that "there is little or no substitute for outright public ownership where a clearly defined public need must be satisfied." [26]

He agreed that the line that separates the "proper role for public ownership and private capital is hazy," but claimed that "it is possible to agree upon some general principles." Public ownership, according to him, rested on the "protection of amorphous values difficult to measure, such as the protection of a watershed or of open space in a metropolitan area." He explained by asserting: "Only a few water uses can generate profits for private capital." There is, he claimed, "no profit in the fields of flood control, or low flow augmentation, or pollution abatement, yet it is absolutely essential for the economic success of a community that such needs be looked after just as effectively as water supply or power," for which there was adequate commercial interest. [27]

Maurice K. noted, however, that a claiming official must be able to "make a case" for the project he is proposing. He stated:

> The charge leveled oftenest against public ownership is that it lays a heavy hand on the surrounding economy by ruling out private development and by not contributing its fair share to the local tax base.
>
> If either objection applies to a project, it is a case of bad management. The purpose of public investment in the United States is to reinforce the private economy by providing opportunities for private investment and by protecting land and resource values.
>
> These benefits can be measured through the increased tax revenues, higher land values, new economic growth, or increased resource supplies engendered by the project. [28]

Maurice K. then cited the $7 million spent by the Commonwealth in clearing thirty-six acres of commercial and industrial slum at the tip of Pittsburgh's Golden Triangle. He claimed this new park gave Pittsburgh a very presentable "front door," which made possible private redevelopment that increased the "taxables in downtown Pittsburgh by $100 million."

□ □ □ □

The Pennsylvania State Planning Board was created by Governor Pinchot in July 1934 to study ways to help the commonwealth find employment for idle workers and lead it out of the depression. It was established in part as a response to President Roosevelt's action the previous year in setting up a National Planning Board within the Public Works Administration. The President's executive order specified that the national board's charter was "to prepare a program and plan of procedure dealing with the physical, social, governmental and economic aspects of public policies for the development and use of land, water and other National resources." [29]

Initially the Pennsylvania group concentrated on developing a Philadelphia-Tri-State Regional Plan as well as one for Allegheny County. It studied housing, working conditions, unemployment, mineral and water resources, the "competitive situations faced by industries such as coal and iron," transportation, education and welfare, the "changes occurring in agriculture," and the trends in population. By the 1960s, however, the state Board had expanded its horizons and become a powerful executive body that cut across all departments of state government. Riding the "crest of a national 'new wave' of state planning," as Board member (and later Chairman) Adolph W. Schmidt described it, the Pennsylvania body undertook population and economic studies, prepared river basin plans, developed blueprints for open space utilization and recreation, considered ways to assist depressed areas, such as Appalachia, and instituted a program of mapping the entire state. [30]

The Planning Board divided the state into thirteen planning regions. Project 70, with monies to be used for the *acquisition* of land for conservation, recreation and historic purposes, reached into all thirteen of these regions. It was the first of a three-pronged state government strategy on acquiring and then developing land. Supplementing Project 70 were the Federal Land and Water Conservation Fund Act of January 1965, which authorized grants-in-aid to states for planning, acquisition, and development of land for outdoor recreation, and the subsequent state Project 500 bond issue, which provided funds for the *development* of land acquired under the earlier Project 70 Act.

After Project 70 approval by the voters and the establishment of guidelines by the legislature, the funds were distributed on the basis of a four-sevenths share to the Department of Forests and Waters, a two-sevenths share to local units of government (on a fifty-fifty matching basis), and a one-seventh share, divided between the Game and Fish Commissions. The Board first approved the individual projects in the state's thirteen regions and then sent them to the Governor for final endorsement. The Department of Forests and Waters became the major group managing project review and expenditure of funds under Project 70. (Forests and Waters also handled the acquisition of sites for the Pennsylvania Historical and Museum Commission.) Moreover, the Department worked closely with local entities in suggesting or reviewing proposed community projects. [31]

Philadelphia was one of the communities that quickly applied to participate in Project 70. In November 1964, Mayor Tate forwarded a formal application for matching funds to buy parks and playgrounds at forty locations throughout the city. The largest of these was Pennypack Park at 175 acres, the smallest a one-fifth-acre site at Point Breeze Avenue. The city proposed to pay $10.8 million of the overall land acquisition cost of $21.7 million. As the *Philadelphia Inquirer* described the city's situation: "Already blessed with well over 8000 acres of parks and other recreational areas, Philadelphia hopes soon to add another thousand-odd acres to its total." [32]

❑ ❑ ❑ ❑

Maurice K., John Rex, and William C. Forrey traveled to each of the proposed park sites around the state to go over the Department's development plans at a public meeting. Some of these were acrimonious sessions. Occasionally Forrey would talk, but the usual format was to have John Rex first describe the land package involved in the proposed park, along with its current status — what land the state already owned, or what had been acquired for the state by private groups such as the Western Conservancy — and then what the state's remaining acquisition plans were. At this point Maurice K. would take charge of each meeting, and the instructor in him would take over from the Secretary. He would describe enthusiastically the advantages of the park to the local community, its aesthetic, its flood control (if appropriate), and especially its economic advantages. Then he would field questions from the floor. [33]

Maurice K. insisted on thorough preparation for these meetings. Affected landowners received registered letters of invitation. Prior to the meeting only general information was released. At the meeting, as much information as possible was disseminated: maps

126

showing the main project features, changes in streams, bridges and highways, the proposed project boundaries; an outline of the steps to be followed in the land acquisition process as well as its schedule; the costs of the project, its method of financing; and the anticipated primary and secondary benefits. He considered it vital that the land acquisition work be initiated immediately after the public meeting to prevent rumors and keep land speculation to a minimum. [34]

When it came time for actually "taking" the land, Maurice K. would send John Rex and a team of experts back to the community to explain the process. Rex would have charts and maps available for those being affected. He would describe the project area, especially its boundaries, so everyone knew exactly what land was involved. He would tell land owners about any available lease-back opportunities. It was usually several years before construction started on a new park and, in the interim, the residents were often permitted to rent their properties. Rex would introduce them to the people they would be dealing with: the surveying-party chiefs and the local attorneys who would be involved in the taking process.

He also would explain the method used to calculate the offers the department would be making. Rex told them he would obtain appraisals from two local firms and use the average of the two. In the event there was a wide variation between them, he would secure a third and throw out the deviant appraisal. After warning them that the state's offers were not negotiable, he would explain all the appeal mechanisms they would have available. Finally he would go over the two legal documents the property owners would be confronted with and the time frames for contesting them. The first of these, the Declaration of Taking, would be filed with the local Prothonotary. At this point, title to the property would pass to the state, and the previous owner would be sent the second document, a Notice of Condemnation, which would be filed with the county Recorder of Deeds. The individual had six weeks to either accept or reject the offer and ask for a review of the case.

□ □ □ □

One of the difficult "sells" was for Ridley Creek State Park near Philadelphia. Approximately two thousand acres of the proposed twenty-five hundred-acre park site, being taken in a hostile condemnation, were owned by one family. The public meeting in May 1965 was held in the Indian Lane Junior High School. Maurice K. told the attendees that the site located along Ridley Creek is "an excellent one" and was one the Department of Forests and Waters was interested in "to preserve open space in urban areas." He explained the "In-Lieu-of-Tax" provisions of Project 70 for the benefit of the school district, and then noted that at the time of the referendum in November 1963, "Delaware county residents supported the constitutional amendment by the greatest plurality of all the counties in the Commonwealth." [35]

When it was time for questions, the attorney for the Jefford family stood up and began to read from a list of ten questions he had on a clipboard. According to William Forrey, it was as if Maurice K. were being interrogated on a courtroom stand. One of the questions the lawyer asked was whether or not the state would be able to maintain the land as well as the Jeffords. Although he may have been hoping to trap Goddard into a confused reply or even a prevarication, Maurice K. immediately responded in his loud, gruff voice: "Well, . . . No! Of course not! We don't have their money." From that point the audience was on the side of the presenters, to whom they periodically gave rounds of applause. [36]

At the Department of Forests and Waters pitch for Marsh Creek State Park at Downingtown High School in March 1966, about a thousand people showed up. One of them, a professor from Bryn Mawr College, gave an eloquent speech against the park. Goddard replied in his direct, unpretentious style. The antagonist came forward following the meeting and told Maurice K. he still disagreed with him but was willing to shake his hand. [37] Goddard's honesty, along with his homespun manner, appeared to disarm just about all comers. Even those who disagreed with or disliked him quickly seemed to become aware of these traits: thus his personal integrity was seldom questioned. [38]  For example, after calling him "adroit in the goat dance called the political Fandango," feature writer John Stewart of the Wilkes Barre *Independent,* admitted the reason for Goddard's survival was that "not one breath of scandal has even been whispered about this able administrator." [39]

Many times the three men did not return to Harrisburg from a park presentation until early the next morning.    Nonetheless, Maurice K. expected Rex and Forrey to come to the office on time the following day and do a full-day's work.  It wasn't until  4 AM, for example, that they arrived back from Downingtown and the Marsh Creek presentation.    When they got to the office that morning, there was word for Maurice K. that President Johnson wanted to tour the western part of the state that afternoon to look at some recently flooded spots.  Governor Scranton was out of town and couldn't get back in time for the hastily scheduled flight, so Maurice K. had to meet Airforce One at  Pittsburgh at 2 P.M. and overfly the Ohio River Valley with the President and Governor Rhodes of Ohio. [40]  Flying as low as four thousand feet, they had a "sunlit view of the devastation" — "entire towns that were all but submerged."  The Secretary of Forests and Waters never seemed to tire; after staying up most of the night he was still Goddard-effusive during the flight, smiling as photographers shot pictures of him and the President.

□ □ □ □

Three years later the State Planning Board reported that nearly $60 million had been spent on 443 projects, while matching local community funding increased the total by another $23 million.  The park acreage added, for example, in the key Southeastern Region (which included Philadelphia) was an impressive 17,500 acres for a 48 percent increase.  The color-coded maps of the area in the board's report showed nearly a hundred locations on which state, local and federal funds were being expended. And the map of the Southwestern Region — the counties surrounding Pittsburgh — was only slightly less marked up. Across the state 163,570 new acres were amassed in the first three years of Project 70 acquisitions. [41]

Project 70 bonds were issued as the need for funds arose, thus their maturity dates varied. The last of these was scheduled to come due by the end of the twentieth century. The bond principal and interest are paid each year out of general tax revenues. There is a single line, "General Obligation — Debt Service," in each state budget (under the Treasury Department) to cover all state bond indebtedness. There is no necessity to defend this line during budget hearings, the obligations are paid by the State Treasury in accordance with the Constitution, regardless of whether or not the Legislature approves the budget. [42]

Issuing bonds, in lieu of direct taxation, tends, of course, to divert taxpayer attention from the cost of doing something by focusing on the benefits of the action. In an answer to one inquiry from a private citizen, Maurice K. told his questioner, "because of the procedures followed in retiring the bonds, said retirement will not cause any tax increase." [43] While this is literally true for current taxpayers, the repayment of a bond either means that future monies in the general fund are not available for another project, or by postponing the ultimate obligation — while doubling or tripling it for interest - increases the tax bill for later generations.

Not all of the land was bought or condemned, some was donated. In Westmoreland County, for example, Gen. Richard K. Mellon, who owned the Laurel Mountain Ski Area, gave the 493-acre facility to the Commonwealth. And much of the land associated with Ohiopyle State Park was obtained through the monumental efforts of the Western Pennsylvania Conservancy, which in the forties evolved out of the Greater Pittsburgh Parks Association.

With a grant from the A. W. Mellon Education and Charitable Trust, the Conservancy directors began to buy up open space "holding scientific, natural, or recreational value."   By 1982 the Conservancy had acquired eighty-thousand acres; including much of what became Moraine, Laurel Ridge, Oil Creek, and Ohiopyle State Parks.   According to John C. Oliver, president that year of the Western Pennsylvania Conservancy, they were especially interested in preserving rivers which had recreational and natural scenic value. [44]

The Conservancy had the ability to use their private, charitable status to purchase land on a "quicker, quieter, and cheaper basis" than public agencies such as the Fish Commission and the Department of Forests and Waters.  When projects were proposed, and especially when "targets of opportunity" — quality tracts at reasonable prices — became available, one of the important criteria the Conservancy applied in deciding whether or not to buy, was the land's resale potential to the state. [45]  In these determinations they worked closely with Maurice K. and John Rex.

# CHAPTER VIII

# WATER IS FOR FIGHTING OVER

**Acre-foot.** The unit of reservoir volume commonly used in Great Britain and North America. It is a volume of water whose surface area is 1 acre and whose depth is 1 foot. One acre-foot is equivalent to 43,560 cubic feet, or 272,000 gallons. [Norman Smith, *A History of Dams.*]

Dams are among the oldest still-working structures that man has built. They cover the earth from Egypt to China, from Europe to America; they stretch from Antiquity to the present. The dam, for example, of St-Ferreol in France, which was erected around 1667, is still in active use supplying water to the celebrated Canal du Midi. [1] And in the nineteenth century hundreds of dams were used to power the Industrial Revolution in England and America. To many, dams are elegant examples of man's ingenuity, his ability and will to tame nature for the benefit of society; in the twentieth century, they have come to be looked upon by others as, like thieves in the night, silent destroyers of the environment.

Water from ancient reservoirs was used for irrigation and water supply. In modern times power generation, flood control, recreation, and low-flow augmentation have been added to these earlier uses. The two great twentieth-century dam-building organizations in the United States have been the Bureau of Reclamation and the U.S. Army Corps of Engineers. The great dams that have watered the West were the work of the Bureau of Reclamation; the large flood control and low-flow augmentation dams of the East the result of the efforts of the Corps of Engineers. In Pennsylvania alone the Corps of Engineers has built more than twenty dams, in addition to from seventy to eighty flood control levees, dikes, floodwalls and channel enlargements. [2] Both the Corps and the Bureau of Reclamation have been the arms of U.S. Congressional will and, on occasion, irresolution.

❑ ❑ ❑ ❑

The Delaware River rises in New York's Catskill Mountains. It makes a short run of about three hundred miles to the Atlantic — two hundred miles for the nontidal river. "The Delaware River drains a basin one-fortieth the size of that of the Missouri, is one-sixth as long as the Rio Grande, and carries one-fifteenth as much water as the Columbia." The Delaware is small as rivers go — it is usually omitted from lists of great American rivers — yet it is called on to do a job that is seldom asked of other, far-larger streams. The "one standard . . . by which the Delaware ranks first among American rivers, is in the number of people served by its waters and the economic importance of their activities." [3]

Nearly 10 percent of the nation's population is served from the waters of its small drainage area, which is approximately 0.4 percent of the United States's land area. [4] The Delaware is also a key source of water for New York City, which is outside the river's watershed. At the same time, the river's flows must provide sufficient water to maintain the ports of Philadelphia and Trenton. This control over low-water levels is also vital to prevent the salination of fresh water intakes throughout the lower basin, including those of Philadelphia. And the river is asked to carry off the massive amounts of industrial and human waste generated by the area. [5]

The ports of the Delaware, which are scattered along the lower portion of the river, serve one of the largest concentrations of heavy industry in the world. Among them are shipbuilding facilities, steel mills, food processing plants, oil refineries, and petrochemical plants. [6] While this part of the river, which is lined with cities and industries, is the one most people know, other parts have remained pastoral in character and would look familiar even today to the first settlers in the area.

Until early in the twentieth century, the river was able to serve as a waterway for commerce, fishing, water supply, recreation, and sewage disposal. Under the weight of increasing population and industry, the requirements of these conflicting demands began to stretch the need for the river's water beyond its capacity, and the Delaware's neighbors began to fight over access to its water. In principle, the three states, Pennsylvania, New Jersey, and New York had agreed as early as 1908 to the need to cooperate in river basin decisions. Commencing in 1923, representatives of the three states began to meet and eventually developed a series of agreements or compacts. Each, however, ended up being rejected by the legislature of one or more of the signatory states because of perceived advantages it was believed another state, usually New York, would receive. [7]

Thoroughly frustrated after years of negotiation, New York announced in April 1929 that it would build two dams on the upper portions of the Delaware as water-supply reservoirs for New York City. New Jersey immediately filed suit. Although the suit cited several technical points, its primary contention was the "injury" New Jersey would suffer by the diversion of water out of the water basin. Among the specific injuries claimed was the state's lost use of the river for water supply, recreation, sanitation, power-potential, shad fishing, and oyster harvests. Pennsylvania entered the case the following February. While Pennsylvania did not contest New York's right to transfer water out of the basin, the state wanted a Court-specified allocation of the amount New York could take, and the appointment of a master to supervise the diversions.

In May 1931, the U.S. Supreme Court delivered its opinion. Writing for the majority, Justice Oliver Wendell Holmes based the court's opinion on the principle of "equitable apportionment," that a river is a "necessity of life that must be rationed among those who have power over it." The Court's decree specified the amount of water that New York could take at 440 mgd (million gallons per day), not the 600 mgd that had been asked for, and also directed the state to clean up the pollution entering the river at Port Jervis. The court denied Pennsylvania's request for a master. Moreover, it retained jurisdiction over the Delaware for itself, but did give each state the right to apply to the Court for future modification of its decree.

Throughout the thirties and forties, proposals and counter proposals over a mechanism for cooperation were put forward by the states individually and by joint commissions. Early in 1951 — the latest of these interstate groups, Incodel, submitted a plan and draft compact. [8] Although there was optimism throughout the Delaware Valley over the adoption of the plan and compact — it was quickly ratified by Delaware and New Jersey, and the New York Legislature was poised to accept it — Pennsylvania wavered. Governor John S. Fine (George Leader's immediate predecessor) appointed a special panel to review the proposal but since the Pennsylvania General Assembly was not scheduled to meet again until 1952, hope for an interstate compact waned. Although the bill finally passed in the Pennsylvania House, it was never reported out of committee in the Senate. By 1953, the Incodel plans had died. New York filed a petition with the U.S. Supreme Court to increase its water diversion and put together a proposal to build another reservoir without the concurrence of its downstream neighbors. [9]

Incodel, the Interstate Commission on the Delaware River Basin, had been formed in 1936 as a planning and advisory agency. It had no administrative powers. All its recommendations were referred to its supporting state governments for approval and for the setting of procedures for their execution. Its charter permitted it to formulate programs for its four state governments for the "development, utilization and conservation of the waters of the river." Initially its main objective was to develop a program for coping with pollution. This was completed in 1939 and subsequently enacted into law by each of the four states. In 1949,

Incodel was directed by reciprocal legislation enacted by Pennsylvania, New Jersey, and New York to explore the feasibility of carrying out an integrated project for utilizing the waters of the basin by the four states. [10] As we have seen Incodel's recommendations were derailed, however, when Pennsylvania hesitated three years later.

□ □ □ □

Almost from the moment he was sworn in as Pennsylvania's Secretary of Forests and Waters in January 1955, Maurice K. became involved with the state's concerns over the Delaware River. Unlike some, however, he realized that Pennsylvania's interests would be served best by cooperating with its neighbors. The flood in the summer of 1955 drove home to him the necessity for control of the river's waters. At a meeting of Incodel at Pocono Manor the year following the flood, he bluntly told the representatives of the four states "to stop squabbling over water resources and form a bloc to obtain more Federal help." He went on to tell the Incodel members, "We're not giving our lives away if the Federal Government builds us a reservoir." [11]

And when he talked to the group again in September 1957, he renewed his call for cooperation by citing the benefits during that summer's drought of the dams New York had built on the headwaters of the Delaware at Neversink near Liberty and Petacton at Downsville. According to Maurice K., while between June 1 and September 8, 47 billion gallons of waters had been diverted to New York City, another 43.5 billion gallons had been released from the two dams into the river, averting what would have been "an all-time low" at Trenton and Philadelphia. Maurice K. told the more than two hundred water experts, conservationists, and public officials, that this "proved conclusively the tremendous value of reservoirs in river development." [12] It was a position that would continue to influence his thinking throughout his twenty-four-year career managing Pennsylvania's natural resources. It also was part of the thinking incorporated in his 1958 "Water Is Pennsylvania's Future" speech.

According to author Richard Albert in his *Damming the Delaware*, Pennsylvania needed to take the lead in initiating new negotiations since it was the state's foot dragging that had killed the previous Incodel plan. It was Mayor Joseph S. Clark of Philadelphia who got things moving again. Clark's job had been made somewhat easier, as for the first time the governors of the four states were all from the same party.

In February 1955 Governor Robert Meyner of New Jersey met with Clark in Philadelphia's City Hall. Clark and his staff then conferred with George Leader and Maurice K. Within days Governor Meyner traveled to Harrisburg with his water experts for a meeting with the new Pennsylvania Governor. In late April a contingent from both states met in New York City with New York State water officials and laid the groundwork for a summit meeting. On May 17, representatives of the four states and the water departments of New York City and Philadelphia met in Princeton.[13]

In June, Governor Leader signed legislation providing for a reciprocal agreement with New Jersey to build a main-stem dam. The month before, in anticipation of this action, Maurice K. had hired Albright and Friel to update the firm's original plans for a dam at Wallpack Bend that had been developed for Incodel. Although the heavy flooding that hit the Delaware Valley in August 1955 is often credited as the motivating factor behind the drive for a system of flood control dams that followed in the storm's wake, in truth the storm's main significance was to "open the door to massive federal involvement" in the basin.[14]

The amount of support President Eisenhower promised Pennsylvania following the disastrous flooding along the Delaware in 1955 was never fully realized, but the following February Congress did authorize the Corps of Engineers to conduct a survey of the Delaware River Basin. That same month, yet another interstate study group, the Delaware River Basin Survey

Commission, was formed. The idea of additional dams on the Delaware and throughout the basin as well as the idea of an interstate compact were now firmly implanted at all levels.

Among the actions the new group of state conferees took up at its first meeting was one to change its name to the Delaware River Basin Advisory Commission, and — rather than to duplicate the Corps' study — to become the states' review group for the Corps' efforts and to conduct research into only those areas that would complement those of the Corps' study. The new Commission assumed some of Incodel's office space in downtown Philadelphia and, more importantly, the idea that its main purpose was to develop a "comprehensive plan for the control and utilization of the water resources in the Delaware River Basin." [15]

With funding from the Ford Foundation, the Delaware River Basin Advisory Commission went to the Maxwell Graduate School of Public Administration of Syracuse University to review the issue of how to manage a river, the water of which was vital to the four sovereign states. The Syracuse University study was completed by September 1959. The key provision and major departure of the Syracuse Report from earlier proposals was the suggestion that a compact of the four states should include the federal government as an equal partner, not simply as a funding source. This proposed new agency would have control over the development and operation of all water projects in the basin. It would be able to sell water and hydrolectric power, to regulate river flows and diversion, and to raise money to fund projects. [16] Not only was the idea of including the federal government in the Commission a new one; the resulting organization would be a most powerful one.

After careful review of the idea by Incodel, and following a two-and-one-half hour presentation to the Commissioners by the Chairman, John Robin, the group voted to "support the premise that a compact for the development of the Delaware River Basin should include federal participation." [17] In early 1961, the four Governors met in Philadelphia and hammered out the details of the compact legislation needed for enactment in their individual states.

The other three states soon had their legislation in place, but once again Pennsylvania was last. Finally, with Governor Lawrence's promise to have the concerns of the oil and steel industries addressed in the federal legislation necessary for final approval of the compact, the Pennsylvania Legislature approved it. [18]

For the first time all four states were lined up behind a specific proposal. President Kennedy appointed Stewart Udall, Secretary of the Interior, to deal with the federal issues that would arise under a compact between the states and the national government. Then with intense lobbying by the representatives of the four states, and the efforts of Governor Lawrence in gaining the support of the administration — he was credited with having delivered Pennsylvania to Kennedy in 1960 — the bill was passed. On November 2, 1961, the President signed the legislation. At the signing Lawrence sat at the President's right hand and Maurice K. stood behind him.

Stewart Udall was never a strong supporter of the compact idea. He raised questions concerning the constitutionality of the federal government entering in a compact with the states, as well as about an arrangement in which four states would be able to out-vote the lone federal voice among the Commissioners. In many instances, however, Udall or his alternate, abstained over the years from voting on a Basin Commission issue, not because either disagreed with it, but because each claimed that he had not had time to "obtain the various clearances among the concerned federal agencies" — the "twenty-five melancholy babies" with which at one meeting Joseph Clark (by then U.S. Senator) had accused Udall of being surrounded. [19]

❑ ❑ ❑ ❑

Incodel continued to operate for another year after the compact was signed. (And the Delaware River Basin Advisory Commission became the Delaware River Basin Commission.) In addition to the federal-state partnership that the compact had established, a significant added power for the new commission, was the authority that the four state governors serving as its primary members — with men like Maurice K. as alternates — conferred on it. Their presence transformed the group from one of technical review and proposal to one with executive powers. Although the Commissioners of Incodel, for example, included members of the state legislatures and the heads of state agencies such as Pennsylvania's Forests and Waters, the four chief executives brought a new level of importance and influence to the deliberations and decisions of the compact's meetings, that previously had been lacking.

According to R. Timothy Weston (the young attorney Maurice K. took to the meetings as his advisor on water basin issues, and who later became a Department deputy for water basins), the success of the Delaware River Basin Commission sessions, whether a "summit meeting" including the governors or the more frequent meetings of the "alternates," often lay in the social gatherings that followed them. [20]

Mark Twain is reported to have said, "Whiskey is for drinking, water is for fighting over." The Commissioners for the Delaware River Basin seemed to be trying to use the first to avoid the second. By gathering together informally for hors d'oeuvres and drinks, they were able to reduce the extent of their disagreements over access to the river's water. More than simply hale-fellow events, these post-meeting get togethers permitted frank discussions of ideas and positions, of importance as well as of difference. Moreover, Maurice K. was able to forge the links with such men as Governor Nelson Rockefeller of New York and Stewart Udall of the Department of the Interior that led to his assigments to the Land Law Review Commission and as a panel chairman at the White House Conference on Natural Beauty.

Although Maurice K.'s eating tastes were anything but aristocratic — Thomas Jefferson's desire to "improve the tastes of my countrymen" was hardly reflected in Commissioner's Alternate

Goddard — he did usually have a Scotch at these after-session affairs. [21]

□ □ □ □

The hundreds of second- and third-tier water officials, engineers, and state officials connected first with Incodel and now the Delaware River Basin Commission continued to meet in the Poconos for their annual "Water Resources Conference." Assuming that Tocks would be built, Maurice K. changed direction for his speech to the delegates in 1962. He opened his talk by showing them a picture taken at thirty-five thousand feet that covered the area from Chester, Pennsylvania to New York City. "This is the heart of Megalopolis," he told them. "This is the heart and the brains of the American Nation. This is where more people earn more money and produce more goods than anywhere else on the face of this globe. . . . It is the focal point of finance and the arts in the Atlantic Community." [22]

Then drawing on Jean Gottman's book on the region as the first *Megalopolis*, he told them, "This massive urban civilization we have reared is truly unique — the forerunner of other communities in other parts of the world." Quoting Gottman, a geographer on leave from the University of Paris, who was doing research at the Institute for Advanced Study at Princeton, Maurice K. told the conference:

> This region serves as a laboratory in which we may study the new evolution reshaping both the meaning of our traditional vocabulary and the whole material structure of our way of life. So great are the consequences of the general evolution heralded by the present rise and complexity of Megalopolis that an analysis of the region's problems often gives one the feeling of looking at the dawn in a new stage in human civilization. . . . Indeed this area may be considered [the cradle of] a new order in the organization of inhabited space.

Following a long list of the changes Maurice K. predicted would take place in the region's industry, transportation, and

141

general living conditions by the year 2000 (among them that the "automobile will have congested itself into limited utility"), he assured the audience that the "residents of this region will be the beneficiaries of today's wisdom." But he also cautioned them:

> We have, in attacking the problems of the Delaware, come up with some of the physical answers for the world of tomorrow. . . . But who is working on the human challenge? Should there be a commission of politicians, social scientists, and artists working out the answers to the problems of the human mind and the human heart? For it is on these answers that the shape of tomorrow must ultimately depend. [23]

Maurice K. closed his speech by quoting John Dewey's statement that a "culture which permits science to destroy its traditional values, but which distrusts its power to create new ones is a culture destroying itself." He then suggested to the gathering that "finding the values to govern us in the year 2000 is the next order of business."

❑ ❑ ❑ ❑

The idea for a main-stem dam that came out of the Corps' study was not a new one. While New York's interest in the Delaware lay mainly in it as a water-supply source, Pennsylvania, especially Philadelphia interests, was more concerned over flood control and low-water augmentation. This had led to several proposals as early as 1936 for the state to build a dam, first at Tocks Island north of the Delaware Water Gap, and then because of dam siting concerns at Tocks Island at Wallpack Bend .

The Corps' report, which was released in draft form over a two-year period between 1959 and 1960, recommended Tocks Island. It was conceived as a true multi-purpose dam, one that provided: flood-control, water supply, low-flow augmentation, and recreation. While Tocks was to be location of the main-stem dam, the plans also called for seventeen new and two existing but modified major dams along with thirty nine other smaller dams and flood-control projects throughout the Delaware River Basin, principally in Pennsylvania and New Jersey. [24]    In Pennsylvania these were to be mainly on the Lehigh and Schuykill Rivers and their tributaries.  A number of these projects to be integrated with those of the Corps were planned as state-funded flood-control and low-flow augmentation facilities.

Rather than relying on one or two high dams, the Corps planned a "package" of structures and works that were designed to function as a set that would provide the necessary flood-control and low-flow augmentation capabilities. The Corps offered five different arrangements of their proposal.   A small dam included in one scenario might be excluded in another.  But each arrangement was intended as an integrated set that met the objectives of adequate flood control and low-flood augmentation through the year 2010, the year by which population in the basin was expected to double. Maurice K. believed that the Corps' "Plan D." served Pennsylvania best from the standpoint of "total number of reservoirs, and total acre-feet of storage for flood control and water supply."    He favored it because it "affords a better distribution of water supply and flood contol facilities over the basin, and enhances the recreational possibilities."

The reservoir at Tocks Island with a capacity of 765,000 acre-feet of water was planned as a true multiple-use facility with flood control, low-flow augmentation and power generation included in its design.   Its cost was estimated at $93,000,000.   Other major Corps dams in Pennsylvania included Beltzville on Pohopoco Creek, Trexler on Jordan Creek and Aquashicola on Aquashicola Creek.  The total plan  would provide the capability to augment the surface flows of the Delaware by 2,100 cubic feet per second. [25]

After extensive review, the final version of the Corps' Delaware River Basin Report was ready for Congress in the spring of 1962. That October after brief hearings, Congress passed the Flood Control Act of 1962.  Included in the nearly two hundred public-works projects was one for the "comprehensive development of the Delaware River Basin."

With the Corps' recommendations for the Delaware now public, the stage was set for what would be the most contentious and protracted fight over a dam to occur in the eastern United States, one that would rival in intensity the epochal Hetch Hetchy Valley battle fifty years earlier in Yosemite Park. [26] Although a fight was also brewing over a state dam at Evansburg, near Norristown, it would be little more than a preliminary bout; Tocks Island would be the main event, a fifteen-round heavyweight clash that would be contested before a highly partisan national audience. One was either for the dam or against it. There seemed to be no dry middle ground on which to stand. And once again, as a half-century before at Hetch Hetchy, the United States Congress would become the final arena in which a dam siting battle would be fought and decided. This time, however, the dam forces would lose.

◻  ◻  ◻  ◻

Of the planned capacity of 765,000 acre-feet at Tocks Island, the permanent pool was 20,000 acre-feet, the water supply and low flow augmentation 315,000 acre-feet and the flood control 300,000 acre-feet. The methodology employed in designing a reservoir for multiple use is elegant, simple, and seldom understood, especially by the layman. Tireless in his efforts to educate people on conservation issues, Maurice K. explained the principle of a multiple-use reservoir in a letter to a correspondent who had heard him speak at a Kiwanis meeting and had written questioning what Maurice K. had meant when he used the term. Maurice K. replied:

> You misunderstood one point in my talk. I was not referring to three small separate bodies of water in lieu of one large project. Rather, I was referring to three pools or levels of water in the single project: the permanent pool, the summer pool and the flood control pool.
> The reservoir is never drawn down below the level of the permanent, or conservation pool.

The next level, or summer pool, is a segment or layer of water which is used for recreation and to provide for low-flow augmentation and downstream water quantity control.

The flood pool, or top layer, is a section of the reservoir reserved to hold back flood flows. Water is stored in this section only during flood periods. After the flood danger has passed, the water is released as quickly as possible to the top level of the summer pool to provide storage space for the next flood. [27]

Maurice K. then attached a diagram to help his correspondent visualize these three pools or levels. In simplest terms, in a multiple-use reservoir the bottom level is never drawn down; the top level is never filled, except with storm or spring-melt runoff. (At Tocks Island, for example, the inactive pool would have stood 34 feet above the valley floor, the water supply 95 feet and the flood control level 120 feet.) This tiered-pool approach means, of course, that to include recreational use in a reservoir, "permanent" facilities such as docks must be able to float up and down between the conservation and the flood levels. [28]

In late 1958 and early 1959 Incodel had wrestled with the issue of multiple-use reservoirs. Testimony was given, letters written, positions drawn on the appropriateness of using water-reservoirs for recreation. In a long letter to Incodel the American Waterworks Company expounded the commercial view of the issue. [29]  The company held that the protection of water that had been initially stocked as pure water typically water from remote areas rather than that stored for later purification purposes was essential. Thus, to permit recreation on such facilities was an inimical use. However, when water was drawn and required purification before use (for example from a river), then limited and controlled recreational use was permissible. In these instances, responsibility for water purity rested with the purifying organization.

In an effort to secure a government statement on the issue, Maurice K. asked C. L. Wilbar, Jr., the Pennsylvania Secretary of Health and Chairman of the Sanitary Water Board, of which Maurice K. was a member, to prepare a position paper. Wilbar echoed the basic position that the American Waterworks took, but

145

did indicate that for the Board of Health to issue a permit, the purveyor must maintain sanitary conditions in and around the reservoir whether or not he permits recreational uses. These included "strict control of activities on the marginal strips around the reservoir, and prohibition of such activities in the immediate vicinity of intake towers."

❑  ❑  ❑  ❑

The ink was hardly dry on the compact for the Delaware, than a years-long drought began in the northeast. Each summer between 1962 and 1965 saw it grow worse. Each winter the level to which the New York State reservoirs refilled was successively lower. Each year the tension between New York and the other three states heightened. By the summer of 1965 the flow of words between the parties became a raging torrent. Hardly a week went by that Pennsylvania newspapers, especially those in the Philadelphia area, did not weigh in with articles and editorials on the crisis. [30]

The criticism ranged from that over New York's waste of water due to its unmetered distribution system, to charges that the state had failed to live up to the terms of the Supreme Court agreement. The New York papers, on the other hand, tended to ignore the Pennsylvania and New Jersey claims, and after the city curtailed water usage, requiring among other measures no drinking water in restaurants other than on request, seemed to make light of the crisis. One reported the story of a visitor to the city, who in following the usual admonition in a restaurant to "watch his hat" suddenly "discovered his glass of water had been stolen."

Governor Hughes of New Jersey warned of a "water fight"; the respected *Journal* of the Water Pollution Control Federation editorialized: "The Future Is Here"; [31] concerned citizen's groups went door to door giving away bricks to be used to reduce consumption by displacing a portion of the water in toilet tanks, and legislators in several states began jumping into the fray. One Pennsylvania lawmaker even introduced a bill to dig a diversion tunnel from the Susquehanna River to the Delaware. Maurice K. quickly assailed the idea, and that finished any further mention of such a scheme. At the height of the drought, however, he stepped into the middle of the battle with his own intemperate remarks.

The Philadelphia *Sunday Bulletin* of June 25, 1965, ran a long article by Adolph Katz based on an interview with Maurice K. It was headlined, "Goddard Charges New York City with Pirating Water from the Delaware River." While the tone of the article was less inflammatory than the headline, it did quote Maurice K. as accusing New York City of "violating the U.S. Supreme Court decree limiting the amount of water New York may take from the river." (One of the powers given to the Delaware River Basin Commission by the 1961 Compact, provided that "modifications to the release schedules" or "impacts on the diversion allowances" in the 1954 decree had to be approved by the Commission. [32] )

According to Katz's article, New York was required to release water from its reservoir if the flow at the gauging station, which had been set up at Montague, New Jersey, as a result of the decree, fell below 1,525 cubic feet per second. In a June 14 article, the *Bulletin* reported the flow as running below 700 cubic feet. Although the rivermaster appointed in accordance with the Supreme Court decree had ordered New York to release water at the rate of 565 cubic feet per second, Maurice indicated the releases had been at a rate less than 150 cubic feet. [33]

At this point the Torresdale water intake for Philadelphia, which used about 375 million gallons of water each day, was not in danger, but the level of salination was becoming a definite concern. During May and early June the "salt line had moved upstream from the Delaware Memorial Bridge below Wilmington to a point two miles below Chester." [34]

The battle over water raged during the spring and early summer months. Then on July 7, 1965, following a "Crisis Meeting" at which Stewart Udall had asked the Commissioners "to demonstrate statesmanship rather than [go to] court," a compromise was worked out. The Commission declared a water supply emergency

147

throughout the basin in the form of a "Conservation Order." This temporarily modified the release and withdrawal rights of New York City. At the same time, the Commission took control of all the water works in the basin and began to dictate releases of even private reservoirs. Among these were the Pennsylvania Power and Light Company's Lake Wallenpaupack, which holds more than 257,000 acre-feet of water, and the Orange and Rockland Utilities' dam system on the Mongaup River in Sullivan County, New York. [35] By these actions, they were able to water the Delaware to keep the saline line below Philadelphia and also permit New York City to avoid releases that would endanger the city's future drinking supply or might be needed later by the down river communities if the drought continued into subsequent years.

President Johnson stepped into the battle by calling the Governors of the Northeast states to the White House in August and ordering "drought experts," led by Stewart Udall and the Corps of Engineers, to recommend courses of action. The result of this effort was essentially the same, however, as that recommended by the Delaware River Basin Commission following its July 7 "crisis" meeting.

The President declared portions of the four basin states "disaster areas," ordered New York to begin releasing 200 million gallons a day from their reservoirs as a "salt water buffer," the Corps of Engineers to install an emergency pump-pipeline system from Lake Hopatcong in New Jersey, and the Department of the Interior to drill emergency wells in the underground Passaic Lake to develop stand-by water supplies. And he also pledged to provide federal assistance to speed up the modifications to the intake at Torresdale so that Philadelphia could begin to draw water at low tide. [36]

By March of the following year the water supply conditions in the basin were substantially better. Although they were still about 80 billion gallons below what was usual for that time of the year, the amount of water in the New York reservoirs had made a 60 percent return to normal and the worst of the crisis seemed to be over. In the Basin Commission's *Emergency Resolution No. 9*, its earlier emergency declaration was terminated and New York was permitted to begin diverting up to 490 million gallons daily for New York City and to make releases required to sustain the flow at Montague at 1,525 cubic feet per second, which with the quantity in hand could be made without endangering available reserve levels.[37]

The drought seemed to prove the usefulness of the Delaware River Basin Compact. The *Journal* of the Water Pollution Control Federation did observe, however, that "if an organization made up of several states requires this degree of stimulation before difficult decisions are reached, its value and effectiveness will be quite limited." [38] This is not a fair assessment. The Delaware River Basin Commission cut its organizational teeth on the drought of the sixties. It was a new institution with a sizable and untested mandate. That it successfully negotiated the shoals of the drought, rather than collapsed in the face of difficulties, as did its earlier counterparts, was evidence of its strength.

# CHAPTER IX

# WHITE HOUSE CONFERENCE
## on
# NATURAL BEAUTY

*The people have a right to clean air, pure water, and to the preservation of the natural scenic, historic and esthetic values of the environment. Pennsylvania's public natural resources are the common property of all the people, including generations yet to come. As trustee of these resources, the Commonwealth shall conserve and maintain them for the benefit of all the people.*

The Pennsylvania Constitution

In his State of the Union Address, January 4, 1965, President Lyndon B. Johnson told the American people:

For over three centuries the beauty of America has sustained our spirit and enlarged our vision. We must act now to protect this heritage. . . . We must make a massive effort to save the countryside and establish — as a green legacy for tomorrow — more parks, more seashores and open spaces. . . .

A new and substantial effort must be made to landscape highways and provide places of relaxation and recreation wherever our roads run.

Within our cities imaginative programs are needed to landscape streets and transform open areas into places of beauty and recreation.

We will seek legal power to prevent pollution of our air and water before it happens. . . . We will increase research to learn more about control of pollution. We hope to . . . preserve unspoiled stretches of some of our waterways with a Wild Rivers bill. [1]

Several weeks later the President summed up his vision of a new America in a speech to Congress. He told the joint session: "The beauty of our land is a natural resource. Its preservation is linked to the inner prosperity of the human spirit." And he challenged them to regain and to retain the "natural beauty of our country." [2]

It was Johnson's intention, moreover, that this beauty-renaissance be the result of a "fruitful new partnership with the states and cities"; [3] therefore, he called a White House Conference on "natural beauty." [4] More than one-thousand conferees from across the country gathered in the auditorium of the new State Department building in Washington on May 24, 1965. The group was made up of architects, landscape designers, civic planners, members of Congress and the Executive Branch, and a broad range of conservationists. Among the attendees were the author and cities' critic, Jane Jacobs — the *Washington Post* called her a "force that brews lightning" — and to the surprise of the other delegates, Walter Reuther, President of the United Automobile Workers, who "popped up" in one session and suggested that mobilizing public opinion through unions and the churches would be "the key to the great society in which men can have both bread and roses." [5]

Laurance S. Rockefeller served as the conference chairman, but the President and especially Mrs. Johnson were in evidence during the two days. She sat and took notes throughout the conference and attended many of the individual panel meetings. Rockefeller made a few opening remarks at the beginning of the first joint session and then introduced Mrs. Johnson who gave the keynote speech. Following a standing ovation, the First Lady set the tone for the group by declaring:

> Ugliness creates bitterness. Ugliness is an eroding force on the people of our land. We are all here to try to change that.

She asked the delegates to find answers to the question of whether or not a "Great democratic society can generate the concerted drive to plan, and having planned, to execute great projects of beauty?" "Ugliness," she said, "has been allowed too long." Then she called on the Conference "to originate plans and projects both great and small," telling them, "great must be the scope of the major projects to redesign our urban areas, renew and brighten the gateways to our cities, cleanse, set in order, and dignify our riverfronts and our ports." [6]

□ □ □ □

Laurance Rockefeller, who had extensive credentials as a businessman, an environmentalist, and a philanthropist, had begun organizing the conference in February 1965 at the President's request. In choosing 120 panelists out of the three thousand nominations and applications he received, Rockefeller "sought a cross section of varying points of view," and "stressed the individual not the office" [7]

Reflecting the Johnsons' wish for "new and substantial efforts" the administration could take, Rockefeller's direction to the fifteen panels surveying ways to go about the quest for natural beauty was for "concrete, specific proposals for action . . ." Although the individual breakout groups dealt with such topics as parks and open space, noise abatement, historic building preservation, town and city beautification, and the knotty issue of highway billboards, Lewis Gould, a Lady Bird Johnson biographer, observed that Rockefeller [and the President] were especially interested in "intergovernmental relations." [8]

The substance of the intergovernmental relations review fell to Maurice K. and the Federal-State-Local Partnership Panel which he chaired. This group was charged with looking at ways to improve cooperation between federal, state, and local governments in the preservation of the nation's natural beauty.

After two days of discussion, the Federal-State-Local Partnership panel prepared a number of recommendations for the President. At the federal level they proposed: the establishment of a National Council on Natural Beauty and Recreation; the issuance of an Executive Order instructing Federal agencies to consider the environmental, aesthetic, and recreational aspects of their programs; the establishment of a major federal effort to provide programs of technical assistance [to the states], training, and research in the preservation of natural beauty and recreation; and the acceptance of private contributions in support of park acquisitions. [9]

Goddard's group also urged passage of the proposed Intergovernmental Cooperation Act of 1965 which was designed to assure local and regional planning review of proposed federal projects affecting community appearance.

At the state level, the Federal-State-Local Partnership Panel declared that "broad and permissive State enabling legislation" was needed that permitted local governments to finance recreation and natural beauty projects. Moreover, the panelists believed that each governor needed a "staff arm" for coordinating and developing a consistent state policy, and that state legislation was needed governing municipal planning and zoning that specifically would develop and salvage "the beauty potentials of their area." [10]

They also felt that the proposed National Council on Natural Beauty and Recreation should review federal grant-in-aid programs to eliminate conflicts and duplication, thus facilitating state and local participation with a minimum of confusion. They believed that the federal programs of technical assistance, training, and research they suggested would address the shortage of qualified personnel, which they insisted was a major bottleneck in accomplishing the conference's objectives of preserving the natural beauty of the nation.

❑ ❑ ❑ ❑

On the final day, the conferees gathered on the White House lawn to meet the President, but were driven inside to the East Room because of rain. There, in the same room in which — at the first Governor's White House Conference on Conservation fifty-seven years earlier, Harrisburg's J. Horace McFarland had raised a lone voice to claim that "one of America's greatest resources" is "her unmatched natural scenery," and then to link beauty to the nation's economic wealth and spiritual health,[11] President Johnson told those assembled:

> Today I worked and thought about problems in Viet Nam and the Dominican Republic.
> I had to consider decisions which might affect the security of this country . . . . Yet this may be the most important thing that I have done, . . . and I am confident this is the most important group that I will see. For this is part of what all the rest is for. . . .
> Crisis and conflict command the headlines. But it is your work that will shape the future. . . .
> For natural beauty is not a luxury for the satisfied. . . . It is not a pleasant frill or a superficial enjoyment. . . . It is more than a rich source of pleasure and recreations. It shapes our values, It molds our attitudes. It feeds our spirit, and it helps to make us the kind of men and women that we finally become. And the kind of men that we finally become in turn makes this great Nation. [12]

President Johnson then told the conferees that many of the proposals they advanced would be incorporated in next year's legislative program, while others would become the basis for immediate executive action. [13]

Johnson announced that he was sending a bill to the Congress that day designed to "eliminate outdoor advertising signs and junkyards from the sight of the interstate and primary highway systems." . . . This, he said, "is not a use of highway funds for an alien purpose. It is a recognition that a highway is not just a ribbon of concrete . . . it should serve all [our] human needs." [14]

The President also stated that he had directed the Defense Department to hold onto surplus military land until its potential for park and recreational purposes could be studied. This was no trivial idea. That year alone the Pentagon had declared 1.2 million acres of land as surplus, while the total in the National Park system was just 24 million acres. [15]

According to a *New York Times* editorial the next day, the conference was an "extremely useful and stimulating enterprise," but concluded it was inadequate. "Mere beautification is not enough!" stated the paper. "Trees are of little help if the air is polluted and the buildings ugly and misplaced. A flower bed cannot redeem a slum." [16]

Moreover, the newspaper claimed that the Congressmen and most federal officials who took part in the conference showed an unfortunate tendency to repeat the "tired thought" that most of the job had to be done at the local level and that "education was the biggest part of the answer." The editorial stated:

> Education, like more trees, is a value beyond dispute. But no local official or group of private citizens can effectively combat the automobile industry or the interstate highway planners or a syndicate of big investors out to ravage a seashore for private profit. [17]

And while the conferees had been busy Tuesday "getting underway," in an act of seemingly deliberate irony, as if to mock the purpose of the proceedings inside the State Department, workers constructing a new E Street expressway on the northside bulldozed and then chainsawed into pieces a twenty-foot maple that was the "last touch of greenery in a dusty little triangle." [18]

In summing up the two days, *Washington Post* staff writer, Wolf Von Eckardt wrote that a "recurring key word of the Conference was 'coordination.'" This, of course, was the area assigned to Maurice's panel. Von Eckardt quoted William H. Whyte, a Vice President of U.S. Steel and one of Rockefeller's conference lieutenants, as having told the President that "as far as coordinating programs is concerned, we have something of an "inverted pyramid." The burden of seeking out and coordinating all of the many federal and state programs falls most heavily on the groups least equipped to do the job — the local governments. They need help."

This, of course, is exactly the point Maurice had addressed when he oversaw the writing in his committee's final report that the "states must take steps to strengthen their organization, financing, and coordination to play their pivotal role in the Federal-State-local partnership."

A few weeks after he returned to Harrisburg, Maurice received a letter from Whyte. Writing from New York's Rockefeller Center, Whyte told Goddard:

> You did a wonderful job! We knew you would, of course, but it was a pleasure to see such a ticklish assignment handled with such fairness and skill. [19]

And in December of the following year, Whyte invited Maurice K. to attend a "small reception" in Whyte's suite at the Waldorf Hotel in Washington, D.C., following the Pennsylvania Society Dinner that year in honor of Roger M. Blough, U.S. Steel CEO. [20]

Although by May 1965 the rising flood waters of the Vietnam War were beginning to lap at the feet of the Johnson administration, and would engulf it a year later, the conference on natural beauty accomplished more than "a lot of fast running just to stay in place, like Alice and the Red Queen" as the *New York Times* had feared; nor did it "peter out into nonaction." There were achievements, perhaps even significant ones, for such an environment as the politically charged one that swept the nation during the period. Moreover, numbered among its accomplishments were several recommendations of Maurice K. and his Federal-State-Local Partnership panel.

First, President Johnson signed a Highway Beautification Act in October 1965. The act had critics and weaknesses, but for the first time there was public recognition that — in addition to other positive effects — as Mrs. Johnson had said following the signing of the bill, "Highway beautification is now the law of the land."

Then the nation's governors, mayors, and members of Congress each received a summary of the proceedings. Johnson's covering letter expressed the hope "that these recommendations will be studied and put to work to build a more beautiful America." A number of states, including Arizona, California and Pennsylvania, soon called similar meetings.

On May 1, 1966, a year after the conference, President Johnson issued an executive order establishing the recommended President's Council on Recreation and Natural Beauty, and simultaneously set up a Citizens' Advisory Committee on Recreation and Natural Beauty. [21] Such a favorable climate for preservation had been established, moreover, that a National Historic Preservation Act became law in October of the same year. Then two years later, in October 1968, President Johnson also signed a Redwoods National Park bill. During the ensuing years, moreover, he periodically asked his department heads for thorough reports on what they had done about natural beauty.

A year following the conference, Hugh Sidey reflected in *Life* magazine that beautification was probably the "single most successful Great Society venture so far." [22] And in 1984, Henry Diamond, one of the conference participants, told an audience at the Johnson Library that the White House Conference of 1965 was "a bridge from the traditional conservation to the new environmentalism." [23]

The long term-involvement of business, however, that Laurance Rockefeller, the President and the First Lady hoped would result (Rockefeller's chairmanship was intended to stimulate such action), never really developed. His seed-idea that the "concept of beauty as good business can and should be extended to the full range of corporate activity" [24] fell on infertile ground. On the other hand, state and federal cooperation did improve. Maurice Goddard, of course, had embarked in this direction long before May 1965, but the plethora of programs and the federal money that went with them, continued to flow unabated into Pennsylvania under his leadership.

❑ ❑ ❑ ❑

As early as 1958, Maurice had made abundantly clear in his talk "Parks and People" at the dedication of Coover Park in Dillsburg, Pennsylvania that cooperation was a major aspect of his management approach. Dillsburg (which is little more than a village) was hardly a significant forum on which to make such a point, but he emphasized that cooperation between the Department of Forests and Waters and the General State Authority had been essential in the development of the first thirteen state parks under his initial park construction program. Moreover, he declared his department had "established close relationships [with] the agencies of Pennsylvania interested in conservation, outdoor life, natural resources and park and recreation programs." He told the gathering:

> Effective administration requires cooperation and integration of effort between various agencies.

In spite of the Federal-State-Local Partnership Panel's urging to Congress, the Intergovernmental Cooperation Act did not become law until 1968. When the final version of the bill was considered by the Subcommittee on Executive and Legislative Reorganization, every witness who appeared, including top officials from many federal agencies and representatives of the National Governors' Conference, the National League of Cities, and the U.S. Conference of Mayors, favored the bill. It was also endorsed by every correspondent with the committee. [25]

The key word in the bill's title is misleading. Cooperation, like apple pie, is universally considered a good thing. Government agencies, however, like truculent neighbors, often have different, conflicting agendas and only "talk" to each other in formal ways and occasions. Those three anchors of bureaucracies — program, resources, and money — that all compete for, seldom engender any strong need for the recipients to cooperate once they receive their piece of the pie.

The main thrust, however, of the Intergovernmental Cooperation Act (Public Law 90-577) was not to exhort agencies to cooperate with each other, but to provide management mechanisms for all federal assistance, grants or grants-in-aid made to the states and municipalities; and to ensure they were coordinated with the Governor or legislature of the states receiving the assistance, and that Congress received annual reviews from each agency under the law. It also provided rules for the disposal of federal property within an urban area. [26]

The federal tax system had long been recognized as a highly efficient money-machine, but before the 1968 act the ability to distribute these funds back to the states and local governments was tied to many separate grant-in-aid laws administered by different departments often working directly with separate agencies deep within a state's bureaucracy. At the top of both the federal and state level, knowledge of these programs was often lacking. Moreover, a state's awareness of the availability of specific programs and money was also a hit-or-miss thing. The act turned what hithertofore had been a network of bumpy, secondary roads into an smooth Interstate system of largess.

❏ ❏ ❏ ❏

While the academic environment is conducive to developing collegiality among faculty members, the solo nature of classroom instructing does not foster a strong need for close cooperation or teamwork among academics. Maurice Goddard, however, had learned early at SHAEF headquarters, where Eisenhower had insisted that everyone regardless of nationality, position or ideology work together, or be moved, that good results can be assured best from a staff that is harmonious, and between agencies that cooperate with one another. It was the management philosophy that had taken him from SHAEF, to the head of the Forestry Department at Penn State, to the Pennsylvania Secretary of Forest and Waters, and finally to the White House Conference.

Writing for the Conservation Foundation in 1977 concerning the Allegheny National Forest in Pennsylvania's northwest corner,

William E. Shands stated that in the past relations between state officials and the Forest Service had been "cordial," but also had been concerned primarily with "protecting one's own turf," while at the local level "the difficulties were even more severe because of the uncertain income local governments received from the federal lands." By 1977, Shands claimed, "Far fewer collisions and confrontations occur among various levels of governments." Each layer of government is "more secure in its own role." Shands attributed this to the "emergence of a strong state land-use strategy" and a "stabilization of population and fair progress toward handling . . . problems." [27]

While Shands's points appear to be valid ones, this increased cooperation can also be traced at the state level directly to Maurice K.'s ideas on conservation and his fundamental management principles, and, perhaps, indirectly to those developed by his Federal-State-Local Partnership panel at the White House Conference on Natural Beauty in 1965.

Maurice K. believed strongly in working together at all levels even before he went to Washington in 1965 — that was why he was asked to head the partnership panel — but the conference helped bring his ideas into better focus and, more important, gave him a solid platform from which to promote them when he returned to Pennsylvania. They had become, if not the law of the land, the policy of both federal and Pennsylvania state resource agencies.

❑ ❑ ❑ ❑

The next year, Maurice induced Governor Scranton to hold a state conference on natural beauty." The Governor's Advisory Committee on Natural Resources and Beauty, which conducted the meeting at Hershey in September 1966, was chaired by Frank E. Masland Jr., Carlisle manufacturer, conservationist and explorer.

Masland, who had attended the White House conference with Maurice K., was well known within the environmental community.

He had worked with the National Park Service on numerous occasions and was called on frequently by Park Service officials as a member of the National Parks Advisory Committee. He had led several early explorations into the Canyonlands National Park in Utah, where he drew up the boundary maps for the park service. Moreover, he had helped set up the park systems in nations such as Kenya, Uganda, Tanzania, and Ethiopia. [28]

In laying out the objectives for the Governor's Conference on Natural Beauty, Masland told the delegates that "ugliness breeds ugliness, crime, corruption, disregard for law and order" and that the "value of beauty and the price of ugliness can be reckoned in dollars." He asked them to consider that "the kind of environment we provide for our children is the "measure of our culture and our maturity." Then, in a cautionary statement, he told them, "Beauty is not the child of law nor the product of force. Beauty is the fruit of knowledge." [29]

Masland emphasized that the "success of the conference would be judged by what transpires after it is over." It would come only if the participants developed a "continuing program of an effective nature," some "continuing form of activity" that was the result of "specific recommendations from the conference." [30]

Secretary of the Interior Stewart Udall came up from Washington to address the Governor's banquet on the evening of the first day. He emphasized the importance of the delegates' work at the conference in "restoring our natural beauty." But he told them:

> One of the biggest and most costly public undertakings in the next ten years will be cleaning up the nation's streams. Whatever the cost, it must be spent. [31]

While there was a panel at Hershey that discussed the "State and Local Partnership," Maurice served on the one that dealt with "Large Parks, Scenic Roads and Open Space." [32] Dr. M. Graham Netting of the Carnegie Institute Museum at Pittsburgh acted as chairman. Netting claimed that "man cannot conquer nature. We are a part of nature — bigger, more noisy, and more destructive

161

than a mouse but subject to the same natural laws. When the good water is gone, the good soil covered or wasted, the good air tainted, we shall surely perish." [33]

Maurice K. told the group that, while the "alternative to open space in most parts of Pennsylvania is obviously development," there are ways in which the state can reverse the trend. He noted that acquisition through Project 70 funds — which, he asserted the "people of the critical urban counties [had] truly passed for us" — was only one way to protect open space. He declared that Pennsylvania needed legislation authorizing acquisition of "less-than-fee" interest in land. By this he meant that deeds would have provisions for rights-of-way, lease backs, conservation easements, and development restrictions. [34]

The private owner would still be the owner. He would still pay taxes, could sell the land, and could "use it," but he would be prevented from "building it up with motels, gas stations, or other [similar] types of use." And although Maurice did not consider zoning to have been particularly effective in Pennsylvania, he proposed additional zoning law enactments and strict protection and vigorous enforcement against encroachments once they were law. The big "failure" he saw in zoning was that we "do not pay anything for this encumbrance on a man's property." [35]

Maurice closed his remarks by cautioning the delegates that shorter work hours and automation would create increasing amounts of leisure time. While he believed that parks were part of the answer, he told his audience, "The warning is clear; we must raise our sights to ever higher horizons, greater and expanded goals, if we are to meet the future." [36]

◻ ◻ ◻ ◻

Just as at the White House Conference on Natural Beauty, the attendees at Hershey took strong exception to the presence of highway billboards, junkyards and litter on city streets and in the

162

countryside. The summary report of the Roadside Control sub-committee, chaired by Donald C. Wagner of the Fels Institute of Local and State Government, declared that "as all highways are built with public money, . . . the public interest in highway amenities should prevail over any private interest which might use adjacent lands . . . to impair or destroy those amenities." [37]

Echoing the pleas of City Beautiful advocates in the early decades of the century for the elimination of roadside signage, the panel expressed the conviction that the outdoor advertising industry had been unable to "regulate itself." It recommended that all billboards be forbidden that were visible from federally financed Interstate and primary highways and that all on-premise signs in rural and scenic areas come under "stringent regulation." The panelists endorsed a billboard-control bill that had been proposed by the State Highway Department even though they thought that "much stronger regulations" were needed.

Governor Scranton closed the conference by announcing that he was setting up a Citizens Steering Committee and appointing Frank Masland to head it. Formation of this group had been one of the "urgent" resolutions of the conference. The other three were the development of a "statewide planning study and inventory of state lands and waters to help determine long-range reclamation and beautification" needs; "establishment of a centralized state agency to coordinate the work of local citizens and groups"; and "passage of the [newly proposed] bill to spend $500 million . . . to *develop* conservation, recreation, and historical landmark sites" throughout Pennsylvania that had been *acquired* with Project 70 funds. [38]

❑ ❑ ❑ ❑

At both the Federal and State Conferences on Natural Beauty, education, especially of the young, was one of the major panel recommendations. Although Frank Masland put it in the most lyrical language when he told the delegates at Hershey, "Beauty is the fruit of knowledge," heightened public awareness was universally felt to be necessary to educate society and convince legislators to think positively about conservation matters. Moreover, the attendees at both conferences believed that efforts at raising this awareness should start with the very young and continue throughout adulthood. This meant that those involved in environmental concerns had to build bridges to the newspapers, radio and television. The theme of the Teaching and Preaching Natural Beauty Panel at Hershey was that "children have an insatiable curiosity in the wonders of nature and its beauty. That curiosity must be constantly fed so that it lasts a lifetime." [39]

Not only did the President and Mrs. Johnson host a Youth Conference on Natural Beauty and Conservation in Washington during which they asked the young representatives "to dream impossible dreams and to translate the dreams and talk of today into the action of tomorrow," but a number of youth training programs came into being in the states under the Economic Opportunity Act (Public Law 88-452). Although they were designed primarily to help "wage war on youth poverty," they were also intended to be educational in nature.

The Pennsylvania Department of Forests and Waters put together a master plan that included seventy-eight separate projects, forty-five in the state forest districts, and thirty-one in the state parks, along with a few in the agency's Harrisburg headquarters. The Department of Public Welfare selected the enrollees from families that were on public assistance, arranged for physical examinations, sub-contracted with the state YMCA for transportation to and from the work sites. Forests and Waters' employees provided on-the-job supervision and the tools necessary to instruct the participants in the elements of conservation use and the development of the state's natural resources. And in an effort to start turning William Whyte's "inverted pyramid" (where the local governments had the largest burden and the least resources) on its base, the Federal Government provided ninety percent of the program cost. [40]

This program was followed in later years by other federally-funded youth programs: the Youth Conservation Corps (1974) and the Young Adult Conservation Corps (1978). The primary residential camps in Pennsylvania for these programs were in the Delaware and Moshannon State Forests. Corps members were used in forest fire protection work, tree planting, timber stand improvement, trail construction and repair, and wildlife habitat and stream development work. During the life of these programs the Department expended more than five million dollars on them. [41]

□ □ □ □

While "beauty," natural or man-made, is considered a desirable objective for a society, men and women have debated exactly what constitutes civic beauty since the turn-of-the-century City Beautiful movement. Those earlier advocates of beauty developed zoning and building setback ordinances, billboard control measures, and laws establishing governmental agencies to formalize decision making on "protecting" the environment and regulating undesirable development. The implementation of these measures has rarely been considered, however, on the basis of "beauty," which has remained largely a hidden objective. In court decision after court decision where beauty did surface as an issue, it has been considered to exist largely in the eyes of the beholder, thus unenforceable. As a result, those who attempt to enforce beautification laws, generally do so under the guise of public health and welfare, not "beauty."

While some legislative actions, such as the 1966 National Historic Preservation Act, can be considered to have been successful, the beautification battle is still being waged despite the efforts of both the earlier City Beautiful movement and of the Johnson Administration. Mine discharges continue to pollute streams, billboards and junkyards still flourish, land development proceeds at a high rate, and however we define it, "natural beauty" continues to disappear at an alarming pace.

For Maurice K., too, beauty was largely an abstract concept. He appreciated the beautiful in nature — he never forgot, for example, the "spectacular and beautiful setting" of the campsite of the New Church Assembly at Fryeburg, Maine, where he first got to know Ethel [42] — but as did most, he considered its worth, its evaluation to be a subjective issue. He understood scientific matters — reading the science section of the Sunday *New York Times* was a regular activity — but aesthetic matters, especially those on any broad scale, such as deciding what constitutes a beautiful town, were largely beyond rationalization and thus outside his daily deliberations. A lake in a park was important based on the demands placed on it for boating, fishing, and swimming — all measurable activities. Its aesthetic value, its intrinsic worth as an object for contemplation, on the other hand, was not quantifiable and, therefore, not one that the Secretary of Forests and Waters was particularly concerned with when building parks. [43]

The old McGee/Pinchot [44] scientific and professional approach to the solution of conservation issues, one that relied on the measured decisions of legislatures and agencies of the government staffed by technicians, was beginning to unravel. In its place a new environmental movement was emerging, one in which popular groups, often single purpose "community" or "neighborhood based" ones, in the writer Robert Gottlieb's words, began to exert pressure on previously appropriate conservation activities and decisions. They were, according to Gottlieb, beginning to force a "debate around new agendas and the question of values and priorities." [45]

No longer would agency heads be able to merely consult a few powerful, select private-interest groups before implementing their plans. Increasingly the nation's Maurice Goddards would have to anticipate accommodating widely varying personal and emotional issues along with those they could scientifically quantify.

Although the 1965 White House Conference on Natural Beauty was driven in the old conservation-minded mold of "experts" recommending new laws, Maurice K. would find in the coming years that pressure to modify his ideas on conservation and adjust his actions as head of the Department of Forests and Waters, to take into account the lines of the new environmentalism, was greatly intensified.

□ □ □ □

The years of the mid-1960's were not only highly productive ones for Maurice K., they were also ones in which he received wide recognition. He was invited to participate in numerous conferences. Many he declined because of the press of business in Pennsylvania, but others he attended. At the 1965 Water for Texas Conference in November 1965, he was the key note speaker. As reported by the *Houston Post*, he told the conferees that "because needs, uses and interests compete and conflict, there must be a breaking point somewhere. You just can't provide everything for everybody. . . . [The] solution will require the co-operation and co-ordinated efforts of every level of government, as well as the understanding of every individual." He then cited some of the conflicts confronting any water program:

> Should dams be large or small? Which will do the best job? How is the best use determined for a prime dam site? Can reforestation and upstream land treatment for flood control be relied upon completely?
> How are the people's needs reconciled for recreation, water supply, power, agriculture and industry and flood protection? Which of these items should have precedence? [46]

Maurice K. sent his regrets to Gov. Sam P. Goddard of Arizona, who invited him to be the chairman on an "Air and Water Pollution" committee at a statewide Conference on Natural Beauty in August 1965. [47] And rather than attend personally he sent Walter Lyon, Chief of the Division of Sanitary Engineering of the State Department of Health, to the University of Pittsburgh's Seminar on Water Pollution and Water Pollution Control in May of the same year. [48]

The following year, Maurice K. received some unexpected recognition, including an honorary Doctor of Science Degree from the University of Maine, and a Distinguished Public Service Citation from Dickinson College, in Carlisle, Pennsylvania. Ethel and the boys, Kim, who was 16 and Mark, who was 8, accompanied him to Orono for the awarding of the degree. Then they toured the campus. The Dickinson College Citation, which was not quite as prestigious, but perhaps more heartfelt, read in part:

> Dickinson college this day salutes you. . . The art of conservation is one which requires rare talents. In an age of excess, a period of abundance and a time of plenty, extravagance is easy. . . . You have been far seeing — instrumental in acquiring tracts of land for the State and its people; in providing parks and recreational areas in sectors becoming more and more crowded. . . . Dickinson College commends you warmly and with appreciation for your progressive achievements. [49]

Left: Secretary Goddard and Arthur B. Van Buskirk, Chairman of Pittsburgh's Point Park Committee, pose with an artist's sketch of Pittsburgh's Point State Park. The park, one of several urban state parks across Pennsylvania, was developed jointly by the City of Pittsburgh and the Department of Forests and Waters. (photo courtesy of the Pittsburgh *Post-Gazette*.)

Maurice K. and Secretary of Interior Stewart Udall, the U.S. Commissioner to the Delaware River Basin Commission, conferring during dinner at the February 27, 1964 reorganization meeting held in New York City. To Goddard's right is Vernon Northrop, the Alternate Federal Commissioner. This meeting marked the passing of the commission chairmanship from Udall to Governor Rockefeller. (photo courtesy of the Delaware River Basin Commission.)

John Rex and John Oliver of the Western Pennsylvania Conservancy "shake hands" over a Western Pennsylvania land transfer deal between the Conservancy and the Department of Forests and Waters. In 1995, John Oliver became the first Secretary of the Department of Conservation and Natural Resources. (from the private collection of Mrs. John Rex.)

John Rex at his desk in the Harrisburg offices of the Department of Forests and Waters. Rex was the long-time land acquisitions chief for the department and a close associate and frequent traveler with Secretary Goddard. (from the private collection of Mrs. John Rex.)

Right: Secretary Goddard pointing out a feature in the valley below Tharp Knob, Ohiopyle, July 7, 1962. (photo courtesy of the Western Pennsylvania Conservancy.)

Maurice Goddard with John O. Simonds admiring a statue and some of the landscaping highlights for Pittsburgh's Point State Park. Goddard was the guest speaker at the June 1963 meeting of the American Landscape Architects. The meeting marked the occasion of Simonds' installation as the organization's new president. (photo courtesy of the Pittsburgh *Post-Gazette*.)

Maurice Goddard addressing a group gathered at the April 9, 1956 unveiling of the Dr. Joseph Trimble Rothrock Plaque in McVeytown, Pennsylvania. (photo courtesy of the Department of Conservation and Natural Resource, Bureau of State Parks.)

The Secretary discusses an item with two of the participants in the Western Pennsylvania Conservancy outing at Ohiopyle on July 7, 1962. (photo courtesy of the Western Pennsylvania Conservancy.)

The view looking out across the lake from the boat marina at M.K. Goddard State Park. (photo courtesy of the Department of onservation and Natural Resource, Bureau of State Parks.)

Governor Raymond Shafer and Secretary Goddard inspecting the sign for M.K. Goddard State Park at the October, 1969 ceremony honoring Maurice Goddard. It was at this ceremony at the William Penn Memorial Museum in Harrisburg that Governor Shafer announced that Sandy Creek State Park in Mercer County was to be renamed the M. K. Goddard State Park. (photo courtesy of the Department of Conservation and Natural Resource, Bureau of State Parks.)

Maurice Goddard speaking at the 1962 dedication ceremony for the dam on the West Branch of Codorus Creek. This joint Glatfelter Paper Company and Department of Forests and Waters project was typical of the cooperative state and private ventures for which Maurice Goddard was widely known and respected. (photo courtesy of the Department of Conservation and Natural Resource, Bureau of State Parks.)

Maurice Goddard, John Haas, Chairman of the William Penn Foundation, Robert Bartlett and Helga Wagner look over some of the unique characteristics of the Pennypak Watershed Association Wilderness Park, April 24, 1976. (photo courtesy of the Department of Conservation and Natural Resource, Bureau of State Parks.)

Kinzua Dam on the Allegheny River near Warren Pennsylvania. The
construction of this dam, which was erected by the U.S. Corps of Engineers,
engendered years of controversy that eventually reached the pages of the
*New York Times*. Today the dam is the center of a multi-faceted recreational
area. (Photo courtesy of the Northern Alleghenies Vacation Region and the
Allegheny Bean Company.)

# SUMMER 1990
# Pennsylvania
# Forests

EARTH DAY
THE TURNING

**INSIDE:**

PFA Salutes:
    Dr. M.K. Goddard
Penn ReLeaf
Annual Meeting
Forest Fire Wardens

PFA DEDICATION

Pennsylvania Forestry Association

Maurice K. Goddard helping to distribute 10,000 white spruce seedlings, provided by the
Pennsylvania Game Commission, at Harrisburg's celebration of Earth Day in April 1990.

# CHAPTER X

## Public Land Law Review Commissioner

> Our land is more valuable than your money.
> It will last forever. As long as the sun shines
> and the waters flow, this land will be here to
> give life to man and animals. . . . It was put
> here by the Great Spirit and we cannot sell it
> because it does not belong to us. . . . As a
> present to you, we will give you anything we
> have that you can take with you; but the land,
> never. [1] [Unidentified Blackfeet Chief]

By 1966 Maurice K.'s reputation had traveled well west of the Alleghenies, east of the Delaware, and south of the Mason-Dixon Line. Not only was he a panel chairman at the White House Conference on Natural Beauty in May 1965, but the preceding December, President Johnson had named Maurice K. to be one of the four professional members of the Land Law Review Commission.

This national recognition came about for a number of reasons. From his earliest days as the Secretary of Forests and Waters, Maurice K. had been assigned to several interstate study commissions. These assignments entailed working with neighboring states as well as the federal government. While the most important of these was probably the Delaware River Basin Advisory Commission, which placed him in contact with professionals and politicians from New Jersey, New York and Delaware as well as the U.S. Department of the Interior, there were also two other interstate river-basin review groups, those for the Susquehanna and for the Potomac Rivers.

Then, too, Governor Lawrence had close ties with the Kennedy Administration, to which it was believed he had delivered Pennsylvania's electoral votes in the 1960 election. And Lawrence's opinion of his Secretary of Forests and Waters was such that when Stewart Udall suggested the Maurice K. come to the Department of the Interior as an Under-Secretary, Lawrence told Udall that Maurice K. would have a job in Pennsylvania as long as he wanted it.

So when President Johnson announced on December 30, 1964, the appointment of Maurice K. as one of the six public members to serve, with the twelve members from Congress, on the Land Law Review Commission, it was viewed as an appropriate step up for the Secretary of Forests and Waters. The Land Law Review Commission was charged by the President with making a "comprehensive review of the nation's public land laws, practices and problems" and "whether, and to what extent, revisions of those laws are necessary." [2]

Senator Clinton P. Anderson of New Mexico, and Representative Wayne H. Aspinall of Colorado, who were the senior members and Co-Chairmen of the Commission, issued their call for the new group to convene in Washington, D. C. on July 14, 1965. Among the prominent members of Congress named to the group were Senators Alan Bible of Nevada, and Henry M. Jackson of Washington. Of the six Representatives named initially to the group only two remained throughout the five years of its deliberations, John P. Saylor of Pennsylvania and Laurence J. Burton of Utah. Morris K. Udall of Arizona, Stewart's brother, replaced one of the departing representatives.

In their announcement Senator Anderson and Congressman Aspinall pointed out that outside of Alaska there are approximately 354 million acres of public lands being administered by various agencies of the government, of which approximately 175 million acres were uncommitted by legislative authority for any specific use. Additionally, they said there were approximately 364 million acres in Alaska that would come within the scope of the Commission's study. [3]

Among the President's public-member appointments, in addition to Maurice K., were Governor Philip Hoff of Vermont, and Laurance Rockefeller of New York. In his letter accepting the appointment to the commission, Maurice K. told Congressman Aspinall, who was the Chairman of the Committee on Interior and Insular Affairs, that he considered the assignment a "vital task," one he considered to be "the highest honor I have been accorded." [4] And he told an old friend, William E. Towell, the Director of the Missouri Conservation Commission: "Frankly, I consider this one of the most challenging assignments I have ever had."

□ □ □ □

Before he left for the first meeting of the Land Law Review Commission, however, Maurice K. made a critical decision affecting the management of Pennsylvania forests. After years of managing the forests for commercial harvest by the individual-tree-selection method, the satisfactory natural reproduction of many areas and the quality of the residual stands appeared to be deteriorating, rather than improving. Moreover, the U.S. Forest Service and groups such as the Forestry Relations Counsel in Washington, were also of the opinion that in many instances "all-age management [where individual trees are marked for cutting] presents an illusion of good management, even where it is not making the maximum use of the forest acre." [5] With this in mind, Maurice K. made the decision to permit even-aged management — often called "clear cutting" — in Pennsylvania forests. The underlying purpose of "management" was, of course, to optimize production of trees for commercial sale.

There were a number of problems associated with even-aged management. There is little beauty remaining following a clear-cutting of an area. When Richard Thorpe, the State Forester, took

Maurice K. to view the first Pennsylvania clear-cut, a prominent two-hundred-acre slash in the Michaux Forest south of Harrisburg, Maurice K. blurted out: "J___ C____, what did you do?" [6] The unsavory view of an area devoid of all living growth in the middle of a forest did and still does, of course, present a dilemma for the forester. Regardless of the commercial gains to be achieved, the public often sees even-aged management as a desecration of the forest. One writer calls it a "Crime Against Nature." Although the ecological damage can be substantial — to the forest floor, wildlife, and water containment — it makes sense from the forest-as-timber-resource point of view.

Clear-cutting was not a new concept, however, in 1965. The practice had originated in Germany and was known in this country early in the century. Among the words in the *Vocabulary of Forest Terms* used at the State Forest Academy at Mont Alto in 1909 the German terms *kahlabtrieb* and *kahlabschlag* were defined as "clear-cutting" or "clear-felling."

In Pennsylvania, Maurice K. and the Forestry Bureau established guidelines to control the extent of and to minimize the problems associated with clear-cutting, not just those relating to the aesthetics of the remaining forest, but also, those concerning the health of the forest areas surrounding a clear-cut. According to Forests and Waters policy — perhaps resulting from the sight of the first such cut in Michaux — the area a state forester was permitted to mark for clear-cutting was not to exceed a total of one hundred acres; the clear-cutting was not to be done within one hundred feet of a stream or lake, was not to detract from the "asethetics and recreational values of the area," and was not to be in a location such as on a slope that would be prone to erosion. [7]

Each District Forester had to request permission to clear cut an area. Each request had to be detailed as to size and area, and be located precisely on the map of the forest being proposed for such treatment. Each request was reviewed first by a team in the field and then in Harrisburg where it was amended as deemed appropriate. During the first half of 1965, Maurice K. personally responded to each District Forester, either concurring in his recommendation or supplying the necessary revisions to the original proposal.

While we don't know exactly what Maurice K. thought of clear-cutting, we can be reasonably certain he didn't agonize over the decision of whether or not to approve it. His life mantra was: Deliberate, Decide, Do!  And that is what he probably did when the Forestry Bureau first recommended clear-cutting to him.

□  □  □  □

The Land Law Review Commission lost little time getting down to work and set an ambitious schedule at its first meeting on January 24, 1965.  The chairmen scheduled eleven three-day working sessions throughout the remainder of the year. Within a few months, too, the Commission was traveling across the country. Rather than visit each state, however, it met in selected regional locations to discuss the issues and problems of the area with the regional authorities.  When the Commissioners went to New Orleans, for example, they not only discussed riverine issues of the lower Mississippi River states, but also spent a day reviewing off-shore oil operations.

The pattern for many of their regional meetings was established early.  When the group went to Boston to review issues and concerns peculiar to the Northeastern United States, for example, the Commissioners not only met with representatives of the Governors of the Northeastern states, the committee's technical staff met with their local counterparts, and the full committee then held public meetings, which sometimes lasted as long as three days. Following each of these tours, one of the members would be assigned the job of writing up a comprehensive report on the trip.

By early 1966 the commission had traveled across extensive portions of the country.  By that time it had visited Salt Lake City, Boston, Albuquerque, Denver, and Seattle, and during June and

July of that year, the Commissioners also spent several weeks visiting four cities in Alaska. Maurice K. was charged with preparing the full report of the Alaskan meetings for presentation before the Commission at its September meeting in Denver. [8]

The Commission reviewed laws and administrative procedures pertaining not just to land, but to timber, water, fish, wildlife, agriculture, minerals, outdoor recreation, regional and local land use planning, federal land grants to the states, even such issues as the appropriateness of charges and fees being collected from those who used federal lands.

User fees were one of the "hot-button" issues of the day among conservationists and politicians. [9] Maurice K. had a definite, well-formed opinion on the subject of user fees — at least those associated with parks. Maurice K. questioned, for example, whether the "user is the sole recipient" of park benefits. To him the "benefits of a park system are so broad as to accrue to all of our citizens." As he told Governor Scranton when the Pennsylvania House was considering tieing such a "pay-as-you-go" proposal to Project 70 enabling legislation:

> I cannot take exception to the basic philosophy. . . . This is only true, however, when a positive definition of the recipients of the benefits can be made. . . . I assume that a park is considered to be an important element in the local economic frame-work. [10]

And in answer to a memorandum from James Reichley, Governor Scranton's Legislative Secretary, Maurice K. told Reichley that he had studied the question of levying fees on various aspects of Pennsylvania parks program "intensively." He summarized his views for Reichley:

> I believe that the benefits accruing to Pennsylvania from its parks are so many and so varied that all of our citizens should bear the burden of its cost equally. Like our public schools, our parks have such broad and diverse effects upon the well-being of the commonwealth that the fairest method of supporting the program is by direct and total subsidy from the tax income deposited in the General Fund.. [11]

□ □ □ □

The Land Law Review Commissioners took rail and air tours of vast sections of the country. And, in addition to the review of large amounts of reading material such as reports, meeting testimony, and local laws and regulations, Maurice K. brought back lighter regional reading matter. From Helena, Montana, for example, he returned with three books that he was reading "simultaneously": *Cow Country* by Edward Dale, *Footprints Along the Yellowstone* by L. W. Randall, and *The Battle of the Little Big-Horn* by Mari Sandoz.

In a letter to John Willard, who served as a tour guide for the Commission in Montana, Maurice K. wrote:

> You are the best tour guide I ever encountered. You knew the country intimately and you had all the answers. . . . I am envious of the great environment you have. It is truly magnificent country. . . . It was very enjoyable as well as educational.
>
> Maybe the ownership patterns of the public lands and the management problems are not so difficult after all! It appears as though we all have problems of one type or another. [12]

When they visited Colorado they spent two days in Denver, with side trips to Aspen, Gunnison and Craig. The Colorado Host Committee provided the commission members with "pressurized" Fairchild F-27 planes to make certain they enjoyed "maximum comfort and excellent visibility" as they flew from site to site during the field trip phase of their visit. [13]

Maurice K. came back from Colorado "particularly impressed" with the "degree of multiple-use" being employed on public lands, and also with the "lack of really serious conflicts." At the same time, he acknowledged in a letter to C. P. Martin, a land manager for Union Carbide in Colorado, "There are many problems and differences of opinions, but I am confident that the Commission will be able to make some worthwhile recommendations." [14] And after effusing over Denver and Colorado and the treatment he had received, he told Governor John A. Love essentially the same thing, then thanked him for time he had devoted to the visitors. "It was gracious of you to spend so much time with us personally."

During these trips for the Land Law Review Commission, Maurice K. also had an opportunity to visit with old friends and acquaintances. When the commissioners visited Jackson Hole, Wyoming, for example, he and John Mattoon, Assistant Regional Forester of the Intermountain Region of the U.S. Forest Service, spent some time reminiscencing about Penn State and Mattoon's student days with Maurice K. at the Blue Jay Camp.

□ □ □ □

The notion of traveling, seeing, learning about new things and ideas was an important part of Maurice K.'s essential nature. And the one thing aside from his conservation work with the land and water that he seemed to enjoy was reading history or biographies, especially of the Presidents. Following the Land Law Review Commission trip to Montana, for example, he wrote of the state, "There certainly is a lot of interesting history and [I] am only sorry one's life is so short. I am more convinced every day that I do not know very much."

And he often "relaxed" at home by reading technical or scientific books and journals. When, for example, Congressman Wayne Aspinall sent him a stack of briefing material from the U.S. Government Printing Office following Maurice K.'s appointment to the Land Law Review Commission, he wrote back that he had "spent a most enjoyable evening reading a good portion" of it. Then he spent the next finishing it up. And again following the Commission's 1967 trip to Idaho, after writing to tell Senator Len B. Jordan, "I am truly impressed by the diversity and magnitude of Idaho," he mentioned, "Last evening I read a good deal of the literature your associates provided." [15]

His traveling, like Maurice K.'s work, was becoming so pervasive, however, that his relationship with Ethel and the boys, Kimball and Mark, suffered as a result. He had always placed family second to work, but by the mid-sixties his was like a military family during war. He was largely an absentee father. When he wasn't traveling on Commission business, or for lectures to national organizations, it was for state business: speaking to scores of local groups each year, studying sites for parks, forests, or water-supply facilities, assisting in difficult land acquisitions, working on legislation or committee or department proposals, or preparing for appearances before either a state or U.S. Congressional committee as an advocate for positions he or the Governor supported.

In addition to traveling, Maurice K. — either from the press of work or the tension at home — would from time to time, like a state representative from a western Pennsylvania county, take a room in downtown Harrisburg. To Kimball and Mark, their parents both seemed to be consumed by demons: Maurice K. by work, Ethel by drink. Both are demons that may make a person more interesting to the casual observer, but seldom agreeable up close. Mark, the younger of the two boys, suffered especially.

On occasion the family would drive to Pinchot State Park, but they never took a real vacation as a family. Even on these day outings, which were the only times they would see their father "relax," the boys seldom felt close to him; he always seemed distant and unwilling to converse intimately with them. Moreover, Maurice K., the staunch advocate of planning, rarely offered any ideas of things he and the boys might do together. When Kimball would ask, "What can we do?" it was often, "Well, what do you want to do?" And according to Mark, although his father had been on the faculty of Penn State, he made no effort to instruct them in subjects such as tree or plant identification, or on other aspects of the woods, or talk to them of his efforts in the development of water-based recreation facilities like Pinchot State Park. [16]

During Maurice K.'s early years in state government, Ethel had occasionally attended state affairs to which wives were invited, but she soon began declining all such invitations, even those to the Governor's residence.  As a mark of the difficulties at home, Maurice K. sometimes even had these "regrets" sent by Nellie S. Howard, his personal secretary.  In one case, Howard took the extraordinary step of placing the blame on the press of Maurice K.'s work:

> Mrs. Goddard expresses her thanks [but] she has had to cope with the Secretary's difficult schedule, since many activities relating to the Department of Forests and Waters occur during weekends. [17]

And Maurice K.'s close co-workers and friends never saw the inside of the Goddard residence in Camp Hill.  Those who came to pick him up for meetings or to discuss some business were always met at the front door, even when the conversation there was an extended one.  They soon came to believe the reason for the lapse in civility was that Ethel, rather than the house, was not presentable.

□ □ □ □

Maurice K. seemed eager, like a politician, to accept invitations to speak anywhere his schedule would permit.  He spoke to the Water for Texas Conference, to the North American Wildlife Conference in Missouri, and then traveled to Worcester, Massachusetts, to talk on "Conservation, The Neglected Frontier of Research." [18] He told the Eighth Annual Scientific Briefing crowd gathered at the Worcester Polytechnic Institute that all our supplies of raw water "are not going to do us much good unless we get them developed, cleaned up, regulated, and adequately managed." After stressing the importance of efficient watershed management, he told the gathering:

> Industry must learn to re-circulate and re-use water, . . . [and] much more research has to be done about streams and their assimilative capacity problems involving water pollution and the movement of underground water. [19]

And Maurice K. was even flattered with letters informing him that he was a prospective candidate to head a school in Natural Biosciences — a title that "fascinated" him — at a major university. He wrote back to E. J. Dyksterhuis, the chairman of the nominating committee:

> As you probably know, I was recently re-appointed Secretary of the Department of Forests and Waters by Governor Raymond P. Shafer. . . . I am only about half-way through a $70,000,000 bond issue for the acquisition of open space lands, and on May 16, the voters of Pennsylvania acted favorably on a $500,000,000 Land and Water Conservation and Reclamation Fund. . . . In view of these challenges, I prefer to remain in my present position. [20]

□  □  □  □

Maurice K.'s trip to Colorado in September 1966 with the Land Law Review Commission was not his first to that area that year. In May, Walter Lyon, a water quality expert in the Pennsylvania Department of Health, had made arrangements for him to debate Floyd Dominy, who was head of the U.S. Bureau of Reclamation. The topic of their debate was: "Eastern vs. Western Water." It took place at a meeting of the American Society of Civil Engineers at the Denver Hilton Hotel.

Before they began Maurice K. kept pacing around, like a fighter itching to get in the ring, pressing Lyon, "Lets get going!" But people continued arriving well beyond the scheduled start time, so Lyon stalled while they set up more seats in the Hilton Ballroom. By the time the debate began, nearly a thousand people were on hand. [21]

As Maurice K. opened the debate, Walter Lyon was in the Chair and Ray Lindsay of the White House was serving as Referee. Maurice K. took the position that eastern money had been sent westward for several decades to "water the west," to the disadvantage of eastern farmers. According to him, a farmer in

Lancaster was paying taxes to provide water to western competitors, who were being subsidized at a rate as high as $1,000 an acre to outproduce the easterner. He agreed that "watering the west" was important, even necessary, but that eastern agricultural interests should be getting comparable "water dollars." [22]

Maurice K. claimed, after quoting the comparative amounts involved, that "it's ridiculous to keep placing eastern farms in the soil bank, while bringing marginal western land into production by water projects," thus charging the taxpayers twice. We should, he asserted, "put abandoned eastern farmland back into production first." He also felt that it was wrong to justify public power projects on the basis that their "primary purpose" was to produce power to pump water for "questionable irrigation projects." He proposed that private dollars should have been used for such ventures. And then Maurice K. summarized the plight of water management in the East by telling the audience, the "eastern water administrator knows only frustration when he goes before Congress for money for a water project. Many of these have taken over thirty years to get underway." And he got a good laugh, when he told the delegates:

He's handed a crumb and the cake goes West. [23]

Dominy took the position that there really is no East vs. West water problem, but rather what is needed is a broad national perspective on water issues regardless of region. He made the point that it has been the historic role of the federal government to support national expansion, especially where a project was too costly or where it was unlikely that private sources were interested in doing it. Moreover, Dominy argued that there was little "conflict" over crops. According to him, crops raised in the West primarily "complemented" rather than competed with those raised in the East. [24]

The referee for the debate was Ray K. Lindsay of the White House. After declaring that both men were "mostly right," he expressed the opinion that unfortunately the debate was "looking backwards" when it needed to "look ahead." Lindsay claimed that it was necessary to look at other means of controlling water than "dams, levees and aqueducts," the same kinds of facilities that were available to Hammurabi. He cited better flood-plain management, the improvement of food production by technology rather than irrigation, and the reduction of water consumption by improved techniques of manufacturing and methods of personal usage. Then Lindsay added that what was needed was to charge users "based on the true cost of delivering the water to them." [25]

If the debate was a "draw" as Lindsay claimed, Maurice K. could take satisfaction in knowing that his presentation "was a major element in the gratifying success" of the Denver meeting of the American Society of Civil Engineers. In his letter of thanks the Executive Secretary of the Society, William H. Wisely, told him, "We want you to know that we do realize the magnitude of your contribution, and that it is greatly appreciated." [26]

◻ ◻ ◻ ◻

In many respects Dominy and Goddard were similar. Both men were driven, sometimes domineering leaders, and were so self-assured they often displayed an arrogance that intimidated those around them. While in Dominy this self-assurance led to claims that he was ruthless, in Maurice K. it manifested itself more as a persistent, persuasive fact-and-figure-driven arrogance that he used to dispel doubt and dissent, especially any based on "uninformed" opinion. Even his closest subordinates had to be careful what they said in his presence. One of these, the hydrologist Alan Somerville, who worked on river basin issues, described his relationship to his boss as always "touchy." [27]

Dominy's rise was precipitous, his manner presumptuous. He took over the Bureau of Reclamation by forcing out its head, and then instilled a fear-based admiration, not only in the Bureau's employees, but also in many members of the Congress, who paid the bills for the Bureau of Reclamation's immense dam-building projects in the West.

As Marc Reisner relates in his book *Cadillac Desert,* Dominy rose "from dirt sampler to waterlord of the American West in a short thirteen years, and for the last three of those he was the defacto commissioner." According to Reisner, "His strategy was simple. He would settle in a branch with a weak man as chief and learn as fast as he could. Then he would flap up to the ledge occupied by the chief and knock him off." And when he became Bureau Commissioner, "he was merciless to the people around him." [28]

Maurice K., on the other hand, seemed to rise from forestry instructor, to Penn State department head, to become at age forty-three Pennsylvania's chief conservationist, effortlessly, naturally, without art. At each step in his climb, he was seen as the right man for advancement, not only by those making the decision, but by those who worked with, and for him. There were those who were intimidated by Maurice K., and many who would say they were cowed by his grasp and use of information as a tool to get what he wanted; however, almost without exception they respected rather than hated him for it.

❑ ❑ ❑ ❑

As if all these Commission and speaking trips were not enough for one year, two months before his debate with Dominy — just prior to the White House Conference on Natural Beauty — Maurice K. journeyed to Missouri to give a major speech to the North American Wildlife Conference. He described what he called "A New Conservation for an Urban America" for the delegates to the Conference. He told them, "It is no longer enough for American conservation to concern itself solely with the impact of man upon water, land, and wildlife. . . . Conservation must absorb within its province of concerns a much wider preoccupation with human welfare and aesthetics than has hitherto been the case. . . .

182

Our old primary concern was with the land and its resources. Our new concern centers upon people." [29]

But then he sounded a note of alarm:

> The task of conservation in the years ahead is to convert man from a parasite of earth to its steward and its husbandman — not just because we enjoy the beauty and bounty of the earth for its own sake, but because the continued existence of civilized man himself is involved. . . . Ironically, we talk about how to keep wildlife populations in balance while . . . we have yet to keep man's own population in balance." [30]

Maurice K.'s view of conservation, however, was still as the preserve of the professional, not the public. He accepted the public's cries of alarm and welcomed their increasing awareness of the dangers to the environment, but was unreceptive to the idea of stopping the forward advance of the expert approach to conservation, or that of locking up the environment. Rather than a new environmentalism, his idea of what was needed was a revised view of conservation that "mandated" that the old-line resource professions "unite all the resource sciences by embrac[ing] landscape architects, climatologists, urban planners, experts in economic development, social scientists and a host of other professions" . . . to build a "new aesthetic for a new America."

After reciting to the North American Wildlife Conference a long list of all the new tools the conservationist now had at his disposal, namely the laws Congress had been supplying — the National Wilderness Preservation System, the Land and Water Conservation Fund, the Classification and Multiple Use Act, the Water Resources Research Act, the Wild Rivers Preservation Bill, the Water Pollution Control Act, and others — Maurice K. closed his talk on the "'New Conservation" by telling the assembly:

> Our Challenge is whether we can convert modern man from a planetary disease into the most constructive force in nature. Can we be creators instead of destroyers? Are we wise enough to sacrifice a few short-term profits for a long-term profit? Can we finally realize that the rape of a virgin continent has come to an end and that we must learn the art of nurturing a hurt and wounded land back to health?

We have the science. We are getting the public and political support. Have we the will and the know-how to meet this challenge? [31]

□ □ □ □

In June, 1970 after five years of study, the Land Law Review Commission issued its final report to the President and Congress. In a ceremony in the White House Rose Garden, the members presented a copy to President Nixon. In accepting it, the President affirmed that it "will have without question a very great effect on the policy of this country." "It is essential," he continued, " to plan now for the use of the land, not to do it simply on a case-by-case basis, but to have an over-all policy."

Among the changes in land policy being recommended — a number of which displeased many conservationists, and especially the environmentalists — were several of major significance: the shifting of land use decisions from the executive departments to Congress; the revision of public-land laws to facilitate commercial activities such as mining, lumbering and agriculture; the opening of land to the states for urban expansion, and the moving of the U.S. Forest Service from the Department of Agriculture to the Department of the Interior. [32]

In such a massive report, it is impossible to see the hand prints of an individual commissioner; however, Maurice K. certainly would have been in agreement with the emphasis on greater assistance for such commercial enterprises as the timber industry. And of course the report's idea that "timber production should be financed by appropriations from a revolving fund made up of receipts from timber sales," is pure-Goddard in form. At the same time, the report recommended that controls should be established that would "minimize the adverse impacts on the environment" by timber harvesting activities, [33] an idea with which Maurice K. also agreed.

184

Moreover the general premise that environmental quality should be recognized by law as an important objective of public-land management and policy — which should have pleased the environmentalists — was embodied throughout the report. At the same time, such ideas as reconciling all possible uses of a specific tract of land with the "dominant use" to obtain the maximum benefits was bound to disturb the same environmentalists.

□ □ □ □

As the decade of the sixties drew to a close, Maurice K.'s star had risen high above the horizon, far beyond the forests and waters of Pennsylvania where it began its ascent. He was being named to federal commissions. He was being asked to speak around the nation on conservation issues. He had been considered as a possible under secretary in the Department of the Interior, and was even prominent enough in Pennsylvania political life to have been rumored to be a candidate for governor. What is all the more remarkable is that he had no real political base or party to foster such a reputation, only the Pennsylvania Department of Forests and Waters.

Although the department, *his* department, was operating without apparent problems of a serious nature — almost effortlessly it seemed — there were clouds edging their way into Maurice K.'s sky. The new environmentalism was threatening to interrupt his plans for the Delaware River Basin, and was about to change the face of Pennsylvania's resource management by removing it from the smoothly running, highly thought of Department of Forests and Waters and placing it in an immense combined resource and enforcement agency whose ability as well as reputation would be challenged.

# CHAPTER XI

# HIGH DAM, LOW DAM, NO DAM

**Riparian doctrine**. The system of water law historically recognized by the Eastern States. The riparian doctrine protects landowners adjacent to lakes and streams from withdrawals or uses which unreasonably diminish water quantity or quality. Individuals have a right to make use of the stream waters flowing by their lands so long as their use does not substantially diminish either the quantity or quality of the water passing to landowners downstream. [1]

The Secretary of Forests and Waters liked to describe his job as a "race against time." He considered parks, forests, pure water, flood control as necessities not luxuries, so he made conserving natural resources now for future Pennsylvanians "his work." In an October 1965 interview with John Cowan, a Harrisburg *Patriot* staff writer, he declared he was not interested in returning to "the cloistered realm of the academic world at Penn State." Of his job at Forests and Waters, he told Cowan:

> I found it difficult at first. It was hard to keep up with the demanding pace, particularly the speeches and the legislative problems. But once I became acclimated, I found it stimulating. I don't think I could ever go back to teaching again. The academic life is too slow. I couldn't stand the pace. I feel that I can do more for more people here.
>
> I am working for $11\frac{1}{2}$ million people here. In college, I would be working for just a few students. And it is hard to estimate your effect on the students. Here you can see the tangible results. [2]

When Cowan visited him in his corner office on the top floor of the State Education Building there were maps on the wall and standing in the corners; books, magazines, and pamphlets were everywhere: on tables, desks, chairs, windowsills, and the floor. To Cowan, Maurice K. had the "look of an eagle" as he sat among all the clutter. To him the Secretary of Forests and Waters appeared "tall and beaked" as he swooped down on one of the piles for an item that carried some piece of information he needed to make a point. [3]

Maurice K. told him that there are three things that make a community: the functional part (homes, stores, factories); the cultural part (libraries, churches and schools); and the recreational areas. "It takes a blend of all three to make an attractive community." He saw the third of these as his responsibility. Parks were needed for health and for business. (He cited one instance of a firm that moved from the Greensburg area to Ohio when the local community would not build the recreation area that management had requested.) The demand for parks was especially acute in metropolitan areas. "If we live in a wilderness, we take it for granted. If we live in a city, we want to escape the crowded conditions." [4]

❑ ❑ ❑ ❑

But putting together some of the park packages in areas that lay close to heavily developed areas, just where, according to Maurice K. they were needed, often became a quite involved and contentious process. Beginning as early as 1933, regional, state and even federal commissions and planning groups had conducted studies and made proposals and other recommendations concerning an area in the southeastern region of the state along the Skippack Creek in Montgomery County. Eventually it would become Evansburg State Park, but at one point the fight over its establishment appeared that it would cost Maurice K. his job.

At Evansburg, he was hoping to preserve an area of significant size that would serve as a buffer between the already developed areas of the region. Evansburg had the potential of providing a place "of quiet in a noisy world," a place "to leave behind daily schedules" and the "time clocks of daily living," a place of "living libraries of nature," of unspoiled surroundings, and a place to enjoy a "moment of relative solitude" in the midst of a metropolitan area. [5]

Because Maurice K. considered the Evansburg project to be of such importance to the Philadelphia metropolitan area, these background studies, in the face of local opposition to the park, were critical to gaining the approval of the State Planning Board and the Governor. One of the reports, "A Regional Park System in Southeastern Pennsylvania," which was developed by staffers of a joint Montgomery, Bucks, Chester, Delaware, and Philadelphia Planning Commission, had recommended in November 1956 that the Department of Forests and Waters acquire and develop "close in regional parks" over the next ten years. [6]  Then, following public hearings in April and May, 1960 the Army Corps of Engineers published its "Report on the Comprehensive Survey of the Water Resources of the Delaware River Basin." It recommended Evansburg as a recreation and water supply site. [7]

Following the Corps' recommendations, there were a number of studies and comprehensive plans developed locally by the Montgomery County Planning Commission (1962) and the Lower Providence Township (1963) that identified the Evansburg area as an important land and water resource site. There was, however, considerable and powerful local objection to the proposal when it was put forward four years later by the Department of Forests and Waters.

In June 1967, Maurice K. and John Rex braved a crowd of eight hundred gathered at Methacton High School in Lower Providence Township outside of Norristown. According to the headlines on the front page of the next morning's Norristown *Daily Herald*, the audience was "Told of a Vast New Park" with a "6-mile long lake" that would cost "Half a Billion." The report stated the proposed lake would cover 1,120 acres and take land in five townships. Although John Rex assured the communities and school districts that they would receive reimbursement for their lost tax base for an indefinite period, the supervisors of three of the communities as well as one local school board immediately "lined up against the project." [8]

According to the *Daily Herald*'s report, Supervisor William Jenkins announced Skippack Township's opposition by contemptuously describing the plan as one that would produce a "500-acre mud flat," and the president of the Lower Providence Township Supervisors declared, "We are resolved to take whatever action is required to insure that it does not become a reality." There was local belief, too, that the Corps of Engineers' proposal of a high dam was simply to create a reservoir of water to cool down the output of a proposed downstream nuclear power plant on the Schuylkill River at the expense of destroying the Skippack Valley. [9]

Many of the local residents and organizations were interested in preserving the rural character of the area — a review of geodetic survey maps of the time shows that it was sparsely settled — and disapproved of the idea of a dam and lake for swimming and boating. The thought of hordes of city dwellers descending on the county during the summer months alarmed them, thus they fought against a water-based park. The board of Supervisors of Worcester Township, for example, called for a "wilderness type or wooded surrounding area . . . devoid of recreational facilities." To protest this attitude, one local Montgomery County planning official did resign after alleging that the opposition to the dam was racially motivated. [10]

With typical Pennsylvania parochialism, many area residents felt that Philadelphia's park needs should be satisfied within the city. Picking up on this sentiment, Montgomery County Senator Edwin G. Holl, a Republican, linked Evansburg directly to Philadelphia with his suggestion that Evansburg should only "be considered in connection" with development of Philadelphia's Fairmont Park. [11] Holl soon became one of the dissenters' strongest allies. Holl also became and would remain a vigorous Goddard adversary for years to come.

□ □ □ □

Initially Senator Holl's position appeared to be a cautious and flexible one. He and Goddard talked and corresponded on a somewhat cordial basis. In a June 1967 letter, Holl asked the Department of Forests and Waters a long series of questions. In an even longer reply, Maurice K. answered each in detail. The full three-page answer to one question dealt with Holl's request for a "detailed statement on the origin of the idea." In response to the Senator's question of why some up-basin facility in the Pocono Mountain area was not more feasible than the Evansburg proposal, Maurice listed eight reservoirs that were in various stages of acquisition or development in eastern Pennsylvania, among them: Beltzville and Aquashicola in Carbon County, Blue Marsh and Maiden Creek in Berks, Trexler in Lehigh, and Prompton in Wayne. [12]

Each of Maurice K.'s answers was factual and to the point, especially the one to Holl's question about the "planned usage by other than Montgomery County residents." Maurice averred the park would "give Montgomery Countians an advantage over other Pennsylvanians," but quickly noted that "Project 70 enabling legislation prohibited restriction of public use based on place of residence." And to the question of why it was not a better idea to use the money to rehabilitate and develop Philadelphia's Fairmont Park, Maurice told Holl that the city had been allocated $3.5 million from Project 70 and with matching funds from the city and those from the Federal Land and Water Conservation Fund, had a total of $7 million to upgrade Fairmont and twenty-two other sites in the city. [13]

Regardless of the extent to which Holl accepted or disagreed with Maurice K.'s answers, ultimately they were not sufficient to satisfy the Montgomery County forces arrayed against the dam. While the Secretary of Forests and Waters' was a difficult position, it would not be easy to back down at this point, it was a situation of his own making. He could have, perhaps should have, secured

190

firmer local backing for metropolitan parks and reservoirs before publicly announcing them. Holl, on the other hand, had been handed a crisis from which there was no turning away. He was an able and respected Senator, known for "tending the store," as one constituent put it, and although he was a strong supporter of parks, [14] had to respond to electorate demands in some determined fashion.

Unlike the weak assemblage of the Cornplanter Indians at Kinzua, the opposition in the Skippack Valley had the support of powerful interests; one report mentioned eight prominent citizen groups arrayed against the dam. And at Kinzua there were large numbers of clear beneficiaries of the dam — the more than thirty thousand residents of Warren, most of whom lived in an Allegheny River flood plain. Few of them or their representatives were likely to object to the loss of upstream land for their flood protection.

The first serious counter-attack against the high-dam plan by its Montgomery County opponents was the funding of several engineering studies that recommended a series of small dams on the Skippack rather than one large one, but they gained little ground in Harrisburg. The State Planning Board kept postponing its decision, from November 1967 to December, and then again to February 1968, to permit the Department of Forests and Waters to evaluate the small-dam recommendation. Then on March 14, 1968 the Planning Board held an extended meeting during which numerous private citizens, groups and local, county, and Commonwealth officials presented their views on the project.

At the Board's March meeting soliciting public input, the forces on both sides of the issue were arrayed as if they were opposing armies facing each other across the Skipjack. In addition to the anticipated opponents of the park with its dam, a surprising number of local groups appeared as supporters of the plan. Among them were the League of Women Voters of Landsdale, the head of the Clean Streams Committee of Perkiomen, the Penjerdel Open Space Commission, the Wissahickon Valley Watershed Association, the editor of the *Bucks-Mont Courier*, and the Montgomery County

Citizens for Evansburg. William Ager of the latter group also brought with him three hundred statements in favor of the park from individuals living in the surrounding communities. [15]

Following the testimony of both sides, the Board decided to postpone its decision until its next meeting to give the members time to review the presentations. On April 9, without extensive discussion, as they had had months to study the proposal, the Board voted eleven to two to "recommend" that Governor Shafer, who had followed William Scranton into the statehouse, approve the Evansburg project. Their endorsement was of a plan that included several "amendments" to the original project. Maurice K. agreed to reduce slightly the size of the acreage involved in the overall park, and to include a statement that "construction of the Dam and Reservoir will not commence until 1977," but he made no other concessions. [16]

Three weeks later, following Governor Shafer's approval, Senator Holl requested and secured yet another meeting on the park. Holl, Maurice K., Irving Hand, Executive Director of the State Planning Board, and Governor Shafer met on May 15 in a long afternoon session. From 3:30 until nearly 6:00 PM, they discussed the objections of the various Montgomery County antagonists to the plan. Finally the Senator asked for a number of changes. The most prominent of these was a request for a stay by the Department of Forests and Waters in the acquisition of land that had not yet been purchased (approximately two thousand acres). He wanted the administration to defer all action until after the completion of several new studies which were being undertaken by the local groups. In place of one large park, they were now working up a proposal to construct a series of small, single-purpose parks. [17]

Maurice K. refused. Apparently seeing this as simply another delaying tactic, he told Holl he would certainly consider the results of the studies when they were completed, but would continue his ongoing efforts to acquire land for the park as planned. At the State Planning Board's meeting the following day, the members briefly discussed the previous day's meeting between Maurice K., Senator Holl, Irving Hand, and Governor Shafer and their decision of the previous month, but quickly reaffirmed their April recommendation that the state go ahead with the park. They agreed that having reported the plan to the Governor for approval, they could hardly go back to him a month later and withdraw it. [18]

Both sides put the best face on the "compromise." Maurice K. was quoted by the *Philadelphia Inquirer* several years later as having stated: "Even at the first public hearings we said we couldn't build a dam until 1977." [19] And, of course, Senator Holl and the local resident groups were cautiously pleased. They had gained time to find new rams with which to batter holes in the high-dam idea. As we shall see later, on numerous occasions during the next decade, Evansburg State Park and Senator Holl would explode into full blaze, like a wildfire burning deep in the "duff," over the issue of the dam and park. The sparks would come from many directions; Goddard, however, was always the kindling they fell on.

One newspaper article described Evansburg State Park as "Goddard's Last Stand!" The Secretary's dilemma, according to the writer, was "High Dam, Low Dam or No Dam." [20] Both Holl and Goddard outlasted the issue. Thirty-five years later, however. Evansburg State Park, which lies five miles north of Norristown, has hiking and riding trails, fishing and hunting areas, and a youth hostel, but no dam, no lake. More than half of the park is inaccessible to all but horseback riders who must bring their own horse as there are no stables in the park. This of course rules out most city residents.

□ □ □ □

A year before Governor Scranton left office, a conservation program even more ambitious than Project 70 had been unveiled. A new bond issue for $500 million, known as Project 500, was proposed. It followed a scenario of legislative and popular endorsement during the Scranton and Shafer administrations similar to that of Project 70 during the Lawrence years. Originally it was the intention of Secretary Goddard and Governor Lawrence that the *development* costs for the park land acquired under Project 70 would come from the Capital Budget each year during the life of the land acquisition process. [21]   This proved too difficult to achieve, thus it was necessary to go back to the voters again.

When Governor Scranton presented his plan for the new bond issue in December 1965, he alleged that: in spite of a recently enacted strip mine law that was restoring lands at a rate of ten thousand acres a year, there were "still more than two hundred thousand acres of abandoned strippings"; that although three thousand miles of streams had been cleaned of acid waters by prohibiting drainage from operating mines, "more than nine hundred million gallons still flowed each day from those that had been abandoned"; that despite Pennsylvania's leadership in state-subsidized construction of sewage treatment facilities, "many smaller communities were still without the financial means to do the job on their own"; and that although Goddard's aggressive program to purchase land for parks with funds from Project 70 and the Oil and Gas Leases had yielded spectacular results, "many of these recreation areas lay undeveloped." [22]

Maurice K. appeared before the Senate Committee on Constitutional Change and Federal Relationship on March 22, 1966. He told the Committee that there were "acute requirements" in the seventy operating state parks, especially the forty-six that were developed prior to 1945. These requirements included "modern sanitary disposal and water distribution systems, hard surfaced roads, and day use and camping site improvements." It was not sufficient, therefore to consider only the recreational development of new Project 70 areas, but rather the entire State Park System, which, he said, had received very limited capital authorizations over the years. He closed his lengthy statement by telling the Committee:

> It is obvious to all that land acquisition alone cannot fulfill the outdoor recreation needs of our people, that effective development of

appropriate facilities is the next responsive step towards the goals envisioned by Project 70. And in the end analysis, the greatest resource of all — the human resource — will benefit from the assurance of a healthy and productive environment, set aside and developed, for this and future generation's use, enjoyment, and heritage. [23]

The General Assembly quickly put together a "Land and Water Conservation and Reclamation Act" — Senator Holl was one of the sponsors. Because of changes in the Pennsylvania Constitution, the amendment process no longer required the approval of two successive legislatures, so the act moved through much faster than Project 70 had. The referendum measure was approved in May 1966, and Governor Raymond P. Shafer signed the enabling act for Project 500 on January 19, 1968, a year after he took office.

Monies from this *development* project were disbursed as follows: the Department of Mines and Mineral Industries, $200 million to eliminate land scars and stream pollution; the Department of Health, $100 million to construct new and improved municipal sewage treatment facilities; the Department of Forests and Waters, Fish and Game Commissions and the Historical and Museum Commission, $125 million to develop recreation areas on lands acquired under Project 70; and $75 million dollars for Community Affairs to acquire additional county and municipal parks or develop of those already in existence. [24]

The Pennsylvania Department of Community Affairs was created in 1966 to assist local governments and to provide services in areas of inter-governmental relationships involving all levels of public jurisdiction. At the time it was considered to be a unique agency of state government in the nation. The department provided technical and training assistance and administered state and federal aid programs in the areas of housing, urban renewal, and community planning, as well as in recreation and conservation.

Once again, Goddard, Rex, and Forrey went on the park lecture trail. Goddard insisted that Forrey, then head of Park Planning, develop detailed plans (but not necessarily architectural drawings of individual buildings) explaining exactly what they planned to do with the land in developing a park. He wanted the affected communities to know up front rather than complain later that he had done something they were never told about. The Department of Forests and Waters used Project 500 money in the construction of day-use facilities; swimming, boating, and nature/education and hiking areas; as well as administrative complexes.

Virtually all the $500 million was spent within the ten-year time frame specified by the Conservation and Reclamation Act. And by the target year of 1970, the Department of Forests and Waters had seventy-one state parks officially open to the public, as well as fifty-nine natural areas, several monuments and historical parks, and numerous picnic grounds. A total of 190,285 acres were being managed. Twenty more parks were under design or development, while twelve new sites were either in the acquisition or study stage. While the Pennsylvania park system was probably not the most important of all state programs, it was certainly the most visible. More than thirty-one million visitor days were recorded in 1970. This was nearly a ten-fold gain over figures recorded in pre-war years.

Not all of the new Goddard-era parks were built and improved with Project 70 and Project 500 funds. In his history of the state parks, Forrey states that between 1949 and 1975 the General State Authority of the Commonwealth — created by the legislature in March 1949 as the "borrow and build agency" for state projects — poured an additional $51 million into the state park system. And money from the Oil and Gas Fund continued to be used for the erection of parks, such as Gouldsboro in Monroe and Wayne Counties in the northeast corner of the state. [25]

Moreover, nearly $22 million in assistance was secured under the Federal Land and Water Conservation Fund Act of 1965. These monies were used in Pennsylvania to augment those available under Project 70, Project 500, and from the General State Authority. They were applied to thirty-four projects and to restore sixty-one state parks damaged during the 1972 flooding of Tropical Storm Agnes. [26]

The idea behind the Federal Land and Water Conservation Fund Act was to "get money to the east," according to Maurice K. Prior to 1965, virtually all federal money for land went to the West. He liked to point out, for example, that all of the East including Pennsylvania was in a U.S. Forest Service district headquartered in Wisconsin. The result of this bias was that tax money levied against the more populous East went overwhelmingly to western states. The Federal Land and Water Conservation Fund Act authorized the expenditure of $300 million a year that had accumulated from the sale of surplus federal property, from the portion of the gas tax that came from recreational purposes (boats, motor homes), and later from the sale of oil and gas leases from off-shore drilling in the Continental Shelf. The money — it reached $900 million annually by the end of the Carter Administration — was evenly split between the states and federal land management agencies such as the Department of the Interior and the U.S. Forest Service. [27]

□ □ □ □

According to the 1996 Pennsylvania Statistical Abstract, $489 million were raised for "land and water development" under the Project 500 bond issue. By 1995 $383 million of these bonds had been redeemed. Typical of the parks benefitting from Project 500 was Codorus State Park in York County. The land had been purchased with Project 70 funds, but its development proceeded only with the availability of Project 500 funds. It was the first state park to benefit from the "land and water development" initiative. [28]

Many local communities also received monies under the project to acquire and develop county and municipal parks as well as municipal sewage treatment plants. This later effort, of course, was directed at cleaning up the state's streams. And it should be remembered that a number of Pennsylvania historic sites received property-expansion and development funds from Project 70 and Project 500. Among the beneficiaries were the Priestley House in Northumberland, the Robert Fulton Birthplace, the Landis Valley

Farm in Lancaster County and the Bushy Run Battlefield in Westmoreland County.

There is a certain irony in the Goddard drive for greater public ownership of land as the way to protect it from misuse by private interests. Communal ownership with private use of land only at the discretion of all is a Native American idea, not a Western one. Prior to the mid-nineteenth century when individuals such as Frederic Law Olmsted and John Muir, then later William C. Kent, J. Horace McFarland and others began to promote a different view, the sole thought was that the forest should be subdued, the land tamed. [29]  It was American policy prior to that time to sell off public lands or lease their mineral, water and grazing rights to help propel national expansion and economic progress. Only late in the nineteenth century and then accelerating into the twentieth century did a growing public conservation awareness cause U.S. government policy to change. At that point state and federal acquisition of land, to protect what previously had been exploited, became *de rigueur*. The numbers of people hoping to reserve for the common good some small portion of the remaining undeveloped land had become a formidable force.

□ □ □ □

The fight over the dam at Evansburg was just one instance of the "environmental" struggle that was erupting throughout the nation. Moreover, Evansburg was little more than a vexatious foretaste of a battle that was developing over dams on the Delaware River. According to Maurice K.'s intimates, men such as John Rex and R. Timothy Weston, who worked with him on river basin issues, the battle of Evansburg was more an irritant, a "headache" that their boss was anxious to dispose of so he could concentrate on other, more important matters. But more to the point, Evansburg was simply a piece in a much larger puzzle, that of the plans for the entire Delaware River Basin.

From time to time, as the Evansburg situation dragged on, other side issues burst like solar flares to plague Maurice K. It was the practice during the land-acquisition phase of constructing a new park, which sometimes lasted four, five or more years, for the Bureau of Parks to rent individual properties to their former owners, if they wished to remain after the state purchased them, or to others who wanted to live in them.

Both Senator Holl and local residents continued to squabble with Maurice K. and among themselves over the department's handling of rental properties at Evansburg. At one point, Holl charged that "Goddard is guilty of gross mismanagement" of the properties, that he was allowing them to deteriorate so that the public would be less likely to "oppose the demolition of a bunch of old rundown houses." According to Holl, "This is Goddard's way of removing all those old properties to make it easier to get the dam through." [30]

And at another time, Holl charged that state employees who were involved in the development of the park were being allowed by the Bureau of Parks to live there "at a fraction of their value." But when Holl unveiled a bill designed to halt the deterioration of park buildings by raising the rents through legislation, some one hundred local residents met to develop a strategy to derail the bill. As one newspaper summed up the issue, "If the project, as Goddard insists, is only one or two years away, it might be foolhardy to spend money on homes that will eventually be under water. However, if the project, as Holl believes, is 10 or 20 years away . . . then it would apparently be worthwhile to renovate and maintain the homes." [31]

❑ ❑ ❑ ❑

Although the proposed Evansburg State Park was a thorn that Maurice K. was never able to pluck from his side, another contentious Goddard fight that eventually was successful concerned the Susquehanna River Basin. Much of the work had been done during Governor Scranton's term, but, on July 17, 1968, Governor Shafer, signed the compact that made Pennsylvania a party with New York, Maryland, and the federal government in managing the river's resources.

While the Delaware River Basin Compact of 1961 was born out of a need to resolve a serious conflict among the states over the Delaware's water, the Susquehanna River Basin faced no such predicament at the time. There were problems, but compared to the Delaware River Basin the Susquehanna River Basin was considered to be an "undeveloped," underutilized watershed. Thus the compact treating the river's basin was formed to establish a mechanism to administer the anticipated development of its resources and to constrain its tendency to flood. While shortly after the Delaware River Basin Compact was signed, others began talking of the possibility of a similar cooperative effort for the Susquehanna, the eventual signing of a compact was largely the result of Maurice K.'s leadership, initiative, and energy.

As the result of a 1962 meeting in Binghamton, New York (close to the headwaters of the Susquehanna), at which John Robin, Francis Pitkin and Maurice K. met with water conservation representatives from New York, it was decided to form an advisory committee to consider the possibility of an agreement for the Susquehanna River similar to that developed for the Delaware. At a subsequent meeting in Harrisburg, later that same year, the Interstate Advisory Committee (IAC) was formally established. Maurice K. was chosen as the organization's permanent chairman. [32]

Although he provided counsel, advice and general oversight to the IAC subcommittee that was drafting the proposed compact, his greatest involvement came in moving it through the Pennsylvania legislature once a document had been forged that the representatives from the three states — New York, Pennsylvania and Maryland agreed to.

In the words of Clifford Jones, Pennsylvania Secretary of Commerce at the time, Maurice K. expended a great amount of his political capital in the endeavor. And it was a fight that took a large measure of his time and energy between 1962 and 1968. One of the peculiar aspects of the struggle, according to Jones, was the need to "neutralize" the opposition rather than convert opponents to the idea. [33]

The major disputant of the legislative bill approving the draft compact was the Pennsylvania Farm Bureau. The farmers were concerned over the possibility of restrictive requirements covering treatment of farm waste and by the prospect of controls over their rights to water usage — they wanted the compact to assert a change from "riparian" to "appropriation" rights. (Under appropriation doctrine, the system of water law adopted by most western states, a right to water is *acquired* only by diverting the water from a watercourse and applying it to a "beneficial use." Furthermore, an earlier acquired water right has priority over right acquired later, thus giving advantage to the first user, who may take virtually all of the water.) And then, of course, a number of state legislators were wary of the delegation of authority to a commission of appointed bureaucrats, especially one that included out-of-state members beyond their control. [34]

Eventually Maurice K. was able to convince the Farm Bureau and enough legislators "not to come out against the bill" so that those who favored it were able to push it through. The bill approving the compact, which had been endorsed earlier by both the New York and Maryland legislatures, went back and forth in the Pennsylvania House and Senate during the summer of 1968, through sometimes bitter debate, especially over numerous amendments that were offered. Finally, however, it passed the House on July 8 and the Senate on July 15, 1968. [35]

Earlier Maurice K. had also had difficulty "neutralizing" the Nixon Administration's opposition. Even Stewart Udall, President Kennedy's Secretary of the Interior, had thought the Delaware River Basin Compact was an "oddball," setting no precedent for other rivers of the nation, and the Nixon Administration was not at all interested in the idea of federal participation in a compact for the

Susquehanna River. This was the case even though the bill had the backing of the Pennsylvania delegation, including the Senate Minority Leader, Republican Hugh Scott. [36]

Along with other IAC members, Maurice K. spent a day in Washington trying unsuccessfully to convince James Watt, at that time Deputy Assistant Secretary of the Interior for water power and development, of the Susquehanna River Basin Compact's need for federal participation. (James Gaius Watt later served as President Ronald Reagan's Secretary of the Interior.) [37] At one point in the discussion, Maurice K. told Watt, "Hell you guys are trying to cooperate with Russia and can't even cooperate with three states." Eventually the administration agreed not to come out against the bill, if it got to the President for signature. In exchange, the states had to promise that they would not publicize the administration's approval of the legislation. According to Maurice K., President Nixon signed the bill at Camp David on Christmas Eve 1970 well out of the view of inquisitive reporters. [38]

□ □ □ □

The Susquehanna and Delaware Rivers and their basins, and thus their compacts, are, however, different. The Susquehanna River does not form the boundary between a number of states as does the Delaware. The Susquehanna drains approximately 27,500 square miles, 21,000 of these in Pennsylvania, 6,270 in New York, and only 280 in Maryland, with New York controlling the headwaters and Maryland receiving the downstream flow. This means that improvements made by New York and Pennsylvania benefit Maryland out of proportion to the size of the Susquehanna's drainage area in Maryland. Moreover, more than half of the Chesapeake Bay's fresh water flow comes from the Susquehanna River. In a long December 1964 letter to Governor Scranton, Maurice K. had outlined these differences and raised the question of voting rights of the members. "If Maryland is given an equal vote," he told Scranton, "should an understanding be reached which would afford some measure of assurance that Maryland will pay a share of the cost of upstream improvements in New York and Pennsylvania *proportional to the benefits* [author's italics] received?" [39]

Then, with a commission of four members there was the possibility of a tie vote. Among the options, Maurice K. mentioned to Governor Scranton was the possibility that Pennsylvania might be given a fifth and tie-breaking vote. He told the Governor that New York and Maryland would probably accept such a plan, but that the federal government would not. The final version of the compact gave each state one vote. In the thirty years since the establishment of the commission, the concern that Pennsylvania might do much of the work and Maryland would receive the benefits has not materialized. The Maryland legislature has always approved paying its fair share of the costs of running the Susquehanna River Basin Commission. [40]

Moreover, the imbalance in size of drainage areas between Maryland and Pennsylvania has not resulted in a financial burden to the Commonwealth. While Pennsylvania does have numerous flood control works in the basin — they provide protection mainly for its own communities — the state's financial contribution to basin works has been greatly reduced through the projects of the Corps of Engineers. There are five federal dams on the Susquehanna River in New York and eight in Pennsylvania, including Foster Joseph Sayers, Alvin R. Bush, Tioga-Hammond, Raystown and Curwensville.

The Corps of Engineers' dams were built primarily for flood control, the major concern along the Susquehanna River, but in several cases have also had a "low-flow" augmentation added to them. Storage of this additional water is paid for by the large, depletive users, principally the electric power industry. When low-water conditions are encountered, the Susquehanna River Basin Commission directs the Corps to release sufficient water from its reservoirs to make up the shortage. The industry reimburses the Corps (through the SRBC) for storing the water. To meet the

SRBC's low-flow water makeup requirement, for example, two large utility companies in Pennsylvania pay the commission to purchase water storage for them at the Cowanesque Reservoir in Tioga County. In 1968, the SRBC purchased twenty-five thousand acre feet of water storage on their behalf at a cost of $3.4 million per year. [41]

□ □ □ □

There were, of course, bright spots for the Secretary of Forests and Waters even in the Pennsylvania State Park firmament; ones that helped to offset the difficulties in establishing a park at Evansburg and in getting approval of the Susquehanna River Basin Compact. Between 1961 and 1968, Maurice K. was able to announce the opening of fourteen new state parks. Then in 1969 Governor Shafer announced to a crowd gathered in the William Penn Memorial Museum in Harrisburg for a dinner honoring Maurice K. that the Sandy Creek State Park in Mercer County was to be renamed the "Maurice K. Goddard State Park." Shafer explained how this happened to a living honoree.

> I am extremely pleased to announce that three of the four members of the State Geographic Board have agreed with my recommendation that the new state park be named in honor of Dr. Maurice K. Goddard.
> The fourth, member — Dr. Goddard himself who serves as chairman — is, of course, understandably opposed to naming any state park after a person now living. I am certain that he will learn to accept and live with the honor bestowed upon him here tonight.
> For in the minds of all of us, Maurice Goddard ranks with Gifford Pinchot as one of America's greatest conservationists. [42]

And in a special "News Information" release to the press, Governor Shafer asserted that the selection of Sandy Creek State Park was "particularly fitting, . . . for the land on which this new facility is being built was acquired under Project 70 and is now being developed under Project 500 — both landmark Pennsylvania conservation efforts which could not have succeeded without his leadership."

M. K. Goddard State Park, as it is now usually called, lies approximately ninety miles north of Pittsburgh. The park consists of 2,856 acres, which includes an 1,860-acre manmade lake, ten miles long with a twenty-five-mile shoreline. The upper part of the lake is managed by the Pennsylvania Game Commission as part of a State Game Lands. A trail leads from the lower lake to an environmental-education center. The center is a modern facility which permits hourly, daily or week-long programming on conservation subjects. There are three dormitories and a dining hall at the site, which can handle groups of up to 120 people. A "discovery building," an auditorium, nearby trails and the outdoors all complement each other to provide an ideal setting for an environmental-education experience. [43]

Sandy Creek, which traverses M. K. Goddard State Park, was first noted in reports George Washington made during a 1753 trip to Fort LeBoeuf. In 1939, the U.S. Army Corps of Engineers became interested in Sandy Creek because of the recurring floods that plagued the watercourse. Prompted by the Corps' initial flood-control study, the U.S. Soil Conservation Service committed itself to building a dam for flood control and conservation purposes.

There was no problem with the park's neighbors. Roy W. Wilt, House Member who represented Mercer County, wrote Maurice K., "I want you to know that my constituents in Mercer County and I feel deeply honored in having the new Sandy Creek State Park named the "Maurice K. Goddard State Park." . . . I look forward to welcoming you personally to Mercer County and hope that together, we can tour the Maurice K. Goddard State Park." [44]


❑ ❑ ❑ ❑


When Maurice K. "pledged" a full-scale Ohiopyle Park to the Western Pennsylvania Conservancy in 1962, he told the members that besides "providing essential recreational opportunities in an age when people are more recreation conscious than ever before, our state parks exert a definite impact upon the economy of their surrounding areas." He then cited two "very notable examples": Presque Isle in Erie and Prince Gallitzin State Park in Cambria County. According to him, Presque Isle State Park had "transformed the City of Erie into the biggest vacation center on the Great Lakes" [while] Prince Gallitzin State Park had begun to serve as the "nucleus for further development of Cambria County's tourist and vacation business."

By 1995, Pennsylvania ranked tenth in the nation in state park land, with 283,000 acres. [45] Much of this was accomplished through Project 70, Project 500 and the Oil and Gas Lease Fund, which were the instruments of Maurice Goddard's dream to save places of superior scenic beauty for the enjoyment of future generations. In closing his article on "Land Acquisition by Public Agencies" for the Department of Agriculture, he had written: "[S]uch lands take up but a small fraction of the Nation's land surface, yet the vital services performed thereon may determine the economic well-being and security of our country." [46]

# CHAPTER XII

# THE FOREST PLAN
## of
## 1970

**mensuration** — the science involved in measuring the volume, growth, and development of individual trees and stands and the determination of various products obtainable from them.

Herman J. Chapman [1]

In the first book of his trilogy, *The Trees, The Fields, The Town,* Pennsylvania author Conrad Richter tells us that early nineteenth-century settlers heading to Ohio along the Juniata River could walk all day and see no more than filtered light through the leaf canopy that covered their path. A clearing along the trail was like an oasis in a desert. And other writers have reported early westward travelers as being unable to see the stars at night. Another has claimed, "The province was 99 percent forested when the first Europeans arrived." [2] Regardless of the accuracy of such a number, *Penn-sylvania,* or Penn's Woods was, except for the rivers and tidewater areas, virtually all covered with virgin forest when the King granted the land to William Penn.

The early North American settler often saw the forest as a place of danger, one that was feared, thus one that needed to be subdued. One settler described it as "a great cave for animals to live in and for Indians to come up on you so sudden." Another wrote that the trees in the forest were so dense she saw them as "monsters, all crammed together as thick as corn stalks." [3] Until the loggers came, it was a claustrophobic life, especially for the women. While their husbands were off hunting, fishing or trapping, they were often left isolated for days, alone in a cabin located on the floor of a clearing hacked out of a forest of trees 150 or more feet high.

The loggers, then, were usually welcomed to the forest by those who first had settled in it. Only after the land had been stripped bare of trees, and the rains began washing the rich topsoil downstream, did voices such as Joseph Rothrock's and Mira Dock's begin to raise cries of alarm. It was this situation, the condition in which the loggers had left the forest after taking all the trees and chewing up the soil, that led, of course, to the establishment of Pennsylvania's first forest preserves and the founding of forestry schools and even the development of forestry as a professional discipline in the United States.

❑  ❑  ❑  ❑

Man has been a cataloger since the beginning of recorded history. And following Aristotle's lead, identification, naming and counting have been fundamental to scientific endeavor — from the stars and planets in the heavens to the mountains and rivers of the earth, and eventually to the plants and animals in the fields. So it was natural in attempting recovery of the state's forests to begin the process by identifying and counting, at first only of trees and then later of the other elements of Pennsylvania's forests — their soil, water, plant, and wildlife. While earlier efforts such as Joseph Illick's *Pennsylvania Trees* were general rather than specific in nature — applied to species, not individual specimens — the final review and adjustments were being made to a detailed Forest Resource Plan for all of Pennsylvania when Maurice arrived at Forests and Waters. Begun in 1949, under the direction of Joseph Ibberson in a newly established Division of Research, the ten-year plan, which covered each forest district in the state, was the first comprehensive, scientific plan for management of the state's forests.

Aerial photographs were made of each state forest. Each forest district was staffed with enough foresters to produce sample plots and through fieldwork to identify the species stands on the aerial photos. The sample plot data were then recorded on mark sense cards for computer processing in Harrisburg. Using statistical models, density inventories of site, size and forest types were produced. The first plan, to be used as a guide for the others, was developed for Michaux State Forest. [4]

Prior to the development of the 1955 management plan, recovery of Pennsylvania's forests from their near destruction in the nineteenth century was the primary objective of the Department of Forests and Waters. By 1950 it had been determined that they were ready to take on the task of providing a sustained supply of timber and other forest products. One of the goals then of the 1955 plan was to "reach the allowable cut in each district." The goal was for the annual cut to be approximately one half of the annual growth. With the help of the U.S. Forest Service, which calculated the volumes and the other data, and the School of Forest Resources at Pennsylvania State University, which produced the volume tables, tree volume tables in both board and cubic feet were prepared for all of Pennsylvania. [5]   As a follow-on to the plan each commercial species was sampled across the states' four geographic regions. This involved data collection and field measurement of more than four thousand individual trees.


□ □ □ □


Gradually over the years following the plan's implementation, as the understanding of the forest environment as an ecosystem began to grow, the realization set in that the plan was only a start. It was a tree plan not a forest plan. It took into account nothing of the other flora residing in the forest, or of the fauna that the trees sheltered, certainly nothing of the subterranean world that existed on and beneath the forest floor.

While a forest makes trees, trees do not make a forest. To fully appreciate this, to recognize that a forest is much more than a large collection of trees, we need first to think of it as a single organism, one of giant proportions, great depth and tremendous variety. The northern deciduous forest originally stretched from Canada to Texas, from the Atlantic Ocean to the western plains. Before it was sundered into separate forests by the settlers' voracious demand for farmland, it was one vibrant being teeming with myriad forms of life.

This primeval forest was, and its remnants still are, a place in which war is constantly waged among its inhabitants, the mobile and the stationary. Individual species battle not in terms of days, as do men at arms, but in decades — even centuries — for access to the soil, for moisture and air, for a skylight to the sun, for protection from the elements and predators, ultimately for dominance over neighboring species.

The pines were pioneers among the eastern trees. Eventually they gave way in all but the coastal areas of the South to the hardwoods — to the ascendancy of the beeches, maples, oaks. But a complete understanding of the forest can only begin with an appreciation of the soil. In his *The Great American Forest*, Rutherford Platt describes it as containing a "massive system of life," a "series of layers," each containing "limitless galleries" teeming with "energetic inhabitants." He claims that it is "so weird, . . . so fantastic . . . that the sight is comparable to getting a close look at a distant planet hitherto but dimly seen." [6]

After their job as food factory for the trees is over each year, as much as two tons of leaves, still rich in nutrients, fall on each acre of the northern deciduous forest. In damp caverns, deep in the forest's bed of leaves and rot from fallen limbs and trees, crops of algae and fungi grow, making a home for ants, thrips, spiders, mealy bugs, centipedes, and ticks. Snails, earthworms, and the larvae of moths, flies and beetles — game for the meat-eaters of the forest floor — feed on this litter and insect life.

Below this layer, just as at the bottom of the ocean, sunlight barely penetrates the leaf carpet. In the sodden mass at this level, leaf elements such as iron, magnesium and calcium begin dissolving and leaching into the layer of humus beneath. And it is in this humus that crops of rich fungi grow in all directions. These fungi form substitute root hairs for many young deciduous tree species, helping them take on more nutrients than they can on their own.

According to Platt, the entire forest floor teems with "insatiable microorganisms," and it is the "incessant carnage, the mass of dead bodies, that makes forest soils nourishing." These soil organisms form the base of the chain of life which leads to the "forest pageant above ground." [7]

This floor world is a marvelously constructed carpet which provides ample security for its inhabitants. In a mature forest, one that has not been disturbed, the trees break the force of violent storms, while the masses of leaves on the floor rarely are torn apart and washed away by floods. In even the worst downpour, globules of oxygen are trapped everywhere.

□ □ □ □

Under the 1955 Forest Plan the only silvicultural practice permitted in Pennsylvania state forests was improvement cutting. In management by improvement cutting, only individually designated or "marked" trees are removed from a timber stand. After ten years of experience under the improvement cutting approach, however, it became evident that this method was not achieving optimum results. This partial cutting encouraged the establishment of the less desirable, shade-tolerant tree species, while the more valuable ones, red oak, black cherry and ash, were not sufficiently regenerating. Moreover, some timber stands were in such poor condition that improvement cutting was of little help. [8]

So ten years into the fifteen-year management plan, as Maurice K. was preparing for the White House Conference on Natural Beauty, he had authorized even-age management (on a controlled basis) as an acceptable cutting practice for state forest lands. Even-age management involves several methods in addition to clear-cutting, primarily shelterwood and seed-tree cutting. The main objective is to regenerate the stand with desirable, high-quality tree species. [9]

The shelterwood system, which combines features of selective cutting with those of clear-cutting, involves removing a stand in two or three cuts several years apart. The poorest timber is taken first, with the better trees left to supply seed to assure an adequate growth of seedlings on the ground. Only when the seedlings are three or four years old is the final cut of the area made. This method is frequently used with the pines, as such species as white pine, sugar pine, and redwood need to have some shade during their early growth.

The seed-tree method is another variation of clear-cutting, which leaves scattered "windfirm" trees at intervals that will furnish enough seeding for the establishment of a new crop. The trees may be left singly or in small groups, but it is essential that large-crowned, windfirm trees are selected to obtain maximum seeding of the clear-cut area.

❑ ❑ ❑ ❑

During the fifteen-year life of the 1955 management plan, a number of modifications were made to it. These were largely the result of specific problems that arose in executing the plan. After eighteen months, minimum acceptable bids were incorporated into the sale prospectus being distributed. Too many sales were being cancelled, adding to the expense and time to re-advertise them. And three years into the plan, it became necessary to add specific requirements as to width, drainage and driving surface for the contractor's haul roads. Although some of the operators objected to these requirements, in time they saw the advantages of leaving well-constructed and well-drained roads to their logging operations. [10]

The commencement of logging in the state forests prompted complaints, too, from those who used them for hunting, fishing, or general recreation. Operators left large amounts of "slash" (debris) throughout their logging areas and along the roads over which they hauled their cut to the mill. In a long letter to one such complainant, Maurice K. carefully explained that it was only practicable for the logger to remove the "merchantable portion harvested"; that the tops and slash generated during the logging operation "gradually breakdown after a few years and help build up the forest soil." . . . "In the meantime they improve wildlife habitat and at the same time they protect young tree seedlings until they can become established as part of the stand." [11]

As the 1955 forest plan reached the end of its life, ideas for a more comprehensive program were formulated. While the main emphasis during the period of the first management plan was on the timber as a merchantable resource, it was decided to place greater emphasis on multiple use of the forest in the 1970 management plan. Among the important issues other than timber to be covered in the new plan were "water resources" and "recreation potential." The new plan, for example, included an inventory of outdoor activities (hunting, fishing, hiking, and camping), the construction of scenic drives, the provision for protection of and access to sites of unusual or unique geological phenomena, and the leasing of cabin sites to private citizens. [12]

The idea of a plan that would cover all aspects of the state's forest-life — its ecology — grew partly out of the growing awareness of the wholeness of forest life, but it also had strong ties to the multiple-use concept. Just as the early timber men eventually moved away from such single-use ideas as the "barking" of living trees, which left the bare trunk to stand and rot, foresters began to think of how to use all of a forest's resources more profitably. Although Maurice K. considered civil-service status for foresters to be the more important accomplishment of his state career, multiple use of the public's land is the distinguishing feature of his twenty-four-year stewardship over Pennsylvania forests — first as head of Forests and Waters and then as Secretary of the Department of Environmental Resources.

◻ ◻ ◻ ◻

The expression "multiple-use" is seemingly a clear pronouncement; in its implementation as a management objective, however, it is mainly a broad-based policy statement. Multiple-use of what and for whom? And how are disputes over conflicting uses and especially between users to be resolved? While today these are viewed and usually acted upon as complex issues requiring broad public input and consensus management, in the framework of Maurice K.'s time and tenure as custodian of Pennsylvania's forests, such decision making was fairly straightforward. The Secretary was the final arbiter of what constituted multiple-use and who the multiple users of a given resource were to be.

Although Maurice K. received the advice of a coterie of close subordinates within the Department of Forests and Waters and from official groups such as the State Planning Board and the State Forest Commission, what he decided was the last word. And Goddard fully, perhaps even eagerly, accepted this responsibility. While on occasion he solicited input from the public, his relationship with the beneficiaries of his department's resource management actions — the citizens of the Commonwealth — was largely only explanatory or educational.

His willingness to make the tough decision, to be the focal point — rather than the Chief Executive — on unpleasant, even contentious issues, and against quarrelsome advocates in a difficult and rapidly evolving area, may be what made him attractive to a succession of Pennsylvania governors. In his biography of William Scranton, George D. Wolf claims, for example, that Maurice K. "was the butt of the opposition" on Project 70, not the Governor. [13]

The idea of setting aside forest lands and at the same time "using" them was not new with the Secretary of Forests and Waters. Maurice K. simply gave the idea broader scope, a sweeping intent, and such forceful execution that it became the hallmark of his forest management philosophy, even his public persona. The waving finger and the booming voice were only outward signs for his inner resolve. He stood tall figuratively even more than literally.

The rudiments of a multiple-use philosophy were in place prior to the turn of the century. Before Gifford Pinchot first used the word conservation to explain a connected set of problems dealing with natural resources, and then had President Theodore Roosevelt pronounce in his 1901 State of the Union Address that "Protection is not an end in itself, . . . the fundamental idea . . . is perpetuation by use," proposals for managing forest resources for "use" but not "overuse" had been made.

Two years after having established a Bureau of Forestry in 1895, with Dr. Joseph Trimble Rothrock as its head, the Pennsylvania General Assembly enunciated two basic policies for the new bureau: responsibility for extinguishing forest fires, and the establishment of forest reserves at the headwaters of the state's three large rivers. Moreover, the legislature charged Rothrock with making these forest reserves "demonstration areas" for the practice of forestry, and directed him to manage them so as to accomplish three objectives: "furnish timber," "protect the water supply," and "provide recreation areas for citizens of the state." [14]

Although the early thinking about the nation's forests was to treat them largely as timber farms and watershed protectors, the idea of multiple-use was suggested in several states, including Pennsylvania. In his reference anthology, *Forests and Forestry in the American States*, Ralph Widner credits a Pinchot pupil, E. M. Griffith of Wisconsin, as an early State Forester who urged the concept of "multiple-use" of Wisconsin's forest land. In 1906, according to Widner, Griffith proposed linking the use of Wisconsin forest lands as preserves, as well as with watershed control, commercial timber sale, farm woodlots, and state parks.

In Pennsylvania, however, Maurice K. was the first to give such force to the "multiple-use" idea, that the state has, not only accomplished its three legislative objectives of a hundred years ago, but made Pennsylvania a showcase for the nation, Under Maurice K. the state also has added new uses and users to the mix. Now Pennsylvania public lands are open for hunting and fishing, watershed protection, electric power generation, oil and gas exploitation, flood control, and public recreation, as well as for commercial tree and forest product harvest. As another vital use for the state's forests, Maurice K. even took into consideration air purification for the expanding populations of Pennsylvania's metropolitan areas, with their increasingly paved expanses — which he abhorred.

The principles that Maurice K. and others had been practicing for several decades were eventually enacted into law in 1960. In June of that year the Multiple Use Act, Public Law 86-517, directed the U.S. Secretary of Agriculture to "develop and administer the renewable surface resources of the national forests for multiple-use and sustained yield of the several products and services obtained therefrom." These were "outdoor recreation, range, timber, watershed, and wildlife and fish purposes." The establishment of a priority or proportion between these products and services was assigned to the Secretary of Agriculture, although the law acknowledged that a given forest might not yield all of them and the weight given to one product or service over the others would differ from forest to forest and even from time to time in the same forest.

□ □ □ □

The 1970 Pennsylvania Forest Plan was not one monolithic document, but many; with a separate multi-section blueprint developed for each of the state's twenty forest districts. Among these were plans for Tuscarora, Forbes, Rothrock, Gallitzin, Bald

Eagle, Kittanning, Sproul, and Moshannon. The individual plans, each of which was divided into five major sections, covered timber, water, wildlife, minerals, recreation and aesthetics, and not only reflected the condition of the various resources but also included an assessment of the economic and social values that the forest provided. To help achieve meaningful multiple-use of the resources, the plans furnished guidelines to be used to reduce the conflict between the various users.

Like the one for 1955, the Forest Resource Plan for 1970 was scheduled for a complete review and update in 1985, although it was designed so that it could be revised or updated at any time within the fifteen-year management period. The process of developing the plan for each forest consisted of five steps: the "establishment of its objectives," the "inventory of the resources," a "study of past performance" with a "prediction of future demands," the "development of specific management recommendations," and the "weighing of the interactions of the management recommendations in the formulations of a balanced action program." [15]

The five sections of each plan were Report, Watershed Management, Recreation, Timber Management, and Minerals. The Report section, for example, "provided descriptive" (geologic and physiographic) and "historical information" (acquisition, original forest type and influences for change); "summarized the resources (timber, water, mineral, and recreation) of the forest;" and listed "the management objectives and policy statements covering the operations" of the specific forest. [16] It made clear that the objective of each plan was: to provide the maximum sustained yield of high-quality timber products; to protect the watersheds making available the maximum yield of potable water; to provide recreational outlets for the general public; and to permit the development of the mineral resources of the forest.

The Report Section sized and located each forest. For Michaux, as an example, which had 77,036 acres spanning Adams, Cumberland and Franklin Counties, the acreage figures were obtained from a tabulation compiled from the original deed acreage documents on file in the several county courthouses. [17] The totals were then divided into commercial and non-commercial forest acreage. The commercial area was categorized for either even- or uneven-age management, while the acreage of the non-commercial area was broken out by roads, reservoirs, camps, parks, picnic areas and rights-of-way. A map locating the forest in Pennsylvania and another positioning it locally were also provided.

Part three of the plan, the Watershed Management Section, made clear that the Department of Forests and Waters believed that "water is one of the most, if not the most, important resource derived from state forest land." Moreover, that, "like timber, water is a renewable resource when properly managed." Part three also stated that the objective was "to make available the maximum yield of potable water under sound multiple use practices." To accomplish this the forester was to "restrict or limit" activities and development within the watersheds that would "reduce the quantity or impair the quality of water" it yielded. [18]

In support of these policies, the operating portion of the Watershed Management Section furnished detailed instructions on all phases of timber management. Among these were ones that covered the building of haul and skid roads in such places and manner as to minimize their impact on watercourses, "even small springs and seeps." The distance between a stream and road or trail had to be fifty feet plus four feet for each one percent of slope and, when a crossing couldn't be avoided, streams had to be spanned at a right angle on a closed culvert or bridge. The operating plan went on to specify maximum road grades as well as techniques for locating cross drains, and provided formulae to be followed in calculating the minimum allowable distance (along the roadway) between them. [19] Even greater details were provided for the development of recreation sites that might impact on water resources. As the plan stated:

> Recreation development within a watershed constitutes both a pollution and sediment problem. Future development within existing and

potential watersheds must be aimed toward eliminating or minimizing these problems. [20]

Forests and water have gone together in the public mind since Gifford Pinchot and Theodore Roosevelt linked the preservation of the nation's water to that of its forests. In their minds water was the end, the purpose for the nascent conservation movement, and forests were the keystone to protecting it. The literature in the ensuing years is filled with papers and books arguing the extent to which upstream forests do in fact aid either the quantity or the quality of water — whether, for example, and if so how much forests reduce the size of floods — but while trees and timber are linked in the popular mind, forests and water are the backbone of conservation philosophy and effort at both the state and national level.

In the general description of *recreation* as a "forest resource," development was to be "aimed at those segments of recreation that cannot be or are not provided for under other land use or ownership." This, of course, was because the size of the land base within a state forest provides a unique opportunity for informal outdoor recreation that cannot be obtained from small forest areas or from private ownership.

While hunting and fishing were important outdoor activities in almost all state forests there were exceptions. In Michaux, for example, the forest plan claimed that "driving the forest roads" was the major recreation use in terms of visitor days. The network of 124 miles in Michaux was dotted with scenic vistas that made them heavily used, especially in the spring and fall months. [21] Where wildlife was a high value in a forest, positive programs were developed to improve the habitat and increase the wildlife population. Although the Commonwealth realizes no monetary return from the recreational resource, except for camp leases, it promotes recreation because visitors to the forest and any adjacent state parks do have a significant impact on the general economy of the area.

The primary means by which the forest plans coordinated and allocated the five *resources* among the potential users was through a "Land Use and Zoning Policy." Tracts within the forest were zoned for a "primary land use," and then the timber management practices which best protected and enhanced the value for which the land had been zoned were specified. Other activities were permitted, but in case of a conflict were subordinated to the primary land use.

The District Forester not only prepared the Forest Resource Plan for his forest (under the supervision of the Forest Resource Planning Branch of the Forest Advisory Services Division), but was also responsible for carrying out the details of each plan. The documentation for each plan went through a half-dozen levels of review and approval, starting with Joseph Ibberson of Forest Advisory Services. The final signature on each plan was, of course, Maurice K. Goddard's.

❏ ❏ ❏ ❏

During the inventory phase of the 1970 Forest Resource Plan, "unique or unusual biologic, geologic," and "scenic or historic areas" were reviewed for possible Natural Area designation. Natural Area status was deemed advisable whenever other resource development would adversely affect the value of the area. Potential Wild Areas were also located during the inventory process. To be considered, an area had to be relatively free of manmade developments such as roads, rights-of-way, pipelines, camp sites, and mineral ownership; be at least three thousand acres in size; and possess high scenic value. The public is able to visit and use a Wild Area for activities such as hiking, hunting, and fishing, but in which no development of a permanent nature is permitted. No public access roads are constructed into a Wild Area and leases of campsites are not made. Forest trail use is restricted to foot travel, horseback riding and bicycling.

The proposed Natural Areas and Wild Areas located during the development of the Forest Resources Plans were submitted to the Environmental Quality Board in April 1975. Forty-four Natural Areas and thirteen Wild Areas were designated by the Board, including those originally recognized by the State Forest Commission. Maurice K. jealously guarded the state's Wild and Natural Areas. When one resident living near a Natural Area wrote asking permission to remove a wind-thrown hemlock lying on the ground, he responded:

> I regret to advise you that, should I comply with your request, I would be acting contrary to the basic policy established for the administration of [natural areas]. The policy states that, where possible, the management . . . shall be such that "nature's way" shall prevail. . . . Down timber shall be allowed to remain on the forest floor so that the public, when viewing the forest may see evidence of the endless cycle of nature. [22]

❑ ❑ ❑ ❑

Not only did the Department of Forests and Waters complete the new Forest Plan for all of Pennsylvania in 1970, but the Department's Bureau of Engineering, under Clifford McConnell, also finished the monumental task of preparing a water resources planning inventory for the state that cataloged all of the dams, reservoirs and natural lakes throughout the Commonwealth. [23]

Clifford ("Cliff") H. McConnell came to Harrisburg from Minnesota, by sheer happenstance. He was a Chippewa on his father's side and had graduated from the University of Minnesota with a degree in civil engineering. By 1955 he was in charge of operations at the Fort Peck Dam on the Missouri River in northeast Montana. On occasion his job took him to York, Pennsylvania, to inspect equipment destined for installation at Fort Peck.

McConnell and his wife Elizabeth were hoping to provide better educational possibilities for their children than were available in Montana, so he decided to check on the job opportunities in central

Pennsylvania. He simply walked into Goddard's office during one of his trips to York in late 1955 or early 1956 and introduced himself. Cliff and Maurice K. immediately hit it off. McConnell was business-like and forthright, exactly the kind of professional Maurice K. and Governor Leader were looking to staff Forests and Waters. When McConnell left, Maurice K. told those around him, "That's my water man!" [24]

McConnell's *Water Resources Inventory* for the state divided Pennsylvania into six river basins: the Delaware, Susquehanna, Potomac, Genesee, Ohio, and Lake Erie. Each of the basins was further divided into sub-basins. There were, for example, three for the Delaware River Basin, five for the Ohio River Basin and nine for the Susquehanna River Basin. [25]

The water resources inventory was the first piece in the development of a comprehensive State Water Resources Plan, the purpose of which was "to insure the Commonwealth of a systematic development, preservation, and utilization of its water and related land resources." [26] Although the department had conducted an inventory between 1913 and 1920 as a result of a 1913 act of the Pennsylvania Legislature, it had not been kept current. Between the turn of the century and 1970, the state Water and Power Resources Board had granted more than six thousand permits to construct dams or other forms of stream or river obstructions. And during those years, nature had taken its toll; many of the early dams had been breached or dislodged.

The report was detailed. Dams were identified by type of construction: earth, masonry, concrete, rock fill, arch, steel or metal, inflatable or collapsible. And the uses ranged from public or industrial water supply to agricultural, flood control or recreational. The inventory contained geographical information, including the latitude and longitude coordinates of each structure, and in addition to the type of dam, physical data such as the height of the structure, the volume and surface area of the reservoir, the size of the contributing drainage area, the use to which the reservoir was put, the name of the owner and the original Water and Power Resources Board permit number.

❑ ❑ ❑ ❑

The *Forest Resource Plan* of 1970 and the *Dams, Reservoirs and Natural Lakes Water Resources Planning Inventory* of the same year were the culmination, the *magnum opus*, of Maurice K.'s fifteen years at the helm of the Department of Forests and Waters. They reflected the state of Pennsylvania's environmental resources and hinted at the direction that Maurice K. hoped to take in their further conservation. Although both documents were bureaucratic in form and style, they enjoyed one major advantage over most such documents. They were grounded in the substantiality of living objects, the forests and the waters of the Commonwealth of Pennsylvania.

# CHAPTER XIII

## DEPARTMENT OF ENVIRONMENTAL RESOURCES

> *The primary obstacle to conservation in the Commonwealth is not lack of authority but the diffusion of authority and the lack of coordinated planning essential to the proper, efficient exercise of powers already granted by the General Assembly.*
>
> William F. Schultz

Maurice K. seemed to have understood fully the interconnection of conservation disciplines early in his public career. In 1960 he had told the foresters they must take on new tasks, they must become more than woodsmen, that "today's forester" must be a "land-management specialist." And five years earlier, he recognized that the future, at least for him, lay not in academia but in the more active arena of state government. Moreover, he appreciated fully the connection between air, land, and water; their conjunction was part of the thrust of his ring of parks around Pennsylvania's urban areas to "maintain their livability." [1] The parks were needed so the cities could breath — literally as well as figuratively.

He viewed decision making, however, with the eye of an engineer. Floods were a problem; dams were an appropriate answer. Whether or not these statement were true, or the only truth, the U.S. Army Corps of Engineers had the ability, the desire and the means to put up high dams, and Maurice K. had the same ability, desire and means to put up small ones.

He did not seem to grasp completely, or at least to accept the significance of the new "environmental politics," as Samuel P. Hays calls it, [2] that swept over the nation in the sixties and seventies. Maurice K. certainly welcomed the heightened awareness over environmental issues that occurred during the period, but was disturbed by the growing influence of citizens' groups on governmental decision making — their ability to lay waste to the well-developed plans of professional conservationists.

In a 1972 talk, "Antipollution 'crusade' goes too far," at Drexel University in Philadelphia, Maurice K. complained, "It has become progressively difficult to accomplish anything constructive in managing and developing our natural resources; people can be found to object to almost any form of alteration." After citing a quotation of Theodore Roosevelt's, that "conservation means development as much as it does protection," he told his audience:

> I am concerned about the private citizen's input. Much of it is based on fear, emotion, and misunderstanding and not on calm, reasoned thought and a complete understanding of the problems and alternatives." [3]

He had a sense of authority from being a professional that was seemingly coupled with a lack of understanding of human nature. Once, when he had an extra pine tree and no place for it in his yard, he took it to Cliff McConnell's house and planted it right in the middle of his chief water engineer's back lawn. When Mrs. McConnell arrived home, she found Maurice K. sitting on the porch, waiting like a proud little boy to show her what he had done. She was so upset by his presumption that she immediately got a shovel and helped him move it to the side of the property. [4]

❑ ❑ ❑ ❑

Prior to the sixties, influence groups were largely made up of the affluent: often those who had a direct, sometimes even vested interest in the outcome of their lobbying efforts. The power of the previously powerless — that the war in Vietnam seemed to unleash — was now through private, often ad hoc, environmental organizations, forcing government to become responsive to issues such as land abuse, air pollution, and water degradation in ways never before experienced by the professionals. The very term "environmental" was beginning to replace the word "conservation." The old fair-use ideas of Gifford Pinchot and Theodore Roosevelt were finally giving way to a new "aesthetic" dynamic, that of the Muir, McFarland preservationists.

As Franklin L. Kury has written in his *Natural Resources and the Public Estate*: "With the convening of the 1967-1968 [Pennsylvania legislative] session, the environmental revolution became a rising, strong tide that did not fall until 1973." During that period the All Surface Mining Act, the Coal Refuse Disposal Control Act, the Air Pollution Control Act, the Clean Streams Act, the Solid Waste Management Act, the Pennsylvania Scenic Rivers Act, the Land and Water Conservation and Reclamation Act, and Act 120, which required the Pennsylvania Department of Transportation to conduct an environmental evaluation in planning highway projects were all enacted. [5]

In addition, the legislature restructured the state's environmental forces by defining the powers and duties of a vast new agency, the Department of Environmental Resources. It also amended the Pennsylvania Constitution to include a Declaration of Rights article, covering "Natural Resources and the Public Estate." The Declaration asserted that "the people have a right to clean air, pure water, and to the preservation of the natural scenic, historic, and esthetic values of the environment," and that these resources were "the common property of all the people." As Kury explains, the drafters of the Constitution in the eighteenth century were "concerned with the political environment" and were "silent concerning the natural environment." [6]

Kury, who was a freshman member of the Pennsylvania House, believed that we should give "our natural environment the same kind of constitutional protection that was given our political rights," so he drafted and introduced the environmental amendment in April, 1969. It went through a number of changes in the House and Senate Conservation Committees as well as review by, among others, the Secretary of Forests and Waters. Maurice K. suggested changing "preserve" to "conserve" to avoid the interpretation that the amendment intended to freeze the environment in its present state. [7]

□ □ □ □

Late in 1969 at the end of his term, almost at the last minute, Governor Shafer signed the bill, Act 275, that established a new Pennsylvania super-agency for Environmental Resources. While according to the bill's sponsor, Rep. John F. Laudadio, Democrat of Westmoreland County, it "did not make any substantive changes in the existing powers of the state," the act abolished the Department of Forests and Waters and its Mines and Mineral Industries Division and twelve other independent boards and commissions. Laudadio's new agency gathered in all of these as well as other miscellaneous environmental responsibilities scattered throughout the executive branch and thus combined all of Pennsylvania's resource management activities with its control of air and water pollution under one cabinet-level position. [8] According to Governor Shafer,

> The signing of this bill is the first command to all the fragmented environmental forces of state government to band together as an army for the first time in the war against pollution and waste of our environment. [9]

The Secretary of Forests and Waters thought otherwise. Maurice K. was concerned about politics entering the state's anti-pollution efforts and told the reporters exactly what he thought of the idea. Several of the boards that would oversee and assist the Department of Environmental Resources were to be staffed with legislators as well as with independent members and the chairmen of the Game Commission, the state Planning Board, the Public Utility Commission and the Historical and Museum Commission. Maurice K. was afraid that Cabinet members would be unwilling to debate with the legislators on the oversight boards since the department heads had to go to the General Assembly for their budgetary needs. Bluntly, and with some sense of prescience, he stated, "I would not want a setup like this running a state park." [10]

While his objections over the concept of the new super-agency might be considered self-serving — his job was abolished, and a new governor would be taking office in less than a month — Maurice K. invariably said what he thought needed saying. If the idea of the new agency was wrong, then he had not only a right but an obligation to say so. And this he did even though John Laudadio, long-time supporter of conservation and Chairman of the Pennsylvania House Committee on Conservation and Natural Resources, was a good friend. [11] "Jimmy [Rankin, his chauffeur] and I thoroughly enjoyed ourselves at your home. It was a pleasure meeting your husband's brothers and sisters and to have had some time to relax," Maurice K. wrote in a letter thanking Mrs. Laudadio for the hospitality she and her husband had shown them during a stop at the Laudadio home in Jeannette. [12]

❑ ❑ ❑ ❑

In yet another example of Maurice K.'s staying power, however, on January 15, 1971, incoming Governor Milton Shapp appointed him as the acting head of the Department of Environmental Resources. The announcement stated that when the new Secretary was appointed, Maurice K. would become the Deputy Secretary in charge of Environment Resources. [13]

The move was on, however, from the beginning to convince Maurice K. to take the position permanently. His friend Frank Masland, Jr., who had helped draft the bill establishing the new agency, initially omitted Maurice's name from the list he suggested to the Governor because he thought Maurice was not interested. He quickly changed his mind when he found out the Acting Secretary was willing to become its permanent head. "I want you to have what you want to have," Masland told Maurice K. Masland admitted that the new Department would probably be as "cumbersome to administer as the Department of the Interior at Washington," but explained to Maurice:

> I would much prefer to entrust that for which I am responsible to your hands, knowing that any changes you support will be designed to strengthen the administrative process and be the result of your unequaled experience. [14]

Eventually, Governor Shapp came to agree with Masland and nominated Maurice K. to head the new agency. It was to be, however, one of the more protracted nomination experiences that a Pennsylvania governor and his nominee has endured.

□ □ □ □

The idea of a super-agency was hardly new. As early as 1953, when he made his comprehensive survey of Pennsylvania's conservation law and administration, and then a pre-inaugural review of the Department of Forests and Waters' policies for Governor Leader (see Chapter V), William Schultz had proposed that all of Pennsylvania's conservation agencies be placed under a single secretary. Although he felt that the existing state agencies had "sufficient substantive power in the aggregate to carry out an adequate conservation program," he developed a "Model Act" [15] that combined all of the resource activities in a single organization, because, as he wrote in the introduction to his "Model Act," Schultz believed that,

> the primary obstacle to conservation in the Commonwealth is not lack of authority but the diffusion of authority and the lack of coordinated planning essential to the proper, efficient exercise of powers already granted by the General Assembly. [16]

Schultz's concern was over what he called a "prolific source of trouble" in the present organizational arrangement, "the frequent overlapping of functions." He cited the Little Hoover Commission (the Chesterman Committee) that Governor Fine had appointed to study the state's administration, which, according to Schultz, "recognized the principle of simplicity as well as the need for the integration of the conservation agencies of the Commonwealth." In 1953, as a result of the commission's recommendations, Governor Fine had asked the legislature to create a single department of conservation to replace the Fish and Game Commissions and the Department of Forests and Waters, but nothing had come of his proposal. Schultz's Model Act went much further, however, than an implementation of the Little Hoover Commission's recommendations. It combined fish, game, water, forests, parks, mines and minerals, and lands and soils, in a single "Department of Conservation."

In his "declaration of purpose," Schultz wrote that the "wastage, pollution, and loss of such resources through neglect and mismanagement and through the lack of control, supervision, and planning constitutes an immediate danger to the health, safety, and welfare of the Commonwealth and its people." Schultz concluded that,

> the conservation of these natural resources can best be effectuated through a system of unified control and the development of a long-range, integrated, and correlated program for all such resources emphasizing the conservation of each resource and recognizing that the management of one resource directly affects all other resources. [17]

Maurice K. was well aware of Schultz's idea from the time he first took office in 1955. To those who asked about conservation laws in the state, he regularly recommended a review of the Pittsburgh professor's *Conservation Law and Administration* as a good starting point. [18] By the time the super-agency idea had reached political viability in the Shafer Administration, however, the Secretary of Forests and Waters was vigorously against the proposal or, at least, the one as implemented under Act 275.

□ □ □ □

Although Maurice K. disliked the very idea of an agency that combined regulatory and conservation responsibilities, he accepted the job from Governor Shapp determined to make it work. One small but to him important point was his insistence that his former Forests and Waters staff members never refer to themselves as anything other than DER employees.

For a number of years before the establishment of DER, it had been the practice of the U.S. Forest Service to provide funds to the states for the production of a state calendar highlighting Smokey Bear. The calendars had been part of an effective public awareness program built around Smokey that highlighted the danger to forests from fires. Some reports credited the New Mexico bear, who had been discovered as a severely burned cub following a 1950 Lincoln National Forest fire, with reducing such fires by a factor of 90 percent. In 1971 Smokey was at the height of his popularity. According to some surveys, his figure was the second most recognizable after Santa Claus.

The Department of Forests and Waters had taken advantage of the Forest Service's offer for a number of years and produced what was generally acknowledged to be an attractive and effective calendar, one in which the department and especially those who produced it took pride.

Several months following the establishment of DER the man who had created the calendar was called upstairs to see Maurice K. He thought it was to be congratulated, as in past years, on having done another good job. After being ushered into the Secretary's office, he approached Goddard's desk and noticing his Smokey calendar in the Secretary's hand prepared to receive some well-deserved plaudits. Instead, shaking the bear picture at the artist accusingly, Maurice K. asked him: "Are you responsible for this calendar?" On receiving an affirmative reply, Goddard angrily ripped the calendar in half and threw it on the desk, sputtering, "Nowhere does it mention DER!" Then he ordered the stunned fellow to "Get Out!" [19]

It would take more than a dramatic confrontation over publicizing the name of the new organization, however, to make it work. The management problems and complexities were numerous. Where there had been two deputy secretaries and a handful of bureaus there were now five deputies, twenty-two bureaus and six other offices, boards and commissions that Maurice K. had to work with. To complicate his organizational work further, members and units of the department were situated all across downtown Harrisburg. Some were located in the former Hotel Harrisburger, others in the Executive House on South Second Street, and still others in the old Forests and Waters Building on Third Street.

□ □ □ □

Neither William Schultz nor Maurice K. apparently foresaw that the regulatory aspects would consume so much of the time and resources — financial and labor — of the state's conservation concerns and of the new Secretary. Schultz's Model Law simply carried the statements of the regulatory functions of each resource activity forward to his new agency. Furthermore Maurice K. hadn't mentioned any concern over combining the regulatory and management of resources together when Act 275 became law; he was more worried that politics and the merging of a plethora of oversight boards and groups would make the secretary's job of managing such a large agency too difficult. When, years later, he recommended that the agency be dismantled, it was the usurpation of the Secretary's and the Agency's time, and especially the imbalance between appropriations in the budget for natural resource management and for protecting the environment, that was his main concern.

Within the first hundred days of DER's establishment, Maurice K. had not only completed the reorganization and developed responsibility statements, but had developed plans for working with the Advisory Council, Quality Board and Hearing Board, had identified the support personnel to be transferred from the

Department of Health, had begun a compilation of department regulations, and had made preparations in the Bureau of Legal Services for twelve hearings. [20]

Maurice K. broke the Deputy for Enforcement's office into three bureaus: Administrative Enforcement, Legal Services (to act as a general law firm), and the Bureau of Litigation Enforcement, which handled actions under statutes and regulations relating to the alleviation of nuisances, pollution and other damages to the environment. Major cases were transferred to the Justice Department after the investigative phase was completed.

The Bureau of Litigation Enforcement's "Strike Force," as it came to be known, began winning not only high profile cases in air and water pollution and solid waste disposal, but also large numbers of litigations against small companies and communities. In one water-quality management case, Judge James S. Bowman of Commonwealth Court issued a permanent injunction in April 1971 ordering Barnes and Tucker Company to clean up acid mine drainages into the West Branch of the Susquehanna. A natural gas company in Pittston was bound over to the grand jury on a charge of manslaughter arising out of a 1969 explosion that claimed four lives at an underground storage operation of the firm. And action was filed against U.S. Steel Corporation to abate air pollution violations occurring at its Saxonburg plant. [21]

Winning a few big cases, as Maurice K. recognized, meant that the Department would eventually be able to handle more of the problems through negotiation and administrative action. In Delaware County, the Strike Force litigated a few solid-waste-disposal cases, but then negotiated with several disposal sites at Clearview and Folcroft that were encroaching on the Tinicum Marsh. And DER's enforcement activities were corporate-blind — even municipalities came under fire.

The Department began citing firms and communities all over the state: several companies in Philadelphia and Downingtown for exposing their employees to excessive amounts of silica dust, a Montgomery County firm for failure to abide by regulations governing the use of drilling equipment, a Pittsburgh coal company for discharge of untreated mine drainage into the Chartiers Creek, a Northumberland quarry for operating an air track drill without a required positive dust suppression system, several municipalities in Allegheny Country that were polluting Willow Run and Pine Creek, and an Atlasburg firm on charges of noise pollution. The department even forced a York County laundromat to cease operations until it took measures to comply with the Clean Streams Act. [22]

At the same time Maurice K. began to move from litigation to negotiation, he also went out of his way to encourage those who were working to solve pollution problems. On April 29, 1971, he "officially dedicated" a new mine-drainage treatment plant, at Burgettstown, as part of DER's "Operation Scarlift." This plant, which was to be operated by the Smith Township supervisors, was the first of its kind in the country. It not only cleaned up a long-standing scar from past coal mining but also manufactured an anti-skid material for use on highways out of the burned-out mine refuse.

□ □ □ □

According to William Eichbaum, the Deputy Secretary for Enforcement, Maurice K. not only gave him great latitude in running his three bureaus, but also gave Eichbaum's efforts his full support. He was involved, often on a day-to-day basis, especially on the controversial cases. Maurice K. felt it was "extremely important to have good, solid legal representation for the department"; thus he helped Eichbaum weed out those attorneys who were unwilling to work full time for the department or wanted to continue with their private practices. [23]

Eichbaum, who prior to the merger of his position with the Department of Environmental Resources had been an Assistant Attorney General at the Department of Health, recalls that the idea for the Strike Force "grew out of the sad state of enforcing the law as it stood in Pennsylvania before DER was set up."

Eventually, however, a significant number of legislators came to feel that the department lawyers were pressing some of their cases too vigorously. First they introduced resolutions in the House calling on the Governor to curb "the power" of the attorneys, and when these didn't pass conducted hearings on the issue. Hearings were held in Pittsburgh and then in Harrisburg. [24] Eichbaum and Maurice K. both were called to testify. Both men admitted that mistakes had been made, but reassured the committee members that they were making every effort to use the prosecutorial power as fairly as possible. Maurice K. told them:

> I think the record would indicate that we're doing better and I think we're making tremendous progress and obviously, . . . we have differences of opinion, ruffle people's feathers, so I think this is part of that dialogue, . . . to make it work better and we're glad to receive criticism and suggestions to try to make it work better. [25]

Enforcement of environmental and departmental regulations was, however, not something new to Maurice K. In his years at Forests and Waters, he frequently wrote letters to recover damages to Department-managed properties for the destruction of timber by loggers, and to townships that did not honor the agreements under which they accepted state-developed flood control works. In 1959, for example, he submitted a bill to the Pittsburgh Bicentennial Association for damage to the Allegheny River Wharf in Point State Park and the following year ordered the township manager of Cheltenham Township in Elkins Park to correct eleven violations of its maintenance agreement for the flood protection works at Glenside. Among the citations requiring remediation by the township were ones for silting, shrubbery and tree plantings by private citizens on the bank, rocks and debris thrown into the channel, and unauthorized footbridges that had been built across the works. [26]

❑ ❑ ❑ ❑

Although Maurice K.'s reputation as Pennsylvania's leading conservationist would have been known to Governor Shapp, who took environmental issues seriously, even personally, Shapp apparently was pleased with the progress the Acting Secretary of the Department of Environmental Resources had made in his first one hundred days. When he opened his press conference on 16 April, the Governor issued a brief statement that Maurice K. was his choice as the permanent Secretary for the Department of Environmental Resources. Shapp said: "I, and the Commonwealth, have been fortunate" in that Dr. Maurice Goddard "has agreed to take on these difficult tasks on a permanent basis." [27] The first "difficult task," however, that Maurice K. and Governor Shapp would have to face was getting the nomination through the Pennsylvania Senate.

Milton J. Shapp, a Philadelphia industrialist, management innovator, and staunch supporter of human rights, had served as an advisor and consultant on economic development to President Kennedy. Moreover, he was the author of many texts and theories on governmental reform and economies. Two years after he returned from the army in 1946, Shapp with $500 and two employes founded an electronics company. When he resigned in 1966 to make his first unsuccessful effort to run for governor of Pennsylvania, the company was a multi-million-dollar corporation employing twenty-one hundred people in the manufacture of electronics parts and equipment. Shapp not only was a staunch advocate for the employment of the disadvantaged, for women's rights and for labor-management agreements, but also for the environment. [28] In 1970 he finally won election to the governorship, without the backing of the Democratic Party.

For six months after Governor Shapp made the announcement of his selection for a permanent Secretary for DER, the "Goddard Controversy" raged in the papers across the state. The Pennsylvania Environmental Council along with the Pennsylvania Federation of Sportsmens Clubs and the Western Pennsylvania Conservancy came out as pro-Goddard, while the Sierra Club was among the anti-Goddard groups.

The Sierra Club summarized its objections by stating, "his record does not hold promise for the kind of leadership, imagination, and concern required of the head of the fledgling Department of Environmental Resources." Among the twelve "examples" that the club cited to support its contention of "Dr. Goddard's lack of understanding of critical environmental problems" were the following: "Indifferent approach to environmental enforcement of existing laws," lack of response to strip mining and to air and water pollution, the use of "outmoded criteria for design" of state parks "limited to a standardized pattern regardless of setting," support of dams on Bald Eagle Creek and at Tocks Island in the Delaware River, as well as his "inflexible advocacy of the Evansburg Dam." [29]

The Sierra Club's first point of objection in its statement to the Pennsylvania Senate, however, was to cite Maurice K.'s opposition to creation of the Department of Environmental Resources. This was a frequently heard objection to his permanent appointment. The *Reading Eagle* countered this, however, by editorializing: "The fact that he was concerned enough about it to question it should be a point for him, not against him." [30]

But dams — or rather one dam — was at the center of the issue when the Senate voted. The advocates of no dam at Evansburg began to sense that this might just be an opportunity to settle an old score. The Citizens to Save the Skippack Valley came out strongly against the nomination. They charged that Maurice K. was avoiding filing a Federal Environmental Impact Statement because he did not have adequate data to justify the dam, that the dam would destroy the historical and cultural heritage of the Skippack Valley and thus the open space recreational intent of Project 70, that Maurice K. was concealing the total cost of the project because of extensive cost overruns, and that as the senior member of the Delaware River Basin Commission, he failed to use his influence to accomplish a comprehensive water study of the Delaware River Basin, although several millions of taxpayers dollars have been spent.

Senator Holl apparently agreed with the citizens. He and a few other Senators simply exercised their right of "senatorial courtesy" with the full senate and thus kept the appointment from a vote. Maurice K. and Governor Shapp would not withdraw the appointment as the opposition apparently had hoped. Shapp continued to meet with individual members of the Senate, and by early November when the issue "broke into the limelight," told Maurice K. he felt "quite confident that confirmation is but a matter of time." [31] And Maurice K. did receive letters of encouragement from across the Commonwealth. The ninety-three-year-old Judge Edwin O. Lewis, with whom he had worked for years on the Independence Mall State Park in Philadelphia, wrote:

> You are in the midst of that silly objection to your confirmation by three Republican senators, whose heads I would like to knock together for . . . blocking the confirmation of the best public servant on the State rolls. [32]

By the middle of November the hew and cry of editorials and letters to the editor in the papers had reached a fever pitch. "Dr. Goddard is unalterably determined to inundate [the Skippack Valley] with polluted water." [He] has established himself as a political dictator." "The thousands of members of the Bay Committee . . . appreciate his views on economics versus conservation." "One salient fact is seldom mentioned . . . Goddard's arrogant and implacable attitude." [33]

Eventually the sentiment around the state for the Senate to "break [its] dreary tradition of back-room, closed-door caucus politicking," as the *Philadelphia Inquirer* described it, grew too strong; the Chairman of the Executive Nominations Committee was forced to bring the issue to the floor. Maurice K. was overwhelmingly confirmed by a vote of forty-six to four. He received a laconic letter from the U. S. House of Representatives. Its three sentences read like a telegram. It was signed, Daniel J. Flood.

"Congratulations on Senate confirmation. — I can't imagine why it was held up so long. The State is lucky to have you." [34]

And from his friend, Homer Kreider, President Judge of the Court of Common Pleas of the Twelfth Judicial District, came a note of congratulations. After telling Maurice K. that the letter was being sent *nunc pro tunc*, Judge Kreider wrote: "Pennsylvania is indeed fortunate in having such a nationally recognized expert as yourself to guide the implementation of the Environmental Program — with common sense." He had intended to congratulate Maurice K. at a meeting of Harrisburg's Eclectic Club, but was unable to attend. [35]

❑ ❑ ❑ ❑

The full public hearings, however, that the *Inquirer* said were needed — before a vote was taken — to examine whether Dr. Goddard "represents an anachronistic concept of man's relation to his environment," and whether his "traditional conservationist attitudes are outworn" and "actively contribute to the destruction of irreplaceable animal and vegetable life and their natural support systems," were never held. [36] The debate on expanding the meaning of "conservation" to include the new "ecology" would not be taken up by the legislature, it would continue to be framed case by case by the public. Actions would not flow from government policy, rather environmental policy would evolve from a consensus of civic actions.

In the fifties, Maurice K. had changed Pennsylvania's view of conservation from Gifford Pinchot's "use without abuse" (of forests and waters) to multiple-use of an expanded inventory of elements (to include recreation, flood control, and low-water augmentation), along with an emphasis on cooperation. In the seventies, his view was still that "steady and sure results are preferable to a demand for instant results which ends up languishing in the courts for years." His view of the new environmentalists was that they were "preservationists who saw a need to lock up natural resources and

239

make them unavailable for use by anyone." [37]   In a speech titled "Down With Chicken Little," eight years after his confirmation battle, Maurice K. berated what he felt were "doomsday predictions."  His view was that rather than "lifeboat ethics,"  we should adopt a positive attitude of "technological optimism."

> When prices go too high, or we reach the unlikely event of near or absolute depletion of something, research and technology are stimulated to deliver us from the problem through development of an adequate substitute — often one which is cheaper or more efficient than the original. [38]

One should not conclude, however, that Maurice K. subscribed exclusively to a view of conservation as driven by technology. While, for example, engineering works were the more visible evidences of the Commonwealth's flood control efforts around the state, by late in his career Maurice K. had become a strong supporter of non-structural solutions.  Whether it reflected a change in Maurice K.'s basic view of conservation — an acceptance of the impracticability of trying to "engineer" fully an escape from flood damage, or a realization that the tide was beginning to turn away from the professional and towards a preservationist point of view — this "new" Goddard position came to the fore following the 1972 Agnes Flood.

While his department continued to clear streams and erect barriers and other structural works, those efforts were balanced with ones to get legislation passed implementing non-engineering measures. He took the lead, for example, at hearings that started in 1974 by telling the legislature, "we must take a common sense approach" to the problem of flooding.  And then at similar hearings a year later, he told them — taking a hydrologist's view — "We must learn to live with nature."  [39]

The two primary non-structural proposals Maurice K. put forward were for "flood plain" and "stormwater" management. Both were "hard sells" to local communities and their representatives, especially to state organizations of township supervisors and borough managers.  They were reluctant for the

Commonwealth to tell them they had to place controls on construction (either the amount or type) by local property owners, many of whom were influential members of their communities.

Maurice K. sent two of his Deputy Secretaries, Tim Weston (who had drafted both a Flood Plain and a Storm Water Management Act) and Donald Osterling (who was an Elks pooh-bah) across the state to talk to community and fraternal organizations in an effort to solicit grass-roots support. [40]

Finally in 1978, following a series of meetings that Franklin Kury had convened to resolve the impasse between DER and the legislature over the issues, both proposals (along with one on Dam Safety) were enacted. The primary purpose of the Flood Plain Management Act was to "authorize a comprehensive and coordinated program of flood plain management, based upon the National Flood Insurance Program, designed to preserve and restore the efficiency and carrying capacity of the streams and flood plains of the Commonwealth." Among its stated goals was one to "minimize the expenditure of public and private funds for flood control projects and for relief, rescue and recovery efforts." [41]

According to Weston, while the Flood Plain Management Act has been very successful, the Storm Water Management Act, which was designed to reduce downstream flooding caused by upstream storm runoffs, has been less successful. [42]

□ □ □ □

The first years at the Department of Environmental Protection were shaky ones. In a letter to all employees when DER was formed, Maurice K., told them that they would continue to perform their currently assigned duties and responsibilities and to report to their present supervisor. The task of integrating four bureaus from Forests and Waters, three from the Department of Health, and twelve from the Department of Mines and Mineral Industries, as well as the State Planning Board, the Soil and Water Conservation

Commission from the Department of Agriculture, and the Division of Mines, Quarries and Explosives from the Department of Labor and Industry, was a daunting one. [43] (See Appendix D for a complete list.) And when it was all finally running smoothly, there would be no Bronze Star or Legion of Merit, only more hard work.

During the first two years of operations nearly three thousand air pollution problems were referred to the agency. At the same time negotiations were completed with General Electric for a $2.4-million, seventeen-station air monitoring system across the state to help DER prevent air pollution episodes. Maurice K. also reported that there was a gain of 147 stream miles cleaned up in 1971, which equalled the total for the three previous years. As a result of enforcement actions, 83 percent of all sewage cases and 93 percent of all water supply cases were in compliance (or making progress to that end) by the close of 1971. Timber sales covering an area of 7,556 acres were at a high of 22,586,000 board feet of saw timber, and 44,394 standard rough cords of pole timber, however, fire weather during the spring fire season was so severe (with 1,257 fires recorded) that Maurice took the extraordinary step of having Governor Shapp place a ban on open burning on April 16. Moreover, the department was responsible for inspecting trailer parks and migrant labor camps, for developing policies for quarries and explosives as well as for strip mines, and for conducting citizen's hearings around the state on a variety of environmental issues. [44]

To add to all these startup difficulties, on June 23, 1972, Tropical Storm Agnes struck Pennsylvania in what Congressman Daniel Flood called "the greatest civic disaster in the history of the Republic." The damage in Pennsylvania was estimated to exceed $3 billion. Although loss of life was held to forty-four individuals, 20,000 families were displaced, and 110,000 homes and hundreds of industrial and commercial establishments badly damaged or destroyed. [45]

The Susquehanna is the longest North American river draining into the Atlantic Ocean. Its watershed touches forty-three

Pennsylvania counties. Of these thirty suffered significant losses. Although the heaviest concentration of damage was in the Wyoming Valley, the environmental destruction throughout the Susquehanna River Basin was believed to have exceeded that of real property. Forests, parks, water courses, bridges, fish, wildlife, and farm soils received extensive damage.

Although it was estimated to require $612.8 million to fund a total restoration, the federal government authorized $400 million for the Commonwealth. [46] Most of this money went for structure and road repair and equipment replacement, not for forest, park, and stream cleanup.

□ □ □ □

By 1973, however, a year which he still called a "time of testing" for the department, Maurice K. was able to report that "much was accomplished under our current programs [because it was a] blessing that no new laws were adopted mandating new responsibilities." This he claimed, was because "we are having difficulty funding current programs with the appropriation we received." One of his biggest disappointments was not being able to open two new state parks due to a lack of funds to operate them. Maurice K. reported, too, that the legislature was beginning "to weaken many of our air and water pollution control laws." In summarizing, he said that the Department "faces another year in which it must vigorously defend itself." [47]

The Office of Enforcement, however, was finally up to its full complement of 28 attorneys by 1973. Permanent offices were established in Pittsburgh and Philadelphia. That year the office initiated over 174 enforcement cases in the courts, of which 56 were criminal actions. In addition, DER attorneys entered into 220 negotiated stipulations for pollution abatement cases around the state. [48]

By 1973, not only had the legislature's love affair with the environment and the passing of environmental laws begun to wane, but the energy crisis and the associated financial downturn prompted budget restraint across state government. In addition to leaving the two new state parks unopened, it was necessary to close four areas in existing parks because of lack of funds to operate them. And although, for example, no attorneys were laid off, enforcement efforts were to go through several years of running "flat" — careful adjustment of case priorities, limited hiring, belt-tightening in all non-essential areas. [49]

But in August of that year, Pennsylvania did send a large contingent of volunteers to fight wild fires in Montana, northern Idaho and Oregon. Within hours of receiving calls for assistance from the U.S. Forest Service, arrangements were in place for the first forty of a total of eighty firefighters led by two Department employees to fly from Harrisburg International Airport. John McCarty, a forest technician from Forest District 2 at McConnellsburg, led the group. The Pennsylvanians were part of a force of thirty-eight hundred volunteer fire wardens and seventy-seven thousand hotshot crew members responsible that year for firefighting in the state. [50]

Although forestry now seemed to take a back seat to pollution enforcement and water concerns, it was never really lost from his view. When the editors of the *Maine Forester* at Orono asked him to write an article, he told them he would "be most happy to prepare material on the subject 'Employment Opportunities for Foresters,' since this has been close to my heart during my entire professional life." [51] During his administration, first of Forests and Waters and then of the Department of Environmental Resources, Pennsylvania's forest resource picture improved in nearly every categories. Figures for the state's total forested land, commercial forest land, and publicly owned commercial forest land all rose significantly. And most heartening, the amount of land forested in saw timber more than tripled. (See Appendix C.) [52]

By 1973, too, Arthur A. Socolow, who headed the Bureau of Topographic and Geologic Survey, was able to report that detailed topographic map coverage had been completed for the Commonwealth. The project, which had begun in 1946, made available 764 topographic quadrangle maps covering the state's 45,025 square miles. The maps — produced using the latest techniques, including aerial photography and automated terrain plotting instruments — were designed to serve as the base for all land-use activities, including basic conservation and land rehabilitation projects, recreational facilities, river basin planning and individual property utilization. [53]

□ □ □ □

Although in his 1975 *Annual Report*, Maurice K. observed that, "In all candor, life in an environmental agency was not all pure water and clear skies," by the following year he was able to report, "The past year was a turning point in many DER programs." It was the year of the nation's Bicentennial. One of the Department's responsibilities included the Bureau of Community Environmental Control's work with local officials to ensure that visitors to Pennsylvania that year would be served by adequate eating, drinking, camping and sanitary facilities. Maurice K. took pride that the job was accomplished without a major disease outbreak in the state.

That year, too, the development of an Environmental Master Plan, a directive in the act that established the Department of Environmental Resources, reached a milestone with the completion of policy recommendations for the first eight critical environmental areas. The department also won a decision from Commonwealth Court agreeing that DER had the authority to order implementation of approved solid waste disposal plans. Had the case been lost, implementation of the planning requirements established by the General Assembly would have been "impossible." [54]

# CHAPTER XIV

# URBAN CONSERVATION

*The main concern of the true conservationist is, and always has been, the conservation of humanity. People, not trees, are our chief concern and principal resource. Foresters and other conservationists help people, not merely trees.* [Maurice Goddard]

On August 30, 1974, Maurice K. traveled to Pittsburgh for the dedication of the 159-foot-high geyser that is the Point State Park fountain. Calling it a "harbinger of good things to come for Pittsburgh," the city's *Post-Gazette* described it as a "watery exclamation point at the apex of what was once 36 acres of commercial slums." [1]

What promised to be a rainy morning turned sunny in time for the ceremonies, which marked the culmination of a twenty-year Goddard involvement in building an urban park for the city. With whistling tugboats pushing barges in the river, freight trains on the far banks, and the cable cars of the Duquesne Incline for a backdrop, [2] the Secretary of the Department of Environmental Resources told the crowd gathered for the celebration that the park was a "Springboard for the resurgence of Downtown Pittsburgh." [3]

Maurice K. had only been in office as the Secretary of Forests and Waters a few months when he appeared before the House Appropriations Committee to justify his Department's budget of $14.25 million for the years 1955 and 1956. Among the many items he laid before the committee were requests of $1 million to acquire additional property for an Independence Mall State Park and a like amount to continue the development work at Point State

246

Park in Pittsburgh, both of which had been started in a previous administration.

Although these two projects were on his plate when he took office, Maurice K. actively supported both efforts with more than budget line submissions. Over the years he attended untold numbers of meetings and had lengthy conversations with city officers, landscape and building architects, municipal planning officials, and local citizen committees. Five years after Maurice K. became Secretary of Forests and Waters, Governor Lawrence, who had been Mayor of Pittsburgh during much of the city's Renaissance, lavished praise on his conservation chief, not only for Maurice K.'s "enthusiasm and direction," but also for his "talent for gaining cooperation between State agencies, between the State and Federal Governments, and between his own Department and private citizens. "I can testify personally," Lawrence said, "to the excellent spirit of co-operation which exists between the people of Pittsburgh and Secretary Goddard. [4]

□ □ □ □

In March 1951, the Pennsylvania Senate had asked the State Joint Government Commission to "initiate an intensive study of the problem of completion of the Independence Hall Mall." The Commission held hearings and took reports from all those involved in the process including Milo F. Draemel, then Secretary of Forests and Waters; Edmund N. Bacon, the Executive Director of the Philadelphia City Planning Commission; S. K. Stevens, chief historian of the Pennsylvania Historical and Museum Commission; and Oscar L. Chapman, the U.S. Secretary of the Interior. [5]

The Commission's report was an assessment, not a finger-pointing document. It outlined the complex legal arrangements between the City of Philadelphia, the Department of the Interior, and the various executive departments of the Commonwealth, to which the state had become a party in 1946. Under the agreement, the city continued to own Independence Hall and the other buildings in Independence Square, the Department of the Interior took responsibility for developing a three-block stretch from Independence Hall leading to St. Mary's Church near the Delaware River — to be called a "memorial thoroughfare" — and the state agreed to buy and develop the three-block-long area east of Independence Hall, between Chestnut and Race Streets. The Department of Forests and Waters' responsibilities included the blocks in which the Merchant's Exchange, the First Bank of the United States, Carpenter's Hall, and the Second Bank of the United States all were located. When completed, the combined state and federal project would form an L-shaped Mall with Independence Square at its elbow [6]

The Department of the Interior also agreed to occupy the historic buildings for the purpose of preserving, exhibiting, and interpreting them for the American people, to assume full curatorial responsibility for the choice of, care and display of museum exhibits, and to operate and maintain the grounds and buildings after the restoration work was completed. [7]

In 1945 the General Assembly had appropriated $16.5 million for the state's share. During the first years of the Independence Mall project the Department of Forests and Waters under Samuel Lewis made no progress "because of its very heavy work load in connection with the desilting of the Schuylkill River," but by 1951 the Department had expended approximately $3.25 million of the legislature's appropriation in acquiring the first block adjacent to Independence Square. The remaining three-block state acquisition, which was still incomplete when Maurice K. took office, was projected to cost $3.75 million more. [8] The Federal appropriation for the Department of the Interior's part of the effort was estimated at $4.4 million.

❑ ❑ ❑ ❑

Pennsylvania's commercial and cultural axis runs from Philadelphia to Pittsburgh across the center of the state, bypassing

Erie, one of Pennsylvania's larger cities. Isolated in the northwest corner of the state, the city tends to be ignored by the rest of the Commonwealth. But, as Thomas Knepp, a *New York Times* feature writer wrote, "Jutting into Lake Erie like a giant, flexed finger is Presque Isle, a peninsula that protects the city from the storms of the lake and provides [it with] one of the finest harbors on the Great Lakes." [9]

Two and a half centuries ago the French built Fort Presque Isle. The fort, however, was on the site of present-day Erie, not the peninsula. It was the first of a chain of such installations the French hoped would hold the Ohio Valley for them, but in 1759 they abandoned Presque Isle. Although the British took possession, they were driven out three years later by Pontiac and his warriors, who destroyed the fortifications. The first permanent settlement was not laid out until 1795. [10]

The peninsula joined the ranks of historic places when its forests became the source of the timber used to build six of the nine ships in Commodore Oliver Perry's fleet for the Battle of Lake Erie. Following the battle, several of Perry's ships were scuttled in the water between the peninsula and the mainland. The area came to be known as Misery Bay for the suffering his sailors endured during the winter of 1813. [11]

The state of Pennsylvania acquired the peninsula in 1921. And although it was a state park long before Maurice K. became the Secretary of Forests and Waters, its refurbishment became a major undertaking during his state tenure.

In French the name Presque Isle means *almost an island,* but the lake storms and shifting sands have turned it into a true island at least four times since 1819. [12] Stabilizing the shore line thus became one of the important aspects of its park status. The peninsula, which is composed almost exclusively of sand and pebbles, is attached to the mainland at the "Head" about four miles west of Erie. Writing in *Water, Land and Life,* Conservationist O. E. Jennings vividly describes the action of the wind and water on the site:

In dry, windy weather beach sand is blown across the narrow neck into the bay, thus to some extent widening the neck on the bayside; and violent storms occasionally wash sand across into the bay. The prevailing westerly storm waves rush up the beach in a diagonal direction, carrying with them sand and pebbles, and with less excitement flow diagonally back, leaving the sand and pebbles along the beach, each time a little farther to the east. . . . I have watched colored pebbles being carried in and out; they might easily travel the whole length of the peninsula in a couple of days.

Having thus reached the end of the peninsula, the transported material is either carried on out into deeper water, adding thus to the growth of the peninsula, or is carried around the end of the peninsula to build up a curving beach. [13]

According to Jennings, "the average migration of Presque Isle appears to have been, during the past few centuries, about one-half mile per century." He also tells us that, "had it not been for man's assistance Presque Isle would long ago have become a flying sand-spit, a real isle, to have fallen a victim to wind and wave." [14] This, of course, is where the Department of Forests and Waters enters the picture.

"When Dr. Goddard took office" in 1955, according to an *Erie Times-News* editorial, "there was no drinking water on most of the Peninsula, roads were inadequate and many of the beaches were in acute danger from erosion. The present boat marina was a swamp." [15] All of this had changed by the time of the *Times-News* comments, sixteen years later.

Much of the Presque Isle restoration as accomplished in the first five or six years of Maurice K.'s tenure at Forests and Waters. Less than twelve months after he became Secretary, Erie Mayor Arthur J. Gardner wrote Maurice K., "you and the other men of our administration in Harrisburg, have leaned over backward in behalf of Erie." [16] And five years later in 1961, the people of Erie held a testimonial dinner for Maurice K. In an open letter of thanks from "All the People of Erie and Erie County" that was printed in the testimonial booklet, they told him:

> It wasn't too long ago, measured in impatient days and months, that we held our breath and deliberated the ultimate decadence of our Peninsula.
>
> The prevailing northwesterly winds had churned the lake waters to a devastating state that promised desolation and obliteration of a natural haven.
>
> But this was only part of the problem. Years of inertia and indecision had rendered this playspot obsolete. . . . You, sir, took the challenge at face value. You listened, planned, consulted, reported, argued, and in the end reaped the fruits of your sowing: a modern Presque Isle State Park — our Peninsula — all spruced up in a new suit.
>
> For these accomplishments . . . for your untiring energy on our behalf . . . for your limitless interest in a greater and growing segment of our Commonwealth, we say "Thank You, Dr. Goddard, for everything! [17]

In those five years, the Department of Forests and Waters had restored more than seven miles of beaches with sand, which had been dredged out of the lake bottom, erected a wall of stone on the lake side to strengthen and widen the precarious *neck* of the peninsula, as well as built roads, created a marina for boaters and constructed bathing and beach facilities. The work of stabilizing the peninsula shore and protecting the neck was done under the supervision of the U.S. Army Corps of Engineers. Maurice K.'s engineering staff would prepare drawings and specifications for repair to "damaged groins" or for "beach nourishment," and after review and approval by the Corps, advertise the work. And, of course, it was Maurice K.'s responsibility to make sure the funds had been requested and approved by the legislature.

The Corps of Engineers had been involved in stemming the continuous migration of the peninsula since early in the nineteenth century. Between 1829 and 1922 the Corps had successfully closed breaches in the neck four times. Although beach nourishment continues even today as an annual undertaking, fifty-five breakwater segments — put up by Maurice K. — also slow erosion by breaking up incoming waves so that less sand and gravel is carried onto the shoreline and around the peninsula to the east. The breakwaters also reduce the amount of sand that is carried away from the beach by the retreating water.

Maurice K. had insisted that the community first develop a comprehensive Master Plan for the peninsula, and then he assisted the Erie Pennsylvania State Park and Harbor Commission, the Erie citizens committee set up in response to his suggestion, in putting the plan into operation.  It was this committee that honored him in 1961. "Erieites will always remember him" as a "true friend in need," the committee's 1961 testimonial booklet affirmed. "He delivered the sand, the stone, the people that restored life and activity to Presque Isle State Park." [18]

❑ ❑ ❑ ❑

An  executive can stall until a project dies or kill it outright in a variety of ways.  He can give it inadequate or inferior resources; assign a subordinate who has little support in the office, thus no real power or authority in the field; or that ultimate bureaucratic ploy, plead priorities as cause for delays. Samuel S. Lewis, Maurice K.'s predecessor, was charged with being "unreliable" and doing all he could "to block the mall" when he was Secretary of Forests and Waters.  According to Judge Edwin O. Lewis, who oversaw much of the Independence Mall's design for the city of Philadelphia, Secretary Lewis "completely laid down on the mall" and "did nothing for two years." [19]

Maurice K., however, supported urban park development wholeheartedly.  He regularly made the point that "conservation is not for trees and water, it's for people."  And when he talked about what he called the "new conservation," he always linked it, just as he did parks, to people who lived in urban areas.  Project 70, for example, was intended to save rings of land around Pennsylvania's cities for those who lived in them.  People lived in cities; therefore, for Maurice K., conservation must deal with the problems found in metropolitan districts.  And issues of land and water were prominent in his park efforts in three of the state's larger cities: Pittsburgh's Point Park, Philadelphia's Independence Mall, and

Erie's Presque Island. Each, too, had a significant historic element embodied in its development.

His support was genuine. He understood the issues involved, the historic significance, and the importance to Pennsylvania of each of these efforts. When a group forty-five students sent individual letters to Governor Scranton protesting the city of St. Louis's use of the name, "Gateway to the West," which they thought rightfully belonged to Pittsburgh, Maurice K. prepared a well-reasoned and most gracious reply:

> I do not believe that we Pennsylvanians really have any exclusive right to that title. At one time or another, at least five cities made rightful claim to it. It may be difficult to imagine; but, Philadelphia, Wheeling, and Chicago, were claimants of that title along with St. Louis and Pittsburgh.
>
> You will be happy to know that your State government has not been standing idly by watching St. Louis steal the show. . . . It is true that we have no tower as tall as the one in St. Louis. We do, however, have the Portal, a magnificently designed entrance to Point State Park that gives the park visitor a very real feeling of passing through the Gateway to the West. . . . Its clear, low, simple lines veil its tremendous strength. A strength that is truly symbolic of the position of our great Commonwealth as the world's Arsenal of Democracy. . . .
>
> As you emerge on the western side of the Portal, you look out over the meeting of the rivers . . . Directly to the west rises the plume of the fountain that tosses its spray . . . into the air above the meeting point of these two mighty "Forks of the Ohio.
>
> Truly, Point State Park was, is, and always will be the most dramatic Gateway to the West; but I do not think that we should be so selfish as to contest the claims of other cities for a small share of Pennsylvania's rightful heritage. [20]

Maurice K.'s support for urban parks was more, too, than perfunctory political expediency or a good soldier embracing a boss's wish list. In his book, *The Shaping of the Point*, Robert Alberts mentions that during the long delays in the project, "Secretary Goddard followed a policy of maintaining public interest by awarding and announcing a number of small contracts at intervals instead of releasing them at one time or grouping them into a few large awards." Maurice K.'s innovative strategy of spreading the contracting process out drew complaints but generated a continual stream of "news stories" that helped keep up, not only public awareness, but also the interest of the legislators who had to approve the funds to continue the work. [21]

Maurice K. even claimed that erecting the bridge over the Allegheny River to the Northside — which stood idle for years waiting for the completion of the approaches, earning for it the name, "the bridge to nowhere" — was also a good move. He told Robert Alberts during a 1975 interview for Albert's book, "I think it was a wise decision on the part of the highway department, because you had the resources, you had the money. If you [had] put it off, the bridges would have cost twice as much. It also puts more heat on the people to resolve the other issues." [22] Maurice K. was like a general slowly investing some massive fortification, redoubt by redoubt, never losing confidence that ultimately he would reduce the main works.

❑ ❑ ❑ ❑

During the thirty-year life of the Point State Park development effort, there were many delays brought on by disagreements over the design and the handling of elements within the park. As an historic site, groups such as the Daughters of the American Revolution, who owned the Blockhouse at the Point, [23] as well as those interested in the old steel bridges at the Point, fought over how the object of their concern should be treated. Arguments such as whether to move the bridges, how to restore them, who would do the work, and who would pay for it caused delays of several years. And there seemed to be an unending stream of difficulties with property owners over the demolition of their buildings. These disagreements were generally between the city, its planning commission, and the organizations or individuals advocating the specific change and not with the Department of Forests and Waters.

In several instances, however, Maurice K. did have to step in as the final arbiter over a disagreement in order to rescue the state's investment from the straits of community deadlock. There were a number of such issues at Point State Park — with the Weather Service over the need to move its river gauge under the Allegheny River Bridge, with the Daughters of the American Revolution over the Blockhouse, and with the firm that owned the unused trolley tracks over the Point bridge.

Although trolley service had not gone over Point Bridge for a number of years, the owner of the company insisted that the development of the park and the necessary removal of his tracks in the park would interrupt service all along the line. When communities miles away wanted his abandoned tracks removed, he started legal action to avoid paying for taking them up by blaming the shutdown of service on the park. Finally Maurice K. stepped in to avoid any further delay in settling the litigation efforts with the owner and agreed to pay for the work. According to him, the trolley track story was a "book in itself," one "as long the bridges":

> We had a terrible hassle about getting rid of the trolley tracks. We paid for work that was done thirteen miles away from Point State Park . . . Something thirteen miles away, they said was caused because you took the trolley tracks away here [in the park]. Rather than get hung up in court I said, 'OK.' We Macademized over the trolley track to save lawsuits. [24]

On occasion, too, Maurice K. had to step in and thwart the plans of even the Pittsburgh Park Committee. At one point the group discussed the idea of sending a man to Europe to study fountains, and they wanted the state to sponsor the trip. Maurice K. told them, "How do you sell this politically? I can't have a guy running around Europe for six months looking at fountains." And when the chief landscape architect, Arthur Griswold, wanted a wildflower garden with lots of shrubs, Maurice K. stopped him, ostensibly because of the difficulty in maintaining a garden. He told Alberts, however, that he opposed the garden "because shrubs harbor skid row characters," who would "sleep there," and "hippy kids," who "would hide in the shrubbery." [25]

The most protracted and difficult negotiations, however, ones that took years to resolve, were with the women of the DAR over the Blockhouse. They adamantly resisted transferring the small property to the state. They claimed their caretaker role was "a sacred trust." After several years of intricate negotiations — always it seemed with a new set of women — Maurice K. agreed to pay $40,000 for some small adjoining tracts of land which confined the DAR to the little square property the Blockhouse stood on. [26]

According to Ralph E. Griswold, whose firm did much of the design work on Point Park, "the City of Pittsburgh gave all their own land and the County all their own land, streets and so forth at no cost," but "no praise goes to the DAR for any phase of the Park conception. They opposed us in every way they could." [27] When Robert Alberts interviewed him, Maurice K. stated emphatically he would have condemned and torn down the Blockhouse if the DAR had not finally signed an agreement. "We weren't going to allow them to stop that whole project," he told Alberts. [28]

And then late in the development of Point State Park, another citizens' organization, Group STL, emerged to criticize the basic design plans and propose changing the direction the effort was taking. Group STL — the initials meant *Stop, Think, Look* — was made up of a number of prominent Pittsburgh architects, artists, and teachers, who averred "we are passionate men that love Pittsburgh." They first expressed their concern in a full-page "statement" in the *Post-Gazette*. The purpose of their manifesto was expressed by the statement: "Let it not be said of us that we sat idly by watching our city being defaced by thoughtless buildings and projects, . . ." [29]

This was followed by detailed discussions of the group's assessment of the situation in Pittsburgh in six categories: *Music, Sculpture, Painting, Drama, Architecture, Monuments.* The section on Sculpture was mainly a statement condemning the plans for Point State Park. After describing the beauties of the location and those of the Manchester and Point Bridges, the group argued:

> To allow Point State Park to become merely a statement of the past is a mistake. To continue to build imitations of the past and create inadequate symbols, such as the proposed fountain, is to create an urban space that is dead. . . .
>
> Point Park's potential calls for a moratorium on present plans and additional study. The destruction of the existing bridges should not be permitted until it can be shown that they are useless. . . . [30]

Then after suggesting that the bridges be used as a pedestrian link to the Northside Stadium and that they be lined with markets, galleries, and shops, they asked? "Are the Fathers of Urban Renewal going to permit a still-born child?"

Over the years the Pittsburgh Point Park committeemen had carried on an intelligent, continuing program of informing and educating the public, but STL's activities caused concern because they reflected not those of the general public, who might be expected to lack knowledge, but professionals who had only come forward as the project was nearing completion. [31]

The committee, having adopted a position of avoiding controversy, suffered in silence and responded not with public announcements, but only in private letters to those who wrote. There was little real danger, however, from these attacks. The state owned the land and was building the park, and both Governor Lawrence and Maurice K. were more than willing to resist any effort to change direction. In a rare public statement in defense of the park, Maurice K. responded tersely to the STL arguments:

> It is a magnificent plan for a park. What could be better than a fountain? The plans for the park are an old decision. It is not designed to be an art center. I see no reason to change it now. [32]

Maurice K. had to struggle, too, with some of the legislators over expenditures, contracting issues, and whether the legislative authorizations permitted certain actions, or why the state was even involved in specific phases of his urban park projects. Some of these challenges to his decisions rose to the level of investigations by the Attorney General.

When the announcement was made that the Department of Forests and Waters was about to enter into a "professional services" contract with the Academy of Natural Sciences for aid in the planning and design of the Conservation Museum at Penn's Landing in Philadelphia, Maurice K. was forced to answer the Pennsylvania Attorney General, Walter Alessandroni's, questions over the specifics of the funding as well as why the state had any role in the project. After citing the act of the legislature that provided for the "planning and design" of the museum, he defended the size of the planning and design fee, which was charged by the Philadelphia consultant for the project, based on the estimate of $2 million for the construction. [33]

Maurice K. went on to explain that his decision to use "some agency experienced in the design and operation of museums" had been made with the concurrence of the General State Authority, the Office of Administration, and the Pennsylvania Landing Project. He then described how he attempted to manage the funding of multi-stage efforts, such as those at Pittsburgh and Philadelphia.

> I have tried to tailor the requests of this Department to two types: On projects for which the planning and design is already accomplished, I have requested construction money. On projects for which plans are not available, I have requested funds for that purpose only. [34]

If, as Maurice K. wrote in 1963, "the purpose of public investment is to reinforce the private economy by providing opportunities for private investment [while] protecting land and resource values," then the $7 million the Commonwealth spent in clearing thirty-six acres of "commercial slum" at Pittsburgh's Golden Triangle were well spent. According to Maurice K. the state's investment "made possible private redevelopment that increased the taxables in downtown Pittsburgh by $100 million." [35]

❑ ❑ ❑ ❑

In October 1962, the Philadelphia City Planning Commission issued a revised *Independence Mall Redevelopment Area Plan* that had been developed in "close cooperation" with the consultant to the Philadelphia Redevelopment Authority. Because of the "introduction of Independence Mall State Park . . . between the historic and residential districts of the Old City and the intense commercial development of the central core," the city's redevelopment plans were expanded to include the "vastly increased desirability of the adjacent land for both high-grade commercial and tourist-oriented activities." The new plan now covered nine city blocks as well as part of two others. [36]

One of the major incentives for the original project as well as for enlarging the size of the redevelopment area in 1962 was the potential fire hazard to Independence Hall from a possible general conflagration in the Old City. According to the planning commission report:

> Fifty-six percent of the structures are more than 50 years old, with a majority of these approximately 100 years old. . . . The combination of inadequate maintenance with generally non-fireproof construction constitutes a continuing hazard. [37]

The state's responsibility for the four-block, ten-acre Mall was unchanged, however, by the new thinking. By 1962, moreover, the Department of Forests and Waters had cleared and developed the blocks between Chestnut and Race Streets from 5th to 8th Street for the state park. Under the central block of the Mall a 660-car parking garage was planned for visitors and tourists and the office development to the west. [38]

The cooperative agreement between the city, the state, and the federal government provided that the Commonwealth would be responsible for the acquisition and demolition of the existing buildings (in the area to become the Mall), for funding and supervising new construction, and for street widening to permit better connections between the Delaware River bridge approaches and Independence Hall. [39] Thus the Pennsylvania Department of Public Highways was involved in the project along with Forests and Waters.

Of the 60 acres in the redevelopment area, 10.4 were in to be the State Park and 22.6 were in streets. The city's redevelopment plan called for eleven streets to be vacated, two to be reduced in width, and one to be widened. As part of the project, the plan also anticipated highway improvements by the state of the approaches to the Benjamin Franklin Bridge at the north end of the Mall. [40]

Although this dual responsibility for the project by two state agencies caused delays, the "layers of consultants and contractors under the principal architectural firm, Harbeson, Hough, Livingston, and Larson, also set up a logistical challenge." [41] Moreover, Maurice K.'s ability to execute contracts and otherwise advance the state's portion of the work depended on the approval by the legislature of his annual budget submissions. In most instances the legislators were less interested in design considerations than in keeping down the escalating costs. The city, on the other hand, was responsible, through its planning commission, to contract for and oversee the preparation of plans which were subject to the final approval by the Secretary of Forests and Waters.

Judge Edwin O. Lewis, the chairman of the federally chartered Philadelphia National Shrines Park Commission, was the "primary facilitor" for keeping the state park project on track. Over the years his role was perhaps the most influential among the Philadelphia planners and designers. He thought big. As he told those who opposed him, the only way to reverse the two-hundred-year westward migration of the city's center of economic activity was "to cut such a swathe in here that it will lead to rebuilding to the river." [42]

The second block, between Market and Arch Streets, took the longest to design and build primarily because of disagreements over the inclusion of the underground garage and the design of the surface layout. According to one of the key planners, the stalemate

260

over the block took three years to resolve. It was not completed until 1967. "Blocks one and three breezed to completion in comparison." [43]

□ □ □ □

In 1957 the architectural critic, Lewis Mumford, wrote a series of four articles for the *New Yorker*. In them he claimed the mall concept was a "grandiose statement" that was incompatible with the city's "ample squares, uniform roof lines, and its intimate gardens." Mumford seemed to feel the mall intruded on the sense of familiarity, of friendship that he believed Philadelphia projected. "Rather than a sweeping view of Independence Hall from the end of the mall, he recommended shrubbery and trees to create a sense of outdoor rooms." [44] Mumford's assessment apparently influenced the ground plans for blocks two and three, for they were redesigned as if they were two distinct parks after the style of William Penn. In laying out Philadelphia's original rectilinear plans, Penn included a park square in each quadrant of the city.

In an analysis of the character of the Mall in 1994 commissioned by the National Park Service, landscape architect Deirdre Gibson writes that the result of following Mumford's suggestion raises a more serious issue than inappropriateness. Gibson sees the entire area as "three distinct un-integrated and ambiguous spaces to the south of Market Street" (the Park Service's original area) that are "well used," while the mall area to the north is, according to her, usually "deserted." She attributes this and the lack of an unobstructed view of Independence Hall from other than the first block of the state park to the separation of the three Mall spaces by "three heavily trafficked streets," and thus the creation of three "discrete orientations and separate focuses." [45]

The original impetus, however, for the restoration — to keep businesses from leaving the area, which was rapidly deteriorating, and to surround the mall with commercial structures, especially the "home offices of large corporations" [46] — has been more than fulfilled. The buildings adjacent to Independence Mall include, among others, those of the Penn Mutual Life Insurance Company, the *Public Ledger* Building, the First Pennsylvania Bank, Rohm and Haas, the U.S. Courthouse, the William J. Green Federal Building, the Federal Reserve Bank and the U.S. Mint. Thus, while the rationale for designing the Mall as a vast open area with clear sight lines reaching to Independence Hall were never implemented, it serves today primarily as a city park for the commercial interests that surround it.

Although the "Lewis Fountain" never seemed to be operating properly when Judge Lewis visited the mall in later years, he was immensely pleased with the result. In a 1971 letter to Maurice K., he wrote:

> I have not seen or heard from you for so long a time that I fear you have forgotten me. However, I am in my ninety-third year, going pretty strong, except that I cannot walk alone very well for more than a block or two with any confidence.
>
> The purpose of this letter is to praise you and your subordinates for the beautiful condition of Independence Mall . . . On Friday last when we [Mrs. Lewis] went down about five o'clock to spend the late afternoon sitting under the trees, . . . we were both full of satisfaction to find how clean and well kept the Mall is in every respect. . . .
>
> The trees have grown now to such a height that they give real shade and it is altogether a delightful place. . . . There were quite a lot of families walking through from Independence Hall and a fair amount of traffic. [47]

Almost a soon as the Independence Mall State Park was completed, Maurice K. announced that negotiations were being initiated for its transfer to the U.S. Department the of Interior. In a February 1972 edition of the Philadelphia *Evening Bulletin*, Maurice K. told the newspaper that it was the "logical and appropriate thing to do . . . as the state's contribution to the total Independence Hall complex." Although he noted that maintenance would be "easier and cheaper" under one management, he also mentioned what was probably the main reason from his and the

Governor's reason for seeking the transfer: the desire to save the state "a costly burden" of $150,000 a year in maintenance. In making his proposal, Maurice K. underscored the value of the state's contribution by mentioning that $7 million (a total of $14 million had been allocated for the project) had been spent to buy three blocks of urban real estate, and that that price "exceeded the amount paid for Pennsylvania's entire forest holdings." [48]

The state planned to donate the Mall to the federal government in fee simple until it was discovered that the Mall had been placed as collateral for General State Authority bonds used for the park's construction. Enough of the loans had been paid off to allow the transfer of the lawn area of the first block, which was done. The remaining part of the Mall State Park is leased to the National Park Service for a dollar a year. The bonds were scheduled to paid off by 1998, when the Park Service would buy the remaining state portion for a dollar. [49]

Rather than an indication of his lack of interest in the Mall as a state park, his divestiture position was fully consistent with Maurice K.'s attitude on community parks as opposed to those he considered true state parks — those in the second of his three-tier system of national parks, state parks, and local parks. He was happy to assist with the design and construction, as well as the acquisition of the land, for a local park, but he always insisted on turning over its maintenance to the community that had sought the state's help in developing it. This was true whether a park was acquired and constructed with money from Project 70, Project 500, the Oil and Gas Leases Fund — the revenues from which had passed $28 million by 1975 — or from the General State Authority.

Today the only public evidence of Maurice K. and the state's involvement in the project is a plaque set in the sidewalk of the first block of the mall. It reads:

> The People of the commonwealth of Pennsylvania have set aside this ground . . . as a public green and walk forever dedicating its use to the inspiration provided by Independence Hall within which American

patriots founded our nation and conceived our government upon the indestructible spirit and principles of liberty. [50]

A measure of irony is imbedded in the sidewalk along with the state's fine words. In 1816 the Pennsylvania legislature, which owned the site at the time, voted to tear down Independence Hall, divide the property into lots, and sell them to help pay for the construction of a new capitol in Harrisburg. It what may have been the first instance in the United States of a public campaign for an historic building preservation, the outraged citizens of Philadelphia raised $70,000 and bought the property from the Commonwealth. [51]

❑ ❑ ❑ ❑

While there were similarities in the state park developments in Philadelphia and Pittsburgh, Maurice K. declared that there were important differences. On the one hand he described Point State Park as "historic," while on the other Independence Mall was one of "natural resources." [52] He never explained his rationale for making this distinction but probably was thinking of the Mall as separate from Independence Hall, which the Mall fronted, but which was not included as a Forests and Waters responsibility.

At Pittsburgh everything in Point State Park down to the shrubbery and trees was designed (or intended to be designed) in a manner pre-dating the year 1800. This not only provided an historical thrust to the effort, but also gave the designers great leverage in rejecting the suggestions of influential citizens who offered to place statuary or other such items in the park in exchange for personal recognition. The only objects that violated the pre-1800 principle were two small utility buildings, a bronze plaque to David Lawrence that was imbedded in a stone, and the ginkgo trees that surrounded the Blockhouse. The ginkgos were selected because it was believed they were one of the earliest trees in America, but after they were planted someone discovered that Thomas Jefferson had introduced them to the country in 1807. Maurice K. wanted to cut them down but the DAR balked. [53]

The major difference between the Philadelphia and Pittsburgh developments, however, was a management one. According to Maurice K., while there were twenty strong committees and organizations in Philadelphia "vying one with the other" for "leadership" as well as "finances," in Pittsburgh the Allegheny Conference served as the "focal point" in "coalescing the political and economic and civic interests" of the western part of the state. Years later Maurice K. told Robert Alberts, when he was working on his *Shaping of the Point*, that this unified approach was important. "Mayors and governors come and go," he told Alberts, "so you've got to have a strong citizen effort." The Allegheny Conference eliminated the "splintering effect ... remarkably well." [54]

Although the shadow of the banker Richard K. Mellon hovered over everything connected with Point State Park — Robert Alberts describes him as "a shy man but one of great power, influence, and capacity for persuasion" [55] — Maurice K. was quick to point out to the writer: "He still had to have doers. He couldn't have built Point State Park without doers." According to Maurice K., the men who built the park at Pittsburgh were "really unbelievable, dedicated individuals." They possesed "a lot of talent, a lot of skill, a lot of perseverance." [56] And in the Pennsylvania Secretary of Forests and Waters they found a willing compatriot, one who had the skill and perseverance to match their own.

Not long after Maurice K. became involved in the Point State Park project, Arthur B. Van Buskirk, chairman of Pittsburgh's Point Park Committee of the Allegheny Conference, and R. K. Mellon's "front man" on the park, wrote glowingly to Maurice K., the state's *doer* on the Department of Forests and Waters three urban conservation projects:

> I was sorry to have to run off so rapidly last Tuesday night to catch a train, and to be unable to tell you what a really wonderful job you did. Public servants like you are rare, and much appreciated when they are encountered. [57]

# CHAPTER XV

# A POX ON TOCKS

*Life in an environmental agency was not all
pure water and clear skies.*

Maurice K. Goddard

While the drought along the Delaware River between 1962 and 1965 appeared to affirm the need for construction of a main-stem dam, at least in the eyes of its proponents, opposition to it was gathering at the same time. Delays in starting construction as planned occurred for two main reasons: first the Vietnam War, and then concerns over the reservoir's impact on the environment.

To avoid paying for the war in Southeast Asia with a tax increase, President Johnson had directed that, among other items, public works projects, especially "on-going water resource projects . . . be continued at minimum rates." Coupled with the Corps' original, serious underestimates of the dam's cost, which grew in five years from $93 million to $198 million, Congressional support weakened and thus affected its appropriations for Tocks. Although funding was continued for land-acquisition and studies, General Accounting Office and Congressional committees began to look at such items as the Corps' stated benefit-cost ratios for the project, which were suspect. [1] Commencing in 1965, however, the Corps and the National Park Service, which was to convert the area surrounding the dam into a national park, did begin buying up land. In many instances land-acquisition practices, especially those of the Corps of Engineers, created great animosity throughout the valley as well as unfavorable publicity for the dam.

266

The cutbacks in funding and the attendant delays in the start of construction allowed the project to become entangled with other obstacles. During this period and as a component of the protests over the war, environmental concerns had became front page news across the United States. These culminated in 1969 when Congress passed the National Environmental Policy Act, with its requirement for the preparation of environmental impact statements.

This opened officially the floodgates for expressions of concern over such consequences at Tocks as harm to fish, the specter of mudflats ringing the reservoir, the loss of wildlife habitat, the effect of siltation on the useful life of the dam, and especially the potential for the lake to become eutrophic. With the Corps now having to respond openly to these issues by writing environmental impact statements, the several small groups of critics who for a number of years had been opposing the dam or off shoots of the project — such as the pumped-storage facility the electric industry wanted to build at Sunfish Pond overlooking the dam site — now had ammunition as well as time with which to fight their cases.

While issues such as the battle to preserve Sunfish Pond and the letter-writing campaigns and court suits of groups like the Delaware Valley Conservation Association fueled the debate over the dam, the major environmental impediment was the possibility of water-quality problems associated with the reservoir, especially eutrophication. Eutrophication (sometimes described as the "death of a lake") involves an increase in dissolved nutrients, such as phosphates, with an attendant deficiency in oxygen. In 1966, the Delaware River Basin Commission hired an engineering firm to review the potential for water-quality problems especially from the impact of millions of visitors seeking recreational outlets. One of the significant sources of difficulties the contractor foresaw, however, was from nutrients entering the river as waste from New York State cattle and chicken farms.

Governor Rockefeller's reply to the newly established Council on Environmental Quality, which had to approve the Corps' environmental impact statements, claimed that it was unfair to ask New York to pay for cleanup when it was not needed in a free-flowing stream. For this reason, he argued, the expense should be charged to the dam, not to an upstream state that would receive little benefit from either the cleanup or the structure. [2]

□ □ □ □

Although Congress had authorized the Tocks Island Dam Project in 1962 and made the first appropriations for it two years later, the process leading to construction start dragged out until eventually cracks began to appear within the Delaware River Basin Commission itself. At a May 10, 1972 meeting in the Department of the Interior Auditorium in Washington, D.C., recently-elected Governor William T. Cahill of New Jersey spoke at length. He explained that while New Jersey did not question the flood control, water supply, power and recreation benefits of the Tocks Island project, he was becoming concerned over the accelerated growth that would result from it.

He went on to note that New Jersey was one of the most densely urbanized states in the nation and expressed apprehension as to how far the state can go in allowing future population and industrial growth. Then he told his fellow commissioners that he was "not prepared to give assurances to the Council on Environmental Quality of New Jersey's support." Finally he indicated he was ordering a study of the impact of highway and sewage-treatment costs associated with construction of a dam at Tocks. [3]

When Governor Cahill reported in September, he reiterated his previous comments about the value of the dam, but imposed several conditions he wanted satisfied for construction of the dam to receive New Jersey's continued support. The problems of eutrophication, especially that resulting from upstream areas, must be solved; both New Jersey and Pennsylvania must enact legislation regulating land use on the flood plains; the planned park load must be reduced from 10.5 million visitors a year to 4 million; and substantial federal funding would have to be secured to offset the local tax losses from the land-acquisition effort and for new highways needed for access to the park. [4]

With Cahill's summary now publicly, officially affirming the concerns expressed over the previous few years by the opponents of the dam — the new environmentalists — the tide favoring building it reversed and began to run out. It would be some time before either the Commissioners of the Delaware River Basin Commission or the United States Congress would withdraw their support, but the "die was cast for the dam's demise."

□ □ □ □

Because the battle over the dam at Tocks Island was beginning to assume epic proportions, Congress appropriated $1.5 million in 1974 for yet another study. It was to be "an impartial comprehensive analysis, including alternatives, and review of the project." The contract was awarded to URS/Madigan-Praeger and Conklin and Rossant, two New York City consulting firms. In addition to a dam at Tocks Island, the study looked at three alternative programs based on future growth patterns for the area: a high-growth, a medium-growth, and a low-growth situation. This was because it was anticipated that the "project area would suffer substantial adverse environmental impacts," whether or not Tocks was built. [5]

URS/Madigan-Praeger and Conklin and Rossant's high-growth alternative proposed a scheme consisting of seven tributary reservoirs for water supply (six in Pennsylvania and one in New Jersey), expansion of state parks, a combination of gas and fossil-fueled generators for electricity, and also a "dry" dam on the Delaware to be used solely to impound storm waters during floods. Their program for a medium-growth future was similar for water supply and energy to that of the high-growth plan, but with seven tributary reservoirs (five in Pennsylvania and one each in New Jersey and New York). The low-growth alternative (which had the least environmental impact) offered the same electric generating plan but provided for no new water supply or recreation, and only non-structural means for flood control. [6]

URS/Madigan-Praeger and Conklin and Rossant's six-volume final report looked at the three alternatives to the dam, but avoided taking a position on building it. The consultants concluded that the area would probably suffer substantial adverse environmental impact due to existing trends, whether or not Tocks Island dam was built. The study conclusions were mixed, but in general the consultants concluded that alternatives to the dam would be more expensive than putting it up, but "less costly to the environment." [7]

Although the Corps of Engineers forwarded a summary to Congress that recommended that Tocks Island should be constructed as an "engineeringly-sound and economically-justified project whose environmental impacts are outweighted by the benefits," Congress was more interested in the position of the four states and had requested that the Delaware River Basin Commission advise it on whether to continue funding a main-stem dam.

The Commission gathered at an executive session in Newark July 31, 1975 to vote on whether or not to ask Congress to appropriate funds for construction of the dam. Their positions were largely known beforehand. Both the Environmental Protection Agency and the CEQ had urged the Commissioners to vote not to construct the Tocks Island Dam (Maurice K. believed this was an effort to "interfere" in the process), and the URS/Madigan-Praeger and Conklin and Rossant study supported the idea of adverse impacts on the environment, although it made no statement on whether or not the dam should be built. New Jersey, which had raised substantial issues about its impact on the state, and New York, which would benefit only indirectly by its construction and would probably receive the brunt of the clean-up costs necessary to avoid eutrophication of the reservoir, were lined up to vote against the dam. And Delaware, which had the least to gain from the

270

project, had publicly announced it would join the majority to prevent a tie vote.

Thus, with the Interior Department abstaining (because it was a federal project), Governor Shapp, perhaps the strongest supporter over the years of the dam, cast the lone favorable vote. Pennsylvania, the reluctant bride twenty years before, was now the sole advocate. The Commission did approve, however, the establishment of the national recreation area along the Delaware River. On this issue the Interior Department joined New Jersey and New York, while Pennsylvania and Delaware abstained. [8]

A bitterly disappointed Milton Shapp and Maurice K. took little consolation in the idea that such possibilities as state cooperation on water releases, a partial system of small dams on tributaries, individual conservation measures, or flood plain control could take the place of a main-stem dam. Governor Shapp told a reporter at the press conference following the vote:

> I voted for the project because [I] lived through Agnes and saw the devastation created by a major flood. I have great fears that should we have a flood of this proportion now . . . you would have as much as six to eight feet of water in many areas of Philadelphia, . . . and the whole Delaware River would be a scene of destruction. The Tocks Island Dam would have prevented this. I voted for the project because I'm very much concerned about the water supply to Philadelphia. . . If we have another drought as we had in the mid-sixties, our entire industrial capacity in Philadelphia would be threatened. I feel that there are environmental problems; I think these could be handled to protect the environment even with the dam in place. [9]

Governor Shapp and Maurice K. knew that people soon begin to forget the last drought or flood. Rousing them years later to spend tax money for a dam would be difficult; their political memory in such instances is short. The two Pennsylvanians believed their task as professionals was to look out for the citizens of the state and that the Tocks Island Dam was one of the necessary pieces of a responsible plan for the Delaware River Basin. As if to reaffirm his long-held belief that "conservation was for people," Maurice K. wrote to a correspondent following the loss:

Make no mistake, the forgotten man in the so-called Tocks Island controversy is the average citizen of the Basin who knows little, and cares less, about Tocks Island. He won't be heard from until he is flooded, until his tap runs dry, until he travels all day for recreation and gets turned away, or until his power fails.

He takes no part in the "controversy," but expects these things to be provided. [10]

While Congress took no steps to "deauthorize" Tocks Island, the Delaware River Basin Commission began a "sweeping reevaluation of the Delaware Valley's water resource picture." The main recommendation of the Commission's study, which has come to be called "Level B," was the construction of new and enlarged reservoirs throughout the basin that would provide minimum stream-flows to control salinity intrusion and to make up for the projected water losses that would come from not building Tocks.

Enlargement was recommended for three existing sites: Francis E. Walter in the Lehigh Valley and Prompton in the Lackawaxen Valley and at Cannonsville, on the West Branch of the Delaware in the Catskill Mountains. Cannonsville is the largest of New York City's impoundments. After a review of twenty-five possible site locations, the study endorsed the building of a new facility in Warren County, New Jersey at Merrill Creek, and at the same time recommended retaining six long-planned reservoir proposals. These included Tocks Island and a number of dams in Pennsylvania: Trexler in Lehigh County, Evansburg in Montgomery County, Aquashicola in Carbon County, and Icedale on the West Branch of Brandywine Creek in Chester County. Maiden Creek, a federally proposed impoundment in Berks County, Pennsylvania was dropped from the Commission's comprehensive plan. [11]

The report concluded that "conservation should be the cornerstone of future water activity in the Delaware." During time of water shortages, for example, it called for a 15 percent reduction in depletive losses — those that are withdrawn and not returned to the river after use — by water users in the basin. This affected primarily the power industry. The Level-B study also looked at water-quality standards, hazardous wastes, ground and surface water supply, fish and wildlife, recreation, and energy issues. [12]

□ □ □ □

Then at the October 1978 meeting of the Delaware River Basin Commission, Maurice K. unveiled a plan designed to mitigate the effects of having lost the dam. It was a draft resolution that asked the states to enter into "good faith negotiations." Governor Shapp and Maurice K. believed that the designation in November 1978 of the middle Delaware as a scenic river "appears to impair substantially the arrangements for the equitable apportionment of Basin waters set forth in the [Supreme Court's] 1954 decree." [13] By submitting his call for "good faith" negotiations (some members wanted them called *discussions* rather than negotiations), Maurice K. was hoping that a new formula for apportionment would be adopted by the Commission and then submitted to the Supreme Court for approval. [14]

A revised version of Maurice K.'s draft resolution was adopted on December 13, 1978. New York City was included in the "good faith" discussions and the agreement because it had been a party to the Supreme Court Decree. The federal government, of course, was not a signatory.

Over the next three years the negotiators met and prepared a number of suggestions for consideration by the Commission. These involved formulas for equitable division of the available water during drought; a set of interim and long-term salinity objectives; and development of water storage, supply, and flow augmentation projects. The Delaware River Basin Commission considered that the Level B Study and the Good Faith Negotiations were "strongly related processes." [15]

Among the fourteen interrelated "good faith" recommendations that were eventually adopted were several assumptions or standards: that future water-supply decisions were to use the 1960s drought as their benchmark for any future drought, and that the salinity standards would be relaxed somewhat. Several projects were recommended relating to dams, including the addition of a water-supply component to the F. E. Walter, Cannonsville, and Prompton Reservoirs. And each state was to develop a drought contingency plan. By 1983 many of the "good faith" recommendations had been implemented. [16]

According to Timothy Weston, Maurice K. expressed surprise at how much they were able to get from the state and city of New York. By 1983, however, Maurice K. was no longer Secretary of the Department of Environmental Resources or an alternate to the Governor of Pennsylvania on the Delaware River Basin Commission.

□  □  □  □

In February 1978, the final year of Milton Shapp's second term, Maurice K. prepared a long report on the "status and needs of the Tocks Island dam and reservoir project" for the Governor. The report's thirty-one pages make for sobering, if not chilling reading. There was no question where Maurice K. stood on the need for the dam, and the problems that made it necessary. He still believed that "without proper conservation, development, and management, the water resources of the Delaware Basin "cannot be expected to meet present and future demands, particularly during periods of drought." He held that Tocks Island "was, and still is, the key element of the Delaware River Basin Commission's Comprehensive Plan." [17]

Maurice K. believed that, "while all of the Basin's water problems are serious, the most critical in terms of the basin's health, safety, welfare, and economy is water supply." He declared bluntly, "The Delaware Basin faces a natural disaster waiting to happen!" After disagreeing with the 1975 URS/Maidgan-Praeger study's opinion that salinity problems in the Philadelphia area were not serious, he claimed that "maintenance of the target flows at

Montague . . . is not simply a legal requirement, but a physical necessity." He told Shapp that adding up the capacity of all the alternative water-supply reservoirs in Pennsylvania and New Jersey would yield only one-half the proposed yield from Tocks. Moreover, according to Maurice K., they provided "little or no flood control." [18]

He proceeded to explain to the Governor in great detail each of the interim measures that the Delaware River Basin Commission had in place for an emergency, and how these stopgaps would be only partially effective, or have high costs associated with them. He mentioned, for example, that five new power plants in the Delaware River Basin (Limerick, Summit, Hope Creek, Gilbert, and Martins Creek), which were heavy consumers of the basin's water supply, had been constructed with the understanding they were to be put on a "river follower" system. This meant that in the absence of enough water for cooling purposes, they would be required to shut down. And the sum of their generating capacity was about equal to the reserve capacity of the entire Pennsylvania-Maryland-New Jersey interconnect pool. [19]

Further damning the URS/Maidgan-Praeger study's conclusions, Maurice K. claimed that most of the environmental problems raised in connection with construction of the dam were of dubious validity; moreover, they were true whether or not the dam was built. Of the eutrophication issue, for example, (disagreeing with Governor Rockefeller's contention), Maurice K. told the Governor:

> The question of Tocks placing treatment burdens on upstream discharges is misleading. The Federal Water Pollution Control Act of 1972 requires all point discharges, including feed-lots and poultry processors, to implement best practicable control technology and eventually best available control techniques whether or not Tocks is constructed. [20]

A conservationist and a professional to the end, he closed his report to Governor Shapp by stating "unit costs" for water supply from Tocks Island at 2.6 cents per thousand gallons, compared to 4.0 cents from Beltzville, 7.1 cents from Blue Marsh, and 15.2 cents from the proposed Trexler. "Any way you look at it," he told

Shapp, "this is cheap water, and the Tocks is probably the last, really low cost storage site that can be developed in the Delaware River Basin." [21]

□ □ □ □

When Terry Williamson of the Harrisburg *Evening News* interviewed Maurice K. following his retirement in 1979, the Secretary of the Department of Environmental Resources told Williamson that his greatest disappointment was the decision not to build Tocks Island dam. He explained:

> For thirteen years, four states supported it and the federal government supported it. The federal government spent out of its pocket over $125 million buying the land and moving forward with the project and now we stop it without a viable alternate. . . . That has to be a huge disappointment to me. [22]

This, of course, is small wonder. Maurice K. had invested more time and energy, and had greater hopes and plans of providing for Pennsylvania's and the East's water future than for any other single issue that marked his career. From his first days as the Secretary of Forests and Waters until his final ones at the helm of the Department of Environmental Resources, he considered water to be the key to Pennsylvania's future. To have lost such an objective after twenty-four years of concern and effort was a bitter blow. That he came forward after the Tocks defeat with the "good faith" resolution shows not only his ability to recover from such a loss, but also how important the Delaware River Basin was to him.

Probably a million or more pages of reports, studies, testimony transcripts, articles, and books have been produced on the dam proposed for, but never built at Tocks Island. But there are those who believe that the final chapters are yet to be written.

The premise behind all the planning efforts of the Lawrences, Shapps, and Goddards was that as population increased the demand for land and water would grow significantly. For them it was a balancing of the needs of an increasing number of people against those of the environment. It was their belief that being unable to control population growth and the spread of an expanding civilization, we should provide for their increase.

It was also their contention that, without the construction of a main-stem dam at Tocks and the dams on the Delaware's tributaries such as the one at Evansburg, another flood of the proportions of 1955 or a drought of the magnitude of the 1960s would overwhelm the slight margin of excess capacity in the system of dams that had been built and what the Good Faith Agreement would be able to squeeze from them. If they are right, when this occurs the struggles and difficulties of the sixties will pale beside the ones that will surface. Then the "brick in the toilet" will be inadequate and a New York restaurant customer can watch his hat in complete confidence that his glass of water will not be stolen — there won't be one to steal.

We should keep in mind, too, that in their original plans for the Delaware River Basin, the Corps predicted that "based on water demand" many of the dams and structures will not be needed until late in the life of the project. For example, Maiden Creek was shown as required by 1995, Beltzville not until 2000, and Evanburg in 2010.

There is an impression that the dire predictions of future water shortages equal to, or even worse than those of the sixties were simply bad prophecies and, therefore, that there actually is no real problem or need for a solution of the magnitude proposed by the Corps or the Delaware River Basin Commission. The assumptions of the planners at the time were based on a ranking of the power industry, manufacturing, and agriculture as the top three consumers of water. Although power and agriculture are using about the same amounts as was predicted in the sixties, manufacturing estimates turned out to be vastly overstated, primarily because of the drastic decline in water requirements by the steel industry. [23]

But according to R. Timothy Weston, "we don't know what the benchmark drought year really is." The next extended drought period may be more severe. At that juncture, according to Weston, the Good Faith Agreement would be tested to the breaking-point since "the assumption and formulas of what would happen and be necessary to hold the allocation system together were actually 40 percent wrong during the 60s drought." [24]

Weston also believes the western part of the state is equally as deficient as the eastern in dam capability. "There is enough capacity for watering the barges on the Ohio in a drought but industry along the river has its head in the clouds on the issue — most of them are oblivious to the fact there is a potential problem waiting to happen." [25]

When the pale of the next major drought descends on the Delaware or the Ohio River Basins, David Lawrence, Milton Shapp, and Maurice K. may then be seen as water prophets rather than dam pariahs. Although the reservoir at Tocks Island is still on Congress's authorized list and is part of the Delaware River Basin Commission Comprehensive Plan, neither the Corps of Engineers nor the state of Pennsylvania is now actively in the high-dam-for-flood-control or low-flow-augmentation building business.

And the word *dam* seldom, if ever, crosses the lips of water-resource professionals publicly. It lies silent like a dead star in cold space.

# CHAPTER XVI

## CONSERVATIONIST WITHOUT PORTFOLIO

> **shelterwood method** n. [*shelter* + *wood*] a method combining . . . features of clearcutting with those of selective cutting. . . . [N]atural tree reproduction is secured by removing the stand in two, three, or more cuts years apart. [The] openings created allow enough light to stimulate seedling growth, [while] the residual trees serve as continual sources of new seed. . . .
>
> [Stoddard, Charles H. *Essentials of Forestry Practice*]

By the beginning of 1977, which marked DER's sixth year of existence, Maurice K. was able to report to Governor Shapp that the agency had reached a "turning point" in many of its programs. Among the positive things he was able to recount was a signing of an agreement that resolved the long-standing air pollution complaints at U.S. Steel Corporation's Clairton Coke Works. According to Maurice, this "proved the value of our commitment to negotiated settlements." Some negotiations were, of course, unsuccessful. He called it a "substantial victory," but it took an Environmental Hearing Board decision to force the Medusa Corporation to install proper air pollution control facilities at its cement manufacturing facility in York County. At the same time Maurice K. was able to report a "forward looking action" in the awarding of $2.5 million in grants to "four resource recovery projects demonstrating new techniques for large-scale recycling." He summarized the year's activities by telling the Governor:

The longer we work, the more our attention turns to the future and planning for a variety of concerns, including water quality, water supply, wastewater management, costal zones, scenic rivers, outdoor recreation and forest resources. [1]

Then two years later as Governor Shapp's second four-year term came to an end, Maurice K. not only compiled a comprehensive "Transition" document for the next administration, but also a departmental annual report that "indicates what can be achieved when good people and good programs come together to work for the benefit of all the people of Pennsylvania." He told the Governor, "It always has been my philosophy that to make an organization work you must first have good people and then good programs," and he asserted that DER "has been blessed with an outstanding staff." [2]

He cited the completion of a number of major department planning initiatives: in development of the state's Environmental Master Plan, in water quality programs, on the establishment of three scenic-river studies (Pine Creek, the Lehigh and Schuylkill Rivers), and in water resource management for the Allegheny, Ohio, and Delaware River Basins. That year, too, the Bureau of Community Environmental Control paid out $1.1 million in reimbursement grants to municipalities for enforcing the permit provisions of the Pennsylvania Sewage Facilities Act, while members of the Bureau staff completed 12,270 inspections of 17,500 licensed food-service establishments, which necessitated 427 enforcement and legal actions. Among the other facilities at which the department conducted sanitary inspections were public and private schools, day care centers, hospitals and nursing homes and migrant labor camps, as well as 16,500 semi-public water suppliers and sixty-four establishments that bottled or shipped bottled water into the state. And Maurice K. was pleased to report that the efforts by the Office of Deep Mine Safety had led to a reduction in fatalities in 1978 from nineteen to eight.

Maurice K. also reported that while 20 percent of the major-stream miles in Pennsylvania still failed to meet water quality standards, 101 additional miles of streams had been cleaned up in 1978. As part of the continuing effort to clean up the state's streams, the Bureau of Design had completed twenty-six new acid-mine-abatement study projects with an estimated constructed cost of $14 million. [3]

Maurice K. closed his 1978 annual report by stating that the Bureau of Forestry not only executed sixty-one timber-sale contracts for sawtimber and pulpwood, generating $1.5 million in revenue, but also planted 485,500 seedlings on 677 acres during the spring. At the same time, the Department was still brokering new leases for oil and gas exploration on state forest land. In 1978 this brought in $2.8 million in new income. It was also a good year for tree-seed collections in both natural stands and in seed orchards. Yields of white pine cones, Japanese larch and Virginia pine were all above average for these species. And during 1978, the nineteenth year of the use of aircraft for fire suppression, the three millionth gallon of retardant was dropped on a Pennsylvania forest fire. [4]

❑ ❑ ❑ ❑

When Richard Thornburgh took office as governor in January 1979, he wanted a fresh cabinet and decided not to retain anyone from the Shapp administration. Thornburgh was by nature an eremitic executive. Unlike William Scranton, who had seldom "acted without extensive consultation" with his "cabinet, staff, legislative leadership and private contacts," [5] the new Governor rarely met with even his cabinet officers, preferring to have everyone work through his immediate staff, so he sent Clifford Jones to tell Maurice K. that he would not be reappointed.

When Jones arrived at the old Evangelical Press Building on Harrisburg's Third Street, where Maurice K. kept his office, the Secretary of the Department of Environmental Resources guessed why Jones, who was an old friend and had served in previous cabinets with him, was there. Knowing Thornburgh's management style, Maurice K. who had not expected the Governor to telephone either to reappoint or to dismiss him, asked Jones if he had been sent to "fire him." Having confirmed the reason for the unannounced visit, Maurice K. told Jones to tell the Governor he would "go without a fuss, if Jones was appointed to follow him." [6]

Jones had served in the Department of Commerce from 1963 to 1968, first as a Deputy Secretary and then as Secretary commencing in 1967. Next he became Secretary of Labor and Industry and followed this as Republican State Chairman from 1970 to 1974. He had the credentials for appointment by a Republican Governor to follow Goddard at the Department of Environmental Resources (DER), and although Jones had not thought of such an appointment before his meeting with Maurice K., that is what occurred.

When Thornburgh's ideas on his cabinet first became known, newspapers around the state began to question, as if in disbelief. "Will Goddard Get [the] Axe?" headlined an editorial in the Shenandoah *Evening Herald*. After describing Maurice K.'s career as an "unparalleled record of honesty, dedication and public service" and stating that he was sure to "become a legendary figure," the editorial continued:

> No one understands Pennsylvania's natural heritage as well as he does. No one understands the problem of managing those resources as well as he does. And no one understands environmental politics as well as he does. . .
>
> DER has experienced hard times in recent years. . . . The Legislature has consistently cut the department's budget and has refused to fund new programs to address major environmental problems, such as poor quality drinking water and solid waste disposal. . . .
>
> Because of . . . too much bureaucracy and overzealous enforcement, DER lost much of its credibility. . . The image problem wasn't necessarily Goddard's fault. . . . Someone had to make the tough decisions necessary. . .
>
> No one, however, disputes the great contributions Goddard made to Pennsylvania. And if he leaves office, he can walk away proud. [7]

And as Maurice K. prepared to leave office, the questions were pressed with even more vigor in interviews of Governor

Thornburgh, Clifford Jones, as well as of Maurice K. Although Jones saw his job as "pro-environment, pro-business," there were those who viewed it as a political appointment because of his lack of a background in environmental protection. Thornburgh tried to diffuse these assertions by stating he had "leaned on Dr. Goddard's assessment of Cliff, which was very favorable." And when the reporters pursued him on the issue, he told them, "I'd suggest you talk to Dr. Goddard about it." In a subsequent interview Maurice K. told them, "I've worked with Mr. Jones as Secretary of Commerce. I think he's intelligent, cooperative and competent. I found him to be interested in our environmental programs. . . . I think the governor-elect made a good selection." [8]

From his position as Secretary of the Department, Jones was able to see that Maurice K. continued serving on the Susquehanna and Potomac River Basin Commissions. Maurice K., however, eventually resigned these positions. He kept submitting reports, which Jones sent to Thornburgh, to which the Governor's Office did not respond. When Jones (knowing that the Governor did not see even his cabinet officers so would not meet with an appointed river basin Commissioner) refused Goddard's requests to visit Thornburgh to make an oral report of plans and problems, and get the governor's reaction and opinions, Maurice K. grew disgusted over the apparent lack of interest in his activities or ideas and quit. [9] Rather than the petty, personal pique this appears to have been, Maurice K. had learned from his efforts on the Delaware River Basin Commission that, without the Governor's unqualified support and involvement, an inter-state group would be unlikely to accomplish other than marginal results, and thus he decided not to spend time in a futile venture.

Maurice K. did attend one last meeting of the Delaware River Basin Commission after he left office. On May 28, 1980, the Commission held a special ceremony commemorating Maurice K. for "his long record of constructive support of Commission programs." Each member of the Commission spoke of his affection and regard for him and recalled instances of his association with him from the period 1961 to 1979. Then the group unanimously passed a resolution dedicating the DRBC conference room at West Trenton to Maurice K. Goddard:

> — with affection for him as a compassionate, lighthearted and friendly person;
> — with recognition of his untiring efforts and unsurpassed accomplishments in improving the quality of the environment throughout the Commonwealth of Pennsylvania and the Delaware River Basin;
> — with admiration for his fair-minded persistence in furthering the right course as he saw it, while maintaining respect for those who saw things differently;
> — with respect for his professional standards and his success in applying those standards as an effective scholar-administrator;
> — with gratitude for his 18 years of valuable and constructive contributions to the programs of the Delaware River Basin Commission.

□   □   □   □

Six months after Goddard's departure from state government, Secretary Jones dedicated Marsh Creek State Park, near Downingtown in Chester County. At the ceremony for the 1,705-acre facility, he commented that the new facility served to "provide the goal of a state park within twenty-five miles of every Pennsylvanian" and then stated with a sense of finality: "This ceremony marks the end of the state park expansion era in Pennsylvania." [10]

During the next decade Maurice K. kept active in a variety of personal and professional matters. He attended several official DER functions, such as the opening of a refurbished Mt. Pisgah State Park; he helped the Pennsylvania Farm Bureau with its plans for a bond issue to buy up threatened Pennsylvania farm land; he served as a panelist on various forums and seminars held by groups such as the Susquehanna River Basin Commission, and he continued attending meetings of the Eclectic Club, a group of Harrisburg-area professional men who presented monthly talks to each other on areas of personal interest.

He also began spending more time with several of his neighbors who were retired — discussing their gardens, praising them for cutting their grass high to benefit the birds, and helping them with chores, especially his boyhood task of shoveling snow. Now in his seventies, the result took the form of a crooked shovel-wide path rambling down the hillside walks of Camp Hill's 21st Street. And he proudly followed the accomplishments of his two sons: Mark as a doctor and Kimball with the U.S. Geological Survey. According to Maurice K., both his sons, for some unexplained reason, were "Western boys." Kimball was working in Utah and Mark had settled in Seattle. He was especially pleased in 1986 when Kimball was honored for his work on two award-winning projects that made use of his "exceptional ability in the field of hydraulics and water quality." [11]

Maurice K.'s Pennsylvania Farm Bureau involvement began in 1988. Nine years earlier Act 43 had provided for the preservation of farm land through the sale by the owners of easements to the development rights of their land. The legislature, however, provided no money to purchase these rights. This had to be raised through a bond issue that was put on the ballot in 1988. Maurice K. toured the state with the President of the Farm Bureau, Keith Eckel, in the campaign that secured voter approval of the referendum for the $100 million bond issue. Ten years later, 117,000 acres of Pennsylvania farm land were covered by the program. [12]

About this same time, in his continuing unofficial oversight of DER activities, Maurice K. reviewed a Community Advisory Committee study of the state parks. He was astounded to read that the report recommended using $1 million from the Oil and Gas Lease Fund for park acquisition. He immediately began inquiries into what the remaining four or five million dollars were being spent on. The original Act, as he had put it together, specified that the income was to be spent on "conservation and recreation." It was the "liquidation of one asset to buy another," as he described it.

He went to the State Treasurer, the Auditor General, and received nothing more than evasive advisory statements — no real answer — so he hired a private attorney to investigate. Eventually they discovered that DER was using the money for trucks, computers, radio equipment, and maps. The State Treasurer and Auditor General put a stop to the practice, but only after receiving a letter from George Leader confirming that the fund had been set up as Maurice K. indicated. [13]

The days when a forceful department head like Maurice K. could appear alone before the Pennsylvania House or Senate armed mainly with his integrity and a few budget notes are gone. If Maurice K. told the legislature that he would build five parks over the next two years, and that the money for two of them was coming from Oil and Gas Lease funds and the other three from Project 70 monies, they knew that that was what would happen and raised no further questions on the subject. Now the budget is prepared by nameless functionaries and submitted to the legislature by that ultimate bureaucrat the computer.[14] The Secretary involved seldom knows many of the details involved in it.

Maurice K. worked hard, too, for the Pennsylvania Forestry Association and the National Wildlife Federation. In March of 1986, for example, he traveled to Seattle to attend the Wildlife Federation's fiftieth annual meeting. There he presented a report of the Pennsylvania Wildlife Federation's activities. And using the Pennsylvania Forestry Association as a platform, he began to lobby soon after leaving his state position against proposed incursions into the state parks and for the breakup of the Department of Environmental Resources. These included appearances on Capital Hill in Harrisburg, where he was well respected and still highly regarded.

❑  ❑  ❑  ❑

In March 1988, Maurice K. and Senator James R. Kelley, Republican from Greensburg, Westmoreland County [15] put together a lengthy "point paper" for submission to the legislature to present the reasons for separating the functions of resource management and environmental oversight.   Their primary point was that the funding of natural resource management functions, especially that for state parks and forestry, was continually declining, while that for environmental protection continued to grow.  Moreover, top management in DER was directed primarily to working on protection priorities.

Goddard and Kelley offered three reasons for "criticizing the environmental superagency" concept.   They claimed that in a superagency, "there is a point of counter-productivity that is reached when too many programs are mixed within one operational department." As a result, it was their contention that "one program type will dominate another." Although they agreed the reason cited in support of environmental superagencies — that they permit a "broad ecological perspective on resource management and pollution control" — while "theoretically logical," proves "almost impossible to implement in practice."  According to the two men, "sets of programs located in separate bureaus [even within the same department] usually act independently." [16]

Among the specific problems they cited in Pennsylvania's version of the superagency were:  the lack of enforcement of rules and regulations in the state parks; imprudent forced increases in timber sales to raise funds for necessary maintenance work; the need to complete long-overdue, federally-mandated bridge repairs; lack of security in the parks; loss of forty-eight salaried forestry positions since 1975; the closing of two tree nurseries; and the dangerously low replacement rate for Bureau of Forestry vehicles. [17]

Earlier he and Senator Kelley had met with the Pennsylvania Federation of Sportsmens Clubs to sell them on the idea. The Federation was primarily preservationist in their view and wanted things left as they were for the hunters and fishermen.  At that time, however, the Federation was so powerful that no legislation in the environmental area was likely to be considered without the legislature first getting the organization's views. (There were those who believed the sportsmen were so powerful that they credited them with having "delivered" several past elections.) Thus, Goddard and Kelley gained the Federation's support for their proposal before approaching the legislature. [18]

□ □ □ □

Then in June 1989, Maurice K. traveled to the western end of the state to testify before the Joint Legislative Air and Water Pollution Control and Conservation Committee meeting at Ohiopyle State Park. He was irritated that they would not meet in the central part of the state, but was no longer able to prevail in these sorts of issues. The hearings were scheduled to "receive comments" on the "future of the state parks," which by that time consisted of 114 totaling 275,000 acres. Bills were pending in the Senate and House to develop the state parks by building resorts, golf courses, and other recreational facilities in the hope of raising money for park maintenance to offset budget reductions.

Terry Fabian of the Department of Environmental Resources first outlined the problems facing the parks. There was a backlog of $90 million in major maintenance needs within the system. Facilities were deteriorating rapidly, everything from buildings, trails, bridges, marinas, sewer and water systems, to roads. Moreover, in the face of declining budgets from 1978 to 1987, new questions had arisen. How should the state satisfy the growing public sentiment for acquiring additional land around existing state parks? How should unique natural resources such as wetlands within the parks be protected? Who should operate the park's facilities? How should the parks be promoted? And should the state consider expanding recreational opportunities in the parks? [19]

Maurice K.'s comments dealt primarily with the latter questions. He began by asking the attendees to "think of the State Park System not by itself, but as a package." In urban areas and township parks, he told them, we built "artificial types of recreation:" basketball and tennis courts. In county parks "we still installed artificial types of recreation, except on a larger scale: golf courses, skating rinks, baseball and soccer fields." Then he appealed to them to "look at" the state park system as providing "natural types" of recreational activities — hiking, fishing, rafting, bird watching. "We never envision[ed] them as places to build tennis courts or soccer fields." We tried to "make the state park system large enough so that you get a wilderness or natural type of environment." [20] Then he told them:

> Frankly, I would not make a major change in the character of the system. . . . I believe also we may have a moral and perhaps a legal obligation not to develop these lands commercially. One of the specific purposes of Project 70, for example, was to protect the land from development, and we only passed that bond issue by about a 51 or 52 percent favorable vote. . . . I know full well if they [the voters] thought these lands were not going to be protected, that bond issue would never have passed. [21]

After extensive testimony concerning the funding history of the state parks between 1955 and 1979, he agreed that the park budget had increased in total dollars in the previous few years, but pointed out it had shrunk from 25.8 to 14.7 percent of the Department of Environmental Resource's budget. At the same time, the number of employees in forestry had declined by fifty while the full department had added twelve hundred. [22] He attributed this to the superagency problem of mixing "too many programs" within "one operational structure." Even more pointedly he noted that the amount the legislature had appropriated the previous year for all the state parks was about the same as Philadelphia had for its park system.

Then Maurice K. made two strong arguments for leaving "resort development" in the hands of "private enterprise on private lands." Using the kind of data he always seemed to be gathering to support his positions, he took the legislature to task for, having built in the parks two years earlier — over his objections — seventy "modern" cabins at a cost to the taxpayers of $3.5 million; cabins "which would benefit a relatively small number of individuals." Not only he contended would these buildings place a heavy maintenance load on the park budget, they also were costing $240,000 a year in interest on the money borrowed to build them.    Then, with his memory for facts as sharp as ever, he punched a hole in the idea of the parks as money-raising "resorts" by offering the following argument to the committee:

> Many states without a large tourist industry built resorts to attempt to develop tourism.   No such activity is needed in Pennsylvania. Tourism brought in 11.8 billion in 1987, a 14.6 percent increase from the previous year, [while] the occupancy rate of the 200 plus Pocono Resorts fell. . . . Tourism is already our number two industry, second only to agriculture . . . .   Why [would we want to] add to the resorts already in the Poconos?   They're advertising in Harrisburg all the time. Mount Airy Lodge, I know the phone number I hear it so damn often, 1-800-441-4410. [23]

All of the testimony offered during the hearings was in support of park improvements.  The stumbling block, of course, was how to fund them.    Samuel P. Hays, Professor Emeritus of History at the University of Pittsburgh, who was there representing the Sierra Club, took the poisition that funding for enforcement should not be reduced in favor of the parks.  He argued that the bureau should have a professional staff trained in "conservation biology and resources" which is "devoted to both monitoring and management with a biodiversity goal." According to him, "Parks do not constitute merely aesthetic and recreational resources. They are natural biological and ecological resources as well." It was his contention that people in Pennsylvania would be willing to support a modest increase in taxation to help solve park problems.  He mentioned several states that had done so, including Missouri where a one-fourth cent increase to the sales tax had been enacted. [24]

Through subsequent years, the idea of charging admission and of commercializing the parks with hotels, golf courses, and other fee-generating ventures has come up in the legislature.  There has always been enough sentiment, however, for the Goddard view of a three-tier system, with the state parks as natural, free-to-the-public ventures, that none of these has prevailed.

□ □ □ □

Even before he left office, several of Maurice K.'s friends had approached him about possible ways to honor him. Out of these discussions, it was decided to seek funding to establish a chair at Penn State in forestry and environmental resource conservation to be named for him. In May of 1978, a Penn State press release announced a school proposal to establish a Goddard Chair. According to the release, the chair would honor his "educational achievements, his contributions as a member of the Penn State faculty, and his dedicated service to the people of the Commonwealth."

A committee of twenty-five Pennsylvania citizens, headed by Adolph W. Schmidt, former Ambassador to Canada, and Thomas Dolan IV, an environmental consultant of Philadelphia, was named to raise the funds necessary to endow the chair. [25] Money was received from corporations, foundations and individuals, among them the Richard King Mellon Charitable Trust of Pittsburgh, P. H. Glatfelter III, the Armco Foundation of Middletown, Ohio, Mrs. Eleanor Morris of the French and Pickering Creeks Conservancy, the George D. Widener Trust of Lafayette Hill, Pennsylvania, and a large number of alumni and friends.

The establishment of the Goddard Chair in the School of Forest Resources of the College of Agriculture finally became a reality in August 1982 with an announcement by the university President, Dr. John W. Oswald. According to Dr. Oswald, "A chair named for an individual is a prestigious academic honor and to occupy a named chair is one of the highest distinctions that can be bestowed on a member of the school's faculty." [26] A total of $750,000 had been raised by the time of Dr. Oswald's announcement, and by 1997 the Maurice K. Goddard Chair in Forestry and Environmental Resource

Conservation was fully endowed. Its focus is on outreach and policy and is unlike any other faculty position at Penn State. Its mission is "to enhance the University's commitment to the Commonwealth to provide direction in balanced resource conservation and utilization through programs of public service, research, and instruction."

The Goddard Professor is expected to focus on environmental resource issues covering water resource policy, watershed protection and management, forest regeneration and renewal, international trade of forest products, timber harvesting practices, and biological diversity conservation.

In September 1984, Arthur A. Davis, director of resource policy for the Western Pennsylvania Conservancy, was appointed as the first to occupy the Goddard Chair. The early holders of the chair focused mainly on developing "issues rather than products." [27] With the appointment, however, of Steven G. Thorne in 1991, this began to change. Thorne worked on the drafting of legislation to increase the penalties for illegal timber cutting, and co-directed a project to develop a strategic plan for conservation of biological diversity in Pennsylvania. Thorne also served as vice-chair of the Superfund Evaluation Committee for the U.S. Environmental Protection Agency.

Caren Glotfelty, who was appointed to the Goddard Chair in 1995, had worked with Maurice K. from 1974 to 1979, and then came back as the Deputy Secretary for Water Management in the Department of Environmental Resources after his retirement. During her five years in the Goddard Chair, Glotfelty authored a "National Water Policy Charter" for the Interstate Council on Water Policy; organized forums on forest regeneration and renewal problems, and air pollution impacts in Pennsylvania; led various state-level initiatives in ecosystem management and biodiversity; and served as co-chair of Governor Tom Ridge's 21st Century Environmental Commission. [28]

❏ ❏ ❏ ❏

Maurice K. remained close to the Mont Alto Forestry School and its activities. He attended "old-timer" reunions and visited the campus from time to time. On some visits he would speak, on others take tours with groups visiting plants such as the Grove Manufacturing Company in Blue Ridge Summit, or of the Waynesboro watershed he had helped to develop years before. Following a 1992 Gala, at which he spoke, Corrinne A. Caldwell, Campus Executive Officer, wrote to thank him for his "support of the campus and our goals for an even better future." [29]

And on occasion he lectured to William Forrey's students at the Penn State, Harrisburg campus. Constantly gesticulating Buddha-like, with pokes and prods, up, down and to either side, he would talk uninterrupted for hours — without notes. He would describe how the state park system had been built with Oil and Gas Lease, Project 70, Project 500, and Federal Land and Water Conservation Act monies — rattling off the figures associated with each. He would tell the class how President Reagan gutted the Federal Land and Water program, about personally visiting Mrs. Pinchot to get her approval to name the York County park after her husband, how he wrote the Oil and Gas Lease Fund bill in his room at the Harrisburger Hotel, and that the idea behind the act was to "liquidate one asset to buy another." [30]

He was kept busy, too, writing letters of introduction and recommendation for men and women with whom he had worked over the years. He never seemed to lose his interest in or willingness to support others, especially newcomers. When Eleanor Maass, was elected to the Executive Board of the Pennsylvania Forestry Association, she got lost in the maze of offices on the way to her first meeting at the Harrisburg airport. Maurice, who didn't know her, saw her, stuck out his hand, and said: "I'm Goddard. You must be a new Board member." He then took her to the meeting, sat next to her, pointed out the other board members, and introduced her to them. Then, after the meeting was over, he made sure she had detailed directions on how to get back out of the airport. [31]

□ □ □ □

From time to time, Maurice K. updated and reissued his position paper on the proposal to split the Department of Environmental Resources into two agencies. In 1994, he prepared a new version for the Pennsylvania Forestry Association. It was filled with data showing that the Bureau of Forestry's budget had declined in the previous three years, while since he had left, the whole Department had grown in strength from 3,647 to 4,120 positions. This, he claimed, meant that Forestry was only able to harvest 27 percent of the annual allowable timber, at the same time that the demand for timber was "dramatically increasing." And he asserted that the state parks needed $100 million to modernize antiquated physical plants. It was his contention that the state parks and state forests "have a great economic and environmental impact on the entire Commonwealth," and that "programs of this magnitude deserve cabinet-level department-status." [32]

While the funding for parks and forestry had lost ground in the face of a gain in the Department's total budget, it is far from clear that this resulted from an inappropriate organization, rather than a management decision or the mandates of the legislature. The available funds for parks in the Governor's budget did drop in the decade from 1980 to 1990, for example, from 19.3 percent of the department's total funding to 11.8 percent. However, in the previous eight years when Maurice K. had run DER, the park funds had actually increased from 16.5% to 19.3% of the department's available monies. [33]

Soon Maurice K.'s call for the "breakup" of DER was joined by other powerful voices. Prior to this, Maurice K. had remained outside of politics, according to Clifford Jones, but for the proposed spilt of the Department he did all of the politically correct things. [34] By 1994, when the idea began to gain enough momentum to appear capable of accomplishment, he not only continued to line up legislators and conservation groups across the state — those he telephoned were usually greeted with a gruff, business-like,

294

"Goddard here!" — but also announced his support for Governor-to-be, Tom Ridge; then he appeared on the stump with Ridge as an active advocate of his candidacy.

And to keep up the pressure on the legislature after Ridge was elected Governor, he induced Clifford Jones, Peter Duncan and Nicholas DeBenedictis, all former Secretaries of the Department of Environmental Resources, to release a joint op-ed piece across the state. The four men declared:

> As former Secretaries of the Department of Environmental Resources, we all faced different issues as we implemented different environmental policies serving different governors. There was one constant for all of us, however — we never seemed to have enough time to give adequate attention to our 114 State Parks and our 2.3 million acres of State Forests. [35]

The piece closed by stating that "thirty-five other states, including neighbors Maryland and Ohio, as well as the federal government, manage their natural resources in agencies separate from their environmental protection agency. We think it's time Pennsylvania split DER into two cabinet-level agencies. It benefits all aspects of our environment, especially our parks and forests."

In early June, 1995, following Ridge's inauguration by only six months, the Pennsylvania house passed the administration's bill to split the Department of Environmental Resources into two agencies: the Department of Environmental Protection (DEP) and the Department of Conservation and Natural Resources (DCNR). According to the Harrisburg *Patriot*, the lopsided vote of 193 to 6, made the legislature look "like a divorce court judge presiding over the end of a marriage." [36] The Sierra Club came out strongly against the breakup. It was the club's belief that the interconnection between land resources and water resources and environmental protection was so great that management and protection should be in one agency. [37] But their position seemed to carry little weight with the lawmakers.

While the sentiment in the legislature for improving the parks and forests was strong, the power behind the push for the bill lay largely on the enforcement side of the equation. Some saw the bill as a means of facilitating economic growth in the state by curbing DER's enforcement role, while others believed that removing forest and parks, would help "streamline [DEP, the new enforcement agency's] protection and enforcement efforts." [38]

Calling this action an opportunity for "a brighter future for Pennsylvania's natural resources," John C. Oliver of the Western Pennsylvania Conservancy became the first secretary of DCNR. Oliver explained that "people's health and safety were at stake," because under DER the "state's parks, forests, geologic resources and river environments" had been in a "wrestling match, a match which they lost about ninety percent of the time." Now that they had cabinet-level representation, the state's "prime resources" were being managed under principles of "*stewardship, partnership* and *service*." [39] According to Oliver, the *partnership* he envisioned included: individuals, organizations, businesses, municipalities and other governmental agencies. His idea of *service* was one of "continuously improving program quality."

The final Goddard endeavor on behalf of preserving the environment was finished.

# CHAPTER XVII

# HIS LIFE WAS HIS EULOGY

*Mystery! Mystery! The universe is conceived, created, and sustained in mystery! . . . The deepest, obscurest, and most difficult mystery in the universe is not far off among the stars, but within man himself.*

Norman O. Goddard

In 1965, Maurice K. was asked to give the Memorial Day address at his hometown Camp Hill memorial service. Following the march to the cemetery, the invocation, the Pledge of Allegiance, and the playing of the Star Spangled Banner by the Camp Hill High School band, he began his remarks by paying tribute to those heroes who "found their destiny in the sound and the fury, the fire and horror of the war," and then told the crowd that "they lived, they fought and they died for a reason and with a purpose." Maurice K. told the gathering:

> On the day that man is born his ultimate destiny is to die. Many men die without ever having lived. This cannot be said of those we honor here today. They lived and they lived purposefully. In bringing this purpose to fruition they died. No more can be said of any man: let no less be said of us.
>
> Let us leave this ceremony, determined that the world we leave behind . . . will be as fresh and green and as colorful as the one that was left for us. The alternative is a barren wasteland full of hate and despair.

During the thirty years following that Memorial Day, Maurice K. certainly "lived purposefully;" his death, however, seemed to have had no reason to it. Early on the morning of his eighty-third birthday, September 13, 1995, fire — the forest scourge that voraciously sweeps away all in its path, from ground to crown: oak, hemlock, fern, beech, cedar, wild berry, birch, thistle, walnut, jack-in-the-pulpit, smallest insect to largest animal — left the former Secretary of the Department of Forests and Waters with scorched lungs and third-degree burns over 80 percent of his body.

The fire, fueled by gasoline, was confined to Maurice K.'s bedroom. Firemen arrived at 9:24 A.M. Ethel, who had called in the alarm when she smelled smoke, walked out of the house of her own accord. Thirty-six minutes later Maurice K. arrived at the Hershey Medical Center by helicopter. At 12:27, he was transferred to the burn unit at Lehigh Valley Hospital. Amidst protestations of neighborliness, of love — offered as if in atonement for such an appalling act — he lived another day; then succumbed to his "thermal injuries." [1] George Leader's "pillar of strength" had been felled.

There was no evidence of the involvement of any weapon or other device, only fire, according to Chief Gregory Ammons of the Camp Hill Police. But the authorities have made public no firm evidence or information to support their finding of suicide, or discount the involvement of any other party. (Wayne Snyder, Lehigh County Coroner, who ruled the death a suicide, said he would have nothing more to say about "this unfortunate event.") Although immolation is not unknown as a political statement, it is seldom a means of self-destruction. According to another Lehigh Valley Coroner, Scott Grim, there is no "normal" method, however, to kill oneself. [2]

❑ ❑ ❑ ❑

As with riches, greatness is rarely thrust upon an individual; more often it comes only after great labor. Moreover, many people mistakenly believe that abundant wealth and great distinction are their own reward, but individuals are driven to excel, as to become rich, for more subtle reasons than simply acquiring wealth or fame. Frequently the drive stems from a desire to overcome feelings of inadequacy, or to achieve power or control over others or events, or is a way of hoarding riches or authority for old age and by so doing overcoming a sense of obscurity, or that ultimate nullity, death. To gain, as is sometimes described, a place in history.

Yet the self-assured become unsure, and shows of strength can be masks for insecurity. Maurice Goddard was old, apparently depressed, and no longer on center stage. His self-death may have signalled a final effort at taking control, of asserting command over forebodings of having become extraneous, of lessening importance.

As is often the case, however, "facts" do not always lead to a single conclusion. There are those who cannot accept that Maurice Goddard had no more mountains to climb, or desire to scale them. He was actively involved in the work of the Pennsylvania Forestry Association's Legislative and Policy Committee, and was agitated over new bills introduced in the legislature in April 1995 designed to "develop" the state parks — erect motels, restaurants, and golf courses. And shortly before his birthday John Rex, his long-time land-acquisitions section chief, had made arrangements for him to talk to Rex's United Methodist Church Men's group the following month.

Just three months earlier, too, he had "watched proudly," happily as Governor Tom Ridge signed the bill dividing DER into two agencies, the Department of Conservation and Natural Resources and the Department of Environmental Protection. He had attended the June 28 signing with Peter Duncan, who followed Clifford Jones as Secretary of the Department of Environmental Resources. "Doc" told Duncan that he had not been feeling well, but the doctors had been unable to find any physical ailment.

Following the agency split, he and John Oliver, who had been installed as Secretary of the new Department of Conservation and Natural Resources, had made plans "to meet soon about the new department's progress" [3] And the evening before the fire William Middendorf, who had been a Deputy Secretary at DER under

Maurice K., telephoned to check on him. They only spoke briefly, but to Middendorf he sounded "upbeat." [4]

Maurice K.'s making of commitments and plans for meetings and of showing signs of improvement, actually support the suicide theory, rather than negate it. The most dangerous time for an individual, according to some psychiatrists, is not when an individual is depressed, it is when his will to act returns. When an individual is in the depths of a depression, *all* of his or her faculties shut down. Only when he begins to get better are the physical and mental abilities restored sufficiently for him to act. [5]

It is possible, however, that Maurice Goddard may have been making a political statement with a death by self-immolation. As much as he may have been depressed and distressed over age and illness, he may have wanted one last time to shock us into seeing clearly, boldly the "creeping fungus-like growth crawling across . . . the continent." To warn that the highway system was not, as his old boss, Dwight Eisenhower anticipated, ribbons for defense, but rather ropes of destruction. To make a final plea in his life-manifesto for the conversion of man from "parasite of the earth to its steward."

Some of his close neighbors, those he saw nearly every day during the last years of his life, suggest, however, an even different theory. They say that, in spite of some difficulties over eating and sleeping, he seemed to be reasonably well for an eighty-two-year-old man. When he went to the doctor with some complaints in late August over his lack of appetite and sleep problems, he was sent to the hospital, a situation which, for the first time, seemed to alarm him. Before then he hadn't thought of himself as ill.

After a stay of only three or four days, he came home, appearing dazed and truly sick for the first time. He told several neighbors he was on new medication, which they thought might be the cause of his worsened condition. Two weeks later he was dead. Medicine, however, seems an unlikely culprit. Although finding the right medicine and amount for a depressed individual requires time and experimentation, medication alone is not likely to cause a depressed person to commit suicide. [6]

Most of his friends seem uncomfortable, however, with any of these as causes: depression, political declaration, or medicine. They remain puzzled, even dazed, as if there must be some unfound, unthought of, more reasonable explanation. Only John Rex has come completely to terms with the question of Why? He quotes Saint Paul in answer:

> Beareth all things, believeth all things, hopeth all things, endureth all things.
> For we know in part, and we prophesy in part.
> But when that which is perfect is come, then that which is in part shall be done away.
> For now we see through a glass, darkly; but then face to face: now I know in part; but then shall I know even as also I am known. [7]

Maurice Goddard's funeral service was held in Camp Hill's Mount Calvary Episcopal Church, a lovely brick structure nestled in a rustic, woodland setting in a quiet neighborhood. A brook saunters past. Although they were not members of the church, Maurice K. and Ethel had approached the Rev. Calvin Van Kirk Hoyt several years earlier — Mark Goddard and one of Hoyt's sons had been high school classmates — and made arrangements for the service. Ethel had been raised as an Episcopalian in New York City, but neither she nor Maurice K. had maintained ties to a church in central Pennsylvania.

The crowd was large, the ceremony simple. Lawmakers, rangers wearing green uniforms and Smokey Bear hats, foresters, and friends filled the sanctuary, then overflowed into the aisles and the foyer. Kimball Goddard was amazed to see one of the mourners, a grown man, shedding tears. It gave him his first glimpse at a side of his father that Kimball had never seen. He was stunned to realize that, unlike with his sons, his father had relationships of such closeness, such warmth that his passing engendered feelings of great loss. [8]

Rev. Calvin Van Kirk Hoyt kept the church unlit so that the thoughts of the mourners "would naturally gravitate toward the light — outside and into the park." [9] This he felt was fitting for the state's most distinguished conservationist. At the Goddards' request there was no eulogy, but as Father Hoyt told them, "His life was his eulogy." Then, following a few brief comments, he read Walter Rauschenbusch's poem, "For This World," which had been found in Maurice K.'s effects. It was a poem Maurice had used throughout the years to send to the grieving relatives of close friends and fellow conservationists.

Rasuchenbusch's poem-prayer closes:

> When our use of this world is over
> and we make room for others,
> may we not leave anything ravished
> by our greed or spoiled by our ignorance,
> but may we hand on our common heritage
> fairer and sweeter through our use of it,
> undiminished in fertility and joy,
> so that our bodies may return in peace
> to the great mother who nourished them
> and our spirits may round the circle
> of a perfect life in thee. [10]

□ □ □ □

Today Maurice Kimball Goddard is remembered first and most often for his successful crusade to place a state park within twenty-five miles of each Pennsylvanian. He always pointed, however, at the campaign to professionalize the state's forestry bureau as the more important accomplishment. Because the park idea was not originally his, he may have felt he should not claim too much credit for it. Then again, he always remained close to his forest origins, to his mother's beloved trees. Ultimately helping to save the one "natural" thing with which he was intimate may have meant more to him than constructing man-made parks, for all their value.

Those who knew him personally have described Maurice Goddard as having the "heart of a lion." This may be good poetry; it's illusory prose. How much courage does it take to be the fiercest animal in the jungle? The description, moreover, does not fit the physical aspect of the man (although the Kimball coat of arms is a "lion rampant"). Like Gifford Pinchot, who used to "unfold" when he got out of a car, Maurice K. was tall with a touch of the ungainly about him, especially when — unable simply to wave — he flapped his arms like some oversized prehistoric bird in deliberate, awkward takeoff. And his deep, husky voice and guffawing laugh were more moose- than lion-like.

Courage he had, but it was his oak-like longevity in a forest of lesser trees, his unswerving dedication to bringing forth an environment other than asphalt, his endearing, homespun humanity — with all its faults — but above all his towering integrity that mark Maurice Goddard as an uncommon man.

In retrospect it is hard to place Maurice Goddard with accuracy. Was he forester or park advocate, autocrat or democrat, professional or bureaucrat, scholar or eccentric? Or was he a little of each of these, a chameleon who championed many causes, according each greater or lesser importance as it suited him, or — like a parent to children — as they needed him? Once he had professional foresters running the Department of Forests and Waters, for example, he was satisfied to let them handle things and concentrated on other concerns.

But "politician" is missing from this list. Generally Goddard is thought as the antithesis of one; it is simply not one of the labels assigned to him. Perhaps, however, it fits him so readily, so unobtrusively that we miss seeing it. Gifford Pinchot played the part of one even when he was the national forester, although his accomplishments as a forester-cum-politician were not particularly auspicious. Goddard, on the other hand, may have been the superlative politician, one of the few who was so adroit — one writer has described him as the "consummate insider" [11] — that he got the lion's share of his agenda approved, an agenda, moreover, that on the surface looks, but is not, as apolitical as apple pie.

"Multiple use," the key to much of Goddard's program, with its design to appease the greatest number of constituencies, is in reality a bureaucratic-inspired political idea. And a park within driving distance (at 1960s speeds) of each Pennsylvanian, one that caters to the tastes of multiple users, is certainly for a democracy a superlative late-twentieth-century expression of a political notion.

□ □ □ □

Maurice K. possessed his mother's sense of humanity, her love of the earth and its growing things, not his father's spirituality with its yearning for the divine. One has the impression that he looked at a tree more as if it were a log waiting to be harvested than a window to God's face. He was, after all, a conservationist, not a preservationist.

In Goddard's world trees grew and then were cut down; the rains fell and floods came; people worked less and had more time for recreation. Pennsylvanians needed water to survive and land to thrive. It was his job, his duty to see that they got the best of both by putting environmental issues into the proper perspective for their benefit. People were always at the center of his world, but it was more as individuals to be directed (through education), or *for whom* things were to be managed, not as ones at the center of a great, abiding personal love.

Although he is sometimes referred to as a man of vision, Maurice K.'s vision was that of a practical man, not a mystic or visionary of unknown, mythical prospects. His view of tomorrow was more that of a squirrel gathering nuts for the winter, or a raccoon cleaning out its home. His was an earth-centric view, one with the here-and-now sense of the engineer. Maurice K. was more interested in finding a better way to dump several thousand gallons of water on a wildfire than in debating whether it was the work of

God or happenstance. If he was religious, he kept it to himself. Among close associates he was not known to pray or even to use expressions such as "God bless you," or "God help us."

But Maurice K. had come from a home in which "righteousness" was both preached and lived. As Norman Goddard had explained in one of his Saturday sermonettes, righteousness means "doing or acting according with that which is right." Among its synonyms, the elder Goddard listed: just, uncorrupt, virtuous, honest. And these are words that fit his son perfectly. Moreover, as Norman said, righteousness "is freighted with all that is noblest and best in human life." [12] And Maurice Goddard represented both the noble and much of the best in life.

Little of his early exposure to a religious life, or having taken walks through the forests of snow-covered spruces and firs in Maine, or the experience of living under the flaming Kansas heavens and prairie — which according to Ben Hibbs must cause "some dim comprehension of the Infinite" to "enter the heart of a young lad" — ever led Maurice K. to show a reflective nature or introspective interests. But this may simply have been a semblance of the times. The twentieth century has been one for the pragmatic, not the mystic. Scoured by war in its first half, its second has been marked by the most egregious of commercial concerns.

Maurice K. cited Rachel Carson and her work on several occasions, but he did not possess, at least openly, the sense of spirituality in the environment that she felt. His appreciation of the outdoors was largely of the whitewater-kayaking sort: vigorous, masculine, a race around the track, leaping hurdles as each loomed before him. He lacked Carson's poetic grace; her feeling that there was "something infinitely healing in the repeated refrains of nature, the assurance that after night, dawn comes . . . ." Daybreak for Maurice K. was not a signal for waking to serious, solitary contemplation of nature, it was time to renew his Herculean labors. In truth, his nights and days were often simply gradations of the same work-continuum.

To Maurice K. conservation was an *issue* not a *religion*. While he had the zeal of a missionary, it was tempered with the practicality of a soldier. The religious zealot sees only one side of the ledger, while the soldier realizes there are costs in reaching an objective. Pictures of Maurice K. usually depict him, not like Rachel Carson gazing out across the horizon or off into the heavens, but connected with someone, often looking directly at an individual or the photographer. He was invariably shown: leaning against a porch rail talking to friends at the Western Pennsylvania Conservancy, pointing out a distant landmark in Ohiopyle Park, striding down a trail at Prince Gallitzin.

He could be gracious around women, warm and charming, witty and at ease, but his true milieu was with men, the more rugged the better. Perhaps that is why he and his driver Jimmy Rankin got on so well; their's was a mutual respect born of an admiration for the virile. When he was with men, especially the foresters of Forests and Waters, he was like a bull moose surrounded by a herd of admiring cows; it was then that he could be himself, sharing stories, laughing hardily, a robust Teddy Roosevelt leading his troop of roughriders. In this universe, life was, like a piss in the woods, an affirmation of potent masculinity.[13] Moreover, he never was able to let his masculinity mature naturally into old age. In his eightieth winter, he chased a thirty-year-old neighbor from the Goddard roof, from which Maurice K. was busy shoveling the snow. "Get down before you fall!" he hollered. [14]

He had a sense of humor, but it always seemed to retain a touch of the boyish, the impish about it and, while more likely to be called mesmerizing than charismatic — he could frighten first-time acquaintances — he did possess a certain charm and exude a sense of camaraderie, especially among those who knew him well. And it was sincere, not the unctuous, pasted-on preacher or glad-handing politician sort. He was especially attentive to and drawn, like a story teller, to the young. Only with them, one suspects, was he truly at home, had the capacity to give, and receive unreserved love.

Larry Schweiger, who followed John Oliver as President of the Western Conservancy, tells of the time he and Maurice K. were marooned in a Washington, D.C., hotel by a blizzard. Schweiger's daughters, who were with him, grew tired of watching television, and went down to the restaurant. When, after several hours, they hadn't returned, Larry went looking for them:

> I remember going down this glass elevator and looking across the atrium. I saw Goddard with my daughters waving his hands and talking loudly at the lunch table. Coincidentally, he [had run] into my daughters, took them to lunch, and spent hours telling them things about the outdoors — things they had never heard about. My daughters came back and said that was the greatest day they had spent there. [15]

And Chuck Schaefer (Charles, Jr.), who moved next door to the Goddards after Maurice K. retired, recalls the time the eighty-year-old "Doc" helped him fell a mature silver maple tree that rose between their houses. Goddard had him tie a piece of twine about two-thirds of the way up the tree, at about roof-top level, and then stood back, loosely holding the end, while Shafer hacked away at the trunk with an axe. Afraid that the tree would not fall in the narrow break between the houses — where "Doc" said it would — Shafer stopped several times to ask for reassurance. Each time he did, Maurice K. grinned his boyish grin and told him: "Go on! Go on!" Finally the tree fell, exactly where the old forester said it would. [16]

In the end, where Maurice K. Goddard is concerned, we are left with an enigma as much as a man. His life as well as his death is shrouded with unanswered questions, inconsistencies. But, possibly, we should expect no more. Stripped of their mystery, the great would lose much of their brilliance; the uncommon would become common. As Norman Goddard once wrote:

> Mystery! Mystery! The universe is conceived, created, and sustained in mystery! . . . The deepest, obscurest, and most difficult mystery in the universe is not far off among the stars, but within man himself. [17]

What we can say with assurance of Maurice K. is that he was a forester who found himself as an accomplished administrator; one, however, who never forgot that his roots sprang from the forest floor. He was part of a generation of rugged, larger-than-life men. They were weaned on stories of Horatio Alger and Paul Bunyan, came to manhood in the depression, fought their way onto the bitterly contested beaches of Normandy and the islands of the Pacific, and then battled into the heart of the Japanese and Nazi empires. They were the duty-generation. Having been forged in fire, they were willing to face the most difficult of enemies and problems, to dare much, and to attempt the seemingly impossible.

Maurice K. had a view of an improved world, along with the determination, the will, the tenacity to bring it into being. For twenty-four years Maurice Goddard held the stage on which to practice his craft; it was a perfect marriage of man and job. And, to create the world he believed should be, could be, he was willing to risk much, even a walk on the downhill side of the log. [18] For a half a century, he blazed like a wild fire across the Pennsylvania political landscape, his brilliance illuminating all who came near.

When, a hundred years hence, the thousand tints of spring-green herald once again the annual awakening of the land, the people of Pennsylvania may not remember the name of the "good," "hard" man whose ability, dedication, and persistence resulted in state parks such as McConnell's Mill, Gifford Pinchot, Ohiopyle, and Marsh Creek, and to natural areas such as Quehanna, but they will appreciate that such beautiful, significant places were set aside by someone who preceded them. It truth, it may be said of his gifts to Pennsylvania, as he wrote of Ohiopyle in his tenth year as the state's chief conservationist:

> I believe that it is no exaggeration to say that this park constitutes a more valuable legacy to future generations than any school, factory or other institution which might be erected here. [19]

No Pennsylvanian in the second half of the twentieth century placed a greater, more enduring mark on the land of William Penn than did Maurice Kimball Goddard.

Perhaps the most compelling and poignant statement concerning Maurice K.'s life, one that seems aptly to encapsulate it, came from Florence Steward, at whose marriage Norman Goddard had officiated in Pretty Prairie, Kansas in 1919 when Maurice K. was seven. It seems to reflect the persistence of personality, the consistency in thought and deed that was a hallmark of his life.

When she learned eighty years later what had happened to the boy she knew, Florence wrote:

> When I was younger (I'm 97) I did a lot of traveling and visited many parks in the United States. I wish I would have known about the Maurice Goddard Park then. I would have gone there and been happy to see what that "ornery Goddard kid" had accomplished when he grew up. [20]

# APPENDICES

# Chronology of Important Events

1912    Born September 13 at Lowell, Massachusetts.

1914    Father, Norman O., ordained a Swedenborgian minister.

1915    Family moves to Pretty Prairie, Kansas.

1935    Graduates from University of Maine. Appointed instructor
        in forestry at Penn State's Mont Alto campus.

1938    Receives M.S. in forestry management from
        University of California.

1939    Promoted to assistant professor at Penn State.

1940    Marries Ethel Mae Catchpole September 7.

1942    Called to active duty with U.S. Army.

1946    Assumes position of Resident Director, Mont Alto.

1949    Mother, Susan K. Goddard, dies May 12 at Portland, Maine.

1952    Appointed head of Penn State Forestry School

1955    Takes office January 17 as Pennsylvania Secretary of
        Forests and Waters.

        Hurricanes Connie and Diane strike Pennsylvania.

        Promotes Oil and Gas Lease Fund Act 256.

1956    Urges state's cooperation over Delaware River water
        resources.

1956    Father dies December 12.

1958    Pinchot State Park ground breaking.

        "Water is Pennsylvania's Future" speech.

APPENDIX A.

| 1959 | Receives U.S. Army Corps of Engineers' Patriotic Civilian Services Award. |
|---|---|
| 1960 | First use of fixed-wing aircraft for cascading water on forest fires. |
| | "Parks Have Come Out of the Forest" speech. |
| 1961 | Proposes an "urban ring" park system. |
| | Delaware River Basin Compact approved |
| | Named to Water Pollution Control Advisory Board of Public Health Service, by President Kennedy. |
| 1962 | Elected chairman of Tri-state Committee of Susquehanna River Basin Commission. |
| | Creates Bureau of Pennsylvania State Parks. |
| 1963 | Voters approve Project 70 bond measure following vigorous Goddard campaign. |
| 1964 | Named to Public Land Law Review Commission December 31 by President Johnson. |
| 1965 | Chairman of Federal-State-Local Panel at White House Conference on Natural Beauty. |
| | Approves change to even-aged management of Pennsylvania forests. |
| 1966 | Puts together Governor's Conference on Natural Beauty at Hershey. |
| 1968 | Project 500, park development Enabling Act, signed into law. |
| 1969 | Member of Task Force on Resources and Environment urging President Nixon to create a top-level environmental affairs post. |

| 1970 | Codorus State Park established as joint venture with P.H. Glatfelter Company, May 9. |
|------|------|
| | Public Land Law Review Commission submits Five Year survey results to Congress, June. |
| | Pennsylvania State Forest Resource Plan for 1970 - 1985 prepared. |
| | The Department of Environment Resources (DER) established by Act 275. |
| 1971 | Susquehanna River Basin Compact approved. |
| 1972 | Finally confirmed in February as Secretary of DER after months-long fight. |
| 1972 | Tropical Storm Agnes destroys State Forest road system. |
| | M.K. Goddard State Park dedicated. |
| 1974 | Environmental Quality Board approves updated guidelines for administering Natural and Wild Areas. |
| 1975 | Dedication of Pittsburgh's Point Park — a twenty-year Goddard involvement. |
| 1978 | Number of state parks nearly doubled from number in 1955. |
| 1979 | Goddard Chair endowed at Penn State. |
| 1988 | Appeals to Pennsylvania legislature to prevent incursions into state parks. |
| | Tours with Pennsylvania Farm Bureau in campaign for preservation of farm land. |
| | Prepares point paper proposing split of DER into two agencies. |
| 1995 | Dies September 14. |

# PENNSYLVANIA STATE PARKS
## (Openings under Maurice K. Goddard)

| 1955 | Lyman Run | Samuel S. Lewis |
|---|---|---|
| 1958 | Hyner Run | Sinnemahoning |
| | Gouldsboro | |
| 1959 | McConnells Mill | Denton Hill |
| 1960 | Shikellamy | |
| 1961 | Archbald Pothole | Gifford Pinchot |
| | Prince Gallitzin Prompton | |
| | Susquehanna | |
| 1962 | Kettle Creek | |
| 1964 | Laurel Mountain | Memorial Lake |
| | Elk | |
| 1965 | Susquehannock Warriors Path | |
| 1966 | Curwensville | |
| 1967 | Ryerson Station | |
| 1968 | Francis Slocum | |
| 1970 | Codorus | Kinzua Bridge |
| | Moraine | Neshaminy |
| | Ohiopyle | |
| 1971 | Bald Eagle | Nolde Forest |
| | Tuscarora | Yellow Creek |
| 1972 | Belzville | Canoe Creek |
| | Lackawanna | Little Buffalo |
| | Locust Lake | Maurice K. Goddard |
| | Milton | Ridley Creek |
| 1974 | Laurel Ridge | Marsh Creek |
| | Nockamixon | Tyler |
| 1978 | Kings Gap | |
| 1979 | Evansburg | Jacobsburg |
| | Mount Pisgah | Oil Creek |

Note: Evansburg, Jacobsburg, Mount Pisgah, and Oil Creek were not opened until after Maurice K. Goddard left office.

Source: William C. Forrey's *History of Pennsylvania's State Parks*

APPENDIX B.

# THE STATE OF PENNSYLVANIA FORESTS - 1978

Periodically the U.S. Forest Service inventories the nation's forest resources. In Maurice Goddard's last year in state government, the third such report for Pennsylvania was issued. Although like most government documents, it is rather dry reading overall, the opening summary seems to take on a certain elegance when read carefully, thoughtfully.

## *CURRENT HIGHLIGHTS*

### Forest Area

Pennsylvania is 58 percent forested. Ninety-five percent of the forest land, 15.9 million acres, is classified as commercial forest land.

Nearly 22 percent of Pennsylvania's commercial forest land, 3.5 million acres, is publicly owned — the highest total and percentage in the Northeast. The State has the largest holding of publicly-owned commercial forest land.

Nearly half of the commercial forest land is in sawtimber stands. Less than 2 percent is nonstocked.

Pennsylvania's forests are dominated by hardwoods. The oak-hickory and northern hardwoods forest-type groups cover 47 and 40 percent, respectively, of the commercial forest land.

### Timber Volume

Growing-stock volume is 21.8 billion cubic feet — an average of 1,366 cubic feet per acre. Sawtimber volume is 46.4 billion board feet — an average of 2,916 board feet per acre.

Ninety-two percent of the growing-stock volume is in hardwood species. Red maple is the species with the most volume — 3.3 billion cubic feet.

APPENDIX C.

## Timber growth and removals

Growing-stock growth is estimated to be 2.2 times timber removals. Select white oaks is the only major species group showing removals exceeding growth.

Sawtimber growth is estimated to be 2.7 times removals. Northern red oak shows the largest annual growth of any species.

Sawlogs were the major timber product and accounted for 41 percent of all growing-stock removals.

## Sawtimber per Acre

In what was perhaps the most dramatic and important area of improvement (not depicted on the chart) during the Goddard years occurred in sawtimber volume.

For 1978 it was an average of 2,916 board feet per acre. During the Goddard years, this represented a doubling for the state from from 23 billion board feet to 46.4 billion board feet.

In layman's term this means that trees grew bigger in both height and breadth.

Source: *Forest Statistics for Pennsylvania - 1978*, USDA Forest
Service, Broomall, Pennsylvania.

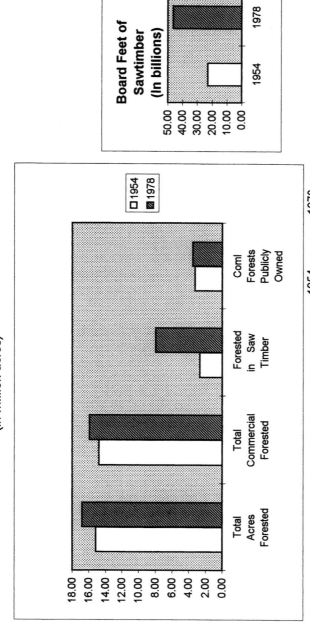

PENNSYLVANIA FOREST GROWTH
1954 - 1978
(in million acres)

Board Feet of
Sawtimber
(In billions)

|  | 1954 | 1978 |
|---|---|---|
| Total Acres Forested | 15.19 | 16.83 |
| Total Commercial Forested | 14.78 | 15.92 |
| Forested in Saw Timber | 2.66 | 7.95 |
| Coml Forests Publicly Owned | 3.25 | 3.51 |
| Board Feet of Sawtimber (in billions) | 23.00 | 46.40 |

Note: Figures, except for sawtimber, are in million acres out of a total of 28.77 million acres in the state
Source: Forest Statistics for Pennsylvania - 1955 and 1978; USDA, US Forest Service

APPENDIX C

# DEPARTMENT OF ENVIRONMENTAL RESOURCES
## Alignment under Act 275

### From the Department of Forests and Waters

Secretary's Office
Bureau of Administration
Bureau of Engineering
Bureau of Forestry
Bureau of State Parks
Comptroller's Office

### From the Department of Health

Deputy Secretary for Environmental
  Protection's Office
Bureau of Sanitary Engineering
Bureau of Housing and Environmental Control
Bureau of Air Pollution Control

### From the Department of Mines and Mineral Industries

Executive Offices
Bureau of Administrative Services
Bureau of Coal Research
Bureau of Mine Land and Water Conservation and Reclamation
Bureau of Appalachia
Bureau of Coal Land Improvement
Bureau of Mine Subsidence Insurance
Bureau of Bituminous Conservation and Reclamation
Office of the Deputy Secretaries - Bituminous and Anthracite
Bureau of Mine Safety
Bureau of Mine Subsidence and Conservation
Bureau of Mine Areas Restoration - Bituminous
Office of the Deputy Secretary - Oil and Gas
Bureau of Inspection
Bureau of Engineering

APPENDIX D.

From the State Planning Board
Bureau of Topographic and Geologic Survey

From the Department of Agriculture
State Soil and Water Conservation Commission

From the Department of Labor and Industry
Division of Mines, Quarries and Explosives

Source:  1970 Department of Environmental Resources Annual Report, Anthracite,
Bituminous, Coal,  and Oil and Gas Divisions.

# GODDARD'S GOOD FAITH RESOLUTION [1]
(As presented to the Delaware River Basin Commission, October 24, 1978)

I think everybody in this room knows I fought as hard as anyone for the Tocks Island project [but] the comments I have to make now have nothing to do with the reservoir. It's pretty clear that when the Congress put this part of the river in the wild and scenic rivers, it was more than a defacto deauthorization of Tocks Island. You're never going to build a reservoir on the main stem of the river. . . . This action would be like trying to build a reservoir in Yellowstone Park or Yosemite Park. We made a valiant effort; the decision was a different one, so I don't want anyone to understand the resolution I'm talking about has anything to do with a new reservoir at Tocks Island; it does not. It has to do with what happens *because* we can't build a reservoir on the main stem either at Tocks Island or at Wallpack Bend as was authorized in the 1954 Decree.

It is the request of Pennsylvania that this [resolution] be placed on the agenda of the November 29 meeting and I can state to the alternate members that the Governor of the Commonwealth will write to the members, including Secretary Andrews [the President's appointee], the first of next week essentially transmitting this proposed resolution . . . so they will be informed:

> *WHEREAS, the States of Delaware, New Jersey and New York, and the Commonwealth of Pennsylvania and the City of New York, were parties to the United States Supreme Court Decree entered in New Jersey v. New York, 347 U.S. 995 (1954) (' the 1954 Decree'); and*
>
> *WHEREAS, the 1954 Decree established a carefully balanced and interwoven arrangement for the equitable apportionment of Delaware Basin waters among the parties; and*
>
> *WHEREAS, in adopting the Delaware River Basin Compact, it was the desire of the signatory States and their respective subdivisions to, if possible, avoid renewed litigation over the equitable apportionment of Basin waters; and*

---

1. SOURCE: Transcript of the *Conference and Meeting Notes* of the Delaware River Basin Commission of October 24 - 25, 1978.

APPENDIX E.

*WHEREAS, to effect that desire, the signatories to the Compact were committed to take no action to impair, diminish, or otherwise adversely effect the provisions of the 1954 Decree without unanimous consent; and*

*WHEREAS, despite said commitments, recent legislation adopted by the United States Congress appears to impair substantially the arrangements for equitable apportionment of Basin waters set forth in the 1954 Decree: and*

*WHEREAS. such action by the United States requires a fundamental reexamination and adjustment of the arrangements made in the 1954 Decree in order to equitably share the limited resources of the Basin and to preserve the basic interests of all concerned; now therefore,*

*BE IT RESOLVED by the Delaware River Basin Commission:*

*1. The Commission calls upon each of the parties to the 1954 Decree to enter into good faith negotiations to seek an equitable reapportionment of the waters of the Delaware Basin;*

*2. In view of the substantial interests of the United States in the Delaware Basin and its status as a party to the Compact, the Commission requests the participation of the United States in any such negotiations;*

*3. The Commission staff shall offer their good offices to assist the parties in negotiations and, if requested, to serve as mediators in such negotiations;*

*4. Said negotiations between the parties should be concluded no later than July 1, 1979, with a unanimous agreement for the equitable reapportionement of Basin waters in a form which can be adopted by the Commission, pursuant to Section 3.3 of the Compact, and thereafter be presented to the United States Supreme Court for approval and entry of an amended decree*

*5. The Secretary of the Commission shall send letters to the chief executive and legal officers of the respective parties to the Decree requesting their written commitment to enter into negotiations consistent with this Resolution.*

6. *If, on or before December 31, 1978, written commitments consistent with this Resolution are not received from all parties, or in the event that such negotiations are unable to reach unanimous agreement between the parties on or before July 1, 1979, the Commission shall be declared unable to resolve the issue of equitably reapportioning the waters of the Basin, and such inability shall be deemed action by this Commission for purposes of Section 3.3 (c) of the Compact.*

*Put very simply in nonlegalistic terms, it is the feeling of the Commonwealth that we were ardent advocates of the Compact to start with. We hope that we could resolve our differences administratively, for example, as we did in the drought of the early 60's, but it says if we can't do that, then we have to go back to the Supreme Court, and have it resolved legally. It is my hope, Mr. Chairman, that this can be acted on at the November 29 meeting of the Commission and we will get the letters out to the members nest week, early next week.*

# NOTES AND SOURCES

---

# BIBLIOGRAPHY

# NOTES

## Chapter I: PRETTY PRAIRIE

1. Lowell remained the center of the nation's textile industry until it moved south near the end of the first half of the twentieth century.

2. Norman Smith, *A History of Dams* (Secaucus: The Citadel Press, 1972).

3. Increase Lapham, "Report on the Disasterous Effects of the Destruction of Forest Trees Now Going on So Rapidly in the State of Wisconsin." Quoted in John Perlin, *Forest Journey, The Role of Wood in the Development of Civilization* (New York: W. W. Norton & Company, 1989), 354 and 355.

4. Ibid.

5. Shelia Connor, *New England Natives* (Cambridge: Harvard University Press, 1994), 137-139.

6. Sig Synnestvedt, "Swedenborg, Emanuel" and "Swedenborgians," *Encyclopedia America*, Vol. 26 (Danbury: Grolier Inc., 1991), 120 and 121.

7. Ibid.

8. Marguerite Beck Block, *The New Church in the New World, A Study of Swedenborgianism in America* (New York: Holt, Rinehart and Winston, Inc., 1932), 144.

9. Ibid., 399.

10. Leonard A. Morrison, *History of the Kimball family in America from 1634 to 1897* (Boston: Damrell and Upham, 1897), 921.

11. One early settler was quoted as saying that when he first passed through there was only one tree between Hutchinson and Pretty Prairie and that was growing along the river.

12. Robert W. Baughman, *Kansas in Maps* (Topeka: The Kansas State Historical Society, 1961).

13. Darrell Albright interview, February 11, 1999. The church is still standing but the parsonage was torn down in the early nineties because of the high cost of upkeep.

14. Eric Zacharias interview, February 12, 1999. Zacharias is the long-time minister of the Pretty Prairie Swedenborgian Church. According to Zacharias, the *natural* is intended to mean the development of a "full appreciation of all that the real or natural world has to offer," while the *celestial* relates to "one's appreciation of and relationship to God."

15. Ibid.

16. The area was first opened by Congress in 1854. Liberty Hyde Bailey, "Kansas" in *Cyclopedia of American Horticulture* (New York: Macmillan Company, 1900), 855. According to Bailey, the trees settlers planted were

often fruit species, and since each settler wanted favorite varieties from his former home, by 1900 over 2,000 kinds of apples alone had been planted in Kansas. Many of these failed.

17.    Eric Zacharias recalls that, when he first arrived in Pretty Prairie, among the many species he didn't know, he did recognize ashs and cottonwoods around the house and church.    Zacharias interview.

18.    Connie McNamara, "PFA Dedication: Dr. Maurice Goddard" (Mechanicsburg: *Pennsylvania Forests*, Summer, 1990).

19.    Bailey, "Kansas."    Bailey gave the acreage of apple trees in Kansas in 1900 as eleven million, cherries 1.6 million, vineyards at .6, blackberries at .3, raspberries at .15 and strawberries at .18.

20.    Although it was a few years before the term "dust bowl" was coined to describe the area from Southwest Colorado through the Oklahoma and Texas panhandles to Southwest Kansas, that part of the continent seldom gets more than 15 inches of rainfall and is swept each spring by high winds.    These sometime reach to the north and east far enough that Pretty Prairie experiences occasional "dust storms."

21.    Caren Glotfelty, ed., "Summary of Accomplishments" from *His Life, Legacy, and Lessons*, program booklet of the Second Pennsylvania Environmental History Symposium of The Pennsylvania State University, (Harrisburg: April 17, 1997), 4.

22.    Patrick Hanks and Flavia Hodges, *A Dictionary of Surnames* (New York: Oxford University Press, 1988), 214.

23.    Zacharias interview.

24.    Ben Hibbs, article "Boyhood on the Prairie," *Reader's Digest*, Vol 85 (Pleasantville: November, 1964).

25.    Albright interview.    Although there was only a morning and evening passenger train through Pretty Prairie each day, there were large numbers of freight trains moving in and out of the town in the 1920s.

26.    Hibbs, "Boyhood on the Prairie."

27.    Hilah Field Young interview, March 10 1999.

28.    Florence Steward interview, March 26 1999.

29.    Hibbs, "Boyhood on the Prairie."

30.    Maurice K. Goddard, *Diary*, 1925.

31.    According to Florence Steward the food, which was always excellent, was the centerpiece of these meetings.    On the frontier people expected to dine in elegance in spite of being in the west, thus tables frequently were set formally with linens and china in even rustic circumstances.    See Craig Miner, *West of Wichita* (Lawrence: University Press of Kansas, 1986), 106.

32.    Goddard, *Diary*.

33.    Stukey interview.

34. According to Swedenborgian Church archive records, Norman Goddard began serving in Toronto in 1924, so the family may have been separated for a period of time between late 1924 and the summer of 1925 when Maurice's diary picks up in Toronto.

35. Goddard, *Diary.*

36. Hibbs, "Boyhood on the Prairie."

37. Hilah Field and Florence Steward interviews. Steward remembers that Susan Goddard attempted to have the New-Church choir chant portions of the service, but the group, which was small, never seemed to be able to do it properly and reverted to singing the anthems.

38. Ethel Goddard interview, May 27, 1998.

39. Robert I Ashman to L. H. Bell, Penn State Director of Public Information, May 8, 1958.

40. Fryeburg New-Church Assembly brochure, August 4 to August 25, 1935.

41. Ethel Goddard interview, May 27, 1998.

42. Ethel M. Goddard interview, April 30, 1998.

43. "Fryeburg New-Church Assembly," in *The New-Church Messenger*, Sep. 23, 1936.


## Chapter II: FROM MAINE TO PENNSYLVANIA

1. "The Maine Bulletin," April 1936 (Orono: The University of Maine Press, 1936), 32.

2. The Penobscot River empties into Penobscot Bay, the largest penetration of water into the state from the Atlantic. The river is navigable to Bangor 60 miles from the Ocean. The name *Penobscot* comes from the Algonquian words for *rocky river*.

3. David C. Smith, *The First Century, A History of the University of Maine 1865 - 1965* (Orono: University of Maine Press, 1979), 142.

4. "The Maine Bulletin," 127-129.

5. Ibid., 96-97.

6. Ethel Goddard interview, April 30, 1998. According to Ethel, it was necessary to replace the tooth. The cost was such a burden to the Goddard budget that Susan Goddard insisted Maurice K. not risk losing another.

7. William C. Bramble interview, September 3, 1997. Although Bramble stated that Maurice K. told him he went as part of a team from the University of Maine, there are no longer any records available at the school of such an invitation.

8.  Cunningham, who in 1936 won a silver medal in the 1500 meter race at the Berlin Olympics while Jesse Owens won four gold medals, had been burned severely as a boy.  The condition of his legs was so grave, his doctors initially felt he might never walk again.  Determined that he would, Cunningham began walking and then running as a means of overcoming his disability. His story was a model of heroic-determinism for boys growing up in the thirties and forties.

9.  *Baird's Manual, American College Fraternities, 14th edition,* 1927 (Menasha, Wisconsin:  The Collegiate Press, George Banta Publishing, 1940), 172-174.

10.  David C. Smith, *The First Century,*  145.

11.  He was also a member of five honorary scholastic societies:  Phi Kappa Phi (general scholastic), Xi Sigma Pi (forestry), Phi Sigma (biological sciences), Phi Epsilon Phi (botany), and Gamma Sigma Delta (Agriculture).

12.  *The Maine Campus* (Orono:  University of Maine, November 11, 1934).

13.  Robert A. Caro, *The Power Broker:  Robert Moses and the Fall of New York* (New York:  Random House, 1974), 169.

14.  Michael Bezilla, *The College of Agriculture at Penn State.* (University Park:  Pennsylvania State University Press, 1987), 42.

15.  Maurice K. Goddard, "Blue Jay Camp," *Sylvan* (State College:  Penn State University, 1940).

16.  Ibid.

17.  Ibid.  The camp was named "Blue Jay" after a settlement which was established north of the camp early in the nineteenth century.

18.  Ibid.

19.  Irving Stone, *There was Light, Autobiography of a University, Berkeley: 1868-1968,* chapter "John Kenneth Gailthbraith"  (Garden City, N.Y.:  Doubleday & Company, Inc., 1970), 21.

20.  Ibid., chapter "Myron Krueger," 289.

21.  Verne A. Stadtman, *The University of California, 1868-1968*  (New York:  McGraw-Hill Book Company, 1970), 289.

22.  Stone, *There was Light,*  22

23.  Russell M. Burns, "Silvicultural Systems for the Major Forest Types of the United States,"  U.S. Forest Service, Agriculture Handbook No. 445, December 1983.

24.  William C. Bramble later married Dorothy Catchpole, Maurice K.'s sister-in-law.

25.  William C. Bramble and Maurice K. Goddard, "Effect of Animal Coaction and Seedbed Condition on Regeneration of Pitch Pine in the Barrens of Central Pennsylvania," article reprint from *Ecology,* Vol 23, No. 3, July, 1942.

# Chapter III: I'M GETTING MARRIED THIS SUMMER

1. *New York Times*, September 7, 1940.
2. Ethel M. Goddard interview, April 30, 1998.
3. Ibid. In a Harrisburg *Patriot* interview after Maurice K. became Secretary of Forests and Waters, Ethel claimed she and a friend went to Fryeburg to use up $30 she had left from a vacation out west.
4. Dorothy Bramble interview, September 3, 1997.
5. M. Eileen Graham, "Goddard The Man," talk at the Second Pennsylvania Environmental History Symposium, *Proceedings of the Maurice K. Goddard Symposium* (Harrisburg: April 17, 1997), 10-11.
6. Henry Wellington Wack, article "The Camping Ideal, The Human Race," *Red Book* Magazine, New York, 1925, pg 2.
7. Army of the United States, "Station List," June, 1941.
8. Ethel Goddard interview, April 30, 1998.
9. M. Allison, *Army Office Training, What everybody should know about Army organization, administration, and clerical procedures* (New York: Gregg Publishing Company, 1942).
10. Maurice K.'s primary and secondary MOSs - that he carried back into the reserves after the war - were 2110 (Adjutant) and 2210 (Classification Officer).
11. Ethel Goddard, "Maurice K. Goddard Event Log." The dating of personal events such as promotions and station changes during his military career was taken from a three-page log, apparently maintained by Ethel Goddard during the war.
12. David E. Eisenhower, *Eisenhower at War* (New York: Random House, 1986), 31.
13. Maurice K.'s position within SHAEF has been established from documents found in his effects after his death. The operational chart for the Military Personnel Branch of the Adjutant Generals Division is annotated with the initials "MKG" on the position of the Executive Officer of the branch.
14. The Walter Bedell Smith quote is from Forrest C. Pogue's interview of General Smith in the manuscript division of the archives of the Army War College at Carlisle, Pa. Following the war, Pogue conducted interviews with many of the high ranking officers who were involved. For Ike's opinion of Barker, see also *The Papers of Dwight David Eisenhower, War Years*, (Baltimore: The Johns Hopkins University Press, 1970), 458.
15. The name of the head of the Military Personnel Branch, Maurice K.'s immediate superior, is unknown. It was probably an officer of the rank of

Colonel and may even have been a British officer. The branch consisted of six sections: Officers Section, Enlisted Section, Distribution and 201 Files Section, Morning Reports Section, Miscellaneous Section, & Awards and Decorations Section and the Emergency Returns Section (of which Maurice apparently had charge before he was promoted to Executive Officer).

16.  During the period Brigadier General Davis was in charge of publicity, Col. Emil C. Boehnke, his deputy, served as SHEAF Adjutant General.

17.  Forrest C. Pogue, *The Supreme Command*, (Washington: Office of the Chief of Military History, 1954), 73 and 74.

18.  Although Pogue does not mention or list biographic sketches in *The Supreme Command* of any key officers other than those of British or American nationality, there were Canadian, French, and Polish units in the field. Therefore, it is more than likely there were middle ranking officers from those countries on the SHAEF staff.

19.  Omar H. Bradley, *A Soldier's Story*, (New York: The Modern Library, 1999), 33.

20.  The actual date of Maurice K.'s assignment as Executive Officer of the Personnel Division is not known.  It is unlikely, however, that he held this position while still a junior officer.  Moreover, it was probably for his service in a subordinate section of the Military Personnel Branch, possibly the Emergency Returns Section, that he later received a Legion of Merit and Bronze Star.

21.  Bradley, *A Soldier's Story*, 30.

22.  Rex Melton interview, April 25, 1998.  Many of the duties General Smith handled were high level.  For example, it was Smith who conducted the negotiations with the German High Command that led to their surrender to the Allied powers.

23.  Unit records (EAM) equipment was in use for automated processing of selected IBM cards.  M. Allison, *Army Office Training*, identifies one such card as the "Report of Change" (W.D., A.G.O. Form 303.) These cards, which reflected changes in duty status for individual soldiers, were extracted from the Morning Reports (probably at the regiment level) to forward to higher headquarters for machine processing.

24.  The "Station and Record of Events" section of a Morning Report recorded the location or assigned station  of an organization and any events affecting its status.  The rations section of the morning report listed each individual who was authorized to draw subsistence for eating separate from the unit.

25.  Joseph E. Ibberson interview, May 1 1998.

26. The figure for Eighth Air Force missing is taken from Andy Rooney's book *My War* [Holbrook, Massachusetts: Adams Media, 1995]. Official figures after the war [cited by Pogue in *The Supreme Command*.] were much smaller,

apparently having been reduced because the men were later declared as "killed in action."

27. Mary C. Harris, "Goddard: The Legacy," talk at the Second Pennsylvania Environmental History Symposium, from *Proceedings of the Maurice K. Goddard Symposium* (Harrisburg: April 17, 1997), 29. The General Eisenhower quote is from Dwight David Eisenhower, *Letters to Mamie*, (Garden City: Doubleday & Company, Inc., 1978), 172 and 175.

28. David E. Eisenhower, *Eisenhower at War*, 157.

29. Dwight David Eisenhower, *Letters to Mamie*, 195 and 197.

30. David E. Eisenhower, *Eisenhower at War*, 349

31. Pogue, *The Supreme Command*, 276-277.

32. William Riley interview, February 1, 1999. According to Riley (a GI who worked in the building, and is now a SHAEF Veterans Association officer) I. G. Farben offices were modern for the day. Riley saw no evidences of laboratories in the building, only offices. Curiously, however, the elevators never stopped running. To get to a different level you had to leap on one as it passed by your floor. When Riley returned to Frankfurt in 1996 for a reunion, the building was still there, but occupied by a firm other than I. G. Farben.

33. The quote from Hilter's speech is from Barbara Miller Lane's *Architecture and Politics in Germany, 1918-1945*, (Cambridge: Harvard University Press, 1968), 147.

34. Harry C. Butcher, *My Three Years with Eisenhower*, (New York: Simon and Schuster, 1946), 856-857.

35. Colbert C. Held, and Hans Arntz, article "Frankfurt an der Oder," (New York: Collier's Encylopedia, Vol. 10, 1996), 326. The Cartel was founded in 1925 out of an earlier syndicate of German Coal-Tar and Dye manufacturers patterned after U.S. Trusts of the nineteenth century. It was the world's largest chemical, pharmaceutical and dyestuff concern. [*Encyclopedia Britanicia*, 15th Edition, Vol. 6 (Chicago: 1974), 245. ]

36. William L. Shirer, *The Rise and Fall of the Third Reich*, (New York: Simon and Schuster, 1960), 664 and 972.

37. Article, "I.G. Farben," *Encyclopedia Britanicia.*

38. James K. Pollock, and James H. Meisel, *Germany Under Occupation*, (Ann Arbor: George Wahr Publishing Co., 1947), 126 and report "Population of the US Zone of Germany, Part I" by the Civil Administration Division, Office of Military Government for Germany, November, 1947.

39. Ethel Goddard interview, April 30, 1998.

40. Maurice K. returned from Europe on March 17, 1946. Shortly, thereafter, he was placed on "terminal" leave, as were many other returning soldiers. This permitted the men to commence their adjustment back to civilian life while still officially in the service and drawing pay (which was considered as a sort of unofficial readjustment bonus).

41. Kimball Goddard interview with Steve Williams, October 31, 1998.

## Chapter IV: MONT ALTO FORESTRY SCHOOL

1. Ethel Goddard interview, May 27, 1998.
2. Elizabeth H. Thomas, *A History of the Pennsylvania State Forest School, 1903-1929* Mont Alto: The Pennsylvania State Forest Academy/School Founders Society, 1985), 21.
3. With her botanical background Dock was one of the few dendrology experts in the United States. According to Elizabeth H. Thomas, she also had an "expert's grasp of theoretical forestry and of forest policy." [Thomas, *A History*, 22.]
4. Rothrock was a medical doctor, but also had been trained as a botanist at Harvard by Asa Gray. He had a varied career in private practice and as a member of several expeditions to the west either as a botanist or medical officer. He served as a Pennsylvania volunteer at Antietam and was wounded at Fredericksburg. In collecting pictures and data after his appointment in 1877 as Michaux lecturer, he was appalled by the conditions he found in Pennsylvania's forests and began the crusade that led to the formation in 1886 of the Pennsylvania Forestry Association, and the legislature's establishment in 1893 of a state Forestry Commission. Rothrock became one of its first members. Dock was appointed to the Commission in 1901. [See Thomas, *A History*, 3-19 for a good survey of Dock and Rothrock's careers in forestry. No full-length biographies of either forestry pioneer exist at this writing. ]
5. Rothrock to Benjamin G. Welch, 4 September 1900. [George H. Wirt papers, Pennsylvania Historical & Museum Commission.]
6. Michael Bezilla, *The College of Agriculture at Penn State* (University Park: Pennsylvania State University Press, 1987), 47.
7. Ibid., 111 and 157.
8. Ibid., 190.
9. Eileen Middleton, "A Goddard Perspective," article in *Pennsylvania Forests*, (Mechanicsburg: Pennsylvania Forestry Association, Summer 1990).
10. Ibid.
11. Bezilla, *The College of Agriculture at Penn State*, 218.
12. After graduating from Penn State, Middleton went to work for the Pennsylvania Electric Company in Johnstown, Pennsylvania. He worked with Maurice K. on several projects including one pioneering the evaluation of appropriate tree plantings under electrical transmission lines.
13. Robert H. Rumpf interview, April 25, 2000.

14. Ralph R. Widner, "Goddard: The Man," talk at the Second Pennsylvania Environmental History Symposium, from *Proceedings of the Maurice K. Goddard Symposium*, (Harrisburg: April 17, 1997), 18.

15. Joseph Ibberson interview, May 1, 1998.

16. Rex E. Melton, "A Few Recollections from the Penn State Years," article in *Pennsylvania Forests*, (Mechanicsburg: Pennsylvania Forestry Association, Summer, 1990).

17. William H. Pfeiffer, "Mont Alto Since World War II," article in *The Sylvan* (State College: Penn State University, 1954).

18. Joan W. Goodwin, "A Kind of Botanic Mania," article in *Arnoldia*, magazine of the Arnold Arboretum, Harvard College, Vol 56, No. 4, Winter 1996-1997.

19. The first female forester was hired by the Pennyslvania Bureau of Forestry in 1984.

20 Pfeiffer, "Mont Alto Since World War II."

21. Rex E. Melton interview, May 14, 1998.

22. Ted Yarosh, "Blister Rust Days," in *The Sylvan* (State College: Penn State University, 1952).

23. "Timber Management and Watershed Protection High Light Annual Meeting," article in *Pennsylvania Forests* (Mechanicsburg: Pennsylvania Forestry Association, July, August, September 1955).

24. "Recent Innovations: TreeP, Sawmill, Chipper," in *The Sylvan* (State College: Penn State University, 1951).

25. Rumpf interview.

26. *The Sylvan*, "Recent Innovations: TreeP, Sawmill, Chipper."

27. Melton interview.

28. Maurice K. was promoted to a full professor of forestry in 1949.

29. Quoted in Steve Neal, *The Eisenhowers, Reluctant Dynasty*, (Garden City: Doubleday & Company, 1978), 210.

30. Ibid., 207.

31. This project was conducted along with the Asplundh Tree Company, Dupont Chemical Company, the U.S. Fish and Wildlife Service, and the Pennsylvania Game Commission. *The Sylvan* (State College: Penn State University, 1954).

32. Robert Stern, "Wood Ute's On Tour," article in *The Sylvan*, (State College: Penn State University, 1952).

33. Ibberson interview.

34. Ibid. According to Ethel Goddard, however, Milton Eisenhower and Maurice K.'s friendship was professional, not social. The Goddards did not, for example, visit the Eisenhower's home during the period they were both at Penn State except for official functions.

35. Melton interview.  Prior to that time, the School of Forestry was a department in the Penn State School of Agriculture.  Bezilla claims that Goddard did not actively support the change.  This seems unlikely, however, as Maurice K. did write enthusiastically in the summer 1953 edition of *Pennsylvania Forests* about the prospects for the upgrade, which were to be part of the change of the college to a university.

36. Leighton P. Stradley, Jr., *Pennsylvania Forests*, (Mechanicsburg: Pennsylvania Forestry Association, Spring 1953).

37. "Committee Report of Progress," *Pennsylvania Forests*, (Mechanicsburg: Pennsylvania Forestry Association, July, August, September 1955).

38.  Ibid.

39.  Maurice K. Goddard  remarks in *The Sylvan* (State College:  Penn State University, 1955).

40.  Maurice K. Goddard speech to the Pennsylvania Electric Association, Sept., 17, 1958.

## Chapter V: MR. SECRETARY

1. George M. Leader inaugural address.   [Quoted in Martin Nelson McGreary's *Pennsylvania Government In Action* (State College: Penns Valley Publishers, 1972), 47.]

2.  George M. Leader interview, November 12, 1997.

3.  George M. Leader, "My Friend, Maurice Goddard," article in *Pennsylvania Forests* (Mechanicsburg:  The Pennsylvania Forestry Association, Summer, 1990).   Blatt, who was a protege of David Lawrence, was one of the earliest active female members of the Democratic party in Pennsylvania.   She was reelected in 1958 as the Secretary of Internal Affairs.  Moreover, she was the first woman to be elected to any state-wide office.  When she was reelected, she received the largest majority cast for any candidate in the election.

4.  Leader interview.

5.  Leader, "My Friend, Maurice Goddard."

6.  J. H. Coffman to George M. Leader, July 8, 1955.   Coffman was Chairman of the Conservation Committee of the York, Pa. Chapter of the Izaak Walton League of America.

7.  Joseph S. Illick  to George M. Leader, January 18, 1955.

8.  George M. Leader, Press Release #12, January 26, 1955.  White's contract specified that he commence cutting by October 1, 1945.  When he did not, the contract was cancelled.  He then filed a claim for damages which was still pending when Secretary Lewis "reinstated" the contract following a meeting

with White. According to the press release Goddard's action resulted in savings to the state of $32,400.

9. Although the story of Lewis's action to "plough under the seedlings" has appeared in print [Crary & Cooper, *The Politics of Progress* (Harrisburg: Penns Valley Publ., 1982), 115.], Joe Ibberson, who ran the Division of Forest Research (but not the nurseries) both for Lewis and then for Goddard doubts its veracity. He does acknowledge that the nurseries were in poor shape when Maurice K. took over Forests and Waters.

10. Leader interview. Martin McGreary, *Pennsylvania Government In Action*, claims that some of the inspectors, who were political appointees, were alleged to have taken payoffs. Moreover, McGreary asserts that removal of the inspectors from the patronage system by Leader was a major step in cleaning up the mines. [McGreary, pg 136.] The mines and the inspectors were not Goddard's responsibility during the Leader Administration.

11. T. T. Darlington, "Department of Forests and Waters - 1957 in Review," article in *Pennsylvania Forests* (Mechanicsburg: The Pennsylvania Forestry Association, Winter 1958).

12. During this period the legislature met on a biennial basis, therefore, department budgets were also developed for the same period.

13. Maurice K. Goddard, article "Excerpts from a Statement by Maurice K. Goddard, Secretary, Department of Forests and Waters, before House of Representatives Appropriations Committee," in *Pennsylvania Forests* (Mechanicsburg: The Pennsylvania Forestry Association, Summer 1955).

14. Ibid.

15. Maurice K. Goddard, testimony before the Joint Legislative Air and Water Pollution Control and Conservation Committee, June 9, 1989, page 45 of the Stenographic Report. Often referred to simply as "The Joint Committee," this group has oversight responsibility for the state parks.

16. George M. Leader, "State recruitment campaign for technical and professional personnel," press release 790, October 4, 1956.

17. Goddard to Joseph E. Ibberson, Aug. 24, 1955. According to Ibberson, the Secretary appeared in his office the same day the letter was prepared. Ibberson had seven days to assume all responsibility for the nurseries in addition to his current assignments.

18. The first competitive state civil service examination for Foresters was held on January 11, 1958.

19. Kenn Marshall, article "Dr. Maurice K. Goddard, Environmental Patriarch" (Harrisburg: *Apprise* magazine, WITF, Inc., May 1993).

20. "Pennsylvania's Resource Renaissance," editoral, *American Forests* (Washington D.C.: American Forestry Association, October 1959), 17.

21. Lester A. DeCoster, *The Legacy of Penn's Woods, A History of the Pennsylvania Bureau of Forestry* (Harrisburg: Pennsylvania Historical and

Museum Commission for the Department of Conservation and Natural Resources, 1955), 81. (In its Oct. 1959 editorial *American Forests* states that Goddard "brought back" Wible; DeCoster writes he was "retained.")

22. Goddard was an Independent, although one writer describes him as an "Independent-Democrat."

23. Goddard testimony before the Joint Committee, 45.

24. George B. Stevenson served in the Pennsylvania Senate from 1939-1962.

25. William F. Schultz, Jr., *Conservation Law and Administration, A Case Study of Law and Resource Use in Pennsylvania* (New York: The Ronald Press Company, 1953).

26. Richard R. Thorpe, *The Crown Jewel of Pennsylvania, The State Forest System* (Harrisburg: Department of Conservation and Natural Resources, 1997), 21; and Goddard, testimony before the Joint Committee, 46.

27. *New York Times*, August 21, 1955, page 1. The Delaware crested at 40 feet, 16 feet above flood stage.

28. Ibid.

29. Maurice K. Goddard testimony before the Select Committee on Water Resources, U.S. Senate, Philadelphia, Pa., October 30, 1959.

30. Leader interview.

31. The Department of Forests and Waters was authorized to alleviate flood damages and provide flood prevention facilities by Act 195 of Jun 5, 1947. The Division of Flood Control, which was set up to execute the purposes of the Act, was, of course, in existence at the time of the flooding in 1955.

32. Department of Forests and Waters, Division of Flood Control, Biennial Report, June 1, 1958 to May 31, 1960.

33. Maurice K. Goddard, article "Department of Forests and Waters - 1958 in Review" in *Pennsylvania Forests*, (Mechanicsburg: Pennsylvania Forestry Association, Winter 1959), 4.

34. In February 1955, Dr. Eisenhower arranged with postal officials to establish a separate post office, "University Park," for the campus. This followed an unsuccessful effort on his part to have the town change its name from State College, which Eisenhower felt had connotations of a "cow town."

35. Henry Clepper, article "Pennsylvania Forestry's Ten Most Influential Men," in *Pennsylvania Forests* (Mechanicsburg: The Pennsylvania Forestry Association, Fall 1964), 56.

36. "50th Anniversary of Penn State-Mont Alto," *Pennsylvania Forests* (Mechanicsburg: The Pennsylvania Forestry Association, Spring 1957), 76.

37. Maurice K. Goddard, report "Pennsylvania's New State Parks" to the 1957 General Assembly on Act 256," April 15, 1957, 5.

38. Ibid., 12.

39. Ralph C. Wible, article "New State Park" in *Pennsylvania Forests* (Mechanicsburg: The Pennsylvania Forestry Association, Fall 1957), 94 and 95.

40. Ibid.

41. Johnstown *Tribune-Democrat*, December 2, 1960. Maurice K. also let the newspaper know that he was "most pleased" with their coverage of the event. [Frank G. Sayut, superintendent, Prince Gallitzin State Park, to John Rue, The *Tribune-Democrat*, December 12, 1960.]

42. Ralph C. Wible, "New State Park."

43. When the park was completed "Pinchot Road" actually became part of the northwest boundary of the park.

44. Goddard testimony before the Joint Committee, 44.

45. Bureau of State Parks, "A Recreational Guide for Gifford Pinchot State Park," Department of Conservation and Natural Resources, as rev. May 1998.

46. Ethel M. Goddard interview, April 30, 1998. Kimball Goddard was born in 1950 and Mark in 1957.

47. Kimball Goddard interview with Steve Williams, Oct. 31, 1998.

48. Goddard, "Pennsylvania's New State Parks," 17. Bendigo State Park was already in existence as a picnic area. It was included as a "new" park because of the addition of a swimming area.

49. Department of Forests and Waters Biennial Report, May 31, 1958. During the next biennium, 265 additional properties were appraised, 136 tracts of land acquired for state park and flood control purposes. [Forests and Waters Biennial Report, May 31, 1960.]

50. Ibid.

51. John C. Rex interview, February 11, 1998.

52. Widner, "Goddard: the Man," *Proceedings of the Maurice K. Goddard Symposium*, 18. According to Widner, Dr. Charles Lewis, head of the Western Pennsylvania conservancy, and Marshall Stalley, who worked with Maurice K. on Pittsburgh's Point Park project arranged for the award by the college.

53. William C. Forrey interview, April 21, 1998.

54. Widner, "Goddard: the Man," *Proceedings of the Maurice K. Goddard Symposium*, 15, 16. Widner never returned to the *New York Times*. He went on to run a variety of organizations including the Appalachian Regional Development Commission, Fairfax House International, and the Civic Network Television.

55. Leonard A. Morrison, *History of the Kimball family in America, 1634 to 1897* (Boston: Damrell and Upham, 1897), 3-4.

56. Thorpe, *The Crown Jewel*, 22.

57. Leader interview.

# Chapter VI: AIR BOMBING WILDFIRES

1. Maurice K. Goddard, "Water is Pennsylvania's Future," speech to the Pennsylvania Electric Association, Sept. 17, 1958.
2. Ibid.
3. Michael P. Weber, *Don't call me boss, David L. Lawrence, Pittsburgh's Renaissance Mayor*, (Pittsburgh: University of Pittsburgh Press, 1988), 171.
4. Ibid.
5. Thomas Donaghy interview with Genevieve Blatt, Sept. 25, 1974, 6. [quoted in Weber, *Don't call me boss*, 172.]
6. Weber, *Don't call me boss*, 353. According to Weber the deficit was $141 million in addition to nearly $400 million in bond obligations. *Don't call me boss,* 348.
7. Ibid., 349.
8. Kenn Marshall, article "Maurice K. Goddard, Environmental Patriarch" (Harrisburg: *Apprise* Magazine, WITF, Inc., May 1993).
9. Maurice K. Goddard, speech "The Citizens Role in Meeting Today's Resource Challenge," to the American Forestry Association, Bedford Springs, Pa., October 13, 1959.
10. William Middendorf, "Goddard: the Legacy," talk at the Second Pennsylvania Environmental History Symposium, from *Proceeding of the Maurice K. Goddard Symposium* (Harrisburg: April 17, 1997), 34.
11. Staff article, *Pennsylvania Forests,* Summer, 1959, 71.
12. Editorial , *American Forests*, October 1959.
13. Ibid., 17. With the establishment of the Department of Environmental Resources in 1971, the duties of the Pennsylvania Forestry Commissioners, who had been appointed by the governor, were absorbed by the Environmental Quality Review Board. Inspections of forests were discontinued.
14. Ibid.
15. McGreary, *Pennsylvania Government in Action*, 134-135.
16. Rex interview, February 10, 1998. John Rex, who was a 1939 forestry graduate of Penn State, later became the long-time head of Forests and Water's Land Acquisition Section.
17. Clifford Jones interview, February 2, 1998. Jones served as Secretary of Commerce and Secretary of Labor and Industry between 1967 and 1970 during the Shafer Administration. In 1979, Governor Thornberg appointed him to follow Goddard as Secretary of Environmental Resources.
18. Norman L. Lacasse to Ernest Morrison, Jan. 5, 1998.
19. The Pennsylvania Administrative Code of April 9, 1929, authorized the Department of Forests and Waters to set aside - within the state forests - such

areas that are "worthy of permanent preservation," . . . and to "dedicate them in perpetuity to the people of the State . . ." By May 1994 there were fourteen designated "wild areas" in the state forests encompassing 110,341 acres.

20. Joseph A. Dague, Jr., article "The Quehanna Wild Area" (Mechanicsburg: *Pennsylvania Forests*, March 1975).

21. Goddard, testimony before the Select Committee on Water Resources, U.S. Senate, Philadelphia, Pa., Oct 30, 1959.

22. Ibid.

23. Ibid.

24. Maurice K. Goddard, letter. "Kinzua Dam Upheld," (New York: *New York Times*, March 26, 1960). The U. S. Supreme Court did not actually hear the case, but refused to review a U. S. Court of Appeals decision. No statement by the court accompanied the order. [*New York Times*, June 16, 1959.]

25. *New York Times*, June 10, 1962 and July 17, 1962.

26. *New York Times*, July 17, 1962.

27. Paul A. W. Wallace, *Indians in Pennsylvania* (Harrisburg: Pennsylvania Historical and Museum Commission, 1986), 167.

28. *New York Times*, June 10, 1962.

29. Goddard, "Kinzua Dam Upheld."

30. Ibid.

31. Goddard to Sheldon A. Taylor, March 30, 1964 and Goddard to Susan J. Schneider, April 5, 1965.

32. Goddard to Joseph Cehovin, July 12, 1960.

33. Ibid.

34. *New York Times*, December 14, 1965.

35. Fire fighters are now assisted by bulldozers, but the axe, hoe, shovel, mattock and rake (supplemented by the chainsaw) are still basic tools on the fire line.

36. *Pennsylvania Forest Fire Warden's Manual*, (Harrisburg: Department of Conservation and Natural Resources, Bureau of Forestry, 1968).

37. *The Sylvan*, (State College: Penn State University, 1952).

38. *Pennsylvania Forest Fire Warden's Manual*, 102-105.

39. *Twenty-Five Years, 1960-1984, Air Operations on Wildfires in Pennsylvania* (Harrisburg: Department of Environmental Resources, April, 1984), 2.

40. Goddard to Martin H. Brackbill, August 5, 1960.

41. *Twenty-Five Years, 1960-1984*, 3-4.

42. Goddard to Brackbill.

43. By the time Maurice K. left government, 8 aircraft were in operation. During March, April and May of 1980 almost 328,000 gallons of water and retardant was cascaded on 227 fires in 1,083 drops. [*Twenty-Five Years, 1960-1984*, 35]

44. Although the helicopters were used in bombing active fires, their capacity was relatively small (40 to 50 gallons) while the fixed wing aircraft could deliver as much as 800 gallons. Helicopters were often effectively pressed into service, however, airlifting men and equipment to the scene of a blaze.

45. *Twenty-Five Years, 1960-1984*, 3 and 10.

46. Goddard to James Kepler Davis, March 30,1964.

47. Ibid.

48. Stephen J. Cummings interview, March 3, 1999.

49. Goddard to Otis B. Morse, February 28, 1963.

50. Cummings interview.

51. Goddard to William M. Norris, February 5, 1965. See also Samuel S. Cobb (Chief of the Division of Forest Protection) to Mr. Carl Hinson, February 18, 1965.

52. For articles about and by Maurice K. see *Water Land and Life*, (Pittsburgh: Western Pennsylvania Conservancy, October, 1959, Summer, 1960, and Winter 1961).

53. Maurice K. Goddard, article "Conservation for Self-Preservation," *Water Land and Life* (Pittsburgh: Western Pennsylvania Conservancy, October, 1959).

54. Ibid. Cook Forest, known as the "Black Forest" of Pennsylvania is located in the northwestern part of the state. It is believed the existing virgin timber began growth following a severe drought and forest fire in 1644. Three different virgin timber tracts remain in the forest: the Swamp Area, Seneca Area and Cathedral Area. Trees over 200 feet tall and 3-4 feet in diameter exist.

55. Ibid.


## Chapter VII: THE PARKS COME OUT OF THE FOREST

1. Maurice K. Goddard, address, "State Parks for the Future," *Proceedings of the Society of American Foresters* (Washington, D.C., American Forestry Association, November 16, 1960), 73, 74.

2. Ibid.

3. Ibid.

4. Ibid.

5. Harrisburg *Patriot*, November 8, 1961. At the time of the announcement, the Federal Government had not agreed to fund the Raystown dam project.

6. William C. Forrey, *History of Pennsylvania's State Parks* (Harrisburg:: Bureau of State Parks, Department of Environmental Resources, 1984), 41.

7. David L. Lawrence, "Special message to the General Assembly," January 16, 1962. [from the booklet "Project 70, A Proposal to the People of Pennsylvania," (Harrisburg: State Planning Board).]

8. *New York Times*, January 28, 1962.

9. Robin came from Pittsburgh where he was Mayor Lawrence's "right arm" in advancing the city's renewal. He served a year as Secretary of Commerce in the Leader administration and then went to the Pennsylvania State Planning Board. After leaving Harrisburg he became an executive Vice President of the Old Philadelphia Development Corporation. [Ralph R. Widner, "Goddard: The Man," talk at the Second Pennsylvania Environmental History Symposium, from *Proceedings of the Maurice K. Goddard Symposium*, (Harrisburg: April 17, 1997), 19-20.]

10. Harrisburg *Patriot*, November 8, 1961.

11. The amendment to the constitution required the majority vote of two separately elected Legislatures. The Senate first approved Project 70 by a vote of 44 to 3 on February 19, 1962; the House of Representatives voted 198 to 2 in favor of the plan February 28, 1962. During the 1963 legislative session the Senate voted 48 to 0 for the project on March 12; and the House followed July 1, with a 174 to 14 vote of approval. [Forrey, op. cit.]

12. Harrisburg *Patriot News*, December 6, 1961.

13. *Philadelphia Inquirer*, December 25, 1962, 25.

14. Ibid. William Bramble eventually gave up waiting for Maurice K., resigned as interim head of the Forestry School, and accepted a position as Director of Forest Conservation at Purdue University.

15. Maurice K. Goddard, Department of Forests and Waters Press Release #89, Sep. 19, 1962.

16. Maurice K. Goddard, Department of Forests and Waters Press Release #80, Aug. 24, 1962.

17. Harold F. Alderfer, *William Warren Scranton Pennsylvania Governor, 1963-1967* (Mechanicsburg: Local Government Service, 1976), 32.

18. Harrisburg *Patriot*, August 28, 1963.

19. *Water Land and Life*, March, 1963 (Pittsburgh: The Western Pennsylvania Conservancy, 1982), 6.

20. James A. Ream to Goddard April 17, 1964 and Anita A. Summers to Goddard May 4, 1964. Summers was president of the League of Women Voters of Lower Merion Township.

21. Pennsylvania Constitution of 1968, Article VIII, "Taxation and Finance."

22. Goddard to George R. Jenkins, April 26, 1965.

23. Forrey, *History*, 41-42.

24. Leonard A. Green, "Goddard: The Legacy," talk at the Second Pennsylvania Environmental History Symposium, from *Proceedings of the Maurice K. Goddard Symposium*, (Harrisburg: April 17, 1997), 24.

25. Goddard to Mrs. Erwin C. Manz, February 19, 1965.

26. Maurice K. Goddard, article "Land Acquisition by Public Agencies," *The Yearbook of Agriculture 1963* (Washington: U. S. Department of Agriculture, 1963), 449-453.

27. Ibid.

28. Ibid.

29. Pennsylvania State Planning Board, *Preliminary Report*, (Harrisburg: December, 1934), v.

30. Pennsylvania State Planning Board, "Biennial Report, (Harrisburg: July 1964-June 1966).

31. Ibid. By 1965 the board had approved 350 projects, ranging in size from one-half to five thousand acres, that involved approximately $30 million.

32. *Philadelphia Inquirer*, January 3, 1965.

33. Forrey interview, April 21, 1998.

34. Goddard, "Land Acquisition by Public Agencies."

35. Maurice K. Goddard, Department of Forests and Waters' press release, May 14, 1965.

36. Forrey interview.

37. Ibid.

38. Only once was Goddard actually "embarrassed" by not being able to responded positively to a questioner. At the hearing for Mt. Pisgah State Park, one of the smaller parks located in the northeast part of the state, Goddard was asked if he had looked at the site. After admitting that he had not, he vowed never to let that happen again. [ William C. Forrey interview, op. cit.]

39. John Stewart, "Goddard Made a Deal," article in the Wilkes Barre *Independent*, September 2, 1975.

40. Forrey interview. Also see the *Washington Post*, March 14, 1964.

41. Annual Report 1968, "Land Acquisition and Development Programs" (Harrisburg: Pennsylvania State Planning Board, 1968).

42. Art Hielman interview, February 11, 1998. Hielman is from the Pennsylvania Department of Revenue Budget Office.

43. Goddard to Allen T. Mallow, Feb. 27, 1964.

44. Tim Palmer, *Youghiogheny, Appalachian River* (Pittsburgh: University of Pittsburgh Press, 1984), 161-163.

45. John Oliver, "The Next 50 Years," chapter in *50 Years of the Western Pennsylvania Conservancy* (Pittsburgh: The Western Pennsylvania Conservancy, 1982).

# Chapter VIII: WATER IS FOR FIGHTING OVER

1. Norman Smith, *A History of Dams* (Secaucus: The Citadel Press, 1972), 263.

2. *Water Resources Development in Pennsylvania 1989* (New York: U. S. Army Corps of Engineers, North Atlantic Division Corps of Engineers, 1989).

3. Roscoe C. Martin, *The Problem of Water Resources Administration, With Special Reference to the Delaware River Basin* (Syracuse: Report submitted to the Water Research foundation for the Delaware River Basin by the Syracuse University Research Group, September 1, 1959), 37.

4. Nearly sixty rivers in the United States are longer and thirty-two of these carry more water. The Susquehanna, for example, discharges more than double the amount of water that the Delaware does. [See Richard C. Albert, *Damming the Delaware: The Rise and Fall of Tocks Island Dam, The* (University Park: Pennsylvania State University Press, 1987), xiii and 1.]

5. Among the largest wasteload users of the Delaware River in 1975 were Philadelphia, E. I. Dupont de Nemours, Wilmington, Delaware, Camden, N.J., Monsanto, Sun Oil, and Mobil Oil. [*The Delaware River Basin, An Environmental Assessment of Three Centuries of Change*, Council on Environmental Quality, August, 1975, 13.]

6. Ibid. 9.

7. See Albert *Damming the Delaware*, 17-21 for more extensive coverage of these events.

8. Incodel was formed at a conference Pennsylvania called in April 1936 to discuss stream pollution with New York and New Jersey. Delaware joined two years later. [Albert, 32.]

9. Albert, 42-43.

10. Unpublished four-page brochure, "Incodel," apparently issued as a publicity item by the Commission. [Copy in Record Group 43, Delaware River Basin Commission minutes, the Pennsylvania State Archives.]

11. *New York Times*, Sep. 28, 1956.

12. *New York Times*, Sep. 20, 1957.

13. Albert, 48-50.

14. Ibid., 52.

15. Statement on Incodel's primary purpose is taken from the Executive Secretary's report of the group's business meeting held in Philadelphia, December 9, 1958.

16. Martin, *The Problem of Water Resources Administration*, 460-465.

17. Incodel "Summary of Minutes," December 8, 1960.

18. Albert, *Damming the Delaware*, 60. According to Albert, the industry concerns were addressed in Section 15.1(b) of the federal compact legislation.

19. Albert, *Damming the Delaware*, 61.   See the Delaware River Basin Commission minutes of Oct. 22, 1968 for Vernon Northrop's comment regarding his voting "instructions" from Udall.

20. R. Timothy Weston interview, April 25, 1999.   Weston was hired initially to work for William Eichbaum but, because of the legal ramifications involved in an inter-state compact, especially one that included the federal government, he was soon traveling with Maurice K. as his advisor on water basin issues.

21. To Patrick Henry's comment that Jefferson returned after five years in Paris, "so Frenchified that he abjured his native victuals," Jefferson replied, "I believe he likes to go out in the woods and eat bear meat."

22. Maurice K. Goddard, "The Delaware Basin in the Year 2000," address to the Delaware River Basin Water Resources Conference, Pocono Manor, Pennsylvania, October 15, 1962.

23. Ibid.

24. In an "Information Sheet" issued with its 1958 plans for the Delaware River Basin, the Corps indicated they surveyed 19 different Federal agencies, 14 interstate agencies and 43 state departments, boards or commissions "having some concern with water resources of the Delaware." The sheet also stated there were more than 250 public and private water companies associated with the Delaware.

25. *Philadelphia Inquirer*, June 24, 1960 and an "Information Sheet" issued with the Corps of Engineers 1958 plans for the Delaware Basin.   Neither Trexler or Aquashicola were built, however, both dams along with Tocks are still on the Corps' list of  Congressionally "authorized" dams  [See *Water Resources Development in Pennsylvania 1989.*]

26. See Holway R. Jones, *John Muir and the Sierra Club, The Battle for Yosemite* (San Francisco: Sierra Club, 1964) and Ernest Morrison, *J. Horace McFarland, A Thorn for Beauty (Harrisburg: The* Pennsylvania Historical & Museum Commission, 1996) for fuller descriptions of the fight over a dam in Yosemite's Hetch Hetchy Valley.

27. Goddard to William W. Sieg, February 6, 1963.

28. In a federal reservoir, the Corps of Engineers is authorized by the Water Supply Act of 1958 to provide additional storage for municipal and industrial water supply, provided the requesting authority pays for the cost, and the Corps may also provide storage capacity for irrigation, if the local community is willing to pay half the cost.

29. The American Waterworks was a conglomerate or holding group of several water and power companies.

30. For a sampling of the coverage see among others the following:  The Harrisburg *Patriot* Jul 9, 1965, Aug 12, 1965, Aug 19, 1965, Sep 3, 1964, and Sep 14, 1965, The Scranton *Times* Sep 3, 1965, The *Philadelphia Inquirer*

June 20, 1965, Jun 25, 1965, Jun 29, 1965, Jul 11, 1965, Aug 19, 1965, Sep 2, 1965, Sep 9, 1965, Sep 12, 1965, Oct 8, 1965, Dec 26, 1965, and Dec 30, 1965.

31. *Journal*, (New York: Water Pollution Control Federation, v. 37, n. 8. 1965).

32. Maurice K. Goddard, "Statement of the Commonwealth of Pennsylvania to the Delaware River Basin Commission," February 23, 1977.

33. Philadelphia *Bulletin*, June 27, 1960.

34. Ibid.

35. According to the 1970 Pennsylvania inventory of dams there were 342 dams in the Pennsylvania portion of the Delaware River Basin. While five of these were U. S. Army Corps of Engineer dams, and others were the property of the Fish and Game Commission or the Department of Forests and Waters, many of these were small privately owned stream dams used for irrigation or industrial purposes.

36. Harrisburg *Patriot*, August 12, 1965 and "Statement by the President" of August 18, 1965 [from the files of the Delaware River Basin Commission].

37. Delaware River Basin Commision Resolution 66-4, March 2, 1967.

38. *Journal*, the Water Pollution Control Federation.


## Chapter IX: WHITE HOUSE CONFERENCE on NATURAL BEAUTY

1. Lyndon B. Johnson, "State of the Union Address," January 4, 1965.

2. Lyndon B. Johnson, February 1965 message to Congress. [quoted by John A. Baker in an article, "The New Conservation in a Changing America" in *Pennsylvania Forests* (Mechanicsburg: Pennsylvania Forestry Association, Jan-Jun 1965).]

3. Johnson, "State of the Union Address."

4. According to Maurice K., it was the President's Task Force on the Preservation of Natural Beauty, of which he was a member, that recommended the White House Conference idea to Johnson. [Maurice K. Goddard to Chester A Kunz, April 6, 1965.]

5. *New York Times*, May 25, 1965.

6. Wolf Von Eckardt, *Washington Post*, May 25, 1965.

7. Lewis L. Gould, *Lady Bird Johnson and the Environment* (Lawrence: University Press of Kansas, 1988), 70-71.

8. Ibid.

9. Maurice K. Goddard, "The Federal-State-Local Partnership," Report to the President, White House Conference on Natural Beauty, Washington, D.C., May 24 and 25, 1965.

10. Ibid.

11. Ernest Morrison, *J. Horace McFarland, A Thorn for Beauty* (Harrisburg: The Pennsylvania Historical and Museum Commission, 1995), 132.

12. President Johnson's Response to the conferees the White House Conference on Natural Beauty, Washington, D.C., May 25, 1965.

13. Jack Elsen, *Washington Post*, May 26, 1965.

14. Ibid.

15. Ibid.

16. *New York Times*, May 26, 1965.

17. Ibid.

18. *Washington Post*, May 26, 1965.

19. William H. Whyte to Maurice Goddard, June 4, 1965.

20. William Wyte to Maurice Goddard, November 23, 1966.

21. Lewis L. Gould, *Lady Bird Johnson and the Environment*, 165-167, 211 and 214.

22. Ibid. 221.

23. Ibid. 243.

24. Laurance Rockefeller to the Seventieth Annual Congress of American Industry, December 1965. [Reported in Lewis L. Gould, *Lady Bird Johnson and the Environment* 211.]

25. Intergovernmental Cooperation act of 1968, House Report No. 1845, "Hearings."

26. Intergovernmental Cooperation Act of 1968, Public Law 90-577; 82 Stat. 1098.

27. William E. Shands and Robert G. Healy, *The Lands Nobody Wanted: policy for national forests in the Eastern United States* (Washington: Conservation Foundation, 1977), 260-261.

28. The Carlisle (Pennsylvania) *Sentinel*, August 1, 1994. C. H. Masland was founded in 1866 as a dye company by Charles Henry Masland, a returning Union cavalryman. By the end of the century the firm had switched to making carpets. Frank E. Masland, Jr. served as president of the company from 1930 to 1960 and then until his retirement in 1971 as chief executive officer.

29. Report of "The Governor's Conference on Natural Beauty," September 12 and 13, 1966, Hershey, Pennsylvania, 7-9.

30. Ibid., 9.

31. Frank E. Masland, Jr., article "More Beauty in Pennsylvania," in *The Shuttle* (Carlisle: publication of C.H.Masland & Sons, Carlisle, Pa), Vol. 33, Bk. 3, October 1966.

348

32. In addition to those mentioned, there were panels at the Hershey Governor's Conference on The Pennsylvania City, The Complete Highway, Pennsylvania's Water Resources, The Pennsylvania Suburbs, Protection and Reclamation of Mining Area, Utilities and the Landscape, The Pennsylvania Countryside, and Citizen Action.

33. Report of "The Governor's Conference on Natural Beauty,"   190.

34. Ibid., 191-192.

35. Ibid., 192.

36. Ibid., 193.

37. Summary Report of "The Governor's Conference on Natural Beauty," September 13, 1966, Hershey, Pennsylvania,   35.

38. Masland, "More Beauty in Pennsylvania."

39. Summary Report of "The Governor's Conference on Natural Beauty," 44.

40. Ralph C. Wible, article "Work Training Program for Youths" (Mechanicsburg: *Pennsylvania Forests*, July-August 1966), 12.

41. Richard R. Thorpe, *The Crown Jewel of Pennsylvania*, 31.

42. Goddard to F. Gardiner Perry, January 6, 1964.

43. One Forests and Waters park formula, "Design Load," took into account picnicking, swimming, boating, parking, sanitation, food concession, as well as some miscellaneous items such as roads.  Moreover, swimming (in the formula) was broken down to consider that 30 percent of the people were in the water and 70 percent on the beach.   And although another park design formula used to calculate anticipated visitations at a park did use a variable, "general attractiveness of the area," a value of 1.00 was always assigned to it.

44.   Gifford Pinchot claimed that William McGee of the Inland Waterways Commission was the "scientific brains" behind the conservation movement. [Gifford Pinchot, *Breaking New Ground* (New York:  Harcourt, Brace and Company, 1946), 325 and 359.]   It was McGee who convinced Pinchot to link forests and water conservation and to see that control over the monopoly of natural resources was nearly as important as preventing their destruction.  See also  Ernest Morrison, "McGee, William John," article in the *Encyclopedia of the American West* (New York:  Macmillan Publishing Co., 1996).   The idea of the link between forests and water (especially stream flooding) has been much debated since it first surfaced in the late nineteenth century. The result of all the studies seems to be that the effect of a forest is only one of - and probably a minor one - in controlling floods. [see Ashley L. Schiff, *Fire and Water*, (Cambridge:  Harvard University Press, 1962.]

45.   Robert Gottlieb, *A Life of its Own, The Politics and Power of Water* (San Diego:  Harcourt Brace Jovanovich, 1988), 203.

46.   The *Houston Post*, November 23, 1965.   The conference was held at Texas A&M University.

47. Sam Goddard to Maurice K. Goddard, August 3, 1965.
48. James A. Crabtree to Maurice K. Goddard, April 30, 1965.
49. Dickinson College News Office Release, October 8, 1966.

## Chapter X: PUBLIC LAND LAW REVIEW COMMISSIONER

1. Unidentified Blackfeet Chief, quoted in an insert in *The West Virginia Archaeologist*, March, 1950.
2. *New York Times*, December 31, 1964 and Clinton P. Anderson, and Wayne H. Aspinall, joint publicity release, "Public Land Law Review Commission to Meet," June 29, 1965.
3. Anderson and Aspinall.
4. Goddard to Wayne N. Aspinall, January 6, 1965.
5. Albert G. Hall, "A Consultant Looks at Even-Age Management of Hardwood" (Mechanicsburg: *Pennsylvania Forests*, Jan-Jun, 1966).
6. Norman Lacasse interview, May 22, 1997.
7. See Goddard to Robert Coy, April 27, 1965, Goddard to Ralph Schmidt, April 19, 1965, and April 26, 1965.
8. Goddard to William F. Clinger, Jr., July 15, 1966.
9. See Marion Clawson, "How Much Should Users of Public Lands Pay?", *American Forests*, April, 1965, p 39, and Marion Clawson, "Public and Private Interest in Public Land," in Howard W. Ottoson, ed., *Land Use Policy and Problems in the United States* (Lincoln: Univ. of Nebraska Press, 1963), 359.
10. Goddard to Charles A. Auker, April 8, 1963 and Goddard to William W. Scranton, April 5, 1963.
11. Goddard to James Reichley, April 5, 1964.
12. Goddard to John Willard, July 21, 1967.
13. John A. Love to Goddard, September 1, 1966. Love was governor of Colorado.
14. Goddard to C. P. Martin, October 7, 1966 and Goddard to John A. Love, October 7, 1966.
15. Goddard to Len B. Jordan, September 12, 1967.
16. Steve Williams interview with Mark K. Goddard, October 31, 1998: Penn State School of Agriculture video.
17. Nellie S. Howard to R. P. Morningstar, October 12, 1965.
18. H. P. Storke to Goddard, April 3, 1964.
19. Peter P. Donker, article "WPI Parley Told Disorganization Hurts Water Resources Program," Worcester *Telegram*, April 1964. Copy attached with

Storke to Goddard, April 3, 1964. [In the Goddard Collection at the Pattee Library, Pennsylvania State University.]

20. Goddard to E. J. Dyksterhuis, June 27, 1967.

21. Walter Lyon interview, June 24, 1998.

22. *Debate on East - West Water*, American Society of Civil Engineers, Denver, May 1966, Bureau of Reclamation cassette tape of debate, from the private collection of Walter Lyon.

23. Ibid.

24. Ibid.

25. Ibid.

26. William H. Wisely to Goddard, May 25, 1966.

27. Alan J. Somerville interview, June 1999.

28. Marc Reisner, *Cadillac Desert* (New York: Viking, 1986), 228, 234.

29. Maurice K. Goddard, "A New Conservation for an Urban America," talk to the 30th North American Wildlife and Natural Resources Conference, March 1965.

30. Ibid.

31. Ibid.

32. *New York Times*, June 24, 1970.

33. Ibid.


## Chapter XI: HIGH DAM, LOW DAM, NO DAM

1. Charles F. Luce, *Water Policies for the Future. Final Report to the President and to the Congress by the National Water Commission* (Washington: U.S. Government Printing Office, 1973).

2. Harrisburg *Patriot*, October 2, 1965. The University trustees authorized numerous continuations of leaves of absence for Maurice K. - usually to coincide with his successive reappointments by incoming governors - until 1978, when he was retired with the rank of "professor emeritus of forestry."

3. Ibid.

4. Ibid.

5. "A Regional Park System in Southeastern Pennsylvania," Report by the Southeastern Pennsylvania Regional Planning Commission, November, 1956 [cited by Forrey, *History of Pennsylvania's State Parks*, 46.]

6. Forrey, *History*, 46.

7. Ibid., 47.

8. Norristown *Daily Herald*, June 16, 1967.

9.  Although there is a measure of truth in the nuclear power plant assertion, according to R. Timothy Weston, Goddard's deputy for water basins, Maurice K. was most certainly more interested in "watering" the Delaware than worrying about the Schuykill.   The threat during a drought of saline encroachment on fresh water intakes in the Philadelphia area was, and still is a major concern.  [See Chapter XIV regarding Tocks Island and the damming of the Delaware for a further discussion on this subject.]

10.  Howard Grossman, deputy director of the Montgomery County Planning Commission, charged that, "There's a history in this county of citizens opposing anything that would attract blacks in the area."   The *Philadelphia Inquirer*, June 10, 1971.

11.  Norristown *Daily Herald*, June 16, 1967.

12.  Goddard to Edwin Holl, July 25, 1967.  These dams were all part of a comprehensive plan for the entire Delaware River water basin. [See note 9 above.]

13.  Ibid.   As we saw in Chapter VII, Philadelphia initially planned extensive park improvements under Project 70 costing $21,677,982, of which the city expected to pay almost half.   At the time, Philadelphia, which was "already blessed with well over 8000 acres of parks and other recreational areas," hoped to add with the state's help another thousand acres at forty sites across the city.   [*Philadelphia Inquirer*, January 3, 1965.]

14.  Senator Edwin Holl was the first named of nine sponsors of Senate Bill 509, the "Land and Water Conservation and Reclamation Act," that in 1967 became known  as Project 500.

15.  Pennsylvania  State Planning Board minutes,  March 14 1968.

16.  Pennsylvania  State Planning Board minutes,  April 9, 1968.   See also Forrey, *History*, 50.

17.  See the Pennsylvania  State Planning Board minutes of May 16, 1968 for a description of the meeting on May 15.   Irving Hand had been appointed Executive Director of the State Planning Board in November 1964.  He served in that position until 1970.

18.  Pennsylvania  State Planning Board minutes of May 16, 1968.

19.  *Philadelphia Inquirer*, April 13, 1972.

20.  John Stewart, Wilkes Barre *Independent*, September 8, 1975.

21.  Governor David L. Lawrence message to the General Assembly, January 16, 1962.   [from the booklet "Project 70, A Proposal to the People of Pennsylvania" (Harrisburg:   State Planning Board)]

22.  Goddard, "Statement before the Senate Committee on Constitutional Change and Federal Relationships," March 22, 1966.

23.  Ibid.

24.  David L. Lawrence message to the General Assembly, January 16, 1962, 53.

25. Ibid., 54 and 37. In 1975, the General State Authority's responsibilities were incorporated in the newly created Department of General Services.

26. Goddard, "Major Outdoor Recreation Programs in Pennsylvania," Department of Environmental Resources Pamphlet, January 1974.

27. Goddard, Penn State lecture, 1990. [personal video tape of William C. Forrey.]

28. Forrey, *History*, 53.

29. William C. Kent was the Independent California Congressman who submitted the bill that established the National Park Service in 1916. Kent believed in public ownership of all land, with private tenancy and access only to the proceeds from any improvements made to the land. The "father" of these ideas in America was Henry George, who in *Progress and Poverty* espoused a "single tax" theory.

30. See the Pottstown *Mercury*, August 7 and August 22, 1975; the Montgomery County *Today's Post*, August 22, 1975, and the Norristown *Times Herald*, August 23, 1975. By the time of the controversy over houses, the Bureau of Parks was in the newly established Department of Environmental Resources.

31. Ibid.

32. William Voight, Jr. *The Susquehanna Compact: Guardian of the River's Future*, (New Brunswick: Rutgers University Press, 1972), 74-75.

33. "Public Forum," Susquehanna River Basin Commission video (Harrisburg: October 21, 1992. Video tape of the proceedings.

34. Voight, *The Susquehanna Compact* and "Public Forum."

35. Voight, *The Susquehanna Compact*.

36. Ibid.

37. Maurice K. Goddard, comments during the Susquehanna River Basin Commission "Public Forum."

38. Ibid.

39. Goddard to Scranton, December 31, 1964.

40. Gil Hirschel interview, September 16, 1999. Hirschel is the Environmental Outreach Coordinator for the Susquehanna River Basin Commission.

41. Susquehanna River Basin Commission Information Sheet, "Storing Water for Low Flows," October, 1996.

42. *Union Press Courier*, October 2, 1969.

43. Department of Environmental Resources Recreational Guide for M. K. Goddard State Park.

44. Roy W. Wilt to Goddard, October 6, 1969.

45. *Statistical Abstract of the United States*, 1997, 252.

46. Goddard, "Land Acquisition by Public Agencies."

# Chapter XII: THE FOREST PLAN of 1970

1.  Herman H. Chapman, and Walter H. Meyer, *Forest Mensuration* (New York: McGraw-Hill Book Company, Inc., 1949).

2.  Richard R. Thorpe, *The Crown Jewel of Pennsylvania, 2.*

3.  William Dietrich, *The Final Forest* (New York: Simon & Schuster, 1992), 86.

4.  Thorpe, *The Crown Jewel of Pennsylvania*, 20a-20c.

5.  Ibid, 20d.

6.  Rutherford Platt, *The Great American Forest* (Englewood Cliffs: Prentice-Hall, 1965), 134-135.

7.  Ibid., 158-159.

8.  Thorpe, *The Crown Jewel of Pennsylvania*, 22.

9.  Ibid.

10.  Maynard H. Hench, "Report on First 15-Year Management Plan for the State Forests," *Pennsylvania Forests* (Mechanicsburg: Pennsylvania Forestry Association, Summer, 1970).

11.  Goddard to Myles Brazill, March 22, 1963.

12.  Hench, "Report on First 15-Year Management Plan."

13.  George D. Wolf, *William Warren Scranton, Pennsylvania Statesman* (State College: The Pennsylvania State University, 1981), 70.

14.  Ralph R. Widner, ed., *Forests and Forestry in the American States* (Washington: The National Association of State Foresters, 1968), 29-30.

15.  The 1970 *Forest Resource Plan* (Harrisburg: Department of Environmental Resources, 1971).

16.  Ibid.

17.  Ibid.

18.  Ibid.

19.  Ibid.

20.  Ibid.

21.  Ibid.

22.  Goddard to Newton D. Yant, February 20, 1963.

23.  There were approximately 2,500 dams and obstructions in place throughout Pennsylvania at the time of the inventory.

24.  Elizabeth McConnell interview, July 21, 1999. According to McConnell, Maurice K. was intrigued by both her husband's ancestry and the fact that he was from the "border" or lake country.

25.  *Dams, Reservoirs and Natural Lakes Water Resources Planning Inventory No. 1* (Harrisburg: Department of Forests and Waters, 1970).

26.  Ibid, 1.

# Chapter XIII: Department of Environmental Resources

1. Goddard address, "State Parks for the Future."
2. Samuel P. Hays, *Beauty, Health, and Permanence, Environmental Politics in the United States, 1955-1985* (New York: Cambridge University Press, 1987).
3. Philadelphia *Bulletin*, March 29, 1972.
4. Elizabeth McConnell interview, April 29, 1999.
5. Franklin L. Kury, *Natural Resources and the Public Estate, A biography of Article I, Section 27 of the Pennsylvania Constitution* (Harrisburg: Reed Smith Shaw & McClay, 1985), 2-3. Kury was also the primary sponsor of the Scenic Rivers Act, the flood Plain Management Act, and the Storm Water Management Act.
6. Ibid., 1.
7. Ibid., 4.
8. Harrisburg *Patriot*, December 4, 1970.
9. Ibid.
10. Ibid.
11. Laudadio, who had graduated from Carnegie Institute of Technology, was an electrical worker with more than 30 years of active civic, conservation and labor experience. In January 1966, Mrs. Lyndon B. Johnson honored him as "National Conservation Legislator of the Year." Laudadio died in 1977 while still in office.
12. Goddard to Mrs. John F. Laudadio, Sr., April 28, 1967.
13. Governor's Office Press Release, January 15, 1971.
14. Frank E. Masland Jr. to Maurice K. Goddard, February 22, 1971.
15. William F. Schultz, Jr., *Conservation Law and Administration* (New York: The Ronald Press Company, 1953), 576-577.
16. Ibid.
17. Ibid.
18. William W. Scranton [written by Goddard] letter to Thomas Hansen, April 10, 1964.
19. Norman E. Lacasse interview, June 8, 1997.
20. Department of Environmental Resources Report, "The First 100 Days," April 29, 1971.
21. Ibid. Three years later the Department attorneys were still spending "substantial amounts of time" on the Barnes and Tucker case and it wasn't until 1976 that Maurice K. was able to report the signing of an agreement with U.S. Steel settling the air-pollution issues at the corporation's Clairton Coke Works. [Department of Environmental Resources Annual Reports, 1973 and 1976.]

22. Ibid.

23. William M. Eichbaum interview, April 25, 1999. According to Eichbaum, the "Strike Force" was composed of attorneys from both the Administrative Enforcement and Litigation Enforcement Bureaus.

24. Ibid. Although it does not appear in the official transcript of the hearing, according to Eichbaum, Maurice K. told the Committee, "If Eichbaum goes, so do I."

25. Verbatim Report of Public Hearings by the House Conservation Committee, July 22, 1976.

26. Goddard to Mr. J. Stanley Purnell (Pittsburgh Bicentennial Association), Nov 9, 1959, Goddard to Harold C. Pike (Cheltenham Township), August 29, 1960, and Goddard to the P & N Coal Company, March 18, 1963, over the unauthorized removal of 10,670 board feet of saw timber from the site of their strip mine operation.

27. Governor Milton J. Shapp, *Statement*, April 16, 1971.

28. The *Pennsylvania Manual*, 1972-1973, 404.

29. Harold A. Lockwood, Sierra Club statement circulated to members of the Pennsylvania Senate.

30. Reading *Eagle*, November 7, 1971.

31. Shapp to Goddard, October 28, 1971.

32. Edwin O. Lewis to Goddard, August 9, 1971. See Chapter XIV (Urban Conservation) for more on Judge Lewis and his role in the development of Independence Mall State Park.

33. Unidentified newspaper article in the Goddard archives at Penn State.

34. Daniel J. Flood to Goddard, November 17, 1971.

35. Homer L. Kreider to Goddard, November 23, 1971. The Eclectic Club is a select collection of central-Pennsylvania businessmen who meet regularly to present papers to each other. The format is similar to that of the Torch Club.

36. *Philadelphia Inquirer*, November 8, 1971.

37. Maurice K. Goddard, "Down With Chicken Little," article in Torch magazine, Reading Pa., Fall 1978.

38. Ibid.

39. Caren Glotfelty to Scott Kurtzman, March 29, 2000 and Timothy Weston interview, April 10, 2000.

40. Weston interview.

41. Flood Plain Management Act of October 4, 1978.

42. Weston interview.

43. Maurice K. Goddard to "All Employees, DER," January 18, 1971.

44. Department of Environmental Resources Accomplishment Report, 1971-1972.

45. *Tropical Storm Agnes: Long-Range Flood Recovery*, Report of The Mitre Corporation, August, 1973.

46. Ibid.

47. Department of Environmental Resources *Annual Report*, 1973.

48. Ibid.

49. Eichbaum interview.

50. *Pennsylvania Forests* (Mechanicsburg: Pennsylvania Forestry Association, Spring), 74.

51. Goddard to Messers, N. J. Dinenn and David Thompson, December 31, 1963.

52. *Pennsylvania Forests*, Spring 74

53. Ibid.

54. Department of Environmental Resources *Annual Reports*, 1975 and 1976.

# Chapter XIV: URBAN CONSERVATION

1. The *Pittsburgh Post-Gazette*, August 31,1964. The height of 159 feet for the fountain is a quote from the *Post-Gazette* article. Others have estimated it at up to 150 feet on a still day. It spouts about 6,000 gallons of water a minute.

2. Ibid. The state first committed itself to a park at the point in October 1944. For a detailed description of the history of the park's construction see Robert C. Alberts, *The Shaping of the Point: Pittsburgh's Renaissance Park* (Pittsburgh: University of Pittsburgh Press, 1980).

3. Alberts, 4.

4. Staff article, *Pennsylvania Forests* (Mechanicsburg: Summer, 1959), 71.

5. *The Independence Mall*, Report of the Joint State Government Commission to the General Assembly of the Commonwealth of Pennsylvania, Session of 1951.

6. Ibid.

7. Ibid.

8. Ibid.

9. *New York Times*, June 7, 1964.

10. Ibid.

11. Ibid.

12. Bill Bailey, *Pennsylvania State Parks* (Saginaw: Glovebox Guidebooks of America, 1996), 285.

13. O. E. Jennings, "Presque Isle's Last Stand," *Water Land and Life* (Pittsburgh: Western Pennsylvania conservancy, Spring 1960).

14. Ibid.

15. Erie *Times-News*, October 25, 1971.

16. Arthur J. Gardner to Goddard, January 27, 1956.

17. Program booklet, "Thank You, Dr. Goddard," Erie, Pennsylvania, October 10, 1961.

18. Ibid.

19. Deirdre Gibson, *Cultural Landscape Report Independence Mall* (Denver: U.S. Department of the Interior, June 1994), 68.

20. Goddard to Judith Wheeler, April 3, 1964.

21. Alberts, *The Shaping of the Point:* 138.

22. Goddard interview with Robert C. Alberts, October 27, 1975, 11.

23. The "ownership" of the Blockhouse by the Daughters of the American Revolution was questionable according to Ralph Griswold. Griswold told Alberts, it actually had been bought by an individual and deeded to the DAR as "caretakers." [Griswold interview with Robert C. Alberts.]

24. Goddard interview with Alberts, 10. See also Griswold interview with Alberts, 19.

25. Alberts interview of Goddard., 8.

26. Alberts interview of Griswold.

27. Ibid.

28. Alberts interview of Goddard.

29. *Pittsburgh Post-Gazette*, April 6, 1967, 38.

30. Ibid. When the bridges were finally taken down, their condition was so deteriorated it was apparent they would not have supported "markets, galleries, and shops."

31. Alberts, *The Shaping of the Point*, 189-190

32. Ibid., 191.

33. Goddard to Walter E. Alessandroni, April 29, 1963.

34. Ibid.

35. Goddard, "Land Acquisition by Public Agencies," *Yearbook of Agriculture 1963* (Washington: U.S. Department of Agriculture, 1963), 449-453.

36. *Independence Mall Redevelopment Area Plan*, Philadelphia City Planning Commission, Philadelphia, Pennsylvania, October, 1962.

37. Ibid., 4. According to William Forrey, the city of Philadelphia was so concerned over the possibility of a fire destroying Independence Hall that they buried a large tank of water in the ground near the building for emergency use.

38. Ibid.

39. Deirdre Gibson, *Cultural Landscape Report Independence Mall*, 64.

40. *Independence Mall Redevelopment Area Plan*, 10, 19-20.

41. Gibson, *Cultural Landscape Report Independence Mall*, 64.

42. Edwin O. Lewis interview with Melford Anderson, August 7, 1956, [quoted in Gibson, *Cultural Landscape Report Independence Mall*, 61.]

43. Gibson, *Cultural Landscape Report Independence Mall*, 65.

44. Lewis Mumford, *New Yorker*, November 17, 1956, February 9, 1957, April 6, 1957.  [quoted in Gibson, *Cultural Landscape Report Independence Mall*, 81.]  Mumford wrote major studies on architecture and urban planning especially dealing with their social aspects as related to human needs and aspirations. He was the visiting professor in regional planning at the University of Pennsylvania at the time of his *New Yorker* articles.

45. Gibson, *Cultural Landscape Report Independence Mall*, 109.

46. *Independence Mall Redevelopment Area Plan*, 11.

47. Edwin O. Lewis to Goddard, August 12, 1971.

48. The Philadelphia *Evening Bulletin*, February 16, 1972.  See also Gibson, *Cultural Landscape Report Independence Mall*, 92.

49. Gibson, *Cultural Landscape Report Independence Mall*, 92.

50. Ibid., 91.

51. Ibid. 12.

52. Goddard to Walter E. Alessandroni.

53. Griswold interview with Alberts, 20.  A whole row of mature sycamores that had been planted years before by a women's club as a memorial were, however, cut down because of the 1800 rule.

54. Goddard interview with Alberts, 8.

55. Alberts, *The Shaping of the Point*, 6.

56. Goddard interview with Alberts, 12.

57. Arthur B. Van Buskirk to Goddard, November 21, 1955.


## Chapter XV:  A POX ON TOCKS

1. Richard C. Albert, *Damming the Delaware: The Rise and Fall of Tocks Island Dam* (University Park:  The Pennsylvania State University Press, 1987), 75-75.

2. Ibid., 109.

3. Delaware River Basin Commission minutes, May 10, 1972.

4. Irene Taviss Thomson, "The Tocks Island Dam controversy," chapter in *When Values Conflict*, ed. Laurence H. Tribe and Corinne S. Schelling, (Cambridge:  Ballinger Publishing Co., 1976), 45-46.

5. Annual Report, Delaware River Basin Commission, 1976.

6. Ibid.

7. Thomson, "The Tocks Island Dam controversy," 41.

8. Ibid. 43.

9. Milton Shapp, transcript of the Delaware River Basin Commission Press Conference, Newark, N.J., July 31, 1975.

10. Goddard to Harold A. Feiveson, December 19, 1974. [Quoted in Harold A. Feiveson, *Boundaries of Analysis, An Inquiry into the Tocks Island Dam Controversy* (Cambridge: Ballinger Publishing Co., 1976), 79.]

11. Annual Report, Delaware River Basin Commission, 1981.

12. Ibid.

13. Scenic River designation was seen by many individuals as defacto deauthorization of Tocks Island Dam. However, when Pennsylvania agreed to the provisions of the Supreme Court decree for diversion of water to New York City and to New Jersey, it was in exchange for their support for a main-stem dam. This seemed to place the Scenic River designation in direct conflict with the Supreme Court decree.

14. Delaware River Basin Commission minutes, October 25, 1978.

15. Annual Report, Delaware River Basin Commission, 1981.

16. Albert, *Damming the Delaware*, 167-169.

17. Maurice K. Goddard, "Current Status and Needs, Tocks Island Dam and Reservoir Project," A Report to the Honorable Milton J. Shapp, Feb.. 15, 1978.

18. Ibid.

19. Ibid.

20. Ibid.

21. Ibid.

22. Maurice K. Goddard as quoted by Terry Williamson, Harrisburg *Evening News*, reviewed in *Pennsylvania Forests*, Spring 1979.

23. R. Timothy Weston interview, April 25, 1999.

24. Ibid. One of the difficulties in the sixties, according to Weston was that, following several consecutive years of drought, New York's reservoirs were unable to refill during the winter and thus aggravated the crisis as the drought continued into succeeding years.

25. Ibid.


Chapter XVI: CONSERVATIONIST WITHOUT PORTFOLIO

1. Maurice K. Goddard, Department of Environmental Resources 1976 Annual Report, Harrisburg, Pennsylvania, December 31, 1976.

2. Maurice K. Goddard, Department of Environmental Resources 1978 Annual Report, Harrisburg, Pennsylvania, December 31, 1978.

3. Ibid.

4. Ibid.

5.   George D. Wolf, *William Warren Scranton, Pennsylvania Statesman* (University Park:   The Penna. State University, 1981),   80.

6.   Clifford Jones interview, February 3, 1998.

7.   Shenadoah (Pennsylvania) *Evening Herald,* December 26, 1978.

8.   Dave Milne, *Pennsylvania Forests*   (Mechanicsburg:   Pennsylvania Forestry Association, Spring, 1979).

9.   Clifford Jones interview.

10.   Forrey, *History of the Pennsylvania's State Parks,*  pg 81.

11.   Rapid City, South Dakota, *Journal*, March 2, 1986.

12.   William A. Adams interview, June 11, 1998.

13.   Goddard, Penn State lecture, 1989.

14.   Paul B. Beers interview, August 7, 1998.

15.   James Kelley was later appointed to the Pennsylvania Commonwealth Court.

16.   Maurice K. Goddard and James Kelley, Concept Paper:   "Creation of a Department of Natural Resources and a Department of Environmental Protection," presented March 24, 1988 before the Pennsylvania Task Force on Government Efficiency.

17.   Ibid.

18.   James R. Kelley interview, January 24, 1998.

19.   Joint Legislative Air and Water Pollution Control and Conservation Committee, "Stenographic report of hearing held at the Old Western Maryland Railroad Station," Ohiopyle State Park, June 9, 1989, 4-5 & 14-16.

20.   Ibid., 53 and 55-56.   Evansburg State Park does have a golf course.   The original Goddard plans called for the commercial facility to be flooded by the lake, but it was retained after state acquisition of the land when the dam option was dropped.   The course is run by a concessionaire.

21.   Ibid.

22. Two years after the Department of Environmental Resources was split, natural resource management (the Department of Conservation and Natural Resources) was receiving 35 percent of the dollars ($72 million vs. $131 million) and 29 percent of the personnel (1,304 of 3,169 positions) allocated to the Department of Environmental Protection.   [Jere Martin, *Pennsylvania Almanac* (Mechanicsburg: Stackpole Books, 1997),  66-67.]

23. Joint Legislative Air and Water Pollution Control and Conservation Committee, "Stenographic report . . .,"   99.   The report reads that the interest on the $3.5 million was $240 million.   This must certainly be an error in the transcript.

24.   Ibid.

25.   Pennsylvania State University press release, May 2, 1978.

26.   Ibid.

27.   Caren Glotfelty interview, July 23, 1998.

28. Ibid.

29. Corrinne A. Caldwell to Goddard, June 24, 1992.

30. Goddard, Penn State lecture.

31. Eleanor Maass, "Remembering Maurice K. Goddard," *Pennsylvania Forests* (Mechanicsburg: Pennsylvania Forestry Association, Spring 1996).

32. Maurice K. Goddard, concept paper "Creation of a Department of State Parks and Forestry and a Department of Environmental Protection, November, 1994.

33. In 1971-72, park funding was $7.9 million against $47.9 million for the full Department of Environmental Resources. In 1979-80 it was $20.7 million against $107.6 million, and in 1990-91 $39.2 million against $332.5 million. [Governor's Executive Budget]

34. Jones interview.

35. Goddard, Jones, Duncan, DeBenedictis op-ed release, "Four Former DER Secretaries Support a Department of Conservation and Natural Resources," May 15, 1995.

36. Harrisburg *Patriot*, June 8, 1995.

37. Joint Legislative Air and Water Pollution Control and Conservation Committee, "Stenographic report . . . ," 111.

38. Harrisburg *Patriot*, June 8, 1995.

39. John C. Oliver, "A Brighter Future for Pennsylvania's Natural Resources" *Pennsylvania Forests* (Mechanicsburg: Pennsylvania Forestry Association, Spring, 1996), 9.

## Chapter XVII: HIS LIFE WAS HIS EULOGY

1. Harrisburg *Patriot News*, September 14, 1995.

2. Pennsylvania coroners are elected officials, not medical or forensic professionals.

3. *Pittsburgh Post-Gazette*, September 15, 1995.   Previous to his appointment by Governor Tom Ridge, John C. Oliver III of Pittsburgh was the president of the Western Conservancy and a member of DER's Citizens Advisory Council.  He and Goddard had worked together closely for 25 years.

4. *Philadelphia Inquirer*, September 24, 1995.

5. John B. Logan, M.D. interview, May 20, 1998.

6. Ibid.

7. 1 Corinthians, Chp. 13.

8. Kimball Goddard interview with Steve Williams, October 31, 1998, Penn State School of Agriculture video.

9. Rev. Calvin Van Kirk Hoyt interview, April 14, 1998.

10. Walter Rauschenbusch, 1861-1918, was an American clergyman from Rochester, New York. His books include *Christianity and the Social Crisis* and *The Social Principles of Jesus*.

11. William W. Warren, Jr., *Tribute to Secretary Maurice Goddard*, at the Annual Meeting of the Pennsylvania Bar Association's Environmental Mineral and Natural Resources Section, Harrisburg, Pa. May 1, 1996, 7.

12. Norman O. Goddard, "Righteousness," Saturday Sermonette, February 1936.

13. At one time, Pennsylvania law required that a state official appear at the site of any property that was condemned and, like an explorer, "claim" it for the state. At one such "taking," Goddard himself happened to be there. He opened his trousers, urinated on the ground, and jocularly proclaimed: "I take this property for the Commonwealth of Pennsylvania." [Rex interview.]

14. Charles Schaefer interview, November 7, 1997.

15. Larry J. Schweiger, "Goddard: The Lessons," talk at the Second Pennsylvania Environmental History Symposium, from *Proceedings of the Maurice K. Goddard Symposium*, (Harrisburg: April 17, 1997), 48.

16. Charles Schaefer interview.

17. Norman O. Goddard, "The Mysteries of Life," article written for the Portland Evening newspapers, January 25, 1936.

18. Woodsmen and foresters always walk on the up-hill side of a fallen log. This way, if the log starts to roll they can jump away from it rather than down-hill and into its path.

19. Maurice K. Goddard, "Goddard Pledges 'Full-Scale' Ohiopyle Park," *Water Land and Life*, (Pittsburgh: Western Pennsylvania Conservancy, June 1965).

20. Florence K. Steward to Ernest Morrison, April 20, 1999.

# BIBLIOGRAPHY

## MANUSCRIPT SOURCES

The Pennsylvania State Library, Harrisburg, houses a large amount of relevant Pennsylvania state government materials from the years Maurice K. Goddard was a member of the governor's cabinet. Among these are the Annual Reports of the Department of Environmental Resources, transcripts of the various Governor's Press Conferences, News Releases, and Speeches, as well as many of the reports and studies of the Delaware River Basin Commission, the Susquehanna River Basin Commission, and the Pennsylvania State Planning Board.

The Pennsylvania State University, Mont Alto, maintains a collection of materials associated with the early years of the campus as an independent forestry school and also from the period Maurice Goddard was the school's Resident Director.

The Archives Division of the Pennsylvania Historical and Museum Commission, Harrisburg, houses official documents of the various state administrations between the years 1955 and 1979. Among these papers are the speeches of the Secretary of Forests and Waters, the Executive Orders of the Governors, and other official documents of the Executive Department of Pennsylvania. The collection also includes a partial set of the minutes and the resolutions of the Delaware River Basin Commission.

The Library of the Department of Conservation and Natural Resources, in the Rachel Carson Building, Harrisburg, has a comprehensive set of forestry and water resources books and journals available. These include both theoretical and practical publications. Copies of various annual reports on forestry, mining and other official functions of the Departments of Forests and Waters, Conservation and Natural Resources and Environmental Protection are also available. Among these are complete sets of the Forest Plans for 1955 and 1970.

The Library of Delaware River Basin Commission at West Trenton, New Jersey maintains complete records of the commision meetings, annual reports, texts, journals and materials on water quality and supply management, as well as various consultant's studies and reports related to the Delaware River Basin.

The Pattee Library of The Pennsylvania State University has extensive holdings of both personal materials on Maurice K. Goddard and Norman O. Goddard as well as the "Reading Files" and the "Secretary's Files" of the Department of Forests and Waters for the years between 1955 and 1970. Much of the correspondence cited throughout the "Notes" was found in either the "Reading" or "Secretary's Files" at the Pattee Library.

The archives at the Western Pennsylvania History Center, Pittsburgh contain materials associated with the development of Point State Park. Among them are the files of the Allegheny Conference and Robert C. Albert's interviews of many of the principals, including Maurice K. Goddard, Arthur Griswold, and John Robin.

The library of the U.S. Army Military History Institute at Carlisle, Pennsylvania contains an extensive collection of World War II materials. Among the items are the Army of the United States "Station Lists," training and instruction manuals, military histories, and various manuscript collections including Forrest Pogue's notes of his interviews of high-ranking officers involved in the European Theater of Operations.

# PRINTED SOURCES

Albert, Richard C. *Damming the Delaware: The Rise and Fall of Tocks Island Dam.* University Park, Pa.: The Pennsylvania State University Press, 1987.

Alberts, Robert C. *The Shaping of the Point: Pittsburgh's Renaissance Park.* Pittsburgh, Pa: University of Pittsburgh Press, 1980.

Bezilla, Michael. *The College of Agriculture at Penn State.* University Park, Pa.: The Pennsylvania State University Press, 1987.

_____. *Penn State, an illustrated history.* University Park, Pa.: The Pennsylvania State University Press, 1985.

Block, Marguerite Beck. *The New Church in the New World; A Study of Swedenborgianism in America.* New York: Holt, Rinehart and Winston, Inc., 1932.

Cahn, Matthew Alan. *Environmental Deceptions, The Tension between Liberalism and Environmental Policymaking in the United State.* New York: State University of New York Press, 1995.

Clawson, Marion. *Forests for Whom and for What?* Baltimore: The Johns Hopkins University Press, 1975.

_____, Held, R. Burnell, and Stoddard, Charles H. *Land for the Future.* Baltimore: The Johns Hopkins Press, 1960.

_____, and Stewart, Charles L. *Land Use Information, A critical survey of U.S. statistics Including possibilities for greater uniformity.* Baltimore: The Johns Hopkins Press, 1966.

Clepper, Henry. *Professional Forestry in the United States.* Baltimore: The Johns Hopkins Press, 1971.

Cooper, Richard J. and Crary, Ryland W. *The Politics of Progress.* Harrisburg: Penns Valley Publishers, 1982.

Cupper, Dan. *Our Priceless Heritage, Pennsylvania State Parks.* Harrisburg: The Pennsylvania Historical and Museum Commission and the Bureau of Environmental Resources, 1993.

Dana, Samuel Trask, and Johnson, Evert W. *Forestry Education in America Today and Tomorrow.* Washington, D.C: Society of American Foresters, 1963.

DeCoster, Lester A. *The Legacy of Penn's Woods: A History of the Pennsylvania Bureau of Forestry*. Harrisburg: Pennsylvania Historicial and Museum Commission and the Bureau of Environmental Resources, 1993.

Dietrich, William. *The Final Forest*. New York: Simon & Schuster, 1992.

Feiveson, Harold A., Sinden, Frank W., and Socolow, Robert H.. editors. *Boundaries of Analysis: An Inquiry into the Tocks Island Dam Controversy*. Cambridge: Ballinger Publishing Company, 1976.

Forrey, William C. *History of Pennsylvania's State Parks*. Harrisburg: Bureau of State Parks, Department of Environmental Resources, 1984.

Gibson, Deirdre, *Cultural Landscape Report Independence Mall*. Denver: U.S. Department of the Interior, 1994.

Gloyna, Earnest F. and Butcher, William S., editors. *Conflicts in Water Resources Planning*. Austin: The University of Texas, 1982.

Gottlieb, Robert. *A Life of Its Own, The Politics and Power of Water*. San Diego: Harcourt Brace Jovanovich, 1988.

Gould, Lewis L. *Lady Bird Johnson and the Environment*. Lawrence: University Press of Kansas, 1988.

Hays, Samuel P. *Beauty, Health, and Permanence, Environmental Politics in the United States, 1995-1985*. New York: Cambridge University Press, 1987.

Kazmann, Raphael G. *Modern Hydrology*. New York: Harper & Row, 1965.

Kinney, J. P. *The Development of Forest Law in America*. New York: John Wiley & Sons, Inc., 1917.

Kury, Franklin L. *Natural Resources and the Public Estate*. Harrisburg: Reed Smith Shaw & McClay, 1985.

Leopold, Luna B. *Water, A Primer*. San Francisco: W. H. Freeman and Company, 1974.

Little, Charles E. *The Dying of the Trees*. New York: Viking, 1955.

Luce, Charles F. *Water Policies for the Future*. Final Report to the President and to the Congress by the National Water Commission. Washington, D.C.: U.S. Government Printing Office, 1973.

Mason, Robert J. and Mattson, Mark T. *Atlas of United States Environmental Issues*. New York: Macmillan, 1990.

McGreary, M. Nelson. *Pennsylvania Govenment in Action: Governor Leader's Administration (1955-1959).* State College: Penns Valley Publishers, 1972.

Osmaston, F. C. *The Management of Forests.* New York: Hafner Publishing Company, 1968.

Ottoson, Howard W. *Land Use Policy and Problems in the United States.* Lincoln, Nebraska: University of Nebraska Press, 1963.

Platt, Rutherford. *The Great American Forest.* Englewood Cliffs, N.J.: Prentice-Hall, 1965.

Pereira, H. C. *Land Use and Water Resources in Temperate and Tropical Climates.* New York: Cambridge University Press, 1973.

Pinchot, Gifford. *Breaking New Ground.* New York: Harcourt, Brace and Company, 1946.

Rodgers, Andrew Denny III. *Fernow, Bernhard Eduard, A Story of North American Forestry.* Princeton: Princeton University Press, 1951.

Schiff, Ashley L. *Fire and Water, Scientific Heresy in the Forest Service.* Cambridge: Harvard University Press, 1962.

Schultz, William F. Jr. *Conservation Law and Administration, A Case Study of Law and Resource Use in Pennsylvania.* New York: The Ronald Press Company, 1953.

Shallat, Todd. *Structures in the Stream.* Austin: University of Texas Press, 1994.

Shands, William E. and Healy, Robert G. *The Lands Nobody Wanted: policy for national forests in the Eastern United States* Washington: Conservation Foundation, 1977.

Smith, Norman. *A History of Dams.* Secaucus, N.J.: The Citadel Press, 1972.

Smith, Reed M. *Government in Transition: Reforms of the Leader Administration, 1955-1959.* Philadelphia: University of Pennsylvania Press, 1961.

Stoddard, Charles H. *Essentials of Forestry Practice, 3rd edition.* New York: John Wiley and Sons, 1978.

Thomas, Elizabeth H. *A History of The Pennsylvania State Forest School, 1903-1929.* Mont Alto, Pa.: Pennsylvania State Forest Academy/School Founders Society, 1985.

Thorpe, Richard R. *The Crown Jewel of Pennsylvania, The State Forest System.* Harrisburg: Department of Conservation and Natural Resources, 1997.

Tribe, Laurence H., Schelling, Corinne S. and Voss, John, editors. *When Values Conflict.* Cambridge: Ballinger Publishing Company, 1976.

Udall, Stewart, L., Conconi, Charles and Osterhout, David. *The Energy Balloon.* New York: McGraw-Hill Book Company, 1974.

_____ . *The Quiet Crisis and the Next Generation.* Salt Lake City: Peregrine Smith Books, 1998.

Voigt, William, Jr. *The Susquehanna Compact: Guardian of the River's Future.* New Brunswick: Rutgers University Press, 1972.

Weber, Michael P. *Don't call me boss, David L. Lawrence.* Pittsburgh: University of Pittsburgh Press, 1988.

Widner, Ralph R., ed. *Forests and Forestry in the American States,* Washington, D.C. The National Association of State Foresters, 1968.

Williams, Michael. *Americans and their forests: A historical geography.* New York: Cambridge University Press.

Wolf, George D. *William Warren Scranton, Pennsylvania Statesman.* State College: The Pennsylvania State Unversity, 1981.

Worrell, Albert C. *Principles of Forest Policy.* New York: McGraw-Hill Book Company, 1970.

# INDEX

373

Lewis, Edwin O., 238, 252, 260, 262
Lewis, Samuel, 69-70
Lowell, Massachusetts, 1
Lyon, Walter, 179

Maass, Eleanor, 293
McConnell, Clifford H., 83, 221-222
McConnell, Elizabeth, 221, 225
McFarland, J. Horace, 154, 226
Maine, University of, 18, 21
  forestry instruction at, 20-21
Marsh Creek State Park, 128, 284
Masland, Frank E., Jr. 160-161, 163-164, 228
Maurice K. Goddard State Park, 204-205
Mellon, Richard K., 265
Melton, Rex, 41, 56, 60
Michaux State Forest, 50, 171
Middleton, Eileen, 54
Middleton, John B., 54, 56
Mont Alto Forestry School, 49, 51-52, 293; struggle with Penn State, 52
Morgan, Arthur, 102
Multiple Use Act of 1960, 216
Mumford, Lewis, 261

National Historic Preservation Act of 1966, 157
National Wildlife Federation, 296
Nixon, Richard M., 184

Ohiopyle State Park, 130
Oliver, John C., 296
Orono, Maine, (see Maine, University of)
Oil and Gas Lease Act. See Goddard, Maurice K., oil and gas lease fund

Pennsylvania state parks. see Goddard, Maurice, K., parks; see also user fees
Pennsylvania Farm Bureau, 201, 284-285
Pennsylvania Forestry Association, 64
Pennsylvania State Planning Board, 78, 114, 116, 124, 129, 191
Philadelphia City Planning Commission, 259
Pinchot, Gifford, 53
Pinchot State Park, 84-85
Pitkin, Francis, 200
Point State Park (Pittsburgh), 71, 246, 253-257264-265
Pittsburgh Point Park Committee, 257
Potomac River Basin, Interstate Commission on, 90
Presque Isle 249-250
Presque Isle State Park, 249-252
Pretty Prairie, Kansas, 5-6
  harvest time, 9
Prince Gallitzin State Park, 82, 83, 206